The
Twentieth
Century
1880–1939

MODERN BRITISH FOREIGN POLICY

General Editor: MALCOLM ROBINSON
Headmaster, Queen's College, Taunton

Tudor Foreign Policy   P. S. CROWSON
Stuart and Cromwellian Foreign Policy   G. M. D. HOWAT
The Eighteenth Century, 1688–1815   PAUL LANGFORD
The Nineteenth Century, 1814–80   PAUL HAYES
The Twentieth Century, 1880–1939   PAUL HAYES

By the same author
Quisling: The Career and Political Ideas of Vidkun Quisling, 1887–1945 (1971)
Fascism (1973)

MODERN BRITISH FOREIGN POLICY

The Twentieth Century 1880–1939

Paul Hayes

ST. MARTIN'S PRESS
NEW YORK

© 1978 Paul Hayes

All rights reserved.   For information write:
St. Martin's Press, Inc., 175 Fifth Avenue, New York, N.Y. 10010
Printed in Great Britain
Library of Congress Catalog Card Number 77-93695
ISBN 0-312-82409-2
First published in the United States of America in 1978

Contents

Here's to the songs we used to sing,
Here's to the times we used to know;
It's hard to hold them in our arms again
But hard to let them go.
Neil Diamond in 'If you know what I mean'

For E. A. S.

Preface and Acknowledgments

The Eurocentric world vanished for ever during the war of 1914–18. The world was profoundly changed, and almost everywhere for the worse. The outbreak of war in 1914 was a watershed in world history. Economic power thenceforth lay outside Western Europe. New views of politics, fiercely contemptuous of the cultured liberalism of the late nineteenth century, came to dominate the world. The classical evolution of the arts was subjected to violent interruption—to changes far more dramatic than those already effected by Richard Strauss, Vincent Van Gogh or Filippo Marinetti. Before 1914 the world was not ideal; it was, for the most part, preferable to the new world. It is, therefore, important to understand the processes which helped contribute to the tragic events of 1914 and the cataclysmic postscript of 1939–41: important, in fact, to see how the 'terrible ifs' accumulated.

British influence was vital throughout this period—until 1914 because Britain really was a great power and after 1918 because she remained a great power by courtesy of the temporary weaknesses of other powers. The study of British foreign policy, its strengths and weaknesses, its consistency and variability, its arrogance and timidity, is central to comprehension of the collapse of the old order. The decision to fight in 1939 was probably Britain's last truly important independent decision. These factors are quite sufficient to warrant detailed attention and study.

It may be apparent from the above that this book has been a labour of love—of an abiding interest in a world for ever vanished. It might most accurately be described as a personal view of the events of 1880–1939, and has all the imperfections that naturally result from an intense feeling of involvement. I was born in 1942 and the developments of these preceding years shaped the world in which I have lived; as a student of history I am acutely aware that the destinies of my generation have been shaped by an unusually dramatic historical process. Throughout my studies I have been forcibly reminded of John Donne's injunction 'And therefore never send to know for whom the bell tolls; It tolls for thee'.

All those who have been close to me in the past twenty years have been aware of my fascination with this period. They, belatedly, are those whom I wish to thank for their encouragement and tolerance. I owe an especial debt to an inspiring tutor, Miss Agatha Ramm, Fellow of Somerville College, who first interested me in the diplomatic complexity of the pre-1914 world. My chief regret is that I do not have her unrivalled knowledge of the period or her facility for accurate and economic communication of that knowledge.

Valuable ideas and encouragement have also been provided by a whole host of undergraduate and postgraduate friends and pupils; to them I am very grateful. Mention must also be made of Malcolm Robinson, an old school friend and now Headmaster of Queen's College, Taunton, without whose prompting this book would never have been written. All the hard slog of typing was done wonderfully well by Mrs Stowell and her small band of helpers in the History Faculty Office, Oxford University. No author could have received more kindness and consideration.

Most important, however, are those who have provided points of stability at times when life has been difficult in one way or another. In particular I think of my parents, my sister Judith and her family, and my former wife Lynne. Two Keble colleagues, neither of them historians, Dr Raoul Franklin and Dr Denis Meakins, have always urged me to write and research. Ralph Feltham, Sub-Warden of Queen Elizabeth House, and David Smith, now a Keble graduate, have given me more aid and comfort than they will ever know. I owe an unrepayable personal debt to some very good friends, Dr Jenö Takács and his family, and Mrs Renée Bloch. They have always been exceptionally kind, and as expatriates (from Hungary in 1956 and Germany in 1938 respectively) have been only too well aware of how the world has changed. Finally, and perhaps appropriately for a book which is so largely concerned with 'if onlys' and 'what might have beens', most of all I think of the one to whom this book is dedicated.

1 Liberalism or Imperialism? 1880–85

You should avoid needless and entangling engagements.
Gladstone's speech at West Calder, November 1879

The period of Gladstone's second ministry provides one of the most intriguing and perplexing tales of muddle and incompetence in foreign affairs, unsurpassed in modern political history until the days of Grey and, later, Neville Chamberlain. To some extent the confusion has been artificially created by those historians who have persisted in regarding Gladstone as an archetypal isolationist who occasionally abandoned isolationism in order to support humanitarian and nationalist causes. It is now rather more widely understood that Gladstone's foreign policy was based upon a set of positive propositions. However, although the premier made a full and firm declaration of his principles during the campaign of 1879–80 it is clear that in practice they were sometimes thrown over. As in the past, political necessity rather than an elaborate and systemic philosophy determined the evolution of foreign policy.

Nevertheless the importance of ideas must not be overlooked. Great emphasis was placed on the Concert of Europe—as A. J. P. Taylor has shown: 'His "right principles of foreign policy" all came from the common Radical stock: economy, peace, no needless entanglements, equal rights of all nations, a love of freedom. All except one: the Concert of Europe . . . the one on which Gladstone laid most stress. It was the one which opened the way to British leadership and British action on the highest moral grounds'.[1] Inconsistency, then, was to be expected. The task of subordinating principles to political requirements was not easy.

There existed exceptional difficulties. Gladstone was not his own Foreign Secretary, that post being held by Lord Granville throughout

References are printed on p. 27.

the life of the ministry. Granville was vastly experienced in foreign affairs but was not wholly in sympathy with his party leader. He was more cautious and less willing to risk giving offence. In the first weeks in office Granville described Gladstone's attacks on Austria as 'quite wrong [and] in opposition to what we agreed ought to be our line'.[2] Within the Cabinet there were several jarring factions. Hartington, Secretary for India (1880–82) and later Secretary for War (1882–85), was leader of the Whiggish element, which on the whole held ideas on foreign policy fairly close to those of the Tories. Hartington usually received support from Kimberley and Northbrook. At the other pole stood Bright, Chancellor of the Duchy of Lancaster (1880–82), until his resignation on a matter of foreign policy. Bright was frequently upheld in his views by Harcourt and Childers. If these represented the extremes of the spectrum, the opinions of Derby, Dilke, Chamberlain, Forster, Trevelyan and Gladstone himself provided a bewildering kaleidoscope of colour in between. Alliances formed between individuals on foreign affairs were often shattered by disagreement over the many contentious domestic issues which faced the Cabinet. Indeed, preoccupation with Ireland and franchise reform during these years frequently prevented the government undertaking any action on the international front.

The influence of the Queen was also an important factor. During these five years her views often coincided with the public mood, thus leading her into conflict with the government. Victoria had long admired Disraeli's style in foreign affairs and feared the worst when his party lost the election of 1880. In April she recorded in her journal, 'I could not give Mr. Gladstone my confidence. His violence and bitterness had been such, the way in which he had, in times of great anxiety, rendered my task and that of the government so difficult, and the alarm abroad at his name being so great, it would be impossible for me to have the full confidence in him I should wish, were he to form a government'.[3] He was never to enjoy her full confidence and many M.P.s knew that in 1880 the Queen had shown a marked preference for Hartington as premier. This hardly made for an easy relationship, particularly when the Queen felt so strongly about foreign affairs. In the days following the Conservative defeat she expressed her views unambiguously:

'There must be no democratic leaning, no attempt to change the Foreign policy (and the Continent are terribly alarmed), no change in India, no hasty retreat from Afghanistan, and no cutting down of estimates'.[4] This was pure Disraeli and predictably unacceptable to Gladstone. The election had been fought largely on foreign policy and at a time of Disraeli's choosing, so Gladstone was hardly likely to agree that the result should not affect that policy. The Queen, however, was made of stern stuff and thus her 'relations with the Liberal Government over foreign affairs reached their nadir between 1880 and 1885'.[5]

The most important areas of conflict were two: Europe and the Empire. Britain had few possessions in Europe (Cyprus, Gibraltar, Malta and Heligoland) but great potential influence on the balance of power. Elsewhere Britain held vast territories, as in India and Africa. The basis of British power, however, was trade not territory, and Britain always had difficulty in bringing pressure to bear in any area where armies were more important than a navy. The debate in foreign policy centred on two important issues: whether Britain should act as a European power and the extent to which imperial advancement should be pursued. Since 1814 British activity in Europe had varied considerably, according to public mood, economic prosperity, the views of the Foreign Secretary and other less significant factors. Outside the Empire little discretion was granted to the Foreign Secretary because of widespread distrust created by the bitterly contested debates over imperial advancement. Some areas where Britain had regularly played a prominent rôle hardly impinged on international affairs in these years. Relations with the United States were smooth and cordial; in China trade developed, but there was political calm before the rush for concessions in the 1890s. But the future of Empire was a central issue in politics. Derby and Carnarvon had resigned from the Conservative government in 1878 owing to their dislike of Disraeli's jingo policy. Their views were shared by many Liberal M.P.s. They were not supporters of moral arguments against imperialism, rather they believed particular policies were wrong. The opinions of the 'middle group' were well put by Carnarvon, who saw the purpose of imperialism as 'wise laws, good government, and a well-ordered finance . . . to

supply a system where the humblest may enjoy freedom from oppression and wrong equally with the greatest'.⁶ This differed little
from Gladstone's faith in the British constitution and the desirability
of its duplication elsewhere in the world.

Despite wide agreement among men of all parties as to the need
for an imperial mission which would 'lead the world in the arts of
civilisation ... [and] act as trustees for the weak',⁷ there were divided
views on expansion. Gladstone held that 'the responsibilities of this
great empire . . . are sufficient to exhaust the ambition or strength
of any minister or of any parliament, and we do not wish to over-
load them or break them down'.⁸ Yet this parliament witnessed
major imperial expansion and acceptance of wide new responsibilities.
Nor could British acquisitions be easily justified on humanitarian
or 'civilising' grounds. For all his high moral tone Gladstone was
ready to put aside sentimentality in the face of necessity. He was
perhaps less honest than Bismarck, who once observed 'When I
hear of the sufferings of a negro in China or in some other remote
part of the world, I may mention him in my prayers, but I cannot
make him an object of German policy',⁹ but on occasion just as
determined.

Almost as soon as the Liberals took office compromises with principle began. It was in relation to the Ottoman Empire that weakness
of direction first became apparent. The decay of formerly strong
Muslim-dominated states (Turkey, Persia and India) had slowly
compelled Britain to assume greater responsibilities in an area stretching from Egypt to Afghanistan and had brought her face to face
with two other major powers, Russia and France. The situation
required delicacy and tact and it was British failure to control
developments in these areas which produced the isolation and weakness of 1883–85. There the responsibilities of Europe and Empire
met and became the subject of dispute not only at home but among
the chancelleries of Europe. Committed by their election tactics,
the Liberals first sought to amend the settlement of 1878 or, rather,
to implement those parts which referred to the desirability of Turkish
reform. The fact that this was an impossible task and one likely only
to cause friction did not prevent optimistic references in the Queen's
Speech. Granville feared if the Sultan were pressed too hard Turkey

'might crumble in our hands',[10] thus reviving the Eastern Question. In truth the weakness of the Sultan was his strength, but too much political capital had been made for the reform of Turkey to be quietly dropped. Gladstone had scathingly denounced taking 'possessions which, like Cyprus, never can become truly British, because they have acquired indelibly an ethnical character of their own'.[11] Cyprus might have been gained as part of a corrupt bargain to uphold the Sultan, but the Liberals abandoned their obligations, not the island. British influence at the Porte was swept away in return for the chimerical gain of the favour of an assortment of unstable Balkan principalities.

From the very first the government aroused distrust. Granville assured Turkey that 'to dissent from the expediency of an international arrangement was a very different thing from reversing it after it had been concluded',[12] but subsequent attempts to undermine the settlement by covert means fanned Turkish suspicions. The Cabinet held that the major powers, operating through the Concert of Europe, should work together to promote reform in Turkey and to secure implementation of the treaty provisions regarding Greece and Montenegro. Unfortunately this enthusiasm was not shared by other powers, especially Austria. The co-operation of Vienna was essential if Britain was 'to press, in concert with Europe, for the full execution of the conditions of the Treaty of Berlin'.[13] The Austrians did not wish to coerce Turkey, fearing the consequences of further strengthening of independent Balkan states. Furthermore, there was strong resentment in Vienna at Gladstone's attacks on Austria during the election campaign—particularly his remark that 'Austria has ever been the unflinching foe of freedom in every country of Europe. . . . There is not an instance—there is not a spot upon the whole map where you can lay your finger and say: "There Austria did good." '[14] Granville persuaded Gladstone to withdraw some of his inflammatory remarks but there remained a major difference of opinion between the two men, summed up in 1883 as, 'Our difference is this: that you are more afraid of Austria and I of Russia'.[15]

Dissension between the powers enabled the Sultan to engineer the failure of an ambassadorial conference which met at Berlin in

June 1880. After much tedious wrangling the powers agreed to a naval demonstration off Ragusa in September, but this hardly proved a potent weapon for coercion as Austria, France, Germany and Italy let it be known in advance that they would not fire a shot unless first fired upon. As the Sultan was abundantly satisfied with great power passivity the exercise was, in Salisbury's words, as much use as sending 'six washing tubs with flags attached to them'.[16] The agreements between Turkey and Greece (May 1881) and Turkey and Montenegro (November 1880) owed little to British pressure. There had been those within the Cabinet who had argued for stronger action, perhaps the seizure of Smyrna or Salonika and confiscation of the customs. In September Gladstone himself proposed definite coercive measures and was supported by Odo Russell, the Ambassador to Berlin, who advised 'if Austria, Germany, and France decline to go to Smyrna, you will think it a sufficient excuse for proposing the Dardanelles instead, and going there with or without allies'.[17] In October the Cabinet decided on an expedition to Smyrna. Attempts to enlist the support of other powers failed when on 9 October Granville's proposals were rejected by Austria, Germany and France. The following day the Sultan made concessions to Montenegro as he had not been informed of the rejection of British proposals and feared concerted action. Bismarck's duplicity in this matter had saved Britain from an awkward situation, but the German did not conceal his dislike for Gladstone's radical initiatives, referring contemptuously to the 'crazy professor' who played in 'the revolutionary quartet on the G string'.[18]

In the long term, consequences were serious. Germany reaped great advantage from the crisis. Goschen, Ambassador to the Porte, had made himself thoroughly unpopular with the Sultan, Abdul Hamid II (1876–1909), who henceforth regarded the British with suspicion. Austria distrusted Gladstone and Russia Granville. In the Levant Britain was out of step with both France and Italy. Bismarck took advantage of this situation by reviving the conservative coalition on a basis of mutual recognition of spheres of Balkan interest by Russia and Austria. On 18 June 1881 the *Dreikaiserbund* was signed at Berlin, thus completely undermining the foundations of traditional British policy in the Near East. Bismarck was not

slow to realize what a coup this was: 'I have been the first in Europe
to break with that old tradition with which the Western Powers
have inoculated all the cabinets: namely, that Constantinople in
the hands of Russia would be a European danger. I consider that
a false idea, and I do not see why an English interest must become
a European interest'.[19]

At this point Britain became further embroiled with the Porte
over Egypt. This led to conflict with the other major powers,
particularly France. Since the purchase of the Suez Canal shares in
1875 Britain had claimed some seniority of interest in Egypt but
under Disraeli the two western powers had managed to co-operate.
During the reign of Khedive Ismail (1863–79) government indebtedness had increased at a rapid rate and in 1876 the *Caisse de la Dette
Publique* had been set up. The Khedive's inability to satisfy the demands of European bondholders led to joint intervention in August
1878 when he was compelled to accept a French Minister of Public
Works and an English Minister of Finance. In July 1880 his successor,
Tewfiq, was subjected to the indignity of an international commission of enquiry on Egyptian finances and, through the Law of
Liquidation, a limit on administrative expenditure. As Milner
put it, 'The Powers stepped in to save Egypt from bankruptcy,
but in return they put her into a strait-waistcoat of the severest
kind'.[20] It was the high point of Anglo–French co-operation.

Opinion among the other powers varied. Russia was reluctant
to see any strengthening of British influence in the area, while
Turkish hopes of re-establishing Ottoman authority in Egypt were
dashed. Germany, on the other hand, favoured western involvement
in North Africa. In January 1881 Bismarck told Odo Russell 'England's interests are in Egypt and Asia, as those of France are in Syria
and Tunis; . . . neither should busy themselves about the Sultan's
European dominions, which do not concern them as they do
Germany's neighbours, Austria and Russia'.[21] International concern
over Egypt, together with local unrest, made it impossible for the
western powers to localize the dispute and, ultimately, to work
together.

In September 1881 a nationalist revolt under a discontented army officer, Arabi, made the Khedive a prisoner of anti-foreign feeling. The possibility of a protectorate was immediately canvassed by the press in both Paris and London, although such a scheme had been dismissed by both Derby and Disraeli in 1876. At first it seemed unlikely that Gladstone would jump in where the Tories had refused to dip their toes. On 7 November Granville clearly defined his position in a letter to Lyons: 'the only event which could make Great Britain depart from her attitude of non-intervention would be the existence of anarchy, or some attack on the Canal'.[22] This attitude soon changed under the pressure of developments in Egypt, despite the realization that there would be problems with France and Turkey. Turkey could, perhaps, be ignored unless she was supported by one of the other major powers, but it was quite otherwise in the case of France. As Granville had earlier observed, 'We wish to act cordially with France without allowing her any predominance',[23] but unless the two western powers did act together the problem was bound to take on an international character.

At first internal political developments in France favoured Britain. In November 1881 Ferry was succeeded by Gambetta, who was anxious to promote a joint Anglo–French intervention. On 6 January 1882 there was a long debate in the Cabinet and two days later the Khedive was assured of Anglo–French support in resisting the pretensions of the Sultan and the nationalists. As Morley commented, 'The general effect was mischievous in the highest degree. The Khedive was encouraged in his opposition to the sentiments of his Chamber. The military, national, or popular party was alarmed. The Sultan was irritated. The other European Powers were made uneasy. Every element of disturbance was roused into activity'.[24] Then, on 26 January, Gambetta fell from power. His successor, Freycinet, was much less enthusiastic about a 'forward' policy, fearing to send troops to Egypt thus leaving France exposed to German pressure. Matters also took a turn for the worse in Egypt where a nationalist ministry was formed on 5 February.

Britain was now in an exposed position. The consul-general in Egypt, Sir Edward Malet, backed by an influential party in England, clamoured for action. Gladstone's preference was for a revival of the Concert of Europe and in this had the support of Freycinet.

The possibility of Turkish intervention to restore Tewfiq's power was acceptable only to the Porte and Berlin. For admittedly different reasons, both Gladstone and the bondholders wished to keep Turkey out of Egypt. Granville, having failed in his attempts to work with France, now favoured intervention by Britain. In May, encouraged by the promise of an Anglo-French naval demonstration, Tewfiq dismissed his ministers but was soon forced to take them back. On 11–12 June there was serious anti-European rioting in Alexandria. Immediately the clamour for intervention revived, spearheaded by Hartington in the Cabinet. Granville accepted intervention as now inevitable. Odo Russell (recently created Lord Ampthill) suggested that 'if we are compelled to protect our interests ourselves, then Prince Bismarck will side with us, because his sympathies are always on the side of force'.[25]

Opposition to intervention was strong, particularly from Bright and the Radicals. The Prime Minister himself told Granville on 21 June: 'The more I reflect the more I feel unprepared to take any measure with regard to the Suez Canal single handed, or in union with France, apart from any reference to the authority of Europe'.[26] Furthermore, there was strong pressure within the Liberal Party to avoid an issue which could only be divisive at a time when the government was wrestling with Irish problems. On 3 July the Cabinet reluctantly decided that further work by the nationalists on the fortifications at Alexandria must be prevented. This decision was taken in the knowledge that the ambassadorial conference meeting at Constantinople was deadlocked. On 6 July the conference invited Turkey to restore order in Egypt, a task quite beyond Turkish resources. This gave the French an excuse to withdraw from the naval squadron and their ships steamed away. On 11 July Admiral Seymour obeyed instructions and bombarded Alexandria. His action was immediately followed by riots throughout Egypt.

Sir Evelyn Baring, already an expert on Egypt, recognized that the responsibility for the ordering of that country had now devolved on Britain. It proved more difficult for the government to see the truth of the matter. Bright resigned upon reception of the news of the bombardment and Gladstone wished to avoid further defections. It was at once plain that the canal was now in more danger than before the bombardment. The Cabinet was hopelessly divided. Gladstone and Harcourt argued for co-operation with France to protect the canal; Chamberlain, Dilke and Hartington pressed for a complete takeover. Fortunately for Britain the Freycinet government put no obstacles in the way at this stage, while Bismarck became 'simply furious at the mere mention of the Egyptian question. . . . "Let the Powers interested settle it as they please, but don't ask me how; for I neither know nor care." '[27] Britain was left with a free hand, though Gambetta urged on his countrymen the necessity for joint action. Gambetta's policy was rejected at Clemenceau's insistence on 29 July. It had become apparent even earlier that Freycinet would do nothing and on 20 July the Cabinet had ordered an expeditionary force to Egypt, under the command of Sir Garnet Wolseley. All notions of working with Turkey or Italy were put aside. The Italian refusal to act pleased Granville considerably: 'I have just received . . . the refusal, which delights me. We have done the right thing; we have shown our readiness to admit others; and we have not the inconvenience of a partner'.[28] Public opinion backed action and on 28 July the House of Commons voted war credits by 275 votes to 19.

During the next few days much time was wasted in attempts to reach agreement with Abdul Hamid II, who still hoped to regain the control of Egypt lost by Mahmud II a half-century before. The Queen was firm in her refusal to countenance a revival of Turkish influence, finding herself, unusually, in agreement with Gladstone—'she has seen with satisfaction the firm tone manifested by the Government. She trusts that we shall get clear of the Turks altogether'.[29] By now French bondholders, dreading an increase in British influence, were backing Turkey, though they received no encouragement in official quarters. President Grévy remarked 'Panislamism is a factor of great weight in the future and I consider it of the highest importance that there should be no doubt, even for a moment, that Musulman or Arab troops cannot resist Europeans in the field'.[30] On 30 July Dufferin, Ambassador to the Porte, was instructed to inform the Sultan that Britain considered herself invested with the duty of protecting the canal. Further deliberations were plainly futile and on 14 August the ambassadorial conference broke up. The next day Wolseley arrived in Egypt and on 13 September he destroyed the army of Arabi at Tel-el-Kebir.

Reaction to these events was mixed. The Porte was hostile, for Egypt was still technically Turkish territory, and British action led to a further cooling of the previously close Anglo-Turkish relationship. What were the Turks to make of a government which advocated leaving Cyprus in 1881 but which a year later occupied Egypt? The Liberal ministry was depicted as simultaneously weak and grasping, timid and imperialist. Hostility in France increased, fanned by De Lesseps and the bondholders. As Anderson has commented, 'The dominant position in Egypt's cultural life and the very important one in its economic life which history had given France seemed on the point of being snatched away, and by an already envied and far too successful rival. A sullen ill will towards Britain, a desire to force her out of Egypt by making difficulties for her there, was henceforth to be a dominant influence in French policy in the Near East'.[31] Again the official reaction was more favourable; Duclerc, Freycinet's successor, told Lyons, 'The sober good sense of France felt that the success of England against Arabi was also a solid gain to the rulers of Algeria'.[32]

In Germany the British advance was welcomed. On 10 September Bismarck's son, Herbert, told Granville 'his father would not oppose even annexation . . . but, if he were in our place, he should avoid annexation, which, although it would not be opposed, would leave a fruitful source of quarrel with the French, who would not forget it'.[33] The occupation of Egypt strengthened Germany's position considerably. In Turkey, German influence increased as British diminished. In Europe the association of the western powers was further weakened.

Wolseley's success was well received by the public and British bondholders, but occupation opened up a new range of diplomatic problems. The duration of occupation, the legal status of Britain, the system of administration and the future of Tewfiq were all matters of the first importance. Power could not be restored to the Khedive, for he had not only shown incapacity but also vulnerability to pressure. Furthermore, a fresh problem loomed threateningly on the horizon—in 1881, following almost a decade of unrest in the Sudan, the Mahdist revolt had broken out. What action, if any, should Britain take against the Mahdi?

Initially it was believed that occupation would be temporary, though there was always opposition to this view. On 17 September the Queen told Granville, 'I think you should be very cautious in speaking of early withdrawal of troops. We must bind ourselves to nothing. We have not fought and shed precious blood and gone to great expense for nothing. Short of annexation we must obtain a firm hold and power in Egypt for the future. A large force will have to be left there for some time; and some troops, doubtless, indefinitely. If you bind yourselves beforehand you will be hampered as you were by the Conference . . . we shall be laughed at and despised by all Europe if we do not hold a high tone'.[34] Bismarck echoed the Queen's opinions: 'In regard to Eastern affairs, Bismarck has never concealed his anxious desire to see Austria occupy Bosnia, France occupy Tunis and England occupy Egypt; and now that those wishes have been realised, his next wish is that the occupation may last, and thereby minimise the ever-recurring danger to Europe of another Oriental crisis and all its consequences. In his opinion a gradual dismemberment of the Turkish Empire is the only pacific solution to the Oriental question'.[35]

Despite these views the government pressed ahead with plans for withdrawal. Gladstone told Granville he wanted 'the withdrawal of the foreign occupation as early as possible'.[36] Yet the old system of dual Anglo-French control was ended and it was clear this was a way 'of consolidating a permanent influence for Britain'.[37] A timetable for the withdrawal of forces was prepared but serious differences within the Cabinet caused Dufferin to be sent to Egypt to report on its feasibility. His instructions show the complexity of the situation; 'while desiring that the British occupation should last for as short a time as possible, [H.M.G.] feel bound not to withdraw from the task thus imposed on them until the administration of affairs has been reconstructed on a basis which will afford satisfactory guarantees for the maintenance of peace, order, and prosperity in Egypt, for the stability of the Khedive's authority, for the judicious development of self government, and for the fulfilment of obligations towards foreign powers'.[38] While Dufferin investigated the government acted. On 4 December it was decided to end the association with France and on 3 January a circular informed the powers that Britain formally claimed a leading position in Egypt. On 6 February 1883 Dufferin's report recommended leaving the Khedive at the head of the government, but that key places should be occupied by Britons in order to ensure proper administration. A stable government would thus be created and the withdrawal of troops would follow.

Later in 1883 it was decided to reduce the number of troops in Egypt to 3000 as the first step in a phased withdrawal, but in September Baring arrived to direct the faltering administration. He was asked by Granville to let him know if there was 'any objection to an early diminution of the troops'.[39] Soon Baring replied that if the government decided 'on a policy of evacuation, they must be prepared to turn a deaf ear to the cries which would . . . be raised both in Parliament and in the press, when the Egyptian government proceeded to govern according to their own lights'.[40] This was a strong argument against leaving a political vacuum, given particular force as Baring was no Tory jingo. Indeed, in 1884 he told Granville, 'I hope you will fully understand that what I am chiefly aiming at is eventual withdrawal, and although the policy will now take longer than we originally hoped, I see no reason why it should not eventually be carried out, if only you will keep the Tories out of office'.[41]

Unrecognized at the time though it was, Baring's arrival signalled the permanent occupation of Egypt. The need for good government compelled British presence. Events in the Sudan reinforced this impression. In May 1883 Tewfiq instructed Hicks Pasha, his general, to reconquer Kordofan, one of the provinces of the Sudan. In London some members of the Cabinet, notably Childers, felt this challenge to the Mahdi was unnecessary, but nothing was done to prevent it. On 3 November the Egyptian army, including Hicks and his European officers, was annihilated at El Obeid. The disaster convinced the Cabinet that Tewfiq's régime would never be stable while he was allowed to squander resources on the Sudanese adventure. In December the Khedive was told to give up the Sudan as lost. This decision ended what remained of Tewfiq's reputation in Egypt and possibly promoted the Mahdist cult. As Northbrook realized, 'We have now been forced into the position of being the protectors of Egypt'.[42] Despite widespread criticism in the press the government stuck to its decision, though as Egyptians now declined to serve the Khedive this now meant further British involvement. Britain could not act decisively in Egypt lest France be offended, but public feeling demanded decisive action.

In the spring of 1884 long negotiations with France enabled Britain to promise to evacuate Egypt in three-and-a-half years' time, provided there was political stability. This enabled Britain to proceed to administer Egypt and on 2 April even Gladstone admitted 'We have done our Egyptian business, and we are an Egyptian government'.[43] It proved an optimistic forecast. On 18 January Gordon had been sent to relieve the beleaguered garrisons near Khartoum, but further reverses in the following weeks rendered the Egyptian position there untenable. As the situation worsened the Cabinet got into a terrible tangle. Forster and Goschen joined in the Tory attacks while the Radicals mounted a separate campaign on the left. Majorities fell and eventually disappeared. In panic, Harcourt demanded, 'We must get out of Egypt as soon as possible at any price'.[44] Public opinion demanded that Gordon be saved, but how could this be done without increasing the 'ill will towards England'[45] which existed in Paris? In June the international conference on Egypt was wrecked by disagreement between the western powers; the agreement of the spring was abandoned. On 31 July Selborne and Hartington, now firmly in favour of staying in Egypt, threatened to resign unless an expedition was sent to rescue Gordon. Northbrook was sent to report on the situation but his view that it would be unsafe to fix a time limit for evacuation was rejected at a Cabinet meeting on 19 November. Debate continued throughout the winter of 1884–85, while Gordon envisaged ever more lunatic and ambitious schemes for crushing the Mahdi. In January 1885 France proposed measures which would have increased international responsibility in Egypt at the expense of British commitments. Seeking an escape route from their problems, Gladstone and a majority of the Cabinet accepted these proposals, overruling Hartington and Northbrook. Scuttle was the order of the day, for acceptance 'means the start of international control for Egypt. After . . . will come the question of neutralising Egypt and consequently the British evacuation of the country',[46] wrote Waddington triumphantly.

On 5 February the news reached London that Gordon was dead and Khartoum captured. A wave of indignation swept the country, shared by the Queen, who telegraphed *en clair* several of her ministers, informing them 'These news from Khartoum are frightful, and to think that all this might have been prevented and many precious lives saved by earlier action is too frightful'.[47] Baring concurred: 'The Nile expedition was sanctioned too late, and the reason why . . . was that Mr. Gladstone would not accept simple evidence of a plain fact, which was patent to much less powerful intellects than his own'.[48] The Cabinet now abandoned its attempts to please France and tried instead to placate public opinion. Wolseley was ordered to defend Egypt at Berber, but on 15 April this policy was reversed once more when evacuation of the whole of the Sudan was ordered. Derby and Harcourt made it plain they thought it a mistake ever to have gone into Egypt. Fortunately for the government the Conservatives were much less belligerent than the general public and did not call for permanent occupation of Egypt and the Sudan. Had they done so grave embarrassment must have been caused.

The government was now tottering to its fall, but in the meantime made final efforts to extricate itself from Egypt. In March the foreign loan administration, through the *Caisse*, was guaranteed by an Anglo-French agreement; the foreign loan to Egypt which resulted was internationally financed. Some of France's *amour propre* was thus saved, and after the fall of Ferry relations between the western powers slowly improved. In June the Liberal government fell and responsibility passed to Salisbury and the Conservatives. Almost as soon as Salisbury took office the Sudanese problem became much less urgent for on 22 June the Mahdi died and on 30 December his successor was heavily defeated at Qinis. Fears of an invasion of Egypt were thus ended and public attention was diverted elsewhere.

British concern over the fate of Egypt arose primarily because of that country's strategic position on the route to India. The ministry of 1880–85 was similarly concerned about Afghanistan, the small state which protected the approach to India from the north-west. As in Egypt, Britain found her policy opposed by a major power—in this case Russia. In 1880 the area was in a state of unrest and political turmoil. The Liberals tried from the very start to establish a better relationship with Russia in order to reach a settlement in Afghanistan and began by replacing the aggressive Lytton as Viceroy with Ripon. Ripon neither possessed his predecessor's diplomatic style nor did he agree with his ambitious schemes for the annexation of Afghanistan. In London Granville, despite personal suspicion of Russia, pleaded for understanding: 'We wish to be good friends with Russia. We do not think there need be any ostentation about it, and we do not propose to make any concession excepting with a view to our own interests as well as to hers. But I can conceive no worse policy than to be always nagging, and always trying to play each other tricks'.[49]

Local developments, however, contributed substantially to poor relations with Russia in these years. During 1880–81 a power struggle was fought out in Afghanistan between two local potentates, Ayub and Abdur Rahman. British troops were inevitably involved in the conflict, being defeated by Ayub at Maiwand on 27 July 1880 but routing him at Kandahar in September. Eventually, in September 1881, Ayub was conclusively defeated by his rival who proceeded to occupy Herat and Kandahar, unifying the country and creating an effective buffer state. The new Amir, a former Russian pensioner, was well acquainted with Russian aims and was determined to prevent penetration of Afghanistan. The immediate threat to Indian security was thus removed, but left unanswered the question of the future British rôle in Afghanistan. Imperialists and annexationists argued that the country should be taken completely under British protection rather than being left to fend for itself with covert backing from Simla. Hartington disagreed; 'It turns, in my opinion, entirely on the degree of importance which is to be attached to the idea, possibility, or danger of Russian invasion of India. If we are to look on Russia as a power which may, in some not remote period, undertake the invasion of India, I conceive that the strategic advantages of holding Kandahar . . . are enormous; and not to be overborne by the expense and inconvenience which would be incurred. But if we do not hold this to be a contingency to be seriously taken into our calculations, all the arguments about trade, prestige and so forth seem to me to be utterly inconclusive. I confess I am not as clear and positive on this vital point as Northbrook, Norman and the other anti-annexationists, but on the whole I am inclined to think that the balance of opinion of reasonable men is on their side'.[50]

Despite the friendly attitude in London and Simla, Russia kept on feeling her way to the Afghan boundary. In 1882 she conquered the Turkomans, persuading Ripon to advocate a treaty by which Britain conceded Russian advance to Merv in return for a promise not to interfere in Afghanistan. Granville disagreed, arguing in 1883 'There is no doubt of the Russians moving on and feeling their way towards the frontier of Afghanistan. The question remains how this can best be met. It is doubtful whether any understanding with Russia would be really efficacious, and it seems certain that the Russians do not desire to come to an understanding'.[51] In 1884, despite assurances by Gorchakov in 1882 that it lay outside the sphere of Russian influence, Merv was occupied. Granville now favoured a more aggressive policy, as did the Queen, but the Cabinet could only agree to send a joint commission to demarcate the Russo-Afghan boundary. Once more Russia failed to honour her pledges and a large force was discovered close to the Zulfiqar pass, which was essential to the defence of Afghanistan. In February 1885 Russian troops arrived at Penjdeh within Afghan territory. Granville protested vigorously and the Queen sent a personal telegram to the Tsar. She was already most displeased with government policy, lamenting 'this want of decision and firmness . . . which gives . . . the greatest anxiety for the future'.[52] On 30 March Russian troops crushed the Afghan forces at Penjdeh. Complaints at British passivity poured in from India and were echoed in the press. The government demanded credits and war fever grew. Britain was too involved in Egypt to act boldly in Afghanistan and in May a preliminary agreement was signed which left the Zulfiqar pass in the Amir's possession. As Gladstone told Granville, 'the Russian government itself has sanctioned in terms the basis *Zulfikar contra*

Penjdeh, and this is not fulfilled unless there be exclusive control by the Afghans of the main portion of the passage'.[53] It was left to Salisbury, on 10 September, to ratify the preliminary agreement, but the crisis had emphasized British isolation. Other powers had shown no sympathy for Britain, particularly after her bold occupation of Port Hamilton, off the Korean coast, as a threat to Vladivostok. The Cabinet contrived in this crisis, as in Egypt, to create suspicion in Europe by its strange oscillation between provocation and surrender.

Another area of critical importance for Gladstone's government was South Africa. Policy was mishandled at almost every stage. In 1877 the Transvaal Republic had been annexed, with the object of achieving three goals: confederation of the settled area, greater control of the Zulus, and increased security for the strategically important base at Simon's Bay. In 1879 Sir Bartle Frere, the energetic and expansionist High Commissioner, authorized Wolseley to crush the Zulus. Defeat of the Zulus at Ulundi removed the only potent lever against the Boers and the result was that 'Carnarvon's attempt to consolidate British supremacy had provoked a dangerous Afrikaner national challenge'.[54] Gladstone was not the man to deal with the situation; already he had criticized Disraeli's handling of the issue, expressing sympathy to the Boers in a fashion which misled their leaders concerning expectations from the new government. In office, Gladstone kept Frere in order to push on with federation. He told parliament that 'Confederation is the pole star of the present action of our government'.[55] The pleas of Kruger and Joubert had no effect save the recall of Frere in August 1880.

At the close of the year an armed rebellion took place and a new republic was proclaimed. This caused consternation in London and helpless confusion in Cape Town, where the arrival of Frere's replacement, Sir Hercules Robinson, was still awaited. The Queen expected the government to take 'energetic measures to assert her authority in those parts of the Colony which have revolted. The Boers are a dangerous foe . . .'.[56] The Cabinet could agree on nothing. Some ministers, notably Chamberlain, Bright, Dilke and Gladstone, sympathized with the Boers. Hartington and Kimberley proclaimed it was in the national interest to suppress the rising. Forster and some others, with uncanny prescience, were most concerned by the prospect of Boer oppression of the native peoples if the Republic were allowed to go its own way. By early 1881 the groups favouring suppression of the rebellion had carried the day and on 27 February General Colley opened hostilities at Majuba Hill. The British forces were routed and Colley killed. News of the defeat incensed the public and the coercionist party was greatly strengthened, though in the Cabinet the doves prevailed by threatening resignation unless peace were made. Bright and his allies saw the danger of the Orange Free State's declarations of sympathy for the rebels and feared international complications which an over-stretched Britain would be unable to handle. On 6 March Sir Evelyn Wood agreed an armistice and on 22 March this was converted into a peace.

The Queen remained hostile to any form of negotiation, observing, 'I do not like peace before we have retrieved our honour.'[57] Kimberley, however, justified peace in practical terms: 'We know that if we conquer the country we can only hold it by the sword.'[58] To the apostles of Gladstonian liberalism this would have been anathema. In the years that followed the Cabinet preferred to negotiate rather than fight, despite the fact that the Pretoria Convention worked very poorly. Meanwhile some changes of attitude took place. The imperialist yearnings of the Transvaal Republic came into conflict with British ambitions. Even Derby, who replaced Kimberley at the Colonial Office in 1882, became concerned at the future of Bechuanaland. In February 1884 he was able to reach agreement with Kruger, delimiting the Bechuanaland border with the Transvaal in return for concessions which made the Republic virtually independent of all British suzerainty. But much trouble for the future was stored up in Derby's analysis of the constitutional relationship: 'Whatever suzerainty meant in the Convention of Pretoria, the condition of things which it implied still remains; although the word is not actually employed, we have kept the substance'.[59] The blunders of Gladstone's ministry, although they temporarily avoided conflict, were to cause a major war within twenty years.

Heavily involved as it was in Afghanistan, Egypt and South Africa, the government was unable to exercise influence in the traditional way elsewhere. The government was regularly, and accurately, accused of being unable to sustain Britain's position as a major power. Throughout these years Germany was the dominant force in international politics and Britain was obliged to give way at almost every turn. It is true that Bismarck was at the height of his power, but the incapacity of Granville and the multitude of conflicting voices within the Cabinet played an important part. The ideal Bismarckian world was 'a political situation in which all the powers except France would need us, and would be deprived of the possibility of coalition against us by their relations to each other'.[60] By 1882 this dream was fulfilled. Russia, Austria and Italy, as well as a number of lesser European states, were bound to Germany by alliances. Turkey already regarded Germany rather than Britain as her mainstay. France and Britain were bitterly divided by rivalry in North Africa; Britain and Russia by rivalry in Central Asia. Nowhere was there any flexibility in the international system, save that permitted by Bismarck.

The impotence of Britain was partially self-created. The conduct of foreign affairs was erratic. The Queen, who had never really liked Palmerston, was driven to observe in 1883, 'She has no doubt that Lord Granville feels as Lord Palmerston did; who with all his many faults, had the honour and power of his country strongly at heart, and so had Lord Beaconsfield. But she does not feel that Mr. Gladstone has'.[61] Gladstone was not the only offender. Baring was equally severe in his strictures on Granville: 'His power of eluding the main point at issue was quite extraordinary. Often did I think he was on the horns of a dilemma, and that he was in a position from which no escape was possible without the expression of a definite opinion. I was generally mistaken. With a smile and a quick little epigrammatic phrase, Lord Granville would elude one's grasp and be off without giving any opinion at all'.[62] This ill-assorted pair were no match for Bismarck, but they made the task still more herculean by helping break the understanding with France which had so frequently been of benefit to both nations since the days of Talleyrand and Liverpool.

Some sources of weakness were beyond control. Britain was already over-extended in 1880 and new responsibilities taken on by the

Liberals made matters worse. Trade stagnated while commercial competition from other countries grew. As trading interests suffered, the areas under British control came to seem more important and the need to protect them more urgent. Clamour for expansion (often on strategic grounds) grew rather than diminished, though it was the cause of weakness rather than its cure. This made it increasingly necessary for Britain to remain on good terms with other powers and ever less likely to succeed. The free hand of the past had disappeared, but politicians and public alike were slow to recognize facts.

A very real problem for other great powers was that British policy in these years was a strange mixture of power politics and idealism. Lack of understanding helped undermine the traditional bases of policy. The first casualty was the Anglo-French understanding, though strain had already begun to show in the days of Disraeli. Britain feared and dreaded the collapse of the Ottoman Empire, whereas France saw herself as the natural heir in North Africa. As a Mediterranean and colonial power France might hope to regain the prestige and authority lost at Sedan. Bismarck naturally favoured these pretensions, which he saw as a diversion from *revanche* and potentially embarrassing for France as likely sources of conflict with Britain and Italy. A better understanding of French aspirations might have saved the *entente*, but quarrels over Tunis began the process of alienation which the Egyptian conflict completed. The struggle between France and Italy for supremacy in Tunis distressed Britain on two counts: she disliked dismemberment, and it was bound to be difficult to remain on good terms with both powers if the *status quo* were upset. French feeling was, however, that Britain was welshing on a bargain. Deschanel believed in 1878, 'In exchange for our support, England gives us *carte blanche* in Tunisia, in agreement with Bismarck, who is delighted to find this opportunity to embroil us with Italy'.[63] When the crisis of 1881 arose Britain did nothing, Granville observing, 'I suppose our best policy is to do nothing to irritate the French unnecessarily and at the same time nothing to reassure them as to possible results'.[64] Gestures were made in the direction of a Concert of Europe, but nothing was done to prevent the Treaty of Bardo of 12 May 1881 which secured French primacy. Britain had barked but not bitten; France had been offended but not incapacitated. The old trust was destroyed. France saw Britain as a well-endowed rival trying to make further encroachments in an area of strong historic French interest. Britain saw French interest in Egypt as a wish to cut vital links to India. Germany rejoiced and profited.

Colonial expansion and conflict became the normal pattern. Indeed, a veritable colonial mania gripped the major powers. France and Germany made the running, but the seizure of Egypt merely accelerated the pace. It was British presence in Egypt which enfeebled Britain in her resistance to the drive for colonies. Needing the help of other powers in the administration of Egypt's shaky finances, Britain did not dare resist colonial claims. In 1881 Granville and Kimberley at last began to realize the gravity of the situation. Rivalries of traders and missionaries were causing Britain problems everywhere in Africa. Ignoring the demands of the imperialists, Granville tried to negotiate a delimitation of frontiers with France in West Africa, but involvement in Egypt killed the plan. Expansionists rejoiced. They had powerful allies in the Foreign Office who 'pressed on Lord Kimberley . . . the view . . . that England should annex all unoccupied territory between Lagos and the French settlement of the Gaboon'.[65] The Colonial Office rejected these arguments, though there was great anxiety about the economic future of British West Africa.

Suspicion and fear were further increased by French and Belgian activity in the Congo. In an attempt to restrain the ambition of these powers Britain resorted to a device which only exacerbated relations. In a treaty of 26 February 1884 Britain recognized Portuguese claims to the Congo and its hinterland. Waddington correctly described it as 'a security taken by Britain to prevent either France or an international syndicate managed by France from establishing itself in the Congo Basin . . . Britain . . . would rather partition it with Portugal, whom it can readily influence, rather than leave France with an open door'.[66] The British attempt to use the feeble Portuguese as a shield to protect her own interests aroused French hostility, while the trading lobby in London attacked the government for abandoning British interests. In the face of a refusal by other powers to recognize the treaty, it was abandoned on 26 June 1884.

This spectacular defeat for the leading trading and naval power heralded a dreadful year for British diplomacy. The government was worried lest intransigence over colonial matters hurt British interests in Egypt. The months that passed showed that it could and did. As Milner observed, 'Everything . . . seemed bent upon going wrong at one and the same time. Alike in military matters, in diplomacy, and in politics, Great Britain was simply haunted by the Egyptian Question'.[67] In Africa Britain faced a coalition of Germany and a French government inspired by Ferry's belief that Alsace and Lorraine were irrecoverable. The only factor which limited French determination to press colonial claims against Britain was that even Ferry hesitated to enter into a serious conflict because its inevitable result would be total supremacy by Germany in Europe. The root of Germany's association in a combination against Britain was irritation over a number of colonial matters. The dispute over Angra Pequena, a desolate area near Walfisch Bay, showed how clumsily Bismarck was handled by Granville. In 1883 the Chancellor enquired what British claims were, but received only an evasive reply: 'Britain . . . considered that any claim to sovereignty or jurisdiction by a foreign Power between the southern point of Portuguese jurisdiction at latitude 18°S and the frontier of Cape Colony would infringe their legitimate rights'.[68] Bismarck rejected this shadowy claim, asking what institutions Britain had there and how she could protect merchants and missionaries. On 24 April 1884 Germany annexed the area.

The real German complaint was not in relation to any specific territory but rather the British attitude. In a letter to Münster, Ambassador to London, the German gravamen clearly emerged: 'the explanations which several English statesmen have given, with the purport that England has a legitimate right to prevent settlements by other nations in the vicinity of English possessions, and that England establishes a sort of Monroe Doctrine in Africa against the vicinage of other nations'.[69] In 1884–85 Germany was in the box-seat. Britain was dependent on international aid in Egypt and Bismarck was able to use this weakness to appease the anglo-phobia of imperialist and commercial lobbies in Germany, where an election was imminent.

On 5 May 1884 Bismarck urged Münster to press the German claim to Heligoland, suggesting 'We believe . . . our attitude to her enemies or rivals is of more importance to British policy than the possession of Heligoland and all the trade rivalry of German and British firms in distant seas. England can secure for herself the continuance of our active support for her political interests through sacrifices, which she would hardly feel'.[70] Even Granville could not look upon this proposal with equanimity, for he knew that polite blackmail would not be well received by the public. For once he was firm: 'Count Münster said it was as good as impossible that Germany and England should ever be at war, but the cession of Heligoland would strengthen the good feeling of Germany towards this country to an extraordinary degree. I said I supposed the cession of Gibraltar would strengthen our good relations with Spain; but the Count denied that there was any similarity in the two cases'.[71] The Queen was even more indignant and her fury was fanned by a letter from her daughter, the Crown Princess of Germany, which reported the strength of anti-British feeling: 'The German Press has been so rude and so impertinent lately about England. . . . If I may say, the Germans are of an arrogance that one longs to see put down, especially their tone towards England'.[72] Nothing came of Bismarck's manoeuvre except increased ill-will on all sides.

After this rebuff Bismarck showed he was in earnest by beginning serious co-operation with France. The claim to Angra Pequena was widened and in August 1884 the whole of South West Africa was conceded to Germany. Elsewhere in the world Britain was forced to retreat before German pressure. Claims were conceded in Togo, Cameroon, Zanzibar, Samoa and New Guinea. Granville hoped that relations with Berlin would now return to normal, but conflict with Russia in Central Asia and with France over Madagascar made German support more vital still. In late 1884, at the Berlin conference on the future of West Africa, Britain found her position on the Niger under threat from France. Initially bereft of German support Britain was compelled to make wide concessions in Africa. Madagascar became French and British hopes in the Congo were destroyed. On 12 March 1885 Gladstone revealed the extent of this humiliation in welcoming Germany as a colonial power 'in the execution of the great purpose of Providence for the advantage of mankind'.[73]

From this time onwards the anti-British alliance slowly faded away, though Bismarck did use his influence with the Porte to prevent any chance of a passage of British ships through the Straits at the time of the Penjdeh crisis. On 31 March Ferry was forced out of office after reverses in Indo-China, and anti-German groups returned to power. On 1 June the Chancellor admitted to his Cabinet, 'For us the French will never become even dependable defensive allies . . . in the end we could hardly do otherwise than go over to the side of the English'.[74] In France Freycinet 'realized . . . how dangerous it would be for France to emphasize a policy by which she risked at any moment finding herself alone and face to face with a hostile England and an indifferent Europe'.[75]

Anglo-German relations were never to be quite the same again. The humiliations of 1884–85 were never entirely forgotten. It is true that men like Derby thought little of these events, but then he was a stern critic of the imperialists. When Germany put forward her claims in the Pacific the Australian government objected vigorously, but Derby brushed their protests aside: 'I asked them whether they did not want another planet all to themselves? The magnitude of their ideas is appalling to the English mind. . . . It is hardly too much to say that they consider the whole Southern Pacific theirs *de jure*; the French possession of New Caledonia they regard as an act of robbery committed on them. It certainly is hard for four millions of English settlers to have only a country as big as Europe to fill up'.[76] Derby was not typical. Public reaction to Germany's demands was immediate and hostile. In December 1884 pressure for building new ships to protect British interests became so intense that an extra £5.5 million was voted. The government was forced into annexing Bechuanaland, St Lucia and parts of New Guinea in order to appease public wrath at the truckling to Germany. Even the pacific Granville felt obliged to take open issue with various of Bismarck's statements.

If public reaction was hostile, so too was that of many politicians. The imperialism of Chamberlain seems to have been born during this year of diplomatic reverses. There had always been opposition in the Cabinet from the Whigs, but now Gladstone and the party favourable to Germany found themselves opposed by men like Dilke and Chamberlain. Initially the objections of the Radicals seem to have been based upon tactical considerations. In late 1884 Chamberlain told Dilke, 'I don't give a damn about New Guinea and I am not afraid of German colonisation, but I don't like being cheeked by Bismarck or anyone else'.[77] Gradually the Radicals began to take a new attitude towards empire as they saw British trade stagnating and the condition of England no longer seemed so enviable. New methods and new answers were required. The collapse of belief in the inevitability of progress produced a readiness to adopt new ideas. The fact that Germany played a major part in the humiliations of the 1884 conferences on Egypt and West Africa left many members of the Gladstone Cabinet with hostile memories. Dissensions within the Cabinet helped bring down the government and, paradoxically, more suspicion existed in regard to the false friend than the enemy. Men of the future, like Chamberlain, never forgot their baptism of fire in international politics.

By 1885 the government was in a parlous condition. Riven by dissension over the Franchise Bill and Ireland, colonial problems provided a mortal blow. A total lack of statesmanship by Gladstone and Granville convinced many people in public life that the government should resign. In Lyons' view, England's only card was 'the reluctance of the French to be thrown irretrievably into the clutches of Bismarck by a distinct quarrel with us'.[78] It was Lyons too who saw that 'Bismarck and Ferry are *jouant au plus fin* with each other at our expense; each seems to think that he can use the other to help in thwarting us, without risk to himself'.[79] In March 1885 the government weakly agreed to a continuation of international control of Egyptian finances, thus condemning Baring to another two decades of vexation. It was the last and most momentous surrender, for it invalidated the whole direction of governmental policy since 1881.

In June 1885 Gladstone's government collapsed. Neither Queen nor country had regrets. Victoria's views on the two leading personalities involved in the conduct of foreign affairs were probably shared by the mass of the general public. 'Mr. Gladstone', she wrote, 'has alienated all other countries from us, by his very changeable and unreliable policy—unintentionally no doubt'.[80] Victoria also wrote Granville's political epitaph: 'Look at our relations abroad! No one trusts or relies on us and from '74 to '80 especially the last three or four years of that time England stood very high. It is a terrible grief to her. The Queen blames Lord Granville very much for he is as many say "quite past"—weak and indolent and not able to work hard'.[81] These were savage strictures, but apt commentary upon a government which with a historic rôle to play in the world had elected instead to live by expediency and time-serving for five years.

REFERENCES

1 *The Trouble Makers* by A. J. P. Taylor. p. 78.
2 *The Life of Lord Granville* by Lord Edmond Fitzmaurice. Vol. II. p. 203. Granville to Hartington, 5 April 1880.
3 *Letters of Queen Victoria* ed. G. E. Buckle. Second Series. Vol. III. pp. 80–1. 22 April 1880.
4 ibid., Vol. III. p. 76. Victoria to Ponsonby, 8 April 1880.
5 *The Political Influence of the British Monarchy, 1868–1952* by F. Hardie. p. 30.
6 *Fortnightly Review* Vol. XXIV. December 1878. Speech of 5 November 1878.
7 *The Imperial Idea and its Enemies* by A. P. Thornton. pp. ix–x.
8 *Hansard*. House of Commons. 17 March 1882.
9 Quoted in *European Alliances and Alignments* by W. L. Langer. p. 209.
10 Fitzmaurice, op. cit., Vol. II. p. 199. Granville to Odo Russell, 5 May 1880.
11 *The Nineteenth Century* Vol. IV. September 1878. Article by Gladstone.
12 Granville to Goschen, 10 June 1880. F.O. 78/3074.
13 Buckle, op. cit., Second Series. Vol. III. p. 93. Granville to Victoria, 1 May 1880.
14 *Annual Register, 1880.* p. 47. Speech of 17 March 1880.
15 Fitzmaurice, op. cit., Vol. II. p. 205. Granville to Gladstone, 5 October 1883.
16 Quoted in Langer, op. cit., p. 204.
17 Fitzmaurice, op. cit., Vol. II. p. 218. Odo Russell to Granville, 9 October 1880.
18 Quoted in Langer, op. cit., p. 204.
19 *Konets avstro-russko-germanskogo soiuza* by S. Skazkin. Vol. I. pp. 142–3.
20 *England in Egypt* by Viscount Milner. p. 55.
21 Fitzmaurice, op. cit., Vol. II. p. 225. Odo Russell to Granville, 26 January 1881.
22 ibid., Vol. II. p. 252. Granville to Lyons, 7 November 1881.
23 ibid., Vol. II. p. 252. Granville to Dufferin, 15 October 1881.

24 *Life of Gladstone* by J. Morley. Vol. II. p. 237.
25 Fitzmaurice, op. cit., Vol. II. p. 262. Ampthill to Granville, 30 June 1882.
26 Gladstone to Granville, 21 June 1882. Granville MSS., P.R.O. 30/29/125.
27 Fitzmaurice, op. cit., Vol. II. p. 268. Ampthill to Granville, 15 July 1882.
28 ibid., Vol. II. p. 271. Granville to Paget, 28 July 1882.
29 Buckle, op. cit., Second Series. Vol. III. p. 317. Victoria to Gladstone, 1 August 1882.
30 *Modern Egypt* by Lord Cromer. p. 237.
31 *The Eastern Question, 1774–1923* by M. S. Anderson. p. 246.
32 *Lord Lyons* by Lord Newton. Vol. II. p. 293.
33 Buckle, op. cit., Second Series. Vol. III. p. 332. Granville to Victoria, 10 September 1882.
34 ibid., Vol. III. p. 334. Victoria to Granville, 17 September 1882.
35 Fitzmaurice, op. cit., Vol. II. p. 273. Ampthill to Granville, 30 September 1882.
36 Gladstone to Granville, 15 September 1882. Granville MSS., P.R.O. 30/29/126.
37 Malet to Granville, 3 September 1882. Granville MSS., P.R.O. 30/29/160.
38 Quoted in *Africa and the Victorians* by R. Robinson and J. Gallagher. pp. 126–7. Granville to Dufferin, 3 November 1882.
39 *Lord Cromer* by the Marquess of Zetland. p. 88. Granville to Baring, 31 August 1883.
40 Cromer, op. cit., p. 735.
41 Zetland, op. cit., p. 92. Baring to Granville, 7 January 1884.
42 Memorandum to the Cabinet, 24 December 1883. P.R.O. 30/29/139.
43 Robinson and Gallagher, op. cit., p. 138.
44 *Life of Sir Charles Dilke* by S. Gwynn and G. Tuckwell. Vol. II. p. 43. Harcourt to Dilke, March 1884.
45 Newton, op. cit., Vol. II. p. 328. Lyons to Granville, 27 May 1884.
46 Waddington to Ferry, 22 January 1885. *Documents diplomatiques français*. First Series. Vol. V. No. 533.
47 Buckle, op. cit., Second Series. Vol. III. p. 597. Victoria to Hartington, 5 February 1885.
48 Cromer, op. cit., pp. 473–4.
49 Fitzmaurice, op. cit., Vol. II. p. 416. Granville to Dufferin, 24 May 1880.
50 *Life of Lord Ripon* by L. Wolf. Vol. II. pp. 40–1. Hartington to Ripon, 30 September 1880.
51 Fitzmaurice, op. cit., Vol. II. pp. 419–20. Granville to Victoria, 9 February 1883.
52 Buckle, op. cit., Second Series. Vol. III. p. 617. Victoria to Gladstone, 1 March 1885.
53 Fitzmaurice, op. cit., Vol. II. p. 443. Gladstone to Granville, 3 June 1885.
54 Robinson and Gallagher, op. cit., p. 64.
55 Morley, op. cit., Vol. II. p. 196.
56 Buckle, op. cit., Second Series. Vol. III. pp. 166–7. Victoria to Gladstone, 26 December 1880.
57 ibid., Vol. III. p. 199. 6 March 1881.
58 Robinson and Gallagher, op. cit., p. 71. Kimberley's Memorandum, 29 April 1881.
59 Morley, op. cit., p. 213 fn. Derby in House of Lords, 17 March 1884.

60 Quoted in *Germany and England, background of conflict, 1848–94* by R. J. Sontag. p. 187.
61 Buckle, op. cit., Second Series. Vol. III. p. 447. Victoria to Granville, 22 October 1883.
62 Cromer, op. cit., p. 304 fn.
63 *Histoire de la politique extérieure de la France* by P. Deschanel. p. 259.
64 *The Political Correspondence of Mr. Gladstone and Lord Granville, 1876–86* ed. A. Ramm. p. 268. Granville to Gladstone, 27 April 1881.
65 Robinson and Gallagher, op. cit., p. 168. Minute by Meade, 28 March 1883.
66 Waddington to Ferry, 4 March 1884. *Documents diplomatiques français.* First Series. Vol. V. No. 214.
67 Milner, op. cit., p. 74.
68 Fitzmaurice, op. cit., Vol. II. p. 349. Granville to Ampthill, 21 November 1883.
69 ibid., Vol. II. p. 353. Bismarck to Münster, 10 June 1884.
70 *German Diplomatic Documents* ed. E. T. S. Dugdale. Vol. I. p. 170. Bismarck to Münster, 5 May 1884.
71 Fitzmaurice, op. cit., Vol. II. p. 351. Granville's Memorandum, 17 May 1884.
72 Buckle, op. cit., Second Series. Vol. III. p. 505. Crown Princess Victoria to Victoria, 25 May 1884.
73 *Hansard.* House of Commons. 12 March 1885.
74 Langer, op. cit., p. 316.
75 ibid., p. 316.
76 Buckle, op. cit., Second Series. Vol. III. pp. 432–3. Derby to Ponsonby, 23 June 1883.
77 *Life of Joseph Chamberlain* by J. L. Garvin. Vol. I. p. 497. Chamberlain to Dilke, 29 December 1884.
78 Newton, op. cit., Vol. II. p. 338.
79 ibid., Vol. II. p. 341. Lyons to Granville, 20 January 1885.
80 Buckle, op. cit., Second Series. Vol. III. p. 643. Victoria to Granville, 28 April 1885.
81 *Henry Ponsonby, His Life from his Letters* by A. Ponsonby. p. 232. Victoria to Ponsonby, 7 February 1885.

2 The Ascendancy of Salisbury, 1885–95

> The Cecils talked more for amusement than for the expression
> of opinion or for the probing of thought.... They knew what
> they thought on fundamentals.
>
> Viscountess Milner in *My Picture Gallery, 1886–1901*

During this decade, although Salisbury was the dominant figure, there were three other holders of the office of Foreign Secretary. Salisbury combined the posts of Prime Minister and Foreign Secretary throughout the periods of Conservative rule (June 1885–February 1886 and August 1886–August 1892) except for the few months between August 1886 and January 1887 when the Earl of Iddesleigh temporarily held office. Rosebery was Foreign Secretary during Gladstone's last two ministries (February–July 1886 and August 1892–March 1894) and on his succession to the premiership handed over foreign affairs to Kimberley, who remained in office until the Conservative return to power in the summer of 1895.

Despite these changes of personnel, British policy was very largely dominated by the style and opinions of Salisbury. There was a substantial degree of continuity between Conservative and Liberal governments in foreign affairs. On 10 July 1890, for example, Rosebery declared, 'I will never be party to dragging the foreign policy of this country into the arena of Party warfare'.[1] Continuity naturally depended upon the character of the holders of office and in this matter Britain was favoured by the Liberal Foreign Secretaries, both of whom could be described as Liberal Imperialists and hence much closer to the Conservative viewpoint than Gladstone or Harcourt. Yet this continuity of policy was not always clearly

References are printed on p. 60.

perceived or understood by foreign governments. It was assumed by most German statesmen and diplomats that a Liberal administration was more likely to be favourable to France and hence that more pressure needed to be applied to the Liberals in order to secure British co-operation with the powers of the Triple Alliance. Furthermore, until his retirement in 1894, Gladstone's occasional forays into foreign affairs were as little understood abroad in this decade as they had been in the government of 1880-85.

It proved extremely difficult in 1885 to pursue any consistent policy. Constant domestic political turmoil, centring on Irish issues, did not permit any government to speak with real authority on foreign affairs. Divisions within the Liberal Party on issues of foreign policy had not abated and until Randolph Churchill's resignation in December 1886 the Conservatives were similarly disunited. Indeed, the conflict of opinion within the ranks of the Liberals was to remain a consistent phenomenon throughout these years. It was one such conflict that ended Gladstone's political career. In 1893 popular opinion demanded increased naval expenditure to offset the threat to British sea-power. Led by Rosebery and Spencer, the Cabinet moved towards acceptance of the new naval programme. Harcourt was originally the principal opponent, but later Gladstone himself took the lead, seeing it as a stand against militarism. On this issue he was virtually alone and in early 1894 it precipitated his departure from office. Personal animosity and bitter feuding within Liberal ranks rendered unanimity over foreign policy issues almost impossible.

The fall of the Liberal government in 1885 put Salisbury at the head of a minority caretaker ministry. He told Cranbrook 'The prospect before us is very serious . . . the vote on Monday night was anything but a subject for congratulation'.[2] The Conservative team was pitifully short of experience in foreign affairs so on 12 June the premier told the Queen 'he was anxious to be Foreign Secretary as well as Prime Minister, because none of his colleagues were well acquainted with foreign affairs'.[3] The new Prime Minister was horrified by the dangers of the British position; 'The Liberal government', he declared, 'have at least achieved their long desired "Concert of Europe". . . . They have succeeded in uniting the continent of Europe—against England'.[4] Salisbury saw his most immediate task as that of leading Britain out of isolation, though not by concluding alliances. His style was to eliminate friction, being cautious with regard to general engagements but willing to consider specific limited agreements. He was most suspicious of Russia, and in this was not unrepresentative of public opinion. If he had any preference it seems to have been for France, for which nation he had shown sympathy in 1870. In practice, however, he found it most convenient to work with Italy, Germany and Austria, for the interests of these powers (the Triple Alliance of 1882) most frequently coincided with those of Britain.

As soon as the Tories returned to office, pressure on Britain began to ease. German attitudes changed almost overnight, as a conversation between two of Bismarck's aides, Busch and Bucher, makes clear. On 16 June Busch observed 'that Gladstone had defended English interests although in an unskilled and feeble way, and that Salisbury would not suit our purposes any better, indeed, perhaps less, because they would be more energetic. Bucher replied that . . . he might, however, for the moment be more welcome to the Chief than Gladstone, who had been seeking a *rapprochement* with Russia. . . . Salisbury, on the other hand, had spoken too strongly against Russia to leave much prospect of an understanding . . . between the Tories and St. Petersburg'.[5] Bucher's analysis proved correct. On 30 June Salisbury reported, 'Münster brought a message from Prince Bismarck . . . it was expressed with great friendliness, alluding in terms of satisfaction to the Conservative tradition of friendliness with the German people'.[6]

To bring Britain out of isolation it was necessary to improve relations with Germany. In August 1885 a special mission, headed by Currie, was sent to Berlin to ask for help in persuading Russia to agree terms in Central Asia. Currie went beyond his brief, advocating 'A close union between the greatest military power and the greatest naval power . . . would be in the highest degree advantageous to the interests of the two Countries'.[7] Bismarck had doubts about this proposal, fearing to incur Russian hostility for the sake of an alliance with a caretaker ministry. This was to be a regularly recurring obstacle to Anglo-German understanding in the next twenty years, for German statesmen feared a change of government might lead to repudiation of commitments. Salisbury tried to allay these fears by suggesting, 'I think that you may reasonably count on a continuity of policy in this matter'.[8] With an election imminent, this assurance suggests Salisbury knew the Queen would insist on either Rosebery or Kimberley at the Foreign Office in the event of Liberal victory. At no stage, however, did Salisbury intend to offer a general alliance. He preferred a limited understanding, but readiness to enter into continental politics made him more of an internationalist than Gladstone, despite the latter's commitment to the Concert of Europe.

The framework within which British policy operated during these ten years was necessarily simple. Salisbury was compelled to reckon with the hostility of France while Britain remained in Egypt. As France was a colonial power this involved the possibility of conflict all over the world—Siam, Madagascar, West Africa, Canada and East Africa. While Britain sought to protect Constantinople and Afghanistan, Russia was also bound to be hostile. To avoid isolation in Europe a working relationship with the Triple Alliance was obligatory. It was essential to reach agreement with Italy and Germany, particularly where these nations had colonial ambitions. Outside this Eurocentric system Britain found that interests in the Far East involved her in conflict in China, while in Latin America existed the possibility of a collision with the United States. The policy of eliminating friction and conciliating rivals had a great deal to commend it, though there existed always the danger that conciliation might be mistaken for weakness by some aggressive power.

Fortunately, relations with Russia were, on the whole, better in this decade than for many years. On 10 September 1885 an agreement was signed which restored the Zulfiqar pass to the Amir, though Russia kept Penjdeh. The boundary commission continued its work on the Oxus and a protocol was signed in July 1887. The strategic importance of this area, where three empires met, prevented any lasting peace until 1895. One of the problems was, as Salisbury saw, independent action by men on the spot—'each influential person, military or civil, snatches . . . the decisions which such person at the moment wants, and that the mutual effect of these decisions . . . is determined almost exclusively by chance'.[9] Sensible Russian ministers also recognized this difficulty because local leaders defied St Petersburg even more readily than their rivals did London. Successive Viceroys, Dufferin (1884–88) and Lansdowne (1888–93), proved no exception, both favouring 'forward' policies formerly pursued by Lytton. The only factor which held some Russian agents back was 'the certainty that any aggression in that direction must involve war with England all over the world'.[10] This a weak, divided, and developing Russia could not afford.

The advance of railways and roads into the undefined area bordering on Afghanistan led to a series of disputes during 1891–95. In August 1891 rival detachments under Younghusband and Ianov met at Bozai Gumbaz in the Pamirs, whose annexation by Russia triggered off a crisis, though the Ambassador to London, Staal, and his chief, Giers, both favoured peace and argued for delimitation as the 'one hope of escape from dangerous complications'.[11] Yet there were further crises in 1892–94. Salisbury and Rosebery each recognized how difficult the situation was for the civilian and peace-loving party in St Petersburg and each avoided taking stands on inessentials, much to the disgust of the 'forward' party. Even Rosebery, however, favoured British control of the northern slopes of the Hindu Kush. He once referred to Bozai Gumbaz as 'the Gibraltar of the Hindu Kush',[12] a preposterous exaggeration of the importance of both the town and its environs. In March 1895 a frontier line was agreed and Anglo-Russian relations in this area improved markedly.

Attention for the most part was focused on Europe rather than Central Asia. In the Balkans and Asia Minor Britain and Russia came face to face. Changes of ministry made little difference to the policies pursued and the weakened position of Gladstone after the disasters of 1880–85, coupled with the Whig and Chamberlainite defections of 1886, assisted the preservation of continuity. There was a Radical and pacifist party in Parliament, but it was weaker and more discredited than of old. As Rosebery told the Queen in 1893, the younger Liberals 'are more conscious than your Majesty thinks of the necessity of a firm foreign policy. Some of the older ones, who early in their careers imbibed the sanguine and futile gospel of Mr. Cobden on these questions, and who honestly cling to it,

will no doubt remain of their former opinion. All tastes, as the
French proverb says, are respectable ... but he believes it to be eva-
nescent and doomed'.[13] Gladstone's position was so weak in 1886 he
was obliged to bow to the Queen's wish that Granville 'should not
return to the F.O.'.[14] Salisbury and Rosebery shared with the
Queen a suspicion of Russian aims and hence enjoyed a much more
easy relationship with her than Granville or Gladstone. Salisbury
was soon highly regarded for 'the admirable manner in which he has
conducted public affairs ... the triumphant success of his conduct
of foreign affairs, by which he has in seven months raised Great
Britain to the position she ought to hold in the world'.[15] If this was a
trifle optimistic, it did mean there was small cause for the Queen to
interfere with the conduct of policy.

In 1879, following the separation of Bulgaria from Eastern
Roumelia, Alexander of Battenberg had been made hereditary prince.
He visited England and made a favourable impression on the Queen,
though he was advised 'to remember he was a vassal of the Sultan
and no puppet of the Tsar'.[16] In the following years, most seriously
in 1883, he had come into conflict with Russia and it became
evident that the young prince was hoping for British and German
support in his fight against Russian domination. Granville agreed
with the Queen that 'these Principalities ought to be a safeguard
for Turkey against Russian influence and encroachment',[17] but
London would give no more than moral support. In September
1885 Eastern Roumelia revolted and united with Bulgaria. The
Dreikaiserbund powers opposed union as a breach of the Berlin
settlement. Salisbury agreed with the three powers, fearing lest a
big Bulgaria be a Russian satellite. On 21 September he told the
Queen, 'Action of Prince of Bulgaria very ill-advised ... there
will be great difficulty in keeping the war from spreading and perhaps
Turkish Empire itself may be endangered. If he succeeds, he would
be only plucking fruit for Russia'.[18] Traditional fears of a collapse
of Ottoman power and a Russian advance on Constantinople were
thus uppermost in Salisbury's mind.

Salisbury soon changed his views. In November he suggested that
a personal union of Bulgaria and Roumelia under the prince would

meet most of the problems. The influence of Sir William White, Ambassador to the Porte, played a major part in conversion to the notion of an independent Bulgaria as a barrier to Russian advance. It was Russia which now opposed a big Bulgaria, thus reversing the diplomatic postures of 1878. An unsuccessful invasion of Bulgaria by a jealous Serbia in November 1885 further complicated matters by drawing Austria, allied to Serbia, into the dispute. In the end, Austrian intervention aided British aims because it was directed towards avoiding pressure by the Balkan states for compensation at the expense of Turkey. In 1886 Germany, wishing at all costs to avert a Turkish collapse which might lead to Austro-Russian conflict, managed to stabilize the situation on lines similar to those proposed by Britain the previous winter.

Russian determination to unseat Alexander was so strong that in August 1886 he was carried off to Russia and soon after forced to abdicate. The great danger now was that a Russian nominee would rule in Sofia—exactly what Disraeli had prevented in 1878. The Queen was furious, as Russian action ran directly contrary to both her personal liking for Alexander and her view of British interests. She was 'horrified at these news from Bulgaria. On what grounds can this have been done? It is these Russian fiends; but it may rouse a European war'.[19] Salisbury felt 'the conduct of the Russians has been simply piratical',[20] but was far too wary to do anything without guaranteed Austrian support. While Bismarck held the ring for Russia nothing could be done, though the following months saw attempts to create an Anglo-Austrian understanding. The difficulty was that neither power would take the initiative. Dilke hit the nail on the head when he wrote, 'Austria would be delighted to take the first step, as Lord Salisbury proposes, if Lord Salisbury will begin by taking the second'.[21]

Tension with Russia led to dissension in the Cabinet, for Lord Randolph Churchill wanted an understanding with Russia which would secure the frontier in India at the expense of Balkan concessions. The premier would not be moved from his customary caution, asserting in November 1886 that Britain 'will not accept the duty of maintaining those obligations on behalf of others who do not think it necessary to maintain them for themselves'.[22] He also resisted Bismarck's attempts to push Britain into a more active rôle in meeting the Russian danger; this involved no small exercise of skill, as Bismarck had induced the Crown Princess to write to her mother arguing 'if England could only regain her power over Turkey, it would be an immense boon. The sight of our ships alone would affect the Sultan's decisions at once'.[23] The Queen, long a friend of Turkey, sympathized with Bismarck's hope of an Anglo-Austro-Turkish triplice to resist Russian pretensions which could relieve Germany of the odium of doing so alone. In July 1887 the Bulgarian crisis was resolved by the election of Ferdinand of Saxe-Coburg-Koháry as king. This election had the merit of pleasing neither Britain nor Russia, so each power could feel that the other enjoyed no advantage.

The major effect of the Bulgarian crisis was to pinpoint British strategic weakness in the Mediterranean. While Britain was not short of bases in the Near East she lacked close association with any other power, particularly now Turkey was no longer on such intimate terms. France, well placed in Algiers and Tunis, and Russia might be able, in certain circumstances, to cut the lifeline to India. Until British strength in the Levant was restored there was little chance of a return to acting as a world power. Instead, 'England will remain comparatively isolated and her word will weigh less in Europe than it did twenty years ago'.[24] This was, then, the principal long-term ambition of Salisbury and Rosebery in the next decade.

In 1887 the diplomatic situation brightened. Germany and France were poised on the brink of war in January, while there were signs of *rapprochement* between Russia and France. Bismarck was naturally anxious to insure against a breakdown of good relations with Russia and began to urge his partners in the Triple Alliance to come to an understanding with Britain. This would create a counterpoise to Russia if the Tsar tried to take advantage of a Franco-German war to make fresh advances in the Balkans.

These manoeuvres were made at a good time. Britain and Austria were seeking to preserve the *status quo* in the Near East, while Italy, jealous of French successes in North Africa, wished to stabilize the situation, hoping to make progress at a more favourable time. In early 1887 serious negotiations began, though Salisbury was always at pains to point out that 'any promise even of diplomatic co-operation could not be directed against any single power such as France'.[25] On 12 February Britain and Italy exchanged notes, promising to act in concert to ensure 'that the shores of the Euxine, the Aegean and the Adriatic, and the Northern Coast of Africa shall remain in the same hands as now'.[26] Kálnoky, the Austrian Foreign Minister, realized his country's interests lay in the Near East rather than the whole Mediterranean but was ready to enter talks with Britain in view of common interests in Balkan stability. On 24 March the powers found themselves in accord and the first Mediterranean Agreement was concluded.

Later in 1887 Italy and Austria suggested that Turkey be incorporated in the system. In August these powers opened conversations with the Porte. In October, prompted by Bismarck, Kálnoky tried to interest Britain in this wider association, but by this time Salisbury had given up hope of propping up Turkey in the traditional way and saw no merit in trying to build on 'the Sultan's fitful and feeble disposition'.[27] The Prime Minister was also deeply suspicious of German intentions, telling White, 'My own impression is that we must join, but I say it with regret. I think the time inopportune and we are merely rescuing Bismarck's somewhat endangered chestnuts. . . . If he can get up a nice little fight between Russia and the three Powers he will have leisure to make France a harmless neighbour for some time to come. It goes against me to be one of the Powers in that unscrupulous game. But a thorough understanding with Austria and Italy is so important to us that I do not like the idea of breaking it up on account of risks which may turn out to be imaginary'.[28] The alternative of Austro-Russian agreement was much worse; it was better to have a slight commitment to defend Turkey in Bulgaria than to risk division of the Balkans. However, it was not so easy to persuade the Cabinet. Members particularly wanted to know what backing Austria would receive from Germany in a crisis. Salisbury communicated the terms of the Dual Alliance to his colleagues and set these fears at rest. It was agreed that the Sultan should not be informed of the terms of the treaty, as he was believed to be too unreliable. On 12 December 1887 the second Mediterranean Agreement was signed.

The corner-stone of British policy had been laid, and was not disturbed until 1895, though there were more problems than first met the eye. The extent to which Britain was bound by these agreements was not wholly clear. There had been criticism from Harcourt, Labouchere and Bryce as to the propriety of Salisbury's secret diplomacy. On 11 June 1891 Harcourt stated 'we did not and should not recognize any right of the present government to engage the responsibility of England in the future . . . our policy was one of absolute disengagement from Continental combinations of any kind, and that we maintained the right of England to act as her interests demanded when the occasion arose unfettered by any alliances conventions or understandings of any description'.[29] This view was confirmed by Gladstone the following day, when he told Rosebery, 'We all three [Gladstone, Harcourt and John Morley] hold in the strongest form the doctrine that it is the business of England to stand absolutely aloof from these prospective engagements. And such we believe to be the general or universal view of the Liberal party'.[30] Thus, while Salisbury could reach agreement with his ministers by discussion in Cabinet, Rosebery was debarred from so doing. The Liberal Cabinet was never consulted and Rosebery, according to Lowe, 'had taken great care never to read the Mediterranean Agreements, so that he could profess ignorance if questioned by his colleagues'.[31] This attitude caused Gladstone to regret Rosebery's appointment to the Foreign Office: 'The fatal element ... was his total and gross misconception of the relative position of the two offices we respectively held, and secondly his really outrageous assumption of power apart from both the First Minister and from the Cabinet'.[32] In retrospect, taking account of Rosebery's duplicity and the almost total ignorance of foreign affairs so regularly displayed by Gladstone, Harcourt and some other Liberals, the misgivings of the Germans as to the reliability of Britain's bond seem almost justifiable.

Throughout the next decade Salisbury and Rosebery resisted all attempts to turn these agreements into an alliance. A loose association gave Britain what she wanted, especially as there were important side benefits in Egypt. British security in the Mediterranean could never be finally established until the Egyptian Question was settled, but the Agreements did a great deal to ease the rigours of the British commitment, for which Salisbury had never shown much enthusiasm. In October 1885 agreement had been reached with Turkey for a speedy withdrawal of British troops and an Anglo-Turkish commission was sent to Egypt to study the problems. Salisbury's position was simple: 'The end to which I would work is evacuation, but with certain privileges reserved for England. . . . I quite agree with you in objecting either to annexation or international control',[33] he informed Wolff. Negotiations were slow and the French became convinced that Britain did not intend to leave Egypt. Baring found life increasingly difficult as the French representative became more minatory. Freycinet announced that France could 'never entertain the idea that Egypt should pass definitively into the hands of a great European power'.[34] For once even Salisbury was cross with France for her wilful obstruction in Egypt and told Lyons, 'it is very difficult to prevent oneself wishing for another Franco-German war to put a stop to this incessant vexation'.[35] In these circumstances the steady support of Italy and Austria considerably relieved the pressure.

Although it was not until 1904 that any satisfactory arrangement on Egypt was reached, there were a number of earlier attempts. On 22 May 1887 Sir Henry Drummond Wolff concluded a convention with Turkey by which British troops would be withdrawn in three years, though certain conditions were annexed by which limited rights of reoccupation were retained. Salisbury was determined to consolidate British supremacy, whether or not there were to be British troops in Egypt. In 1885 he had told Wolff, 'relief from our hated presence is the one bribe we have to offer. . . . If we once part with that, we practically go into the market empty-handed, a practice of which the late Government were fond, but which I never knew come to any good'.[36] The Wolff Convention reinforced French suspicions that the British were determined to maintain supremacy. When, in return for the Mediterranean Agreements, Britain extracted from Germany a promise of continued support in Egypt, the French decided to act. Joint representations by France and Russia succeeded in bullying the Sultan into rejecting the convention, and all subsequent proposals for evacuation were wrecked on the question of re-entry.

Failure to reach agreement completely altered the diplomatic situation and paved the way for the Fashoda *débâcle* in 1898. Salisbury was convinced that Anglo–French accord was dead and without hope of revival. In the context of this hostility even an agreement of October 1888 concerning the status of the canal meant very little. Most ominous for Britain and Germany were the multiplying signs of Franco–Russian collaboration. The collapse of the *Dreikaiser-bund* and conflict over Bulgaria and Egypt had wrought a diplomatic revolution which was to lead to the Franco–Russian Alliance of 1894. In 1887 all Salisbury could do was to tell Lyons, 'I see nothing for it but to sit still and drift awhile: a little further on in the history of Europe conditions may be changed. . . . Till then we must simply refuse to evacuate'.[37] This viewpoint involved acceptance of permanent French hostility and also committed Britain to the possibility of action in the Sudan, whence a challenge to the occupation was most likely to come. In order to 'sit still' it was probable that Britain's representatives, notably Baring, would have to run very hard.

Acceptance of the permanency of Egyptian occupation compelled a review of former attitudes. After 1887 Salisbury was reluctant to have anything to do with the protection of Constantinople. The premier, who had disagreed with Churchill over this issue in 1885–86, had then said, 'I consider the loss of Constantinople would be the ruin of our party and a heavy blow to the country'.[38] He now told White, 'It would be a terrible blow to lose Constantinople. But have we not lost it already?'[39] Salisbury was now ready to abandon the defence of the route to India at the Straits and to fall back on Egypt. As British determination to defend Turkey waned, so did the need for opposition to Russia and an alliance with Germany fade away.

It remained essential to be on good terms with Germany, whose help in Egypt was still needed. German friendship also gave insurance against the possibility of Franco–Russian naval supremacy in the Mediterranean. In April 1888 there were fourteen French ironclads stationed in the Mediterranean; by 1891 there were twenty. Opinion in Britain was greatly agitated and a campaign was mounted to strengthen the navy, the state of whose readiness was in the Queen's view 'certainly . . . very unsatisfactory'.[40] Salisbury was sufficiently alarmed by these moves to refer to France as 'England's greatest danger'.[41] The result of this panic was the Naval Defence Act of March 1889, which produced increased spending on capital ships and re-organization of their disposition. For the first time Britain was committed to maintaining a 'two power standard'; it was quite evident which two powers were feared.

Although Anglo-German accord reached its height between 1888 and 1892 this did not prevent Salisbury trying to induce a more realistic approach by France to the Egyptian problem. Un-fortunately, Anglophobia reigned in Paris and in 1889–90 French pressure reached dangerous proportions. In November 1889 and again the following summer it proved necessary to reinforce British units in the Mediterranean, but these gestures were sufficient warning to Paris. In the meantime Baring's administration was making real progress. The finances of Egypt were honestly administered and after 1888 deficits ceased. This success eased pressure on Britain in two ways. Firstly, occupation became more tolerable to the British taxpayer and hence less explosive a political issue. In the second place, occupation became more secure, not only because it obviously benefited Egypt but also because the *Caisse* could exert less leverage when new loans were no longer required. Diplomatic pressure was thus relieved and Britain became less dependent upon friendly gestures by Germany, Austria or Italy. It did not, however, solve the outstanding problem of French dislike for the British presence. On 3 August 1889 British security was further strengthened by the defeat of some Mahdist forces at Tushki. In the following decade the Sudanese rebels posed little threat to Egypt as the Mahdist cause degenerated into internal strife and an enervating war on Abyssinia.

In 1889 it was finally made clear to France that Britain intended to stay in Egypt—a matter already understood by all the other powers. Prompted by career diplomats like Waddington, the French government tried in June 1889 to reach an accommodation, basing their offer on an acceptance of the Wolff Convention, which had been so bitterly denounced only two years before. This was no longer enough for Britain. On 15 June Baring had told Salisbury, 'the real reason why the evacuation policy is well nigh impossible . . . is . . . the utter incapacity of the ruling classes in this country . . . the more I look at it, the more does the evacuation policy appear to me to be impossible under any conditions'.[42] A few days later Salisbury told the French Ambassador there could be no withdrawal as originally envisaged, for 'the Khedive will not last for six months'.[43]

Salisbury's view that Britain must temporarily accept French enmity as the price for Egypt was warmly supported by Rosebery and Chamberlain, as well as old guard imperialists who had argued for a protectorate ever since 1882. Even those, like Harcourt, who had upheld evacuation in 1884–85 now understood that security could only be attained by occupation. Furthermore, to hold Egypt it became essential to prevent establishment of other powers on the Upper Nile. In 1890 the Italians, who had sought to increase their influence in the area by the Treaty of Ucciali in May 1889, were warned off. The government was content to use diplomatic methods to exclude other powers and to rely on Mahdist strength in the Sudan to reinforce its arguments. If Mahdist power collapsed, then Britain would move into the Sudan, but nothing would be done to accelerate such a collapse.

Rosebery maintained a strict continuity of policy on Egypt. In 1893 Tewfiq dismissed Lord Cromer (Baring had been raised to the peerage in June 1892) and replaced him with an incompetent who was hostile to British interests. Cromer demanded permission to take drastic action and received the support of Rosebery, who wished to make it clear to the Khedive that British rule was a reality. The Foreign Secretary and Cromer shared the Queen's belief that the Khedive had been 'doubtless egged on by the French and by his grandfather'.[44] But the anti-imperialists, Gladstone and Harcourt, at first carried the day. The premier told Hamilton, 'I would as soon put a torch to Westminster Abbey as send additional troops to Egypt. It cannot be . . . I can see nothing for it but for Rosebery to resign'.[45] Threats of resignation by Rosebery and Cromer brought about a change in the Cabinet and it was decided to land a small force at Port Said. Tewfiq soon found Cromer back in the driving-seat with an enhanced reputation.

The crisis of 1893 had important repercussions. Differences between

Rosebery and Gladstone were openly revealed and from January 1893 until Gladstone's resignation in March 1894 the two men hardly agreed on any aspect of foreign affairs. Once it was clear to the Queen that Gladstone could no longer command undivided loyalty within his own party or Cabinet she did not hesitate to make her views known in forcible fashion. The Liberal Imperialist group was thus strengthened and Rosebery's boast that 'he was almost indispensable to the inherently weak ministry'[46] was justified. The crisis created a frenzy of excitement in France, where it was hoped that British rule in Egypt would collapse. The revival of Anglophobia killed for a decade Cromer's suggestion that 'some *modus vivendi* might be found with the French by combining the settlement of the Egyptian question with that of other questions unconnected with Egypt'.[47]

Although France and Russia were but tenuously linked before 1894 their association forced Germany and Britain closer. As both Salisbury and Bismarck wished to preserve a free hand alliance was out of the question. Yet, in early 1889, Bismarck suggested an alliance; in January he even referred in the Reichstag to Britain as an old, traditional ally with whom Germany had no conflict of interest. The moment seemed well chosen. Only twelve months earlier, Salisbury had told Morier, 'our policy is identical with that of the Central Powers. England and Germany and to a great extent Austria are satisfied Powers'.[48] The events of 1888 could only have strengthened such feelings. When Salisbury consulted the Cabinet he discovered that while there was general agreement as to the desirability of a close understanding there was no deep wish for an alliance. There was suspicion of the young Kaiser and fear lest accession to the Triple Alliance might involve backing wild schemes put forward by Wilhelm II or Crispi, the adventurist Italian premier. Salisbury's reply was polite but firm: 'we leave it on the table, without saying yes or no; that is unfortunately all I can do at present'.[49] Bismarck was wise enough to accept this, for he understood well the value of British friendship.

There were, of course, areas of conflict between Germany and Britain. Africa south of the Sahara proved a regular source of discord. In 1885 the two countries had tried to expunge memories of the Franco-German colonial alliance of 1884 by reaching agreement on Zanzibar. Salisbury believed his concessions worth while: 'I have been using the credit I have got with Bismarck in Caroline Islands and Zanzibar to get help in Russia and Turkey and Egypt. He is rather a Jew, but on the whole I have as yet got my money's worth'.[50] During the next few years it became evident that Bismarck was ready to partition East Africa into spheres of German and British influence. In October 1886 another agreement advanced partition still further, though commercial competition between rival national companies soon made this easy relationship collapse. Salisbury, too, became ever more reluctant to assist in the destruction of any local power anywhere near the Upper Nile. A rebellion in German East Africa in 1889, caused by maladministration, ruined trade in the whole region and further complicated local passions. Neither Bismarck nor Salisbury was able to control the ambitions and rivalries of men on the spot. By 1890 the Prime Minister was aware of the changing relationship and told the Queen, 'any indefinite postponement of a settlement in Africa would render it very difficult to maintain terms of amity with Germany, and would force us to change our system of alliances in Europe'.[51]

By 1890, Salisbury was willing to do a deal with Germany. The fall of Bismarck in March suggested a less tortuous course for German diplomacy. The Kaiser, Marschall and Caprivi seemed anxious to abandon the secrecy of the old Chancellor, though the passage of time was to show how important his finesse had been. It was imperative for Britain to settle the situation in Africa and so Salisbury proposed to exchange Heligoland for Zanzibar. In reality, this represented a further attempt to secure Egypt. The Queen was hostile to the suggestion, for once disagreeing with Salisbury, whom she told on 9 June, 'the people have been always very loyal . . . and it is a shame to hand them over to an unscrupulous despotic Government like the German without first consulting them'.[52] She received unexpected support from Gladstone, Labouchere and the Radicals, all of whom realized that the agreement would prolong British presence in Egypt. Many members of the Liberal Party supported Salisbury, who had already approached Rosebery and some others in an attempt to agree a policy. Accusations by Gladstone that the Royal Prerogative was being usurped were brushed aside. The agreement of 1 July 1890 stabilized the existing situation of a firm working relationship between Germany and Britain. The alternative, as Salisbury saw, was alliance with France, which 'must necessarily involve the early evacuation of Egypt under very unfavourable conditions'.[53]

Nevertheless, Salisbury tried hard to avoid quarrels with France and in 1891 refused to be dragged into opposing her policy in Morocco. German attempts to push Britain into a more active Mediterranean rôle were stoutly resisted and, when persisted with, helped create suspicion in Salisbury's mind as to the true direction of the Kaiser's policy. In Rome and Berlin the British attitude was hardly understood, for the powers expected 'excellent results to be anticipated from the German arrangement with England and the British support of the Triple Alliance'.[54] It was a sad disappointment for Italy's powerful expansionist lobby. Crispi's urge to expand almost killed the Anglo–Italian alliance, especially when Italy showed interest in the Upper Nile. Tornielli, the Ambassador to London, reported that 'common interests of prime importance link our policy to that of Great Britain, if we want . . . the idea to grow here that Italy is her natural ally, we must move extremely carefully, lest we should create the least suspicion of challenging British supremacy in the Nile valley'.[55] The trouble was that British interest in the alliance was no longer as great as in 1887. It seemed likely to diminish still further if it involved support for adventurist policies.

Salisbury was particularly fearful of Italian initiatives which might push him into confrontation with France. He reacted strongly to Italian hysteria at French development and fortification of their naval base at Bizerta. He was not at all worried for Britain's sake, arguing that it would lead to the break up of the French Mediterranean fleet into small squadrons. He dismissed the Italian frenzy as a jealous reaction to French successes in North Africa and, in any event, 'He could not see why Italy felt herself menaced by Bizerta when Toulon and Corsica were much closer'.[56] Salisbury never valued the Italian connexion that highly and told Dufferin in 1891, 'They imagine that their alliance is a pearl of great price which we would do well to secure. . . . To my mind the Italian alliance is an unprofitable and even slightly onerous corollary on the German alliance. Germany and Austria are very useful friends as regards Turkey, Russia, Egypt and even France. They value the Italian alliance greatly, because it means many battalions to them; and for their sake we value it too. But, by itself, it makes our relations with France more difficult: and it is of no use anywhere else'.[57]

The decline of German influence after 1891, once it became clear that some understanding had been reached between France and Russia, caused a reappraisal of the British position. There had always been those in both Liberal and Conservative ranks who favoured Anglo-French accord and the break up of the *Dreikaiserbund* simultaneously increased British security at the Straits and promoted the possibility of British balancing between two power groups. It became possible for pro-French politicians, such as Ripon, to argue that Britain should gradually move away from alliance with Germany towards a more neutral position. The Prince of Wales and his circle even argued for a complete understanding with France. Although the opinions of this party had little influence on the serene diplomacy of Salisbury, he politely turned down the offers of Rudini, Crispi's successor, for British incorporation in the Triple Alliance. It was already clear to Salisbury that Britain was needed more by the Triple Alliance than she needed it. Germany's failure in June 1890 to renew the Reinsurance Treaty with Russia compelled the Triple Alliance to keep in step with the power previously regarded just as a useful auxiliary.

While French naval strength increased Salisbury was wary of breaking with his allies. In 1891 it was revealed that the programme of 1889 was insufficient for Britain to keep pace with Franco-Russian naval construction, and in early 1892 reports from the Admiralty and the War Office painted a very gloomy picture of Britain's strategic position in the Mediterranean. The implication of these reports was that the policy of limited alignment with the Central Powers was no longer an adequate counter to the threat of Franco-Russian co-operation in the Levant. Just before he left office Salisbury informed the Cabinet that British policy had been based for many years on a false estimate of relative naval strengths. The premier even questioned whether a navy should be maintained in the Mediterranean! Salisbury's kite-flying did have the effect of drawing attention to the changing diplomatic situation and he asserted, 'Our foreign policy requires to be speedily and avowedly revised. At present, it is supposed that the fall of Constantinople will be a great defeat for England. . . . It would surely be wise, in the interest of our own reputation, to let it be known as quickly as possible that we do not pretend to defend Constantinople. . . . At present, if the two officers in question are correct in their views, our policy is a policy of false pretences. If persisted in, it will involve discomfiture to all who trust in us, and infinite discredit to ourselves'.[58]

On leaving office, despite this pessimism, Salisbury urged Rosebery to continue working with the Triple Alliance. The new Foreign Secretary was pro-German and Caprivi assured Austria that as long as British policy remained in Rosebery's hands relations with the Triple Alliance would be unaltered. Events were not to bear out this cheerful hypothesis, though at first Anglo-French relations took a sharp turn for the worse. Gladstone and Waddington, the French Ambassador, both wished to improve relations, but events worked against them. Rosebery cordially disliked Waddington's manner, referring to him as 'a churchwarden come round for a subscription . . . he brings nothing, but generally tries to take something away'.[59] Sensing Rosebery's hostility, the ambassador was foolish enough to discuss affairs with Gladstone behind the Foreign Secretary's back. When Rosebery discovered this he told Gladstone, 'He has rendered the transaction of business with him almost if not quite impossible, so far as I am concerned. . . . His proceedings are unprecedented I should think in the annals of diplomacy'.[60] Other diplomats in London, notably Hatzfeldt, saw what was going on and confidently predicted a major clash between the western powers within a short time.

There were plenty of opportunities for strife between the two nations. In 1893 arose a dispute over Siam and both nations behaved foolishly and provocatively. Feeling ran high in Britain and the Germans expected war. On 25 July Rosebery told the Queen,

'Whole history of this French aggression on Siam is unspeakably base'.[61] Victoria urged him to stand firm: 'The honour of my great Empire . . . must be upheld. . . . Are you sure of your colleagues? The want of confidence abroad in your Chief leads to the boldness of the French, I fear'.[62] The problem was that French actions seemed to threaten the security of India on a new frontier—in the south-east. Ever since 1883 France had been frequently reminded of the special British interest in the future of Burma and Siam. In October 1885 the capricious behaviour of King Thibaw of Burma led to a British ultimatum and the formal annexation of Burma on 1 January 1886. In 1889 France proposed that Siam be neutralized, an idea which Salisbury favoured, though no action was taken. In February 1892 the French, well established in Indo-China, laid claim to the territory up to the Mekong River. By this time British negotiations for a frontier settlement between Burma and Siam were far advanced; in December 1892 they reached an amicable conclusion. For no good reason, other than imperialist truculence, the French chose to regard this treaty as an infringement of their rights and in May 1893 declared war on Siam in support of the Mekong claim. Rosebery was extremely irate, later referring to De Lanessan's actions (he was Governor of French Indo-China) as being 'in exact fulfilment of the programme of undisguised aggression and encroachment laid down in his published work on French colonial policy'.[63]

The French attack on Siam confirmed the fears of the party which imagined the operation of a Franco-Russian onslaught on British interests in all parts of the world. The pressure of the French or Russians on Cairo, Constantinople, the Pamirs and the Mekong was believed to be part of a concerted plan to destroy the British Empire. Rosebery hardly needed any encouragement and, on 30 July, sent an ultimatum to France. The crisis was soon ended and, on 3 October 1893, a satisfactory treaty was negotiated. However, the incident had important repercussions. In Germany it was supposed that the conflict would turn the Triple into a Quadruple Alliance. On 14 June Rosebery had reported that 'England's relations with France left much to be desired, and the French government was acting in every way as if its aim were to drive England into the arms of the Triple Alliance'.[64] The Germans were further encouraged by

Curzon, leader of the party which feared a Franco-Russian attack on India, who on 3 August wrote, 'France has behaved criminally, England weakly, Siam foolishly; and when folly, weakness and crime are in competition, it is the last named, as a rule, that wins'.[65] The Kaiser's confidence that Britain would be compelled to fight was misplaced. The readiness of Britain to come to terms was an unwelcome surprise which convinced many Germans that she would be a useless ally, as she could never be relied upon to fight. What the Germans had failed to realize was that France was reluctant to push Britain into a war which France could hardly win, while Britain had no intention of incurring ineradicable French hostility. The too-obvious pleasure of the German statesmen at the poor state of Anglo-French relations gave both French and British career diplomats food for thought.

German pressure on Britain to join the Triple Alliance was not relaxed. Through the medium of Austria it was suggested, 'the psychological moment has come for England not only to increase her navy, but also to make up her mind whether she intends to assert her traditional political authority or whether she will allow herself to be crowded out of the Mediterranean, where British power has hitherto been predominant'.[66] Germany was simultaneously hedging her bets. Holstein believed that a revival of colonial pressure, last used in 1884–85, might bring Britain to heel. He therefore failed to respond to the cordiality which Rosebery and Kimberley showed after March 1894. A whole series of irritating colonial questions arose—in Samoa, the Congo, Uganda and West Africa. This was a complete reversal of Germany's 'New Course' and, as Rosebery told Deym, the Austrian Ambassador, on 14 June 1894, reversal of German policy would lead to a reversal of British. Hatzfeldt, the exceptionally astute German diplomat, saw the problem clearly: 'The danger here does not lie in offending some Minister or other, but in the possible shift of so-called public opinion, which is by the way already making itself felt as a result of the estrangement between us; and even Salisbury will not be able to contend with it if, by the time he returns to office, public opinion has turned decisively against the Triple Alliance'.[67] Crispi, who returned to power in Italy in late 1893, soon found out the truth. When he attempted to come to terms with Britain in East Africa he was told that while support would be given in the Mediterranean there would be no help for aggressive actions in the Red Sea, 'thereby getting into conflict with other powers'.[68]

Trivial colonial disputes soon began to exacerbate Anglo-German relations. In March 1894 Kimberley, the new Foreign Secretary, opened talks with Belgium in order to divide the area of the Upper Nile into spheres of influence. On 12 April a treaty was signed which ceded influence in the Sudan to Britain, and in Equatoria and the Bahr-el-Ghazal to Belgium. There was fierce opposition to this treaty from other powers and within the Cabinet. Harcourt and Morley were furious that the treaty had been concluded without Cabinet agreement and in complete secrecy. Not only was this constitutionally improper but 'The whole thing is a wanton provocation of France, made all the more mischievous by the underhand manner in which it has been conducted. The exasperation produced by this shady proceeding will of course embitter all the questions which we have at issue with France in Egypt, Siam and Uganda. I am of opinion that there is only one safe and reasonable course, and that is to cancel an Agreement which should never have been made if the Cabinet had been allowed to discuss it'.[69] On 13 August, in response to diplomatic pressure spearheaded by Germany and France, a majority of the Cabinet forced nullification of the treaty.

Chronic embarrassment was also caused by events in Uganda. In 1892 Rosebery had suggested annexation, but had been resisted by Harcourt who saw it as certain to cause friction with France and Germany as well as being 'in the highest jingo tune advocating the annexation of the whole country up to the Albert Lakes with a view to the "reconquest" of the Sudan via the Upper Nile'.[70] Rhodes and Lugard, meanwhile, campaigned vigorously against evacuation of the area by the East Africa Company. In despair, the government sent out Sir Gerald Portal to investigate and in November 1893 he advised annexation. On 12 April 1894 the government announced its intention of establishing a protectorate. The imperialists were delighted; the clinching argument was that 'The relinquishment of Uganda to a civilized Power immediately imperils the safety of

Egypt, as the diversion or blocking of the headwaters of the Nile could stop her water supply and starve her population'.[71] These events showed how important the Upper Nile seemed, but British attempts to use Belgium to protect her interests, her clumsy attempts to play off France and Germany against each other, and Rosebery's failure to consult Germany (as he should have done under the terms of the 1890 treaty) convinced the Kaiser that a revival of the Franco-German colonial *entente* was necessary.

The opportunity soon arose in West Africa. Here Britain was on the defensive. During the period 1889–95 British strategy dictated holding back in West Africa in order to advance in Egypt. Salisbury and Rosebery tried to hold what they could, but by 1890 the colonies of Sierra Leone and Gambia, both deprived of hinterlands, were useless encumbrances. West African trade was minimal; there was no impetus from London for empire building. Small wonder that Salisbury saw West Africa as an area where Britain might make concessions to France and Germany in return for favours elsewhere. During 1889–91 a series of treaties defining boundaries in West Africa was concluded with France. All except that of August 1890 were favourable to French claims, but French officers and merchants persisted with their policy of trying to undermine the British position, particularly in Nigeria. Nevertheless, Rosebery at first only reacted cautiously, giving limited backing to Goldie and the Royal Niger Company. In November 1893 agreement was reached with Germany, but the following year a Franco-German treaty left Britain to shoulder alone the responsibility for preventing French advance.

Despite imperialist leanings, Rosebery tried in 1894 to reach agreement with Paris. Kimberley was ready to give up much in West Africa to secure the Nile. In October an agreement seemed possible, but broke down owing to the intransigence of the *Comité de l'Afrique française*. The Foreign Secretary saw the folly of these disputes, remarking 'I often ask myself whether these African disputes are really worth taking seriously . . . a matter of barren deserts or places where white men cannot live, dotted with thinly scattered tribes who cannot be made to work'.[72] But what Harcourt had characterized as '*Sie sollen nicht ihn haben, den freien Britischen Nile*'[73] dominated British thinking. Fearing French incursions into the

Upper Nile Valley, Grey, the Under-Secretary for Foreign Affairs, announced on 28 March 1895 that an advance into the Bahr-el-Ghazal would be 'not merely an inconsistent and unexpected act, but it must be perfectly well known to the French Government that it would be an unfriendly act and would be so viewed by England'.[74] It was clear Britain could not afford to wait much longer before conquering the Sudan. On 10 May Kimberley made a final offer, suggesting an Anglo-Egyptian sphere of influence as far south as Fashoda and a standstill elsewhere in the valley. Hanotaux, France's Foreign Minister refused, and on 12 June negotiations were broken off; a few days later the Liberals fell from power.

Germany took advantage of the deterioration in Anglo-French relations by putting pressure on Britain in South and West Africa and in the Pacific—in a fashion closely similar to that of 1884–85. Unpleasantness first arose over the future of the Samoan islands, which had been administered for some years by a triplice consisting of Germany, Britain and the United States. The awkwardness of this joint administration caused the Americans to declare that they would take full responsibility for one island and withdraw from the others. Germany then put in a bid for the rest of the group, arguing that Britain already had a sufficiency of Pacific stations. Rosebery was intransigent and demanded the continuation of joint control, despite opposition from his own party. Harcourt, indeed, was unflattering in his description of Rosebery's imperialism: 'We have already got the lion's share; why should we insist upon taking the tiger's also? Not to say the jackal's'.[75] On this occasion German initiatives came to nothing, save that Rosebery stood ostentatiously aloof from the Triple Alliance.

There were much more serious and far-reaching conflicts in Africa. After 1885 British policy in South Africa had been directed towards containing the Transvaal's imperialism. Rhodes and the British South Africa Company, on the other hand, pressed on with the aim of securing as much territory in the area as possible. Although Salisbury seems to have had no enthusiasm for the acquisition of new colonies, he was put under great pressure from a number of quarters. Salisbury always made it plain he did not wish to antagonize

German feelings, telling Malet in 1889 that he was afraid Rhodes's new company 'will startle people a little in Berlin. I have ... strongly recommended them in the first instance to confine their proposed region of operations to the south of the Zambesi'.[76] But even Salisbury was forced to accept the gradual extension of British interests, in East Zululand and south of the Zambesi in 1887, Matabeleland, Tongaland and Mashonaland in 1888. The extension of British influence brought renewed conflict with the Transvaal in 1891, particularly when Rhodes put forward a plan to buy the reversion of Mozambique from the Portuguese. Germany was suspicious of these plans, fearing encirclement of South West Africa and British seizure of the Portuguese empire. The good effects of the Anglo-German treaty of 1890 were undone in South Africa. In December 1892 Ripon, the Colonial Secretary, offered to leave Swaziland to the Transvaal if concessions were given to the Uitlanders in the Republic, but Kruger rejected the scheme. Swaziland remained a problem, despite signature of agreements with the Transvaal in 1890 and 1893. In May 1894 Ripon put forward various solutions to the Cabinet, but none was satisfactory. In December 1894 Swaziland passed to the Transvaal, though Ripon denied Afrikaner access to the sea by annexation of Trans-Pongoland and Amatongaland in April and May 1895.

It was becoming increasingly evident to Kimberley and Rosebery that Kruger's stubborn resistance was fed by German encouragement. While these two politicians did not strongly support Rhodes's schemes for Delagoa Bay and Mozambique (which had been revived in 1894) they did resent covert German opposition. Kimberley became very aggressive, particularly when Berlin protested against British attempts to secure an Uitlander franchise. Ripon supported the Foreign Secretary, telling him 'there is little chance of our being able to take a firm line with the Germans in the face of Harcourt's dread of a strong word and of Rosebery's hatred of the French, which throws us inevitably on German support',[77] thus enjoining caution on his colleague. Kimberley conceded the point, but assured Ripon, 'The Germans must be made to understand that while we are most anxious to have cordial relations with them, we will stand no bullying'.[78] Part of the problem was that a substantial party in the

Cabinet not only disliked Germany but disliked still more the notion of colonial pressure forcing changes of a serious nature in British foreign policy. Harcourt put this opinion forcibly, referring to 'These colonial gentlemen [who] expect us to quarrel on their behalf with the great military Powers of Europe, and to add millions to our expenditure, to which they refuse to contribute a single farthing'.[79] Thus in June 1894 Rosebery told Rhodes the ambitious schemes for Mozambique had been vetoed by Germany and must be given up.

The fact that Germany made it plain in 1894 that she regarded herself as an unofficial protector of the Transvaal did more than any other act of the Kaiser to create suspicion in Britain. The exchanges between Berlin and London wrecked good relations. Hatzfeldt was instructed to tell Kimberley that Germany would not permit annexation of Mozambique. Kimberley replied that 'England is a great Sea Power and could in such a matter speak the strongest word'.[80] The German riposte was to threaten trouble in Egypt. Ripon and Kimberley were thoroughly alarmed at German threats in South Africa. The Colonial Secretary insisted 'The German inclination to take the Transvaal under their protection is a very serious thing. To have them meddling . . . would be fatal to our position and our influence in South Africa'.[81] On 30 January 1895 Ripon asked Kimberley to insist that the Transvaal lay within the British sphere of influence, for 'I am afraid that if something of this kind is not done, we shall drift into an unpleasant position with Germany'.[82] These were prophetic words.

Although the relationship between Britain and Germany had deteriorated sharply, the leaders of both nations seemed sublimely unaware of the permanence of the damage. In Germany, Holstein cheerfully assumed that at any point Britain could be bludgeoned back into friendship, if not alliance. In Britain, Rosebery was as optimistic, telling Malet, 'Britain holds the key of the situation. For about five months this year Germany appeared to ignore the fact; and so I had to send her a very plain message through Vienna. Hence, too, the developments when Germany began to talk of being able to pursue a French policy in Africa, while maintaining the Triple Alliance in Europe, it was time to speak out, for they ignored

the central keystone of the situation—through Italy, England.
You will have observed the alarm and annoyance at Vienna and also
at Rome. And now we have a very different tune at Berlin, though
much harm has been done'.[83] Indeed it had, and not least by Rosebery.
The influence of the former Foreign Secretary on relations with the
European powers had been almost totally irritative. Harcourt, always
an acid observer, was for once entirely on target when he told Kimberley, 'It is clear to me that . . . we have to count on the negative
if not positive hostility of Germany. . . . We may be sure that if
Germany has the opportunity of tripping us up, it will be done. . . .
It seems plain enough that the Triple Alliance is used up, and that
fresh combinations are in view . . . we must walk very warily.
We have never been so destitute of friends or so "mal vus" by the
Powers. The less we attempt any move which requires their friendly
co-operation the better—for we assuredly shall not get it'.[84] For
Harcourt and his party, the answer to British problems lay in a
better understanding with France and Russia—an unthinkable
solution for Rosebery.

Events, however, obliged Rosebery to seek agreement with
Russia. In the summer of 1894 massacres in Armenia precipitated
an international crisis. Unrest had been growing among the Armenians ever since 1883 and had troubled both the Turkish and Russian
governments. In 1890 at Erzerum unrest first took insurrectionary
form against the Porte. The return of the Liberals in 1892 convinced
many Armenians that British influence would secure them at least
autonomy, but they had reckoned without the catastrophic decline
in British influence at Constantinople. Insurrection was followed
by repression and an outcry in Britain against Ottoman cruelty.
After long and difficult negotiations Britain, France and Russia
presented a scheme of limited reform in the vilayets of Bitlis,
Diarbekr, Erzerum, Mamuret, Sivas and Van, to the Porte in May
1895. Although the diplomatic initiative ultimately came to nothing
because Russia felt unable to support the use of force in Armenia
and the French, pleased with their new alliance, would not oppose
this view, the association of these powers was displeasing to Ger-.
many. Holstein claimed that the Armenian triplice was insubstantial
and ephemeral. In the event, he was correct, but he would have

done well to take Hatzfeldt's warning seriously: 'the fact remains . . . argue about it as one will, that England is now casting about else-where, a policy that England blames on our alienation of herself'.[85] If the Kaiser had known that Kimberley felt he was 'a very disturbing influence in affairs'[86] and Harcourt wanted 'a good understanding with Russia, a thing we have never yet tried, but which is now happily within our reach',[87] German policy might have received a less fatal orientation in these years.

Difficulties encountered by Britain in the Mediterranean, the Near East, Africa and India, in these years imposed limitations upon the exercise of her power elsewhere. Nowhere was this more obvious than in relations with the United States. After 1870 the Monroe Doctrine and its corollaries gained fresh importance as the Americans became increasingly hostile to European influence in Latin America. In 1870 Grant had predicted a speedy end to the European connexion, though action did not match the belligerence of his words. In 1883 Venezuela provoked a revival of her dispute with Britain over the border between British Guiana and Venezuela, a matter of controversy ever since 1848. It was only the receipt of a British ultimatum in 1887 which compelled compensation to be offered. There was concern in the United States and in December 1886 Bayard, the Secretary of State, offered to mediate and arbitrate. Salisbury regretfully declined the offer because the Venezuelan attitude precluded arbitration. During the next few years there were further attempts made by the United States to rectify the situation. In 1894 President Cleveland decided to act and on 3 December told Congress, 'The boundary of British Guiana still remains in dispute between Great Britain and Venezuela. Believing that its early settlement on some just basis alike honourable to both parties is in the line of our established policy to remove from this hemisphere all causes of difference with Powers beyond the sea, I shall renew the efforts heretofore made to bring about a restoration of diplomatic relations between the disputants and to induce a reference to arbi-tration—a resort which Great Britain so conspicuously favours in principle and respects in practice, and which is so earnestly sought by her weaker adversary'.[88] Stripped of its rhetoric, this statement indicated a determination by the United States to increase its influence in countries where Britain had reigned supreme since the days of Canning. It was a challenge which a Britain heavily committed elsewhere could not meet but only seek to delay. Bayard, now Ambassador to London, met with Fabian tactics from Rosebery and Kimberley, who insisted on keeping all territory to the east of the 1848 Schomburgk line while professing themselves ready to negotiate on the rest. So matters rested when the Liberals fell from power, to be replaced by Salisbury. The truth was that in Latin America Britain no longer felt able to pursue 'gunboat diplomacy' even if she wished so to do. It was a symbolic change in power relationships between Britain and the United States and stemmed not so much from increase in American power but rather from recognition in both countries that British priorities lay elsewhere and that refusal could cause America grave strategic embarrassment.

It was a similar regard for commitments elsewhere which led to a cautious policy in the Far East in this decade. Whereas in the past Britain had been the leader in advancing European claims in China, a passive rôle was now adopted. Salisbury soon abandoned the provocative occupation of Port Hamilton, thus easing Russian fears as well as reducing the anti-European sentiment which was such a strong force in the politics of the area. The corner-stone of British policy was the promotion of trade and this necessitated peace. British control over the Chinese Imperial Maritime Customs gave Britain immense influence at Peking, by providing the finance with which some measure of westernization and reform took place in China. Indeed, according to Young, 'British representatives at Peking displayed an easy, even magisterial, attitude over the direction of affairs, confident in Great Britain's control of over 80% of the foreign trade of China'.[89] Finance and banking remained largely a British preserve, untroubled by foreign rivalry until the founding of the Deutsch-Asiatische Bank (1889), the Yokohama Specie Bank (1892) and the Russo-Chinese Bank (1895). Once commercial competition became a reality the Anglo-Chinese firms were quick to form the China Association in 1889. This body acted in characteristic fashion, demanding that the Foreign Office help sustain a commercial offensive to correct the decline in the value of British exports from £8·57 million in 1885 to £7·10 million in 1895.[90] As in so many other parts of the world, it was German rivalry which was most feared and resented. However, by 1895 this rivalry was not so far advanced that it created serious problems for Britain elsewhere in the world.

In 1894, this year of troubles for Britain, growing rivalry between China and Japan exploded into war. The Japanese were everywhere victorious, capturing Port Arthur and Weihaiwei and penetrating deep into Shantung. Britain believed that mediation was the most likely policy to restore peace and prosperity and on 6 October 1894 Rosebery circulated proposals to France, Germany, Russia and the United States. Circumstances, however, combined to produce indifference or hostility to the British scheme among the other powers, and nothing was achieved. When the scale of the Japanese victory became clear to Russia it also became apparent that Russian interests would not be suited by the probable concessions. In early April Japan and China agreed on the cession of the Pescadores, Formosa and the Liaotung peninsula, as well as independence for Korea. At this point Russia invited the adherence of Britain, France and Germany to a joint intervention. Britain refused, Kimberley telling the Minister at Peking, 'The Japanese conditions do not afford grounds for interference on our part'.[91] The Russians pressed ahead and, backed by France and Germany, on 23 April identical notes were presented to Japan demanding revision of the Sino-Japanese treaty. The Shimonoseki intervention led to the retrocession of Manchuria to China and an amended treaty, signed at Chefoo on 8 May. This was a defeat for Britain and her policy of non-intervention as well as for Japan. It began the process of forcing these two powers together to avoid the isolation which had been so clearly a source of weakness in 1895. Reappraisal of British policy was inevitable when the collapse of tranquillity in the Far East and the resumption of a scramble for concessions put yet another strain upon Britain's already severely stretched resources. In 1895 this was already clear, though a solution had not yet been suggested.

The fall of the Liberal government in the summer of 1895 left Britain with a large number of unsolved problems in foreign affairs.

It would be unjust to ascribe deterioration in Britain's international position since 1892 to defects in Rosebery's diplomacy, though these certainly played a significant part. Rosebery was less of a conciliator than Salisbury and was more emotionally involved with imperialist designs. He also had more opposition within his own party with which to contend, and this made consistency more elusive. Rosebery, too, was less impressive in a wider political sense than his Conservative predecessor. The major causes of change, however, owed little to these personal characteristics. There were important changes in German policy and personnel which made the world of 1895 seem very different from that of a decade earlier. The lapse of the Reinsurance Treaty and the signature of the Franco-Russian Alliance had altered the balance of power in Europe, just as the industrial growth of the United States and the development of Japan had altered that balance in other parts of the globe. As a world power, Britain found her interests challenged and changing everywhere. Salisbury, indeed, was the man most likely to steer a good course in times of rapid change—his experience and unflappable temperament were considerable advantages. The return of the Conservatives was expected to lead to a restoration of the relationships of 1886–92, with adjustments for changed circumstances. Instead, Salisbury was to preside over a diplomatic revolution.

REFERENCES

1 *Hansard*. House of Lords. 10 July 1890.
2 *Life of Robert, Marquis of Salisbury* by Lady Gwendolen Cecil. Vol. III. p. 133. Salisbury to Cranbrook, 10 June 1885.
3 *Letters of Queen Victoria* ed. G. E. Buckle. Second Series. Vol. III. p. 663. 12 June 1885.
4 Cecil, op. cit., Vol. III. p. 136.
5 *Bismarck. Some secret pages of his history* by M. Busch. Vol. III. p. 143.
6 Buckle, op. cit., Second Series. Vol. III. p. 683. Salisbury to Victoria, 30 June 1885.
7 *Persia and the Defence of India* by R. L. Greaves. p. 241. 3 August 1885.
8 Cecil, op. cit., Vol. III. p. 224.
9 ibid., Vol. III. p. 231. Salisbury to Morier, 15 September 1885.
10 *British India's Northern Frontier, 1865–95* by G. J. Alder. p. 204. Ridgeway to Iddesleigh, 8 September 1886.

11 ibid., p. 240. Morier to Salisbury, 2 February 1892.

12 Rosebery to Howard, 13 November 1893. F.O. 65/1470.

13 Buckle, op. cit., Third Series. Vol. II. pp. 299–300. Rosebery to Victoria, 9 August 1893.

14 ibid., Third Series. Vol. I. p. 32. Victoria's Memorandum, 30 January 1886.

15 ibid., Third Series. Vol. I. p. 31. Victoria to Salisbury, 29 January 1886.

16 *King Edward VII. A biography* by Sir S. Lee. Vol. I. p. 500.

17 Buckle, op. cit., Second Series. Vol. III. p. 454. Victoria to Dufferin, 18 November 1883.

18 ibid., Second Series. Vol. III. pp. 690–1. Salisbury to Victoria, 21 September 1885.

19 ibid., Third Series. Vol. I. p. 179. Victoria to Salisbury, 22 August 1886.

20 ibid., Third Series. Vol. I. pp. 191–2. Salisbury to Victoria, 27 August 1886.

21 *The Present Position of European Politics* by Sir C. Dilke. p. 23.

22 Speech at the Guildhall, 9 November 1886.

23 Buckle, op. cit., Third Series. Vol. I. p. 246. Princess Victoria to Victoria, 1 January 1887.

24 Cecil, op. cit., Vol. III. p. 226. Salisbury to Thornton, 21 July 1885.

25 Buckle, op. cit., Third Series. Vol. I. p. 268. Salisbury to Victoria, 2 February 1887.

26 *The Foundations of British Foreign Policy* by H. W. V. Temperley and L. M. Penson. p. 450. Salisbury to Corti, 12 February 1887.

27 Cecil, op. cit., Vol. IV. p. 71. Salisbury to White, 2 November 1887.

28 ibid., Vol. IV. p. 71.

29 *Britain and the Casus Belli, 1822–1902* by C. Howard. p. 123. Harcourt to Gladstone, 11 July 1891.

30 ibid., p. 123. Gladstone to Rosebery, 12 July 1891.

31 *Salisbury and the Mediterranean, 1886–96* by C. J. Lowe. p. 95.

32 *Rosebery* by R. R. James. p. 270.

33 Cecil, op. cit., Vol. III. p. 235. Salisbury to Wolff, 13 August 1885.

34 *European Alliances and Alignments, 1871–90* by W. L. Langer. p. 397.

35 *Lord Lyons* by Lord Newton. Vol. II. p. 386.

36 *Africa and the Victorians* by R. Robinson and J. Gallagher. p. 258. Salisbury to Wolff, 18 August 1885.

37 Newton, op. cit., Vol. II. p. 409. Salisbury to Lyons, 20 July 1887.

38 *Lord Randolph Churchill* by W. S. Churchill. Vol. II. p. 161.

39 Cecil, op. cit., Vol. IV. p. 51. Salisbury to Wolff, 10 August 1887.

40 Buckle, op. cit., Third Series. Vol. I. p. 413. Victoria to Salisbury, 8 June 1888.

41 ibid., Third Series. Vol. I. p. 438. Salisbury to Victoria, 25 August 1888.

42 Cecil, op. cit., Vol. IV. pp. 138–9. Baring to Salisbury, 15 June 1889.

43 Robinson and Gallagher, op. cit., p. 282.

44 Buckle, op. cit., Third Series. Vol. II. p. 209. 21 January 1893.

45 James, op. cit., p. 279.

46 Lowe, op. cit., p. 92.

47 James, op. cit., p. 278.

48 Lowe, op. cit., p. 46. Salisbury to Morier, 1 February 1888.

49 Langer, op. cit., p. 494.

50 Cecil, op. cit., Vol. III. p. 230. Salisbury to Iddesleigh, 24 August 1885.

51 Buckle, op. cit., Third Series. Vol. I. pp. 613–14. Salisbury to Victoria, 10 June 1890.

52 ibid., Third Series. Vol. I. p. 612. Victoria to Salisbury, 9 June 1890.

53 ibid., Third Series. Vol. I. p. 614. Salisbury to Victoria, 10 June 1890.

54 Paget to Salisbury, 25 September 1890. F.O. 64/1233. No. 254.

55 Lowe, op. cit., p. 64.

56 ibid., p. 65.

57 Salisbury to Dufferin, 16 January 1891. Salisbury Papers, Oxford.

58 Salisbury's Memorandum, 4 June 1892. P.R.O. Cabinet. 37/31. No. 10.

59 James, op. cit., p. 272. Rosebery to Gladstone, 19 October 1892.

60 ibid., p. 273. Rosebery to Gladstone, 4 November 1892.

61 Buckle, op. cit., Third Series. Vol. II. p. 284. Rosebery to Victoria, 25 July 1893.

62 ibid., Third Series. Vol. II. p. 284. Victoria to Rosebery, 26 July 1893.

63 *Cambridge History of British Foreign Policy* ed. A. W. Ward and G. P. Gooch. Vol. III. p. 194 fn. Rosebery to Dufferin, 5 September 1893.

64 Temperley and Penson, op. cit., p. 474.

65 *Life of Lord Curzon* by Earl Ronaldshay. Vol. I. p. 197. Curzon to Leiter, 3 August 1893.

66 Lowe, op. cit., pp. 94–5. Kálnoky to Deym, 7 December 1893.

67 ibid., p. 96.

68 ibid., p. 97.

69 James, op. cit., p. 350. Harcourt's Memorandum, 4 May 1894.

70 *Life of Sir William Harcourt* by A. G. Gardiner. Vol. II. p. 192. Harcourt to Gladstone, 20 September 1892.

71 *The Diplomacy of Imperialism* by W. L. Langer. p. 124.

72 Robinson and Gallagher, op. cit., p. 335.

73 Gardiner, op. cit., Vol. II. p. 195. Harcourt to Rosebery, 23 September 1892.

74 *Twenty-five Years, 1892–1916* by Lord Grey of Falloden. p. 20 fn.

75 Gardiner, op. cit., Vol. II. p. 326. Harcourt to Kimberley, 8 December 1894.

76 Robinson and Gallagher, op. cit., p. 228. Salisbury to Malet, 12 June 1889.

77 *Life of Lord Ripon* by L. Wolf. Vol. II. p. 231. Ripon to Kimberley, 21 October 1894.

78 ibid., Vol. II. p. 233. Kimberley to Ripon, 25 November 1894.

79 Gardiner, op. cit., Vol. II. p. 326. Harcourt to Kimberley, 8 December 1894.

80 Robinson and Gallagher, op. cit., p. 417.

81 Wolf, op. cit., Vol. II. p. 232. Ripon to Kimberley, 25 November 1894.

82 ibid., Vol. II. p. 234 fn. Ripon to Kimberley, 30 January 1895.

83 Rosebery to Malet, 6 January 1895. F.O. 363/3.

84 Gardiner, op. cit., Vol. II. p. 324. Harcourt to Kimberley, 16 November 1894.

85 Lowe, op. cit., p. 97.

86 Gardiner, op. cit., Vol. II. p. 325. Kimberley to Harcourt, 21 November 1894.

87 ibid., Vol. II. p. 325.

88 *Life of Lord Pauncefote* by R. B. Mowat. p. 176.

89 *British Policy in China, 1895–1902* by L. K. Young. p. 5.

90 *Anglo-Chinese Commerce and Diplomacy* by A. J. Sargent. p. 251.

91 Kimberley to O'Conor, 8 April 1895. F.O. 17/1242.

3 The Era of Change, 1895–1902

We have a chance now of doing something which will make this Government memorable.

Chamberlain to Devonshire, 23 July 1895

The government formed in the summer of 1895 was strong and united, in marked contrast to its predecessor. Fortified by a majority of 152, policies could be pursued without fear of snap defeats in Parliament. Some very powerful politicians found seats in the Cabinet—Chamberlain, Devonshire, Balfour, Goschen, Hicks Beach, Cross and Lansdowne. There were some able men holding junior posts too, including Curzon, Brodrick and the younger Balfour. Salisbury presided over this government until July 1902 (his mandate being extended in the election of 1900), when his long career in politics ended. Already, in October 1900, he had relinquished the Foreign Office to Lansdowne and had thereafter played a less prominent part in determining foreign policy. There were signs even in 1895 that his enthusiasm for foreign affairs was waning. At the time he wanted Devonshire to take the post but 'the Duke . . . persisted in refusing. . . . He himself thought he must be at the Foreign Office as well as Prime Minister, which I thought would be too much, but he said he would not go on with it if he found it too much',[1] wrote the Queen.

Salisbury's return was generally welcomed abroad, but almost at once he found himself in difficulties. During 1895–97 the Ottoman Empire was seriously challenged in Armenia, Crete and Macedonia. It looked as if its disintegration could not be long delayed. Salisbury was very pessimistic. The optimism of 1880, when he had told

References are printed on p. 105.

Layard 'It would be a great success to defer the fall of Turkey until
the revolution in Russia has taken place; we have everything to
gain by postponing the catastrophe',[2] was gone. The problem of
Turkey was subtly different from 1878. Russia was now in favour of
a conservative solution, it being the general belief in St Petersburg
that 'there is no doubt . . . Turkey will fulfil every demand that we
make upon her and probably in a comparatively short space of
time will place herself entirely at Russia's disposition'.[3] Had this
been the sole problem then Salisbury could have worked either
towards helping Turkey resist Russian pressure, with the aid of
Austria, Italy and, perhaps, Germany, or towards an agreement with
Russia to limit the damage when the crash came. Public opinion,
however, was firmly against the former policy while Lobanov, the
Russian Foreign Minister, was an Anglophobe and killed the alternative plan. The strength of public opinion in Britain against Turkey
seriously handicapped Salisbury, who in 1895 told his Ambassador
to the Porte, 'I do not believe that from Archangel to Cadiz there is
a soul who cares whether the Armenians are exterminated or not.
Here the sympathy for them . . . approaches to frenzy in its intensity'.[4]
Domestic agitation thus played an important part in influencing
British policy towards Macedonia and Crete.

Salisbury, for reasons of diplomacy as well as temperament, preferred the policy of delay, but this was no longer possible. Even if the
Armenian triplice were resurrected, it still might not successfully
protect British interests. A reform programme might accelerate
rather than retard the collapse of the Ottoman Empire. This might
please Gladstone, but it would hardly suit Salisbury. Nevertheless,
an approach was made to Russia in August, but Lobanov rejected
all overtures. Salisbury had no method of putting pressure on Britain's
erstwhile partners in the triplice because Rosebery had committed
Britain to reform without securing a similar commitment from
France and Russia. There was no alternative but to fall back on
securing Triple Alliance support for a programme of limited reform
intended to prolong the Sultan's rule. The Prime Minister had
already discussed the future of the Ottoman Empire with both
Hatzfeldt and the Kaiser, who had visited Britain in early August.
Discussions had really taken the form of a contingency plan by

Salisbury in case the Russians proved unco-operative. Unfortunately the British position had been completely misunderstood. Hatzfeldt was anxious to promote Anglo-German understanding and mis-represented Salisbury's statements in an attempt to head off any deal between Russia and Germany. The Kaiser was given to fits of en-thusiasm for projects which a few weeks later would be abandoned with equal alacrity and chose this occasion to encourage the notion of partition of Turkey. Germany's anxiety to find a final solution for the Eastern Question was understandable and Salisbury committed a serious error in constantly referring to the imminent decease of the sick man of Europe. It is scarcely surprising that the Kaiser was mystified by Salisbury's lack of enthusiasm for German plans for partition.

Despite his rebuff at Salisbury's hands, the Kaiser continued to fly the kite of partition for a few more weeks. He discussed with Szögyény, the Austrian Ambassador to Berlin, what compensation Austria would require for Russian acquisition of Constantinople. Szögyény and the German Chancellor, Hohenlohe, were horrified but powerless. On 29 August the Kaiser sent for Colonel Swaine, the British military attaché, and advocated British action to force change on Turkey. Salisbury did not know how to reply to German suggestions and succeeded only in offending the Kaiser. Currie was even obliged to assure the Austrians that Salisbury had never seriously contemplated a partition which would give the Russians Constan-tinople: 'as to change of policy, I never hinted anything of the kind. I said I was sure the Germans would do it if they had a war with France'.[5]

As a result of these events it seemed plain to Salisbury, 'all Europe is opposed to our Armenian policy. The two German Powers certainly hate it: they think it quixotic and dangerous'.[6] Thus, when crises in the Ottoman Empire recurred, Britain was isolated. In the autumn of 1895 more atrocities took place and the ambassadors in Constantinople forced the Sultan to appoint a reforming ministry. At first this seemed to mark a new era of international co-operation, for Russia was now more willing to act with the other powers. Salisbury even told Deym that in these circumstances it might be possible for the parties to the Mediterranean Agreements to sustain

Turkey, though at the same time he was trying to persuade Nicholas II to give Russian support to the notion of deposing Abdul Hamid II. However, none of the Continental powers, except Austria, could understand Britain's wish to take action. There was thus a general distrust of British motives. Furthermore, it became more difficult to judge what effect the Sultan's protestations in favour of reform would have upon the rickety structure of his empire. As the Queen observed on 5 November, 'Turkish Government seem to have lost all power and control over Civil and Military officers'.[7]

The moment for joint action had passed, though on 11 November Goluchowski did suggest that a European fleet should force the Straits and impose its will on the Sultan. Lobanov, however, wished to keep the powers away from Constantinople and firmly vetoed the plan; backed by Holstein, Russia was in a strong position. As the powers would not act together, Salisbury was obliged to consider the possibility of Britain acting alone. In Cabinet he suggested that Currie be given power to summon the navy from Salonika. Expert opinion in the Admiralty, which had been critical of British naval capacity in 1892, advised Goschen that the proposal was lunatic. Balfour and Chamberlain supported Goschen and the plan was killed. The result was, as Salisbury said, 'In Armenia I have been told by the Cabinet practically to sit still'.[8] Opposed at home and ignored abroad, there was nothing to be done. Even the notion of reviving an *entente à trois* had to be abandoned. Germany would not permit her allies to join with Britain in an attempt to reform Turkey 'unless a binding convention can be arrived at, since otherwise they fear England will not honour her obligations'.[9] Anglo–German mistrust after the unhappy events of the summer was now so deep that on 20 December the Kaiser even told Swaine Britain had suggested the establishment of an Anglo-Russian condominium over Constantinople.

Turkish problems, however, multiplied. In 1895 serious unrest had broken out in Macedonia, where rival cliques backing the claims of Serbia, Bulgaria and Greece competed for influence. The Porte was entirely unable to control the situation, which continued to worsen until by 1897 the province was virtually in a state of anarchy. In February 1896 the activities of a Greek secret society, Ethniké

Hetairia, were crowned with success when a revolt broke out in Crete. The powers wished to preserve the *status quo*, though in Britain there was sympathy for the Greeks. Russia suggested a blockade but the Queen told Salisbury, 'I hope you will not join in a blockade of Greece which Prince Lobanoff now proposes'.[10] Salisbury, with an eye on public opinion, replied, 'The Cabinet were informed that several of the Powers were disposed to suggest a naval blockade of Crete . . . and that Lord Salisbury had declined these overtures on the ground that England traditionally had always refused to interfere by force between insurgent populations and their Sovereign. Lord Salisbury also added that the recent proceedings of the Ottoman Government in Armenia made it very unfitting that England should join in helping the Sultan to subdue his subjects, unless there was some effective guarantee that the Sultan would deal justly and mercifully with his subjects'.[11] Once more, isolation precluded effective action.

In August 1896 a renewal of Armenian massacres roused a storm of protest in Britain, led by W. T. Stead in the *Review of Reviews*. Gladstone urged unilateral action, but Salisbury knew this was impossible. The Continental powers, while shocked at Turkish brutality, had little sympathy for the Armenian revolutionaries behind the trouble. Salisbury agreed with the British Vice-Consul at Van, who reported, 'The more I learn of past events and the present state of this province, the more clearly I see that the criminal actions of these societies have been largely responsible for the terrible scenes enacted here and all over Anatolia . . . much as the Turks are to blame'.[12] The premier looked to Russia for help, as did the Queen, who believed 'if England and Russia went together, there must be peace, and something ought to be done to bring this about'.[13] The moment seemed favourable as Lobanov had recently died and the Tsar was visiting Britain. Salisbury and the Tsar met at Balmoral on 27 and 29 September. In two long discussions Salisbury argued for a revival of the Concert of Europe to prevent anarchy in Turkey, but the Tsar was adamant in his support for the *status quo*. British fears that an unreformed Turkey would collapse were not shared, though the Tsar was pleased by the conciliatory tone of British policy. Salisbury's remark that 'if Austria, France and Italy were in favour of Russia having control of the Straits, England would not maintain her objection alone',[14] was well received. But the limitations of British policy were plainly shown in Salisbury's observation that 'the idea . . . that this control of the Straits should be given to Russia while the Sultan was still at Constantinople, would be exceedingly unacceptable to the other Powers, and would be strongly resisted'.[15] The Tsar disclaimed any desire for territorial acquisition, but could find no way of implementing a satisfactory joint policy.

The problem facing Salisbury seemed insoluble. There was pressure on Britain to act, but not to act alone. Yet it seemed impossible to secure assistance from other powers. In January 1896 Austria had made overtures to Britain for a renewal of co-operation in the Near East, but these proposals foundered on Salisbury's unwillingness to renew Britain's obligation of December 1887 to defend Turkey. Deym reported to Goluchowski that 'public opinion in England . . . was very bitter towards Turkey and it was very questionable if the country would undertake a war on her behalf'.[16] While Salisbury himself made every effort to retain a connexion with Austria, opinion 'even on the Tory side was much more favourable to Russia and much more adverse to the Turks than it used to be'.[17] After the Italian defeat at Adowa on 1 March 1896 Salisbury seized this opportunity to demonstrate that he wished to continue working with the Triple Alliance, but this impressed Rome rather than Vienna or Berlin. The old combination of Austria and Britain was played out.

On 20 October 1896 Salisbury circulated proposals concerning Turkey to all the powers. The burden of his argument was that numerous factors were working towards the dissolution of the Ottoman Empire, while none of the powers wanted change in the territorial *status quo*. The cure was to be reform sustained by the unanimity of the powers. Precise details were to be defined by an ambassadorial conference at Constantinople. First reactions were favourable. Italy and Austria promised support while Germany indicated she would support any plan receiving unanimous consent. France too was co-operative. Hanotaux, the Foreign Minister, realized how great was French financial involvement in Turkey and wished to stabilize the situation. All now rested on Russia, but in

St Petersburg the expansionists, led by Nelidov, Ambassador to the Porte, favoured seizure of the upper Bosphorus. At a Crown Council on 5 December this policy was agreed, despite fierce opposition from Witte, the Finance Minister. Nelidov hoped to be able to square Britain, probably by concessions in the Euphrates Valley. This master plan which might well have involved Europe in war, founded as it was on deceit, was wrecked by the Tsar's timidity and the obstinacy of France. It did not take long before the peace party regained ascendancy at St Petersburg, while in Paris Hanotaux was furious at the failure of Russia to consider French interests. On 12 December he told Mohrenheim that France would only agree to joint action by the powers if the integrity of Turkey was maintained, no individual action was executed by any power, and no condominium established. These events made it imperative for Russia to treat seriously Salisbury's proposition that 'the Powers will . . . come to a definite understanding, that their unanimous decision in these matters is to be final, and will be executed up to the measure of such force as the Powers have at their command'.[18] The ambassadors began work in December and by February 1897 had reached agreement on a reform programme. It was never to be implemented, because in 1897 war between Greece and Turkey broke out, following another Cretan insurrection. The latest crisis caused Salisbury some embarrassment as it fractured inter-party unity on foreign affairs. There was much sympathy for the Greeks and Kimberley rejected Salisbury's policy of concerted action with the other powers. Debate within the Cabinet was acrimonious and on 23 March Salisbury handed over the Foreign Office to Balfour while he had a rest. When war broke out in April Britain refused to support Greece and by the end of the month the Turks had won. However, pressure from Britain prevented too harsh a settlement and in 1898 Crete was made autonomous under Prince George of Greece.

The recurrent crises of 1895–97 forced a complete change of policy by Britain. Public opinion would no longer tolerate support for Turkey. This in turn made nonsense of the Mediterranean Agreements and attempts by Austria in 1896 and 1897 to revive the old understanding failed. If Turkey could not be supported then antagonism to Russian ambitions at the Straits could no longer be justified. Indeed, naval and military experts had, ever since 1892, argued against anti-Russian policy. In 1896 the Director of Naval Intelligence put the position even more strongly: 'Asia Minor will in time become Russian or at least entirely subject to Russian influence. Europe cannot prevent this. When this is done Marmorice will be the naval base of Russia in the Mediterranean. The time therefore for jealously guarding the inviolability of the Dardanelles is passing away, and is not worth any important sacrifice now'.[19] When Austria realized that Britain would 'certainly neither move nor interfere . . . whatever might occur in the Turkish capital',[20] she was forced to make an agreement with Russia. On 5 May 1897 an Austro-Russian agreement was signed which promulgated the principle of non-intervention in Balkan affairs. This suited Britain well enough.

It could not be imagined, however, that such changes left Britain unscathed. Relations with the Triple Alliance were worse in 1897 than they had been for many years, while Russia was hardly an intimate friend. The decision to abandon Constantinople and take a stand at Cairo seemed likely to create fresh difficulties with France. British influence at the Porte was virtually non-existent after 1898. Yet there were benefits to compensate. Turkey no longer seemed so weak. Salisbury had misjudged the capacity of Turkey to survive and admitted his error in 1897: 'the idea that the Turkish Empire is on the verge of dissolution has been dissipated'.[21] The process of concentrating British power and diplomatic activity on areas where interests could be protected had begun. Blanket support for Italy had been abandoned with the *entente à trois*, for she was 'by herself a broken reed to lean on', only useful as 'a link to bind England to a powerful confederation'[22] which no longer existed.

These developments were not unimportant in domestic politics, playing a part in educating members of the government about the realities of the British position. Salisbury was no longer able to dominate totally the making of policy. Defeat over the proposal to give Currie full powers marked a turning point in his relations with the Cabinet. Fuller discussion removed many of the clouds impairing the vision of his colleagues. New and more strident opinions were heard. Chamberlain's suggestion of 1895 that the United States might help introduce reform in Turkey was not repeated in the realistic atmosphere of 1897. Traditional Tory preference for Germany was eroded by familiarity with the Kaiser's erratic diplomacy. Public opinion was a more important force and politicians found it necessary to explain their policies. The central change in British policy in the Near East, the acceptance that 'the only policy which . . . is left to us . . . [is] to strengthen our position on the Nile (to its source) and to withdraw as much as possible from all responsibilities at Constantinople'[23] fitted in well with these new pressures.

Problems at Constantinople suggested a passive policy on the Nile, though Salisbury's wish to avoid conflict with France was not wholly shared by the new Colonial Secretary, Chamberlain. In 1895 negotiations over Siam and West Africa were opened, in the hope that generosity in these areas would improve relations in Egypt. This aim was neither ignoble nor impossible. Hanotaux, the Foreign Minister, and successive French ambassadors, Courcel and Cambon, were reasonable men. But France was neither ready to negotiate seriously on Egypt nor to recognize that 'general French political interests suffered from the prolonged estrangement between the two countries'.[24] Failure to agree in Egypt precluded agreement elsewhere in Africa. The only ray of hope was conclusion of an agreement on Siam in January 1896 which gave France influence on the Mekong while preserving the independence of the Menam Valley—Lansdowne's 'middle of the artichoke'.[25]

For those who wished to promote good relations between Britain and France the years 1896–98 witnessed a most unwelcome rise in tension, culminating at Fashoda in 1898. In West Africa strain first became apparent. When Chamberlain entered office he made his belief clear that commercial prosperity and the possession of empire were closely connected. In November 1895 he informed governors of colonial territories, 'I am impressed with the extreme importance of securing as large a share as possible of the mutual trade of the United Kingdom and the Colonies for British producers and manufacturers. . . . I wish to investigate thoroughly the extent to which . . . foreign imports of any kind have displaced, or are displacing, similar British goods, and the causes of such displace-

ment'.[26] The condition of British possessions in West Africa soon
aroused the Colonial Secretary's anger, for Sierra Leone and Gambia
were cut off from commercial prosperity by surrounding French
territory. In the Gold Coast and Nigeria there were British traders
struggling against French competitors who enjoyed official support
in Paris. Chamberlain's determination to make the struggles of
Goldie and Lugard the concern of Britain made it certain that the
dimension of conflict would be enlarged. In France, Hanotaux was
the prisoner of Etienne and the *Comité de l'Afrique française*. In
April 1896 the Méline government surrendered to the fanatics and
agreed that a concerted attempt was to be made to penetrate
regions claimed (though not effectively ruled) by Britain. Once
established, these expeditionary forces were to 'spread out like a
fan, in order to bring pressure to bear on the disputed points and
to establish the nucleus of a French administration'.[27] This was
aggressive and in bad faith, for, ever since February, negotiations
had been going on in Paris. In May talks were broken off. Chamberlain's grand design—the cession of Gambia and Dominica to France
in return for Dahomey, and the exchange of Dahomey in return
for German agreement for a free hand in the Gold Coast hinterland—
was wrecked.

Chamberlain now became a firm advocate of a policy of counter
pressure on France. His influence in the Cabinet was such that he
could not be lightly overruled; indeed, Salisbury told the Queen
Chamberlain's belligerence risked the destruction of the Cabinet
and that he 'is a little too warlike, and hardly sees the other side of
the question'.[28] The premier was in no position to enforce his views.
His hold on the Cabinet had weakened and Chamberlain enjoyed
a large measure of extra-parliamentary support for his imperial
policies. The Colonial Secretary bombarded Salisbury with notes
and memoranda, complaining in June 1897, 'We have thrown away
all our cards and they keep all theirs in their hands. . . . I firmly believe
that if we do not show that we will not be trifled with we shall
finally be driven into war, with the disadvantage of having already
surrendered much that is valuable'.[29] Chamberlain was not, however,
just a jingo looking for a pretext for a conflict; on 12 September he
told Selborne, 'My own idea was that the only hope of a peaceful

arrangement was to convince the French, from the first, that they had tried our patience too far and that they must give way or take the consequences'.[30] All this was far removed from the Cabinet's original intention of settling as many questions with France as possible. In late 1897 Chamberlain was ready to mount his counter-offensive, despite the opposition of Salisbury, Goschen and Hicks Beach. During early 1898 Chamberlain's West Africa Frontier Force advanced into the disputed areas of Nigeria. The purpose was clear: 'We ought—even at the cost of war—to keep the hinterland for the Gold Coast, Lagos and the Niger territories. We ought not to allow the Gambia and Sierra Leone business to be repeated'.[31]

While representatives of France and Britain struggled in the remote and valueless hinterland of Lagos, the diplomats of the Niger Commission tried to reach a settlement in Paris. Repeated acts of provocation by both sides made it hard to come to terms. Salisbury and his Colonial Secretary were in open disagreement by the summer of 1898, particularly over French claims to two towns—Ilo and Bona. Salisbury's case for giving way was simple: 'It will be a pity if we break off the negotiations, for it will add to our difficulties in the Nile Valley. . . . If you wish to come to terms it would be prudent to do so before we take Khartum. We shall get nothing out of the French Assembly after that event'.[32] Chamberlain's view was coloured by the French practice of upping their demands as soon as a concession had been made—a tactic which was to continue until 1904. On 3 June Chamberlain made it clear he would go no further, saying: 'We are now, therefore, giving them what they asked for—they ought to be content. It is more than I am. . . .'[33] The French finally accepted the British proposals and on 14 June 1898 the Convention was signed. It was with relief that Salisbury told the Queen, 'It is a matter of sincere congratulation that the agreement was arrived at before the resignation of Monsieur Méline's Ministry'.[34] More than Méline's ministry had perished in the Anglo-French conflict. Salisbury's authority in foreign affairs had received a second important check. Chamberlain was now suspicious of Salisbury's weakness, his tendency to truckle to the rivals of Britain, and was determined to reshape British policy. Nor was he alone in believing that Salisbury's judgment was at fault, for there was a good deal of support for the Colonial Secretary within the party ranks. The most influential hardliner was probably Curzon, the Under-Secretary for Foreign Affairs, who later observed of the conflict, 'I never spend five minutes in inquiring if we are unpopular. The answer is written in red ink on the map of the globe. Neither would I ever adopt Lord Salisbury's plan of throwing bones to keep the various dogs quiet (Madagascar, Tunis, Heligoland, Samoa, Siam). They devour your bone and then turn round and snarl for more'.[35] These criticisms were to have their influence on the making of policy in the second Anglo-French dispute of 1898—that of Fashoda.

Fashoda was the scene of the most serious crisis between Britain and France since the days of Napoleon. An insignificant collection of mud huts on the banks of the White Nile became symbolic of the clash of empires. It was not Fashoda which mattered; the struggle was over Egypt, the prize snatched from France's grasp in a moment of weakness in 1882. During the period 1889–96 Egyptian affairs had played only a concealed part in Anglo-French hostility. Under Cromer's capable management Egyptian finances had prospered and minimal offence had been given to French interests. But in both Britain and France there was constant watchfulness. Relations between the two powers could never run smooth until either Britain evacuated Cairo or France accepted the permanency of the occupation. The British decision of 1895–96 to concentrate the line of defence of the route to India at Cairo rather than Constantinople merely advanced the date of conflict.

Events in 1896 conspired to push Egypt into the limelight. After Grey's declaration of March 1895 that the British would view foreign intrusion in the region of the Upper Nile as an act of hostility, the risks of action ought to have been plain enough to France. Yet, in late 1896, Plunkett, the Ambassador to Brussels, reported that a force had left the French Congo bound for the Nile. This expedition, headed by Captain Marchand, had been authorized in November 1895. The object was simple: to establish a French position on the Nile and to force the British out of Egypt. As a policy it was crude, obvious, unsophisticated and, in view of the small size of the expedition, probably suicidal. If it had not been for developments elsewhere the expedition might well have caused nothing more than a newspaper headline commemorating its annihilation at the hands of Mahdist forces. In December 1895 part of the Italian army in Abyssinia had been defeated by the French-equipped and Russian-advised forces of the Emperor Menelik. On 1 March 1896 the whole force had been routed at Adowa. The collapse of Italian power opened the way for Mahdist advances as well as increasing suspicion in Britain that Abyssinia was to be used as a tool by the Franco-Russian alliance to eject Britain from Egypt. The Italians pleaded for a diversionary move by Britain to relieve pressure. This gave the British the excuse for action in the Sudan. As Lansdowne told the Cabinet, 'the ulterior object was to restore a portion of her lost territory to Egypt'. [36] Salisbury was even more specific, telling Cromer 'we desired to kill two birds with one stone, and to use the same military effort to plant the foot of Egypt rather farther up the Nile'.[37] The contingency foreseen almost a decade before, the necessity of occupying the Sudan, had arisen.

The Cabinet decided that an Egyptian army under the command of the Sirdar, Kitchener, should advance as far as Dongola. It was at once seen that this was but the prelude to the inevitable attempt to crush Mahdist power and permanently secure the British position in Egypt by occupation of the whole Nile valley. Reactions to this modest proposal, therefore, were strong. Led by Harcourt and Dilke, the Radicals compared the advance into the desert to the 'madness of Cambyses' and 'breathed dire prediction'.[38] Opposition in France was even stronger and by June French and Russian representatives on the *Caisse* had managed to prevent the subsidy of the expedition. If Salisbury's 'ultimate intention was to go to Khartoum and restore it to Egypt'[39] France was already fighting this more important battle.

The campaigns in the Sudan were controlled by Cromer, a civilian. The reasons for this unusual state of affairs were simple. Among the politicians there was suspicion of '*trop de zèle* on the part of Kitchener'[40] and a fear lest the generals decided to go 'marching into the centre of Africa',[41] thus causing fresh complications. On the diplomatic plane the problem was that 'the military question is in reality a financial question, and, looking at the general Egyptian tangle, it is quite impossible to separate the financial from the political question'.[42] By autumn 1896 the province of Dongola had been recaptured and Kitchener was making preparations for further advance. Cromer was hostile to these plans and told Salisbury in October 1897 that 'no sufficiently important interest is involved to justify the loss of life and money which would be involved in the capture of Khartoum'.[43] Salisbury was in a difficult position, for he was aware that 'by destroying the Dervish power we are killing the defender who is holding the valley for us now'.[44] On the other hand, he was conscious of the 'diplomatic difficulties . . . if any French explorer reaches the Nile before we have taken Khartoum'.[45] In the autumn of 1897 the project of sending a small expeditionary force from Uganda, thus by-passing Mahdist forces, to establish itself at Fashoda collapsed. Salisbury's hand was now forced.

In late 1897 it became evident that Mahdist forces were contemplating an offensive. On 1 January 1898 Cromer suggested that British troops reconquer the Sudan and his request was granted by the Cabinet. On 8 April Kitchener won a significant victory at Atbara and followed this up by routing the Mahdist forces at Omdurman on 2 September. The power of the Dervishes was broken, though it was not until November 1899 that the Khalifa and his emirs were killed. Kitchener's victories brought him face to face with Marchand, who had arrived at Fashoda on 10 July. The stage was set for imperial confrontation. Salisbury had observed in autumn 1897 that 'if we ever get to Fashoda, the diplomatic crisis will be something to remember'.[46] He realized, however, that with the British title based on conquest and fortified by the presence of a large Anglo-Egyptian force in the Sudan there would be little that France could do. Such realism did not penetrate the Quai d'Orsay. Delcassé, who had succeeded Hanotaux on 28 June, had been one of the authors of the Marchand expedition. On 8 February 1898 he had told the Chamber 'it is not I who am to blame . . . if from the banks of the Upper Ubanghi the French flag has yet to be carried to the banks of the Nile'.[47] Once in office the gravity of the situation gradually became clear, particularly when Monson, the British Ambassador, warned him, 'the situation on the Upper Nile is a dangerous one. . . . H.M.G. are determined to hold to the decision already announced . . . they would not consent to a compromise on this point'.[48] Delcassé had the choice between surrender and war.

In reality there was no choice. The press might rave at abject surrender by the government but France could not fight Britain for Egypt. The relative naval strength of the powers was unfavourable to France and it was quite clear to all parties that the Franco-Russian alliance did not apply in Africa. British demands for evacuation by Marchand had to be met and on 3 November, after tension lasting two months, Delcassé caved in, having tried every trick to persuade Salisbury to make concessions. He made threats to cancel the Convention on West Africa and to invoke a Continental League against Britain. He pleaded not to be driven into a corner and suggested that France would prefer an alliance with Britain to one with Russia. All his efforts were in vain. Marchand was withdrawn and on 21 March an Anglo-French declaration defined the spheres of influence of the two powers. There was no place for France on the Nile.

There was great satisfaction in Britain at the outcome of this confrontation. Public and Parliamentary opinion had overwhelmingly supported Salisbury's uncompromising line. Indeed, there were those in the Cabinet who would not have permitted concessions had Salisbury been inclined to grant them. Attitudes differed sharply among the Conservative leadership. While Salisbury wished to avoid humiliating France, warning that too strong a stance 'would probably cost the French ministers their offices',[49] Chamberlain, Goschen and Curzon were much more belligerent. At one point it looked as if Chamberlain wanted war. According to Metternich, the future German Ambassador to London, the Colonial Secretary spoke of needing 'to settle . . . differences once and for ever' and presenting 'our bill to France not only in Egypt but all over the globe, and should she refuse to pay, then war'.[50] Curzon was scarcely less minatory, urging 'no French flag, territory or men anywhere near the Nile'.[51] Liberal imperialists like Rosebery and Grey were equally unyielding in their attitude.

At first the inevitable legacy of this encounter was increased bitterness in France. The Queen's pleasure that the entire valley of the Nile was in British hands found its equivalent in chagrin in France.

But there were hopeful signs too. The Queen and Salisbury had been at one in feeling 'We must try and save France from humiliation'.[52] Now that the permanence of British occupation had been recognized by the French government it could only be a matter of time before relations improved. This both Salisbury and Delcassé desired. As long ago as 1896 Courcel had assured Salisbury that French interest in Egypt was largely sentimental. The colonial lobby had been unenthusiastic about the Marchand expedition once its implications had been revealed, and Delcassé had not lost office in the aftermath of Fashoda. The ingredients of future agreement were there, though they could not at once be utilized. Events conspired to postpone the day of agreement, but the real cause was the poor state of public opinion in both countries. Until other factors began to affect public feeling, relations between the western powers could never improve dramatically. In Salisbury's opinion 'anything like hearty good will between the two nations will not be possible. But I think a mutual temper of apathetic tolerance may be cultivated on both sides, without sacrificing the interests of either'.[53] Until 1903 this was to remain the sorry state of Anglo-French relations.

Just as British involvement in Near Eastern problems indicated the desirability of lowering tension in West Africa and Egypt, so did poor relations with France require an understanding with Germany. Mainly because of South African issues this was not achieved. The growing wealth of the Transvaal intensified political problems and increased the appeal of the party demanding incorporation of all South Africa into the British Empire. In 1895 it became apparent that the Uitlanders were ready to revolt against Kruger. On 1 October Kruger closed the drifts to goods imported through Cape Colony, thus precipitating a crisis. Chamberlain's warning to Kruger about 'a proceeding almost partaking of the nature of an act of hostility',[54] was supported by the Cabinet. Confident of German moral support, but as yet short of arms, Kruger was forced to climb down. Preparations for an Uitlander revolt went ahead, though when it took place on 28 December it was a dismal failure. The next day Dr Jameson launched an invasion of the

Transvaal to sustain the crumbling revolt. His action was at once disavowed by Chamberlain, who described it as 'a flagrant piece of filibustering for which there is no justification that I can see. . . . If it were supported by us it would justify the accusation by Germany . . . that having first attempted to get up a rebellion in a friendly state and having failed, we had then assented to an act of aggression'.[55]

The failure of the raid had serious diplomatic repercussions despite lack of British involvement. Salisbury's feeling that 'no one seems to have anticipated this mad move of Jameson's'[56] was not shared by the German press and public. On 3 January 1896 the Kaiser sent a congratulatory telegram to Kruger. Opinion in Britain was outraged. The Prince of Wales described it as 'a most gratuitous act of unfriendliness'[57] while the Queen was moved to write to the Kaiser saying 'I feel I cannot refrain from expressing my deep regret at the telegram you sent. . . . It is considered very unfriendly towards this country . . . and has, I grieve to say, made a very painful impression'.[58] Opposition and factious malevolence from France and Russia had been expected, but the treason of Germany was much harder to forgive. The motive behind the telegram was clear—to force Britain into dependence on the Triple Alliance. The Austrians were dismayed at this act of folly; Hatzfeldt reported, 'we might yet live to see an *Entente Cordiale* of the Western Powers—new edition'.[59] There was further exacerbation of British feeling when it was realized that the Kaiser had taken advantage of the anti-British tide in Germany to push through a new programme of naval construction.

Serious problems troubled Anglo-Transvaal relations in the next few years. British policy was based upon the Colonial Office Memorandum of 26 March 1896 which advocated a forward policy. The reasoning was clear. The strategic importance of the Cape was vital to Britain, and the existence of an independent Transvaal or a Transvaal which was the client state of another power would imperil security. Economic factors pointed towards annexation, as did imperialist public opinion. Chamberlain and his supporters grew steadily more powerful in the Cabinet and German manoeuvres increased suspicion that Berlin wished to establish Germany as a major power in South Africa. Rhodes was replaced by Milner, after a short interval, as the advocate of expansionist policies. Uitlander discontent became the focus of attention, and the ostensible cause of conflict with the Boers.

Germany was not merely concerned for Boer independence. If the truth be known, the Kaiser agreed with his grandmother that the Boers were 'horrid people, cruel and overbearing'.[60] German aims were to incorporate Britain into her alliance system and, if possible, to inherit part of the Portuguese African Empire. While there was some pressure in Britain for an alliance with Germany—the Queen, for example, dilated on the dangers of isolation in a letter to Salisbury on 14 January 1896—there was no enthusiasm for German colonial ambitions in South Africa. In fact Britain herself started negotiations in order to secure strategically important parts of the Portuguese Empire. Salisbury, however, felt that these talks were doomed to failure, for France and Germany were sure to oppose the cession of Delagoa Bay. By the close of 1896 the impatient Colonial Secretary was forced to agree, 'we have nothing to do but stand on our rights and wait events'.[61] In 1898 the pressure of conflict with France brought Britain round to a policy of conciliating Germany. The moment for which Holstein had been waiting seemed to have come.

Salisbury's illness removed from the Foreign Office the leading opponent of entangling alliances. His deputy, Balfour, favoured an accord with Germany. On 25 March he had a long discussion with Hatzfeldt concerning all Germany's grievances. On 29 March, to the surprise of all, Chamberlain suggested an alliance, telling Hatzfeldt, 'It seemed to me that on these greater issues the interests of Germany were really identical with our own'.[62] Berlin did not know what to make of this offer, though there was suspicion that German help was needed and that as soon as it had been obtained the alliance would be jettisoned. Salisbury's warning that 'the attitude prescribed to us . . . by our popular constitution . . . will not acknowledge the obligation of an engagement made in former years'[63] was recalled. The cool reception of his offer upset Chamberlain. After talking again to Hatzfeldt, he reported, 'I gathered that he thought any attempt to secure a direct defensive alliance between

Germany and England was premature. He assented, but said the opportunity might come later. I reminded him of the French proverb, *le bonheur qui passe*'.[64]

On his return to the Foreign Office Salisbury was horrified at the division which this rash initiative had created. The premier never truly believed in the value of a German alliance, later insisting, 'The liability of having to defend the German and Austrian frontiers against Russia is heavier than that of having to defend the British Isles against France'.[65] Conversely, the Kaiser believed in an alliance only if it extended to Europe: 'Chamberlain must not forget that in East Prussia I have one Prussian army corps against three Russian armies and nine cavalry divisions located close to the frontier . . . no British warship can keep them away from me'.[66] A colonial deal could not, therefore, lead to a full alliance, nor would the strength of public opinion in either country have permitted an arrangement. Holstein's moment had not arrived. Perhaps it had never existed.

Salisbury hastened to disabuse Hatzfeldt of any notion that extensive British commitments made him easy prey for Holstein. On 11 May he told the ambassador, 'I could not recognize that Germany had any claim that we should purchase her support by concessions to which, except for the consideration of that support, we should be adverse'.[67] Meanwhile Chamberlain's speech of 13 May continued to delude Holstein and prevent him evaluating Hatzfeldt's reports correctly. On 2 June negotiations were suspended though on 21 August the Kaiser met Lascelles, the Ambassador to Berlin, and the question of an alliance was fully discussed in a friendly fashion. Nothing came of this either, not least because Salisbury remained ignorant of his ambassador's initiative.

In summer 1898 an attempt was made to placate Germany by opening negotiations over the Portuguese colonies of Angola and Mozambique. Salisbury was hostile to these talks but was compelled to accept them by a rebellious Cabinet. The premier would have preferred to negotiate a loan agreement with Portugal to prop up her tottering empire. The imperialists won the day, sustained by Milner's view that 'I look on possession of Delagoa Bay as the best chance we have of winning the great game between ourselves and the Transvaal for the mastery in South Africa without a war.

I am not sure indeed that we shall ever be masters without a war'.[68]
Negotiations opened on 22 June 1898. The basis of German claims
was that she was well placed to squeeze Britain. Salisbury saw
German pressure as blackmail and even Chamberlain, who advocated the opening of negotiations, observed 'we pay Blackmail
to German*y* to induce her not to interfere where she has no right
of interference'.[69] Wiser than his colleagues, Salisbury saw that once
an agreement for the partition of Portuguese territories had been
made Germany would try to expedite presentation of the bill. As
he told Balfour, 'Germany is trying to induce us to join in putting
the knife into Portugal'.[70] On 30 August 1898 Balfour signed a
convention outlining conditions for an Anglo-German loan to
Portugal and, while professing to wish to maintain the integrity of
the Portuguese Empire, including a secret article providing for the
contingency of partition. In return, Germany was not to oppose
British policy in South Africa. Salisbury felt the agreement was
both morally and politically wrong but had to accept Balfour's
handiwork. At the same time he continued to work to maintain
Portugal, to prevent Germany's 'wish to force the pace of destiny'[71]
and on 14 October 1899 an Anglo-Portuguese Agreement renewed
old British commitments, thus reducing the likelihood of the lapse
into anarchy to which Germany cheerfully looked forward. When
Germany discovered the existence of this arrangement Britain was
wrongly accused of double-dealing.

The Anglo-German Agreement of 1898 made certain that there would
be no outside interference when the time for the reckoning with
the Transvaal came. At the beginning of 1899 it seemed unlikely
Milner's ambitions would be fulfilled. British public opinion had
not yet been roused, but the High Commissioner was confident of
his ability to attract support, telling Selborne, 'If I can advance matters
by my own actions . . . I believe that I shall have support when the
time comes'.[72] The hostility and mutual suspicion of Milner and
Kruger wrecked all attempts at compromise. In early June the
Bloemfontein conference broke down, despite the wishes of the
Cabinet. Shortly before the failure of the conference Chamberlain
had expressed serious reservations about Milner's conduct, thinking

'he requires to be restrained rather than to be encouraged'.[73] In July Kruger made a concession on the franchise, though the imperialist party remained suspicious of Boer good faith. The argument now used by Milner and endorsed by the Cabinet was that it was necessary to maintain pressure on Kruger in order to ensure implementation. Even Salisbury warned Chamberlain 'it is necessary to guard against backsliding'.[74] Only Hicks Beach stood out, hoping 'Milner and the Uitlanders will not be allowed to drag us into war'.[75] In the end the dispute between Milner and Kruger became a struggle for supremacy in South Africa. Chamberlain put this clearly, 'What is now at stake is the position of Great Britain . . . and with it the estimate formed of our power and influence in our Colonies and throughout the world'.[76] The case for sending an ultimatum was still being discussed when Kruger despatched his own on 9 October. Inevitably it was rejected by the Cabinet and war began on 11 October.

The Boer War ended with the Peace of Vereeniging on 31 May 1902. During those years the extent of British isolation and unpopularity became clear. Reverses at the hands of the Boers demonstrated both military incapacity and over-confidence. The stretching of British resources to the uttermost (by early 1902 there were about 300,000 men under arms in South Africa) made Britain vulnerable to pressure. It did not take Germany long to formulate demands, particularly as the manoeuvres of Muraviev, the Russian Foreign Minister, and Delcassé were clearly anti-British. As soon as war broke out Muraviev believed there was 'every prospect of the conclusion of an understanding between Russia, France and Germany'[77] to take action against aggressive British expansionism. The notion of a Continental League did not, however, appeal to the Kaiser. Wilhelm II condemned British arrogance but was more interested in securing concessions than injuring badly a power he still hoped to have as an ally. As it happened, Germany and Britain were in dispute over the Samoan Islands condominium. In May 1899 the Kaiser had written to the Queen complaining about Salisbury's intransigence and in September Hatzfeldt made it clear that his master would not visit England unless the dispute were settled forthwith. Salisbury still did not wish to come to terms and was unimpressed by the Kaiser's assertion that he alone stood between Britain and an upsurge in German feeling which would create a Berlin–Paris–St Petersburg axis. 'I desire to remain friendly to England but . . . I cannot go on sitting on the safety-valve for ever',[78] he told the military attaché in Berlin on 6 November. Under pressure from his colleagues, Salisbury gave way and the Anglo-German convention of 14 November 1899 gave Germany what she wanted.

Although evidence was accumulating of the real lack of goodwill towards Britain on the part of Germany, soon to be given dramatic new impetus by the Navy Bill of 1900, the group within the Cabinet which favoured an alliance still saw Germany as the best candidate. On 30 November Chamberlain, in a speech at Leicester, argued that 'the natural alliance is between ourselves and the great German Empire . . . a new Triple Alliance between the Teutonic race and the two great branches of the Anglo-Saxon race, will be a still more potent influence in the future of the world'.[79] This astonishing speech was made only ten days after conversations with Bülow had revealed the impossibility of such a liaison. It was received without warmth in Berlin and cautiously at home. Yet the Kaiser tried hard to persuade Britain that he was an invaluable friend, warning the Prince of Wales against the machinations of Russia and receiving the warm thanks of the Queen. He was not able to allay Salisbury's suspicions and on 10 April 1900 the premier told the Queen he doubted 'whether a proposal for a combination against England was ever really made by France and Russia to Germany'.[80] Evidence suggests that Salisbury was wrong; the Kaiser did reject Russian overtures in October 1899 and again the following March.

Throughout 1900 alliance proposals remained dormant. Chamberlain had been rebuffed while Salisbury preferred to work outside the framework of a formal alliance. Ill health and the need for a governmental reshuffle following electoral victory in October led to Salisbury's retirement from the Foreign Office and the appointment of Lansdowne on 29 October. It was the Queen's wish that Lansdowne must remain 'entirely under his [Salisbury's] personal supervision',[81] but this proved a mere form. Lansdowne opposed continued isolation and soon told Lascelles, 'we should use every effort to maintain . . . and strengthen the good relations which at present exist between the Queen's Government and that of the Emperor'.[82] Recent agreement with Germany over Chinese affairs seemed to portend happier days.

In March 1901 Lansdowne persuaded the Cabinet that a limited agreement would suit British interests well. Events in the Far East pointed to Germany as the partner. On 18 March Eckardstein, temporarily in charge of the German embassy, offered 'a purely defensive alliance between the two powers, directed solely against France and Russia'.[83] He was acting without authority, though Lansdowne naturally assumed the offer had the sanction of the Wilhelmstrasse. Worse still, Eckardstein then told Berlin that Lansdowne had taken the lead. In an attempt to improve Anglo-German relations the Baron had made them worse. Holstein and Bülow were convinced that 'the English must come to us',[84] while Lansdowne was disconcerted by the variable nature of German policy. This he felt mattered in case of alliance because policy would be 'no longer British but Anglo-German'.[85]

In May Hatzfeldt resumed conduct of negotiations with an increasingly divided government. Two members of the Cabinet, Balfour and Hamilton, strongly favoured a full alliance. Salisbury and Hicks Beach were hostile and the rest of the Cabinet uncertain. The global nature of the commitment worried the faint hearts but pleased Balfour and Hamilton. In April Hamilton had told Curzon, 'we must alter our foreign policy, and throw our lot in for good or bad, with some other Power. On the whole . . . the best alliance . . . would be . . . the Triple Alliance. Such a combination would guarantee the peace of Europe. . . . As we now stand, we are an object of envy and of greed to all the other Powers'.[86] In his memorandum of 29 May Salisbury attacked this analysis decisively. The ageing premier saw numerous objections to the draft treaty prepared for Lansdowne by Sanderson, the Permanent Under-Secretary. He asserted that the democratic nature of the constitution debarred accession to a secret alliance; a future government might repudiate the treaty. More cogently, he suggested that his alliance would 'excite bitter murmurs in every rank of German society' and that 'the bargain would be a bad one for this country'.[87]

In the circumstances Lansdowne decided 'to mark time for a while'[88] until Hatzfeldt himself came forward with an authentic offer. The Foreign Secretary was not himself hostile to an alliance, though it would be 'a big fence to ride at'.[89] In August Edward VII and the Kaiser met at Wilhelmshöhe. The alliance question was discussed and the Kaiser expressed a wish for a binding treaty. The Kaiser's manner, coupled with repeated examples of his backstage attempts to worsen British relations with France and Russia, created a most unfavourable impression and 'the conviction rapidly spread that the Kaiser was insincere in his protestations for an alliance, and that the chauvinist tone of the German press more correctly represented the attitude of Germany'.[90] The two powers were drifting away from an alliance, primarily because of mutual suspicion. Even Holstein, the wrecker of past negotiations, now realized that negotiations might never be resumed. In October he had a frank discussion with Chirol, head of *The Times* foreign news section, but spoiled his case for a re-examination of Anglo-German relations by misrepresentation of Salisbury's rôle in the past. Bertie, the Assistant Under-Secretary, rang the death knell of the alliance proposals in his memorandum of 27 October. 'If once we bind ourselves by a formal defensive alliance, and practically join the Triplice, we shall never be on decent terms with France . . . or with Russia. . . . Treaty or no Treaty, if ever there were danger of our destruction or even defeat, by Russia and France, Germany would be bound, in order to avoid a like fate for herself, to come to our assistance. She might ask a high price for such aid, but could it be higher than what we should lose by the sacrifice of our liberty to pursue a British world policy, which would be the result of a formal defensive alliance with the German Empire?'[91]

Perforce, Lansdowne now returned to the notion of a limited understanding to which 'The objections to joining the Triple Alliance do not seem to me to apply'.[92] Metternich, the new German Ambassador, did not even think this overture worth reporting to Berlin. Meanwhile Chamberlain, the former advocate of the alliance, had provoked German anger by a speech on the Boer War. In subsequent discussions with Deym, the Austrian Ambassador, Chamberlain made it clear 'he saw German hatred becoming more and more intense' leading him 'to despair of attaining his ideal'.[93] Instead of taking this hint, Bülow engaged in a war of words with the Colonial Secretary from which the German emerged the loser, not least because public opinion in Britain now became convinced that Germany was the enemy. Spring Rice observed, 'The change is extraordinary. Everyone, in the Office and out, talks as if we had but one enemy in the world, and that Germany. It is no manner of good trying to assure us unofficially or officially that they are really our friends. No one believes it now, and the only effect is to disgust. The change in Chamberlain's mind is most remarkable'.[94] This was not perceived in Germany, where Holstein saw the upset as the result of a temporary exasperation and the machinations of Salisbury, his *bête noire*. He was wrong. By early 1902 the alliance project was dead, never to be raised again by Britain. The final German mistake, casting into obscurity all previous essays at blackmail, double-dealing and optimistic reasoning, was the rejection of a limited *entente* which might have kept an alliance 'shimmering on the horizon'.[95]

While it is evident that African issues and conflicts of personality played a central part in exacerbating Anglo-German relations, it should not be imagined that these were the sole causes of disenchantment. Events in the Far East played a major part in the collapse of the *entente*. The emergence of Japan in 1895 as a significant force in Far Eastern politics had altered permanently the balance of interests. British commercial interests seemed threatened, though in 1897 trade took a turn for the better after a decade of decline. The basis of the British position was a wish to promote trade in peaceful circumstances and to avert the partition of China. This conservative policy was not shared by any other power save the United States. As Salisbury put it, 'I think other governments if they seek trade, it is in order that they may obtain territory; if the English government seeks for territory, it is in order that it may obtain trade'.[96] The difficulty in China was little different from that in Turkey—the inefficiency and malevolence of the local authorities. Reform had been demanded as long ago as 1869 and Chinese defeat in the war of 1894–95 merely intensified this pressure, while increasing Chinese indebtedness. After 1895 the political rôle of loans became crucial and eventually developed into a scramble for concessions.

The financial struggle which developed in China soon led to demands for territorial concessions. Inevitably, Germany took the lead. She alone of the major powers had no significant territorial base and had, therefore, the strongest desire to upset the *status quo*. Aware of this danger, the China Association had suggested a British accord with France and Russia. It had proved possible to come to terms with France, whose interests in China lay in the south, but not with Russia, where the war party was in the ascendant. In 1896 Russian diplomatic pressure on Peking was intensified, but Salisbury hoped that this would not lead to great territorial demands. Members of the government went out of their way to assure Russia that there was plenty of room for all the powers in the Far East. Regrettably this was interpreted by the Russian activists as a sign of weakness. While *The Times* might suggest that 'surely Asia and Africa are large enough for all of us',[97] Russian action at Peking made an unfavourable impression on British observers. In October 1897 MacDonald, Ambassador to Peking, informed Salisbury 'the Russian government intended that the provinces of China bordering on the Russian frontier must not come under the influence of any nation except Russia'.[98] Germany, however, not Russia, provoked the long-awaited scramble. The result was greatly increased international tension, as Salisbury had predicted in 1891: 'When a nation dies there is no testamentary distribution of its goods, there is no statute of distribution for what it leaves behind. The disappearance of a nation means a desperate quarrel for what it had possessed'.[99]

On 14 November 1897 Germany occupied the port of Kiaochow, ostensibly to secure compensation for some murdered missionaries. In reality the port was intended to serve as a base for the German naval squadron in the Far East and as the centre for economic penetration of Shantung, the province surrounding the port. Richthofen, the German explorer, hit the nail on the head when he drew attention to the value of Kiaochow as a *point d'appui* and the 'vast coal resources of excellent quality . . . fortunately located nearby'.[100] The integrity of China was further threatened when a month later Russian warships established themselves at Port Arthur and Talienwan. In Britain and France pressure mounted for the protection of commercial interests through the seizure of other ports, though such action was bound to be in contravention of well-established policy. The Foreign Office was certainly ready to consider demanding a counterpoise and Curzon told a representative of the China Association 'it is . . . the policy of the Government to resist any action of Russia or Germany that would injure our interests',[101] but was equally anxious to try negotiation first.

Although negotiation was a forlorn hope the Foreign Office took some time to assess the situation. It hoped to reach agreement either with Germany or Russia, but did not realize Germany had encouraged Russia to seize Port Arthur. Hicks Beach more accurately judged the position when he saw the actions of the other powers as indicative of the existence of a Far Eastern triplice: 'the whole drift . . . looks like a *rapprochement* of the Three Powers in their Chinese policy, with the intention of leaving us out in the cold'.[102] This pessimism did not stop Salisbury from opening negotiations with Russia in January 1898. Witte, the Finance Minister, was correctly believed to favour compromise. On 25 January Salisbury suggested an understanding, based upon spheres of commercial interest and excluding territorial partition. By early March it was clear that no accommodation could be reached and pressure in Britain increased for 'a cartographic consolation'.[103] This led to the decision on 25 March 'that Britain should maintain her position in the Gulf of Pechili, and in the neighbourhood of Pekin, by closing with the Chinese offer of the reversion of Wei-hai-wei'.[104] The port was eventually secured for Britain in July, though it never proved much use as a strategic or commercial counterweight.

The reversal of British policy was, perhaps, inevitable. It was serious in its consequences, adding fuel to an already raging fire. A whole host of claims were now put forward by various powers and the integrity of China was seriously threatened. Xenophobia grew apace and culminated in the Boxer Rising of 1900. From the moment Germany seized Kiaochow the scramble had been inevitable and the danger to British interests fully apparent. As well as those who had argued for agreement with France and Russia there had also been a party favourable to working with Germany. Yet another group favoured an *entente* with Japan. Those favouring agreement with Germany and Japan were, of course, giving support to the notion of an alliance designed to keep the Dual Alliance powers under control. Working with Japan seemed in 1898 a leap in the dark, though Chamberlain enquired of Salisbury in late 1897: 'have you considered whether we might not draw closer to Japan . . . in many contingencies they would be valuable Allies . . . in any case they are worth looking after as it is clear that they do not mean to be a *quantité négligéable* in the East'.[105] This idea was echoed by O'Conor, Ambassador to St Petersburg, who observed that 'the possibility of our alliance with Japan haunts them and helps us'.[106] The prospect of working with Germany was much more alluring and made better sense in global strategy, so it seemed sensible to consider that possibility first.

In early February 1898 Chamberlain wrote to Balfour suggesting that Britain work with Germany and the United States. It was another factor pointing towards the alliance proposal which the Colonial Secretary made the following month. The importance of China was evident in the Cabinet discussions on the value of such an alliance and when it became clear Germany would not agree to an Anglo-German protectorate designed to uphold the integrity of China the whole negotiation foundered. While talks continued Germany was encouraging the Russian advance. On 28 March the Kaiser wrote to the Tsar in fulsome terms: 'I must congratulate you most heartily at the successful issue of your action at Port Arthur; we two will make a good pair of sentinels at the entrance to the Gulf of Pechili, who will be duly respected, especially by the Yellow Ones!'[107] Efforts to enlist the aid of the United States were equally devoid of success.

The duplicity of Germany was unknown. Much time could have been saved in the next few years if the Foreign Office had realized that Germany had no intention of ever helping check Russian advances. It was clear, however, that the only prospect of Anglo-German co-operation lay in limited agreement. British interests lay primarily in the Yangtze valley. Priority had to be given to defence of this area despite the acquisition of Hong Kong through the agreement of 9 June 1898. The scramble for concessions to build railways and for favourable tariffs lasted the whole summer, but when autumn came Britain was not too badly placed, though many commitments had been undertaken in order to keep out other powers. The determination shown by Salisbury convinced the powers that perhaps a settlement might be advantageous. In July negotiations began with Russia and Germany. Britain's demands centred round her policy of the 'open door' for trade, modified by guarantees for her special position on the Yangtze in return for a freer hand for other powers elsewhere in China. In September agreement was reached with Germany. American support for the 'open door' was also secured. Talks with Russia dragged on. In August Balfour told Salisbury 'Russia is (I think deliberately) hanging back. . . . I want to drive them into making a distinct offer of spheres of interest (so far as concessions go)—i.e. Manchuria v basin of Yangtze'.[108] The temporary ascendancy of the peace party in Russia hastened agreement which was reached on 28 April 1899. The preponderant nature of British interest in the Yangtze was recognized by Russia.

Throughout the rest of his term as Foreign Secretary Salisbury was anxious to stick to the agreement. Events in China made this difficult, particularly when unsatisfied powers, Italy and the United States, put forward claims. However, overcoming international problems proved easier than dealing with unrest among the Chinese. Stimulated by foreign activity in 1899, following the concessions of 1897–98, the dissatisfied populace turned to the xenophobic doctrines of the sects and secret societies. The disintegrating Chinese government, under the authority of the Dowager Empress Tz'u-hsi, encouraged these manifestations. In summer 1899 the situation worsened and the China Association demanded a full British protectorate of the Yangtze, a demand rejected by Brodrick on the grounds that 'we are not prepared to undertake the immense responsibility of governing what is practically a third of China'.[109] Nevertheless the merchants advised that 'our interests in the Yangtze Region . . . be asserted more decisively, if only in preparation for the *débâcle*'.[110] In early 1900 the full flood of Chinese resentment spilled forth and the Boxer Rising swept the country. The legations at Peking came under siege and the whole fabric of European power was shaken. Salisbury's reluctance to intervene stemmed from

British involvement in the Boer War but was a serious misjudgment. Within the Cabinet there were serious divisions of opinion, some ministers clamouring for an expeditionary force, others arguing for some unspecified action, and Salisbury himself in favour of doing nothing which might encourage Russia to occupy Peking. Fortunately, in August the siege was raised and interventionist clamour died away.

Partition had been revived as a possibility, for instability offered opportunities for a spectacular *coup de main* by any expansionist power. Salisbury's attempts to push forward Japan as a power mandated to protect western interests collapsed because of German objections. International agreement on a joint expedition was secured, though it proved hard to find a suitable commander. Eventually Waldersee was appointed but the Kaiser's manoeuvres had aroused distrust on all sides. Quarrels over these issues obscured the major problem of avoiding annexations during the anarchy. For once, Germany and Britain were in accord. Britain wished to protect the Yangtze; Germany could hope for nothing more than Shantung and was anxious not to lose prestige. Encouraged by the Kaiser, talks began in June. Salisbury was reluctantly persuaded to negotiate by pressure from Chamberlain, Balfour, Goschen and Brodrick. The premier was suspicious of Germany, fearing 'an attempt to make a quarrel between France and us',[111] but the feeling of weakness induced by the Boer War was a more powerful influence on his colleagues. 'I cannot help expressing myself strongly,' wrote Goschen, 'absolute isolation is playing the devil'.[112] By early September the Germanophile group was in full cry. Hamilton saw 'an opportunity such as we have never had before of separating Germany from Russia'.[113] On 16 October agreement was reached. Britain and Germany agreed to try to maintain the 'open door', to sustain territorial integrity, and to recognize spheres of economic influence already defined. The terms were vague and promised trouble. Furthermore, there was still no British understanding of fundamental German reluctance to be pushed into an alliance directed against Russia in the Far East.

While Britain and Germany negotiated, Russia prepared to advance her interests in Manchuria. On 3 January 1901 it was revealed that

Russia was negotiating for the control of Manchuria. Russian machinations made nonsense of the agreement of 1899 though Salisbury tried very hard to pretend that it was being honoured. Lansdowne was much more sceptical and hoped to be able to work with Germany and, possibly, Japan. In fact Japanese policy was changing in a fashion likely to meet with British approval. The growing strength of Russia in Manchuria persuaded the Japanese to support the integrity of China as the only effective form of defence. While the British put their trust in Germany this shift in policy had little impact, but the failure of alliance negotiations begun in March 1901 soon altered the situation. In February Salisbury was already more hopeful of an agreement with Japan than Germany. The premier told Lansdowne he was 'not opposed in principle to an engagement with Japan . . . but we must define the extent of our responsibilities very carefully'.[114] This was much more encouraging than his view of Germany: 'She will therefore never stand by us against Russia; but is always rather inclined to curry favour with Russia by throwing us over. I have no wish to quarrel with her; but my faith in her is infinitesimal'.[115] Despite all efforts of the pro-German party within the Cabinet it became clear that Germany would not help in China. On 15 March Bülow declared, 'There were no German interests of importance in Manchuria, and the fate of that province was a matter of absolute indifference to Germany'.[116] This effectively killed the Anglo-German alliance. As Lansdowne recalled many years afterwards when asked why he had given up seeking agreement, 'It was something to do with Manchuria. I found I couldn't trust them'.[117]

An agreement with Japan now seemed much more attractive than in January when Lansdowne had been 'not much enamoured of the idea'.[118] In spring 1901 Hayashi, the Ambassador to London, realized how favourable the situation was. Japan's chief fear was for the security of Korea, while Britain wished to prevent Russian occupation of Manchuria on a permanent basis. Japanese sentiment, after the events of 1895, could not tamely accept Russian seizure of Port Arthur and Talienwan, so there was some common ground. In April Hayashi spoke to Lansdowne but nothing came of this meeting as the Foreign Secretary was hoping that Russia would come to terms or that Germany could be prevailed upon to help. By the summer Lansdowne was much more receptive. On 19 June Lansdowne told the Cabinet, 'It is of the utmost importance that we should stand well with her in the Far East'.[119] In July he informed the Cabinet of the progress of the private discussions and it was agreed that negotiations should be pursued. Hayashi was delighted and received permission from Tokyo to broaden the talks. On 25 August Lansdowne reported 'some interesting conversations . . . as to the possibility of a closer understanding between us and I think it not at all improbable that we may succeed in arriving at this'.[120] The basis of discussion was that Britain would be committed to holding the ring if Japan fought Russia.

Negotiations halted for some time while the pro-Russian party in Tokyo attempted to come to terms with St Petersburg. This risk of losing the alliance stirred Lansdowne and on 25 October he presented two memoranda to the Cabinet, being a draft treaty with Japan and a proposal for agreement with Russia. The notion of a double bargain was approved by the Cabinet, despite Salisbury's opposition. The premier's feeling that talks with Russia would be useless was dramatically confirmed by Lamsdorff's blunt rejection of the British approach. On 5 November the Cabinet agreed to a Japanese alliance. Determination had been fortified by Russian intransigence and German unreliability. Selborne, the First Lord of the Admiralty, had underlined British naval weakness in a memorandum of 4 September and had played a key part in convincing the doubters.

On 10 December the objections of the peace party in Japan were overcome. The following seven weeks saw some tough bargaining and the revival of doubts within the Cabinet. Chamberlain, Selborne, Ritchie and Hicks Beach proved ready to accept Lansdowne's recommendation, though all were slightly uneasy that Japan was getting the best of the bargain. Balfour was still inanely advocating a German alliance; 'the dangers are less and the gains are greater from joining the Triple Alliance than would follow from pursuing a similar course with regard to Japan'.[121] Salisbury was the real obstacle, insisting, 'I do not think it will be wise to give to Japan the right of committing us to a war, unless the policy which Japan is pursuing has been approved by the British Government'.[122] He did not maintain this hard line as staunchly as he had in the case of Anglo-German proposals of alliance and on 30 January 1902 the Anglo-Japanese Alliance was concluded. The most important provision, apart from recognition of Japan's special position in Korea and that of Britain in China, was that binding the countries to strict neutrality in the event of war unless confronted by the opposition of more than one power, in which case the alliance came into operation. It was a momentous departure from the policy of isolation.

The Anglo-Japanese Alliance marked more than the end of isolation. After 1902 the pro-German party was never again so influential. German hesitation had made a major contribution to the conversion from isolationism; the alliance can thus be depicted as a defeat for Holstein's theory that Germany could wait for Britain to ask for help. Equally it could be regarded as vindication of Holstein's other assumption—that Britain and Russia could never come to terms. Yet the treaty did not cause a major upheaval in international affairs, though it was disliked by most of the other powers. Although the alliance represented a break with Salisbury's confident isolationism and a new awareness of British weakness, it was essentially a practical arrangement intended to meet British needs in the Far East without acquiring unwanted European commitments. In this sense it fitted in well with the old policy of limited arrangements. The weakest point lay in the implicit assumption that Anglo-Russian hostility was almost permanent. In 1902 such a view of international affairs was not unreasonable, given recent Russian opportunist intransigence. Events in the next fiveyears were to show how questionable was this assumption.

Hostility to Russian schemes in China played an important part in changing British policy, but this was but one facet of a global fear of Russia. In addition to machinations in the Near East, Russia seemed to threaten British security in Afghanistan and Persia. The ministries of 1895–1902 most frequently saw weakness as a product of Russian pressure and reacted as strongly as they dared. For a short time after the return of the Conservatives there was little Russian activity on the borders of India. Russian inactivity, however, could not conceal the deep pessimism in London concerning British capacity to defend India. Forthright propaganda emanating from military circles had argued for British adhesion to the Triple Alliance ever since 1890. In August 1898 Curzon was appointed to succeed Elgin as Viceroy in January 1899. The result was a revitalization of the British attitude towards Russia—in Simla if not in London. Curzon despised the passivity of Salisbury. He wanted no more buffer states of doubtful value but a forward policy to ensure British predominance. He was not the man to truckle to Russia. In 1889 he had written, 'Whatever be Russia's designs on India, whether they be serious and inimical or imaginary and fantastic, I hold that the first duty of English statesmen is to render any hostile intentions futile'.[123] Curzon believed in meeting trouble rather than waiting for it and this was to lead him into serious differences of opinion with Salisbury. Curzon's grasp of local and global problems made him a powerful advocate of a hard-line policy as well as a persuasive apostle of the abandonment of isolation.

At the close of the century a direct military threat to India seemed possible for the first time. Under Witte's influence the Russian railway system had been expanded almost to the borders of Afghanistan. This was ominous in view of the Russian belief that 'there are not and cannot be any frontiers for us in Asia'.[124] British control of India was under threat in three areas: Persia, Tibet and Afghanistan. The Cabinet was advised in the winter of 1899 to strengthen the strategic position by expediting the construction of a railway from Quetta to Bandar Abbas, *via* Kandahar. The possibility of the loss of India, or at least the reduction of the sub-continent to anarchy, had to be given serious consideration for the first time, and in a period of mounting concern regarding over-commitment. In India prestige and economic interest were intertwined. It has been estimated that 'the key to Britain's whole payments pattern lay in India, financing as she probably did more than two fifths of Britain's total deficits'.[125] The forward views of Curzon, then, were bound to find extensive support inside both the Conservative Party and the Cabinet.

In 1888 Britain and Russia had signed an agreement by which Afghanistan was defined as lying outside the Russian sphere of influence. In 1900 this treaty looked rather a slender protection when the Russians demanded the opening of direct relations with Kabul. Curzon vigorously opposed Russian demands, believing that a policy of boldness would pay the greatest dividends. Certainly he adhered to the view that 'south of a certain line in Asia, Russia's future is much more what we choose to make it than what she can make it herself'.[126] Unfortunately for the Viceroy powerful factors were operating against him. His own reckless treatment of the Amir had provoked Afghan hostility. The Cabinet preference for the mainten-ance of the independence of the Amir had been ignored until in November 1899 the Viceroy had been peremptorily ordered to obey instructions. Tension in China and South Africa made it desirable to avoid conflict. Furthermore, there was a party in London which preferred to try to come to terms with Russia. Its influence was greatly increased by the support of Sir Arthur Godley, the Permanent Under-Secretary at the India Office, whose opinion on the Russian demand was, 'If we are, as appears likely, going to agree to the proposal sooner or later, I hope (1) that it will be made the occasion of getting a general understanding with Russia . . . and (2) that we should not begin by protesting and saying disagreeable things and then end by backing down'.[127] But in the end Curzon won the support of Hamilton, who informed the Viceroy of the admirable qualities of his despatch and that 'objections to a Russian agent at Kabul are, as you say, insuperable, and to that point we must adhere'.[128]

Successful resistance to Russian demands, however, hinged more on the Amir's personality than the temper of the Cabinet. In October 1901 Abdur Rahman died and was succeeded by his son, Habibullah. The previous July Lansdowne had suggested that on the Amir's death arrangements between Britain and Afghanistan be revised. However, in early 1902 Russia was informed that the new Amir must be allowed to consolidate his power before any revision could take place. Russia was displeased with the stalling tactics of the Foreign Office and in 1902 rumours were rife of trade and arms deals to follow the visit of a Russian mission to Kabul. Curzon even thought it possible that the new Amir had begun this flirtation. In late 1902 St Petersburg announced it intended to enter into direct relations

with Kabul, despite British protests. The Viceroy's irritation proved
to be unnecessary when the Amir, in another change of tack,
rejected Russian overtures. For the moment the issue was closed.

There were also considerable fears regarding Russian activities
in Tibet. At the end of the nineteenth century there had been a number of attempts to conclude an agreement with China. But the frontiers remained undemarcated and the regulations of 1890 and 1893,
concerned mainly with trade, were ignored. In the summer of 1900
Curzon's overtures to the Dalai Lama met with no response. The
following year the Viceroy urged on the India Office 'the adoption
of more practical measures with a view to securing the commercial
and political facilities which our friendly representations . . . failed to
procure'.[129] The urgency of the Viceroy's letter undoubtedly
stemmed from his knowledge of Russian activities in Tibet. In
1900 a Russian adventurer, Dorjieff, had established himself at
Lhasa. The intransigence of the Dalai Lama was believed to be the
result of promises of Russian support. Lamsdorff's assurances that
Dorjieff had no status and had been given no official mission were
greeted with scepticism in the Foreign Office when the *Novoye
Vremya* and other journals openly proclaimed his success in counter-
ing British pressure. The Tsar's reception of Dorjieff at court only
served to reinforce suspicion. In 1902 rumours of a secret agreement
between Russia and China which gave Russia a Tibetan sphere of
influence were rife in Peking. Chinese and Russian disclaimers
did not dispel British anxiety. On 1 October Lansdowne observed
that 'The story of the Russo-Chinese agreement . . . is supported
by a good deal of evidence'.[130] The following month Curzon expressed himself 'a firm believer in the existence of a secret understanding, if not a secret treaty, between Russia and China about Tibet;
and, as I have said before, I regard it as a duty to frustrate their
little game while there is yet time'.[131] The scene was set for a pre-
emptive British advance into Tibet, despite the reluctance of many
members of the Cabinet 'not to quarrel with her [Russia] if it could
honourably or wisely be avoided'.[132]

It was not in Tibet but in Persia that the British position was most
seriously threatened at this time. As in many other parts of the world
local authority had been fatally weakened by European penetration.

The death of the old Shah in 1896 had precipitated the country into near anarchy. Various nations were ready to start the race for concessions. The influence of Britain and Russia was already great, because of geographical proximity. Germany hoped for a foothold at Kuwait and France at Muscat. The strategic importance of the Persian Gulf and Seistan (the area bordering on British India) was such that Britain could not view the collapse or division of Persia with equanimity. In 1898 the situation was grim. Durand, the British Minister, was unpopular with the Shah because of lack of tact and failure to understand Teheran's difficult diplomatic position. Elgin, the Viceroy, had lamented the decline in British influence but had been unable to suggest a remedy. Indeed, his Viceroyalty had been a sad mistake: 'Elgin had been convinced that he lacked the ability that would justify the appointment,' wrote Gopal. 'History has provided us with no reason to differ from his estimate of himself'.[133] It was quite otherwise with Curzon, who from the first flung himself eagerly into the battle for Persia. It was his conflict with London over Persia which made his stay in India so much a source of controversy and which led him to indict the Foreign Office so fiercely.

Persia was, in Curzon's opinion, the critical test of British policy. A show of weakness on the Gulf or at Teheran would have ruinous consequences for the whole Empire. In September 1899 the Viceroy advised the government to seize those areas of southern Persia which were essential to British interests, unless agreement could be reached with Russia. The Cabinet did not agree with his imperious analysis, both Hamilton and Salisbury opposing any move that might precipitate conflict. As Salisbury had wearily observed in relation to Afghanistan, 'Curzon always wants me to talk to Russia as if I had five hundred thousand men at my back, and I have not'.[134] In 1900 the situation took a turn for the worse when Russia made a loan to Persia on condition that future foreign loans could only be raised from Russia. Curzon was furious at British timidity, raging 'Oh, my God, English policy towards Persia throughout this century has been a page of history that makes one alternately laugh with derision and groan with despair'.[135] Only in 1901 did Curzon's diatribes begin to affect British policy and inject a more steely note into dealings with the Shah. The days when he could lament that 'the crash will come, and then my Despatches will be published and in my grave I shall be justified. Not that I care for that. But I long to see prescience, some width of view, some ability to forecast the evil of tomorrow, instead of bungling over the evil of today'[136] were rapidly passing. The lesson of the Boer War had been learned. It was imperative for Britain to strengthen her position in those areas of strategic importance where she had recently been weak.

The advent of Lansdowne had a great deal to do with changes in policy. He saw clearly that understanding with Russia was impossible and this opinion was reinforced by Curzon's despatch of 5 April 1901. The Viceroy reported that 'Within the last 25 years British prestige and influence have never sunk so low . . . we are at present drifting merrily towards another Port Arthur. . . . As a recent British representative at Teheran put it to me, all the while that he was there he felt like a jellyfish in a whirlpool'.[137] Another formative influence was that of Sir Arthur Hardinge, the new Minister to Teheran, who had informed Lansdowne of the great growth in Russian power. In July Hardinge was instructed to inform the Shah of British interest in Seistan and the following September the suggestion of a British loan was put forward. However, this notion was killed by the miserly Hicks Beach, despite Salisbury's support. Indeed the premier was able to assure Curzon 'Our chief interest in the East (after China) has been the movements of the Persian question. . . . In the last generation we did much what we liked in the East by force or threats: by squadrons and tall talk . . . the day of free individual coercive action is almost passed by. For some years to come Eastern advance must largely depend on payment; and I fear that in that race England will seldom win'.[138] Despite this pessimism Hardinge was instructed in early 1902 to inform the Shah that Britain did not intend to surrender her hard-won position in Persia. In particular, Britain would not permit the concession to Russia of a station on the Gulf or preferential trading rights in southern Persia. Plain speaking was much more to Curzon's taste, particularly the thinly veiled threat that if admonitions were disregarded 'it might no longer be possible to make the integrity and independence of Persia the first object as hitherto'.[139] In the summer of 1902 the Shah visited London. After his return to Teheran he was invested with the Garter in an attempt to improve Anglo-Persian relations. This manoeuvre enjoyed some success and by the end of 1902 British influence in Persia had increased substantially.

Although Britain was primarily concerned with affairs in the Far East and Africa during these years, attention had also to be paid to relations with the United States. Unhappily, these were far from smooth. In the last decade of the century new-found American strength drove the government towards an expansionist policy and the construction of a large navy. At the very moment when he returned to office in 1895 Salisbury was confronted by a renewal of claims by the United States to speak for all the American states. Olney, Cleveland's Secretary of State, was principally responsible for this initiative in a despatch of 20 July 1895. Olney dared to assert the sovereignty of the United States in the Americas and that its fiat was law 'upon the subjects to which it confines its interposition'.[140] This unwelcome revival of support for the wild claims of Venezuela caused great offence in Britain. Unfortunately Salisbury's stalling tactics provoked Cleveland into belligerency in his annual message to Congress, delivered on 17 December 1895. The President unwisely observed that 'The dispute has reached such a stage as to now make it incumbent on the United States to take measures to determine . . . what is the true divisional line between the Republic of Venezuela and British Guiana. . . . When such report is received it will . . . be the duty of the United States to resist by every means in its power, as a wilful aggression upon its rights and interests, the appropriation by Great Britain of any lands, or the exercise of governmental jurisdiction over any territory, which after investigation we have determined of right belongs to Venezuela'.[141]

Cleveland's bellicose attitude carried with it the risk of war with Britain, in defence of an extension of the Monroe Doctrine. The Prime Minister was determined not to yield to American demands for arbitration, but at a Cabinet meeting on 11 January 1896 he was overruled. The belligerence of Chamberlain, who believed that there was gold in the disputed area, was likewise ignored. The clear refusal of Harcourt, Leader of the Opposition, to countenance war undermined the party favouring resistance. Within the Conservative Party there were those who had already expressed disquiet at Salisbury's attitude. Selborne, for example, had told Chamberlain, 'the hatred of England by the Americans is to me quite unaccountable. We expect the French to hate us and are quite prepared to reciprocate the compliment if necessary; but the Americans, No!'[142] The result was, 'It was quite clear that the great majority—if not all—the Cabinet would be glad of any honourable settlement'.[143] The crisis passed and the diplomats, Pauncefote in Washington and Bayard in London, set about solving the problem. In late 1896 Pauncefote was authorized to sign an Anglo-Venezuelan arbitration treaty, which the United States forced on a reluctant Venezuela in February 1897. Indeed, the truth of President Montt's (of Chile) remark that 'the United States would make Venezuela pay dearly for any action taken on her account'[144] now became apparent. The arbitration award of 30 October 1899 was very favourable to Britain. All that the Venezuelan affair had really confirmed was the capacity of the United States to intervene in Latin American politics. The British had, in addition, recognized that power and had simultaneously determined not to risk a conflict with the United States when other global commitments were so extensive.

In fact, the crisis of 1895–96 went some way towards improving Anglo-American relations. Some misunderstandings were cleared out of the way and British recognition of American importance satisfied and gratified many citizens of the United States. During the Spanish-American crisis of 1896 and the war of 1898 British sympathies were chiefly with Spain. This attitude was shared by most European nations and Germany tried to create a European bloc against the United States. Britain would have none of this scheme. Balfour told Hay, the American Ambassador, he did not 'propose to take any steps which would not be acceptable to the Government of the United States'.[145] Hay and the pro-British party were suitably grateful. Hay told Lodge that the friendship of Britain had been invaluable 'in the present state of things, as it is the only European country whose sympathies are not openly against us'.[146] Even the seizure of the Philippines caused hardly a ripple in smooth relations. The battle of Manila Bay even gave rise to a legend that the British squadron had manoeuvred to prevent a clash between American and German units. Thus by 1898 relations were much improved.

Reasons for British passivity are not hard to find. Some American commentators thought the British attitude was founded on the new hostility to Germany; others saw it as evidence of waning imperial strength. While there was some truth in these views they hardly represented a full analysis. Britain wanted American co-operation in a number of areas, particularly the Pacific, Canada and China. Good relations were essential. In the Samoan dispute of 1899, for example, British and American forces acted in concert. The British undoubtedly hoped that the American presence in the Philippines would lead to increased interest in China, which Salisbury felt was bound to be of assistance to Britain. Increasing distrust of Germany among every rank of society in Britain certainly made more attractive the notion of co-operation with the United States. Indeed, the views expressed by Chamberlain in his speech of 13 May 1898 represented feelings of an ever increasing number of Britons. Chamberlain's clarion call for closer, more cordial and fuller relations between the two states and his suggestion that 'even war itself would be cheaply purchased if in a great and noble cause the Stars and Stripes and the Union Jack should wave together'[147] found ready response on the far side of the Atlantic.

The powers were far from a true understanding however. There still existed disputes over the demarcation of Canada's boundaries with the United States and Alaska. Problems of naval strategy in 1898 had convinced Americans it was essential to construct a canal across Central America and made it plain that this canal must be constructed by and remain under the control of the United States. In 1899 negotiations were opened, but no progress was made until in February 1900 Pauncefote was instructed to sign a draft treaty providing for American construction of the canal. Wrangling continued throughout the year and into early 1901. The stalling tactics of Lansdowne were clearly designed to produce better terms and were ultimately successful. On 18 November 1901 the Hay–Pauncefote treaty was signed and the United States was to have her canal.

In early 1903 a formula for the arbitration of the Canadian frontier disputes was agreed and Anglo-American relations improved markedly thereafter.

The adjustment of Anglo-American disputes had been accelerated by a realization in Britain that the new power of the United States made the maintenance of the Clayton–Bulwer treaty impossible without war. On 9 December 1898 a memorandum from the Director of Military Intelligence advised an agreement between the two countries. The strains of the Boer War convinced Lansdowne and his colleagues that British naval supremacy could no longer be guaranteed in American waters and, therefore, the prudent course was to give way to American demands for control of the projected canal and to rely on friendly relations to preserve Canadian and Caribbean security and integrity. The War Office might continue to draw up plans for the contingency of war with the United States, but the view of the Foreign Office had prevailed. As an article in the *Spectator* declared, 'we have a community of interests as well as of blood . . . the sooner we come to a frank and generous and sensible understanding with America the better'.[148] This was exactly what Lansdowne did.

The cumulative effect of all the strains placed upon British foreign policy in these years had been considerable. Britain had moved slowly and reluctantly away from dangerous isolation. Instead of reliance on worldwide naval supremacy Britain had begun to base policy on a notion of limited liability. Japan in the Far East and the United States in Caribbean and Pacific waters had been assigned rôles which assumed continued friendship. Salisbury's old principle of limited bargains based upon settlement of local differences had been extended and had led to some diminution of problems. The concept of a German alliance had been exposed as chimerical and support for Austria in the Balkans had been steadily eroded. Efforts to improve relations with France and Russia had been retarded by events at Fashoda and Port Arthur, but agreement in West Africa and the British abandonment of Constantinople as a front line of defence held out some prospect of future agreement. The Boer War had underlined Britain's strategic difficulties and her unpopularity in Europe. These issues had been squarely faced and a start had been made on the most pressing problems. The age of confident supremacy had passed away and the future lay 'with those who thought in terms of continental Europe and of its balance of power'.[149]

REFERENCES

1 *Letters of Queen Victoria* ed. G. E. Buckle. Third Series. Vol. II. p. 525. Victoria's Memorandum, 25 June 1895.
2 Salisbury to Layard, 19 February 1880. Salisbury Papers.
3 *The Times*, 24 November 1896.
4 *Salisbury and the Mediterranean, 1886–96* by C. J. Lowe. p. 101. Salisbury to Currie, 27 August 1895.
5 *Lord Salisbury and Foreign Policy* by J. A. S. Grenville. p. 37. Salisbury to Currie, 5 September 1895.
6 Lowe, op. cit., p. 100.
7 Buckle, op. cit., Third Series. Vol. II. pp. 571–2. Victoria to Salisbury, 5 November 1895.
8 Lowe, op. cit., pp. 104–5. Hamilton to Balfour, 12 January 1896.
9 Lascelles to Salisbury, 21 December 1895. Salisbury Papers.
10 Buckle, op. cit., Third Series. Vol. III. p. 57. Victoria to Salisbury, 31 July 1896.
11 ibid., Third Series. Vol. III. p. 58. Salisbury to Victoria, 31 July 1896.
12 *The Diplomacy of Imperialism* by W. L. Langer. p. 322.
13 Buckle, op. cit., Third Series. Vol. III. p. 82. 24 September 1896.
14 Salisbury's Memorandum, 27 September 1896. Salisbury Papers.
15 Salisbury's Memorandum, 29 September 1896. Salisbury Papers.
16 Lowe, op. cit., p. 111. Deym to Goluchowski, 23 January 1896.
17 Salisbury to Victoria, 19 February 1896. Salisbury Papers.
18 Salisbury's Circular, 20 October 1896. F.O. 83/1453.
19 *British Naval Policy, 1880–1905* by A. J. Marder. p. 579. D. N. I. Memorandum on Naval Policy, 28 October 1896.
20 *Slavonic and East European Review*. Vol. XXXVI. p. 366.
21 Salisbury to Currie, 19 October 1897. Salisbury Papers.
22 Marder, op. cit., p. 576. D. N. I. Memorandum on Naval Policy, 13 October 1896.
23 Salisbury to Currie, 19 October 1897. Salisbury Papers.
24 *Modern Egypt* by Lord Cromer. p. 764.
25 *Life of Joseph Chamberlain* by J. Amery. Vol. IV. p. 183. Lansdowne to Monson, 30 July 1902.
26 *Life of Joseph Chamberlain* by J. L. Garvin. Vol. III. pp. 23–4. Chamberlain's Circular, 28 November 1895.
27 *La politique de la France en Afrique, 1896–98* by A. Lebon. p. 67.

28 Buckle, op. cit., Third Series. Vol. III. p. 209. 14 November 1897.
29 Garvin, op. cit., Vol. III. p. 204. Chamberlain to Salisbury, 6 June 1897.
30 ibid., Vol. III. p. 204. Chamberlain to Selborne, 12 September 1897.
31 ibid., Vol. III. p. 211. Chamberlain to Selborne, 29 September 1897.
32 Salisbury to Chamberlain, 3 June 1898. Salisbury Papers.
33 Garvin, op. cit., Vol. III. p. 221. Chamberlain to Salisbury, 3 June 1898.
34 Buckle, op. cit., Third Series. Vol. III. p. 256. Salisbury to Victoria, 17 June 1898.
35 *Life of Lord Curzon* by Earl of Ronaldshay. Vol. I. p. 254. Curzon to Selborne, 9 April 1900.
36 Lansdowne's Memorandum, 24 March 1896. Salisbury Papers.
37 *Lord Cromer* by the Marquess of Zetland. p. 223. Salisbury to Cromer, 13 March 1896.
38 Garvin, op. cit., Vol. III. p. 171.
39 Buckle, op. cit., Third Series. Vol. III. p. 39. 8 April 1896.
40 Garvin, op. cit., Vol. III. p. 170. Chamberlain to Salisbury, 11 March 1896.
41 Zetland, op. cit., p. 225. Cromer to Salisbury, 11 April 1896.
42 ibid., p. 228. Salisbury to Cromer, 24 April 1896.
43 Grenville, op. cit., p. 119.
44 *Lord Lansdowne* by Lord Newton. p. 148. Salisbury to Lansdowne, 22 October 1897.
45 ibid., p. 148.
46 Langer, op. cit., p. 549. Salisbury to Cromer, 29 October 1897.
47 *Théophile Delcassé and the Making of the Entente Cordiale* by C. Andrew. p. 91.
48 *British Documents on the Origins of the War, 1898–1914* Vol. I. No. 137. Monson to Salisbury, 18 September 1898.
49 *New French Imperialism, 1880–1910* by J. J. Cooke. p. 87. Salisbury to Chamberlain, 17 September 1897.
50 Garvin, op. cit., Vol. III. p. 232. 4 November 1898.
51 ibid., Vol. III. p. 229. Curzon to Chamberlain, 26 October 1898.
52 Buckle, op. cit., Third Series. Vol. III. p. 305. Victoria to Salisbury, 30 October 1898.
53 *The end of Isolation* by G. W. Monger. p. 16. Salisbury to Curzon, 8 April 1899.
54 Garvin, op. cit., Vol. III. p. 44. Robinson to Kruger, 3 November 1895.
55 Chamberlain to Salisbury, 31 December 1895. Salisbury Papers.
56 Grenville, op. cit., p. 99. Salisbury to Devonshire, 4 January 1896.
57 Buckle, op. cit., Third Series. Vol. III. p. 7. Knollys to Bigge, 4 January 1896.
58 ibid., Third Series. Vol. III. p. 8. Victoria to Wilhelm II, 5 January 1896.
59 *Africa and the Victorians* by R. Robinson and J. Gallagher. p. 343. Hatzfeldt to Holstein, 21 January 1896.
60 Grenville, op. cit., p. 102. Victoria to Empress Victoria, 8 January 1896.
61 Chamberlain to Salisbury, 19 December 1896. Salisbury Papers.
62 Garvin, op. cit., Vol. III. p. 259. Chamberlain's Memorandum, 29 March 1898.
63 Salisbury to Lascelles, 10 March 1896. F.O. 800/9.
64 Garvin, op. cit., Vol. III. p. 274. Chamberlain's Memorandum, 25 April 1898.
65 *Foreign Policy of Victorian England, 1830–1902* by K. Bourne. pp. 462–3. Salisbury's Memorandum, 29 May 1901.
66 Langer, op. cit., p. 500.
67 Salisbury to Lascelles, 11 May 1898. F.O. 64/1436.

68 Garvin, op. cit., Vol. III. p. 311. Milner to Chamberlain, 5 July 1898.
69 ibid., Vol. III. p. 315. Chamberlain to Balfour, 19 August 1898.
70 Grenville, op. cit., pp. 193–4. Salisbury to Balfour, 19 August 1898.
71 ibid., p. 197. Balfour to Lascelles, 1 September 1898.
72 ibid., p. 239. Milner to Selborne, 31 January 1899.
73 ibid., p. 247. Minute by Chamberlain on Milner's telegram, 27 May 1899.
74 Garvin, op. cit., p. 419. Salisbury to Chamberlain, 19 July 1899.
75 Hicks Beach to Salisbury, August 1899. Salisbury Papers.
76 Chamberlain's Memorandum, 6 September 1899. Salisbury Papers.
77 *British Documents on the Origins of the War, 1898–1914* Vol. I. No. 287. Monson to Salisbury, 27 October 1899.
78 ibid., Vol. I. No. 154. Grierson to Gough, 6 November 1899.
79 Garvin, op. cit., pp. 507–8. Speech of 30 November 1899.
80 Buckle, op. cit., Third Series. Vol. III. p. 527. Salisbury to Victoria, 10 April 1900.
81 ibid., Third Series. Vol. III. p. 611. Victoria's Memorandum, 23 October 1900.
82 Newton, op. cit., pp. 196–7. Lansdowne to Lascelles, 11 November 1900.
83 Amery, op. cit., Vol. IV. p. 153. Lansdowne to Lascelles, 18 March 1901.
84 ibid., Vol. IV. p. 149. Bülow to Wilhelm II, 21 January 1901.
85 Newton, op. cit., p. 200. Lansdowne to Lascelles, 18 March 1901.
86 Monger, op. cit., p. 36. Hamilton to Curzon, 25 April 1901.
87 Bourne, op. cit., p. 463. Salisbury's Memorandum, 29 May 1901.
88 Grenville, op. cit., p. 355. Lansdowne to Lascelles, 9 June 1901.
89 Monger, op. cit., p. 38. Lansdowne to Lascelles, 28 August 1901.
90 *King Edward VII. A biography* by Sir S. Lee. p. 131.
91 Bourne, op. cit., p. 469. Bertie's Memorandum, 27 October 1901.
92 ibid., pp. 470–1. Lansdowne's Memorandum, 11 November 1901.
93 Amery, op. cit., Vol. IV. p. 169. Metternich to Bülow, 26 November 1901.
94 *The Letters and Friendships of Sir Cecil SpringRice* ed. S. Gwynn. Vol. I. p. 350. Spring Rice to Miss Lascelles, 17 April 1902.
95 Amery, op. cit., Vol. IV. p. 170. Bülow's Memorandum, 1 November 1901.
96 *London and China Telegraph,* 15 June 1896.
97 *The Times,* 4 February 1896.
98 MacDonald to Salisbury, 19 October 1897. Parliamentary Papers. China. No. 1. 1898.
99 *Life of Robert, Marquis of Salisbury* by Lady Gwendolen Cecil. Vol. IV. p. 385.
100 *Colonial Zeitung,* 6 January 1898. See also *British Policy in China, 1895–1902* by L. K. Young. p. 45.
101 *Old China Hands and the Foreign Office* by N. A. Pelcovits. p. 213.
102 Hicks Beach to Salisbury, 27 December 1897. Salisbury Papers.
103 Garvin, op. cit., Vol. III. p. 249. Salisbury to Chamberlain, 30 December 1897.
104 Buckle, op. cit., Third Series. Vol. III. p. 238. Balfour to Victoria, 26 March 1898.
105 Garvin, op. cit., Vol. III. p. 249. Chamberlain to Salisbury, 31 December 1897.
106 O'Conor to Salisbury, 26 January 1898. Salisbury Papers.
107 *Briefe Wilhelms II an Den Zaren, 1894–1914* ed. W. Goetz. p. 308. 28 March 1898.
108 Balfour to Salisbury, 30 August 1898. Salisbury Papers.

109 *Hansard.* House of Commons. 9 June 1899.
110 Pelcovits, op. cit., p. 255. Gundry to Bertie, 5 July 1899.
111 Salisbury to Bertie, 24 August 1900. Salisbury Papers.
112 Amery, op. cit., Vol. IV. p. 139. Goschen to Chamberlain, 2 September 1900.
113 Young, op. cit., p. 201. Hamilton to Curzon, 5 September 1900.
114 ibid., p. 285. Salisbury to Lansdowne, 16 February 1901.
115 Monger, op. cit., p. 17. Salisbury to Curzon, 17 October 1900.
116 Young, op. cit., p. 290. Bülow's Speech, 15 March 1901.
117 *Salisbury, 1830–1903* by A. L. Kennedy. p. 393.
118 Lansdowne to Salisbury, 15 January 1901. F.O. 17/1499.
119 Lansdowne's Memorandum, 19 June 1901. Salisbury Papers.
120 Young, op. cit., p. 304. Lansdowne to Satow, 25 August 1901.
121 Bourne, op. cit., p. 473. Balfour to Lansdowne, 12 December 1901.
122 ibid., p. 478. Salisbury's Memorandum, 7 January 1902.
123 *Bayonets to Lhasa* by P. Fleming. p. 25.
124 ibid. p. 29.
125 *Studies in British Overseas Trade, 1870–1914* by S. B. Saul. p. 62.
126 Fleming, op. cit., p. 30.
127 Ronaldshay, op. cit., Vol. II. p. 125. Godley's Memorandum, 8 February 1900.
128 ibid., Vol. II. p. 126. Hamilton to Curzon, 15 June 1900.
129 Fleming, op. cit., p. 35. Curzon to Hamilton, 25 July 1901.
130 ibid., p. 48. Lansdowne's Memorandum, 1 October 1902.
131 ibid., p. 48.
132 Monger, op. cit., p. 7. Selborne to Curzon, 19 April 1901.
133 *British Policy in India, 1858–1905* by S. Gopal. p. 180.
134 *Records and Reactions, 1856–1939* by Earl of Midleton. p. 193.
135 Gopal, op. cit., p. 229. Curzon to Godley, 15 March 1900.
136 Ronaldshay, op. cit., Vol. II. p. 101. Curzon to Mrs Craigie, 8 January 1900.
137 Newton, op. cit., pp. 230–2. Curzon to Lansdowne, 5 April 1901.
138 Monger, op. cit., p. 5. Salisbury to Curzon, 23 September 1901.
139 Grenville, op. cit., p. 426. Lansdowne to Hardinge, 6 January 1902.
140 Bourne, op. cit., p. 170. Olney to Salisbury, 20 July 1895.
141 *Life of Lord Pauncefote* by R. B. Mowat. p. 184.
142 *Transactions of the Royal Historical Society* Series V. Vol. XVII. p. 156. Selborne to Chamberlain, 18 December 1895.
143 Garvin, op. cit., Vol. III. p. 161. 11 January 1896.
144 *Transactions of the Royal Historical Society* Series V. Vol. XVII. p. 161. Kennedy to Salisbury, 26 February 1896.
145 Grenville, op. cit., p. 203. Balfour to Pauncefote, 6 April 1898.
146 Mowat, op. cit., p. 205.
147 Garvin, op. cit., Vol. III. p. 302. Chamberlain's Speech, 13 May 1898.
148 *Great Britain and the United States, 1895–1903* by A. E. Campbell. p. 79. The *Spectator,* 27 January 1900.
149 *The Foreign Office and Foreign Policy, 1898–1914* by Z. S. Steiner. p. 70.

4   Towards Disaster, 1902–14

> The story begins long before that—years before sometimes—
> with all the causes and events that bring certain people to a
> certain place at a certain time on a certain day. . . . And
> then, when the time comes—over the top! Zero hour. Yes, all
> of them converging towards zero.
>
> Agatha Christie in *Towards Zero*

Long before the fateful summer of 1914 the British had become
involved intimately in the European power system. Asquith asserted
'we are under no obligation . . . and our actions must depend upon
the course of events';[1] but this technically correct statement had little
to do with the political realities of August 1914. Violation of
Belgium's neutrality played an important part in resolving the
opinions of both the uninformed mass of the British people and the
class of the politically influential, but in reality there was no free
hand for Britain. There was a wish to avoid war, but if there was
war Britain could only fight Germany. Policies pursued since 1902
would have made it illogical and undignified to stand aside in 1914.
Britain's position as a world power seemed at stake.

Yet it is clear that in 1902 there was no general wish for conflict
with Germany. Hopes of an alliance had been dashed but there was
no reason to suppose that bitter rivalry was the alternative. The
Kaiser and Lansdowne wanted understanding, but in London and
Berlin were groups deeply suspicious of each other. Resentment at
recent German conduct in international affairs was particularly strong
among Tory and Radical ultras. Curzon held typical views: 'In
my opinion the most marked feature in the international development of the next quarter of a century will be . . . the aggrandisement
of the German Empire at the expense of Great Britain; and I think

References are printed on p. 172.

that any English Foreign Minister who desires to serve his country well should never lose sight of that consideration'.[2] This background of mistrust was to have a serious effect in undermining Anglo-German amity.

In 1902 Britain was awkwardly placed. Events at the turn of the century had convinced policy-makers that traditional relationships must be revised. It was widely assumed that the interests of Germany and Britain were hardly anywhere in conflict and that the sensible course was to improve relations with France and Russia. It was not expected that this new course would make relations with Germany more difficult, though this possibility was not entirely unforeseen. Indeed, there was an ever growing body of opinion which believed that Germany did not wish for good relations with Britain. The German Navy Acts of 1898 and 1900 convinced Lascelles, the Ambassador to Berlin, that 'the German navy is professedly aimed at that of the greatest naval power—us'.[3] The Kaiser was strongly advised against expansion of his fleet by his ambassador in London, but protests were in vain. On the eve of the Navy Bill of 1908, Metternich observed, 'There can be no mistake that the German naval programme has awakened the vigilance of the British in the highest degree, and that England intends to maintain her supremacy at sea without question. It is to the interest of good Anglo-German relations, that there should be no illusion about this in Germany'.[4] Illusion there was, and naval rivalry played an essential part in creating demands for a new alignment of powers.

In the months following the treaty with Japan, it was impropitious for Britain to seek improved relations with Russia. France shared Russian views of the treaty. Cambon, the French Ambassador, told Lansdowne 'he could not see what object we had in tieing ourselves by a hard and fast bargain to a yellow ally, who might involve us, in spite of ourselves, in troublesome quarrels'.[5] Yet it was plain that Cambon wished to improve relations with Britain. In early 1901 he had raised the question of some kind of colonial bargain and, later in the year, Lansdowne had told Cromer, 'I have been struck by the comparative friendliness of the French. . . . Their manners are better and in substance they are easier to deal with than the rest'.[6] The group within the Cabinet favouring improved relations with France was reinforced in early 1902 by Chamberlain, the rejected suitor of Germany. In January Metternich reported that 'Chamberlain has proposed to the French Ambassador that the outstanding colonial differences between the two powers should be treated not one by one but as a whole. . . . Cambon seems to be very keen to secure a definite agreement with the British Government upon these questions'.[7] Metternich was mistaken, but his account proved merely to be a few weeks premature.

Events conspired to bring Britain and France to the negotiating table. The Boer War had persuaded Lansdowne and a majority of the Cabinet that British resources were seriously stretched. The growth of the German Navy had created a new threat in home waters. The difficulties of Cromer embarrassed the Foreign Office. In France there was an awareness that colonial disputes with Britain had impaired the French bid to be a major European power. Quarrels with the greatest naval and trading power in Siam, West Africa, Egypt, Newfoundland and the Pacific hardly advanced the recovery of Alsace-Lorraine. Furthermore, events in Morocco, an area of great interest to France, had led to a deterioration in political stability. Spain, Germany, Italy and Britain also had North African interests and the colonial party in France was anxious to protect those of French merchants and settlers. Fashoda had made it plain that the Dual Alliance would be of little or no help in a colonial quarrel, so it was possible for the party favouring compromise with Britain to grow in influence.

Within Britain the group favouring an understanding with France was already formidable. Edward VII wanted peace with Germany, but as he told Eckardstein, a German diplomat, 'We are being urged more strongly than ever by France to come to an agreement with her in all Colonial disputes, and it will probably be best in the end to make such a settlement, because England only wants peace and quiet and to live on a friendly footing with all other countries'.[8] The King was surrounded by a pro-French circle, including Francis Bertie, at this time Assistant Under-Secretary, and Charles Hardinge, then attached to the St Petersburg embassy. Salisbury had always believed in the value of limited negotiations to smooth away disputes. Chamberlain led the group favouring a binding alliance, though his mercurial temperament made him an uncertain quantity. Ministers primarily concerned with defence problems (Balfour, Brodrick and Selborne) also favoured an agreement. Curzon, the Viceroy of India, hoped to use France as a moderating influence on Russia. Against this powerful combination could be set only Lansdowne, who remained desirous of agreement with Germany, and Sanderson, the Permanent Under-Secretary, who had absorbed much of Salisbury's caution. Even these key figures were not anti-French and both accepted the validity of Cromer's argument that 'We must make a serious effort to get rid of the *Caisse de la Dette*'.[9] In sum, informed British opinion favoured agreement with France, and the retirement of Salisbury in July 1902 removed the last powerful figure opposed in principle to binding alliances.

In France the spirit of compromise and conciliation was less obvious. Delcassé was still undecided as to the value of an agreement, being unduly suspicious of British intentions in Morocco. However, the Anglophobia of the colonial party, at a peak in 1898, was much diminished by 1902. The *revanchards*, led by Clemenceau, had never believed it possible to compete simultaneously with Germany and Britain. Nevertheless, the legend of British perfidy in Egypt was still strong, and, but for Cambon, might have continued to exercise a decisive and disastrous effect on Anglo-French relations. In 1901 and early 1902 the ambassador was apparently 'acting on his own initiative and in actual defiance of Delcassé's instructions'.[10] French diplomatic style seems to have permitted unofficial initiatives of a kind unimagined by the British service. Indeed, Monson, the Ambassador to Paris, was correct to suggest, 'I believe that he plays very much for his own hand; and counts upon being approved and supported without waiting for definite instructions'.[11] Despite these limitations, Cambon played a vital part in creating a climate of amity. He constantly pressed Delcassé towards compromise and away from confrontation and he convinced Lansdowne and the Foreign Office that attempts to come to terms would meet with a warm French response.

In 1902 it was impossible to reach agreement, or even to negotiate seriously. The British were still thinking in terms of limited agreement. Lansdowne envisaged settling the troublesome dispute over the Newfoundland fisheries by concessions to France in West Africa. Cambon thought on a larger scale, realizing that relations could never be smooth until major obstacles, such as Egypt and Morocco, had been cleared out of the way. He was already considering an Egypt–Morocco barter, though as a skilful negotiator he did not intend to raise the possibility of concessions in Egypt until forced to do so. The essential weakness of his approaches in 1902—and he had important talks with Lansdowne on 23 July, 6 August and 15 October—was that until both parties could be induced to discuss issues in similar fashion, no real progress could be made.

Lansdowne made it clear to Cambon in March 1902 that he was ready to consider 'the idea of reasonable "give-and-take" arrangements in regard to . . . possessions in different parts of the world'.[12] Unfortunately Cambon was preoccupied with the Moroccan Question to the exclusion of all else. In 1894 a young Sultan had succeeded to the throne in circumstances of economic decline and increased international intrigue. The commander of his forces was Kaïd Maclean, a Briton, and it was feared in Paris lest he play a Cromer-like part in leading Morocco gently under British control. In 1900 Delcassé had resolved upon a forward policy in Morocco and subsequently attempted to purchase the acquiescence of other powers. Agreement with Italy was reached in December 1900, but a treaty of September 1902 with Spain was not ratified owing to Spanish fear of British displeasure. An attempt to disarm Britain, in March 1901, met with failure. Chamberlain told Lansdowne, 'If we are to discuss such a large question as Morocco please bear in mind that the Germans will have something to say—and both they and we will want compensation'.[13] Failure in 1902 stemmed from Cambon's unwillingness and inability to offer anything substantial in return for concessions in Morocco. Consideration of the question was bound to open a Pandora's box of international rivalries and Britain had to be offered the right price for running the risk of Italian, Spanish and German wrath.

In retrospect Lansdowne's judgment seems correct. In 1902 Morocco was not in chaos and, as the Foreign Secretary told Cambon, 'I did not see what opening there was for any transaction between us. The country in question did not belong to us, nor did I see how either of us could announce to the world that we had come to terms on so questionable a basis'.[14] The hints thrown out by Cambon of an Egypt–Morocco barter thus met with a poor response. More than once Lansdowne observed that he was 'not prepared to discuss a possible "liquidation" of Morocco'.[15] Uppermost in his mind were fears of further extending British commitments and antagonizing interested powers. In 1902 pressures were not sufficient to make these risks a justifiable gamble for either power.

Towards the close of 1902 the Cabinet realized that the situation in Morocco was deteriorating. Despite Delcassé's professed preference for stability, French pressure on the Sultan steadily increased. At much the same time Turkey permitted Russian torpedo-boats to pass through the Straits, thus raising once again the spectre of a challenge to the precarious British naval predominance in the Mediterranean. Attempts to rebuild a coalition on the lines of the 1887 agreements met with an unfavourable German reply. No action could be taken by Britain alone, so Russia won a minor diplomatic triumph. The consequences were far reaching. The weakness of Britain in the Levant was fully exposed by the failure of Germany and Austria to support her. Agreements with France and Russia seemed increasingly attractive to the Foreign Office.

Chamberlain now took a hand in the game. On his way to South Africa he visited Cairo to talk to Cromer. In turn, Cromer reported these discussions to Lecomte, the French *chargé d'affaires*. Lecomte gave valuable support to Cambon's pressure on Delcassé, revealing that Chamberlain 'now believes that the time is ripe to enter into negotiations. At the least, if the desire for an entente is reciprocated, the task of making it fruitful should begin by an exchange of obligations. . . . Mr. Chamberlain has already thought it right to expound this conception of his to the Cabinet'.[16] In private Chamberlain was even more enthusiastic, telling his son Austen, 'I am sorry to hear that Delcassé is likely to go. He seems to me to have done much to make possible an "entente cordiale" with France, which is what I should now like'.[17] Thus, at the beginning of 1903, there existed a diplomatic situation favourable to Anglo-French co-operation and readiness in London and Paris to negotiate seriously.

On 1 January 1903, following the virtual collapse of the Sultan's government in Morocco, Lansdowne and Balfour agreed to try to work with France and Spain. Correspondence with Durand, Ambassador to Madrid, shows how anxious was the Cabinet to avoid disruption in Morocco and poor relations with France. The French attitude was less clear, though apparently Delcassé already accepted that Britain 'would ask for either a territorial compensation or the parallel settlement of the Egyptian question'.[18] It was to be some time before this private recognition became a public stance.

Royal initiative suddenly changed the situation. Edward VII, who was to make a Mediterranean tour, decided to visit Paris. The French were easily persuaded to make his visit official. President Loubet told Monson, 'a visit from the King would . . . do an amount of good which is probably not realized in England'.[19] Cambon and the *chargé d'affaires*, Geoffray, believed that press and public thoroughly understood and approved the purpose of the visit. Geoffray asserted that 'Edward VII reflects the wish of the great majority of his subjects: to live on good terms with France'.[20] The royal visit of May 1903 was a great success and Loubet was invited to a return visit in July. It was widely believed that these meetings eased Anglo-French relations; certainly other powers were impressed. Russian reaction was favourable, the meetings being seen as a snub to the Kaiser. In Berlin, Bihourd, the French Ambassador, perceived confusion and dismay, reporting that the visits were seen as 'more than acts of international courtesy . . . they cannot fail to impress William II strongly'.[21] It was generally assumed that France and Britain intended to resume the happy relationship which had existed before 1882.

Negotiations were not completed until April 1904. In the meantime there was some tough bargaining. Geoffray attributed this to the pro-German party in Britain: 'some important groups have remained faithful to the policy of understanding with Germany and nothing will diminish their hostility to our cause'.[22] This was a misjudgment. Sanderson favoured Germany, but the unyielding attitude stemmed from French reluctance to accept that the Egyptian Question had to be settled. Only at the end of 1903 did Delcassé openly accept the validity of the British case.

Delcassé accompanied Loubet on his official visit in July 1903 and serious negotiations began on 7 July when he told Lansdowne he was 'entirely in favour of a comprehensive settlement, and that the Egyptian Question formed part of the larger African Question which could . . . be disposed of satisfactorily if only we could come to an agreement as to the position of France and Morocco'.[23] This studied ambiguity was to lead to strain between Cambon and Lansdowne, for on 21 July Delcassé still insisted that 'this political question had not been touched upon'.[24] Equivocation held up agreement. The French remained outwardly convinced that theirs was the stronger bargaining position. On 11 October Cambon told Delcassé the British were trying to exchange 'what they did not possess in Morocco . . . [for] the advantages and rights of which we were already in full possession in Egypt'.[25] The fact was, Delcassé feared adverse public reaction in France to concessions in Egypt. He also saw that negotiations would prove abortive unless a major gain in Morocco could be assured. This was impossible without British consent, as Spanish refusal to acquiesce in previous schemes showed. Further, on 5 August, Lansdowne had removed all cause for doubt by telling Cambon, 'My Cabinet colleagues agree with me that we cannot settle the matters of interest to us without including the Egyptian question'.[26] On 24 October Delcassé bowed to the inevitable, telling Cambon, 'It is evident that time has worked against us, for little by little England has transformed her precarious hold . . . into a veiled protectorate'.[27] A few days later Cambon made firm proposals involving French concessions in Egypt. The Egypt–Morocco barter had been accepted by both sides.

Some issues proved easy to settle. A compromise was soon reached over Siam and the New Hebrides, but the question of residual French fishing rights in Newfoundland proved more difficult. These rights were of little practical value, but Delcassé held out for substantial territorial compensation in West Africa. He wanted the cession of Gambia, but the Cabinet would have none of this suggestion. On 11 December Lansdowne was instructed to tell Cambon that Britain 'finally refused to part with the Gambia even upon the conditions which M. Delcassé had suggested'.[28] The government's opinion was that demands were too high, though in the end the Îles de Los (off French Guinea), a small strip of Gambia and part of northern Nigeria were ceded. These details were settled in March 1904.

At the heart of the agreement of 8 April 1904 was the exchange of interests in Egypt and Morocco. Britain received a free hand in Egypt and a promise of French support for proposed changes in financial arrangements. In Morocco the French agreed to respect Spanish rights and to forego fortification in the coastal strip opposite Gibraltar. Otherwise France had a free hand in Morocco and assurances of British diplomatic support. Both powers thus surrendered a capacity to obstruct the other, though Britain also gave up effective commercial supremacy in Morocco. It was a fair exchange and was recognized as such by both Parliament, which approved the treaty without a division, and the Chamber of Deputies, where Delcassé's recommendation was carried by 436 to 94 votes.

Yet the negotiations showed how far Britain and France were from a true understanding. The French had repeatedly and erroneously assumed that they had the upper hand. They failed to understand that if the worse came to the worst Britain would continue to tolerate obstruction in Egypt, whereas disorder in Morocco might soon destroy French aspirations. Delcassé forgot that since 1899 Britain had steadfastly refused to 'contemplate the fall'[28] of Morocco and in agreeing to French rule over the whole of North Africa, was making a considerable concession. It was Cambon, the architect of understanding, who had argued, 'I am of the opinion we should yield nothing, we should not show ourselves pressed for time. We have the right to be awkward; the English have more interest in coming to terms with us in Egypt than we have with them in Morocco. They will become impossible if they once think us anxious'.[29] During negotiations France encouraged Russia to complete the Orenburg–Tashkent railway—an act hardly calculated to please London. On 1 March 1904, Delcassé even assured his colleagues that a defence system had been prepared in the Mediterranean against a possible British attack. French diplomats tried to use Cromer's anxiety for an Egyptian settlement as a lever in the talks. Cromer did press Lansdowne to make concessions, arguing that 'the French concessions to us in Egypt are in reality far more valuable than those we are making to them in Morocco'.[30]

When talks broke down in January 1904, Cromer promised that 'although it was difficult for him to advise on questions outside his competence, he would do what he could'.[31] Cambon even tried the *ballon d'essai* of 1898, arguing for concessions as 'no other politician in France . . . would dare consider the Egyptian questions'.[32] These manoeuvres made little impression on Lansdowne, who had a good grasp of the realities of the power relationship.

The *entente* of 1904 was not, then, the finished product of a deeply considered revision of attitudes. It was a bargain. Its usefulness would be judged as much by the spirit in which the terms were executed as by the letter of the treaty. Relations had improved but were hardly close. Rivalry had been too bitter for too long for a total and immediate reversal of attitudes, though the western powers now shared an interest in making their bargain worth while.

The understanding was strongly favoured by those involved in the planning of British defence, which had acquired new dimensions since the creation of the Committee of Imperial Defence. Balfour, who chaired the first C.I.D. meeting on 18 December 1902, was influenced by Admiralty fears of growth of the German Navy and supported Lansdowne against the more cautious members of the Cabinet. Willingness to accede to French demands in Morocco stemmed, in part, from fear of German ambition. In 1905 Fisher assured Lansdowne, 'the Germans would like a port on the coast of Morocco, and without any doubt whatever such a port possessed by them would be vitally detrimental to us from the naval point of view, and ought to be made a *casus belli*'.[33] Cambon had already perceived this hypersensitivity, observing that Lansdowne 'is well aware of the German plan to establish a coaling station and perhaps a base on the Mediterranean coast between the Spanish outposts'.[34] Britain was prepared to let France into Morocco to keep out Germany. The basis of the *entente* was a common apprehension rather than a feeling of shared purpose.

The strength of the *entente* was soon to be tested. A deterioration in Russo-Japanese relations in the winter of 1903–04 led to war in February 1904. At the risk of creating distrust at St Petersburg and Tokyo, Cambon and Lansdowne sought to preserve their relationship. They agreed 'to do all in their power to keep the peace' and to 'pour as much cold water as possible on the embers',[35] Their efforts as peacemakers were futile, though perhaps the outbreak of war expedited conclusion of the *entente*. Both western powers found the diplomatic situation delicate, as neither wished to see an ally humiliated nor to become involved itself. The only hope of preserving both new and old agreements lay in promoting peace in the Far East, but this seemed a herculean task in the spring of 1904. As Bompard, French Ambassador to St Petersburg, put it, 'Our conduct at the conclusion of peace will be the touchstone by which it will be judged whether this *rapprochement* is compatible with the Franco-Russian alliance or whether, on the contrary, it is favourable to it. That will be a difficult moment for us, and it will need all your dexterity and *savoir-faire* to surmount it'.[36]

The outbreak of the Russo-Japanese War created a particularly dangerous situation for France. Defeat for Russia might mean the end of the 1894 alliance, or, more probably, its weakening into uselessness. Fortunately for Delcassé the mood in Britain favoured compromise, though how much this owed to widespread under-estimation of Japanese strength is hard to calculate. Since 1902 the party in Britain favourable to compromise with Russia had grown, but conciliatory attitudes derived from fear of the Russian colossus, rather than from a sincere desire for friendship. British strategic problems in Asia, it was felt, necessitated an arrangement with Russia. Balfour, who was closely in touch with the military planners, affirmed, 'I do not personally believe that Russia is vulnerable in any mortal spot except her Exchequer'.[37] The anti-German party in the Foreign Office believed an agreement with Russia to be indispensable and shared Edward VII's anxiety to promote good relations. On 14 April 1904 the King had a long and friendly discussion with the Russian Minister at Copenhagen, Izvolsky. Writing to the Tsar a few weeks later, Edward assured Nicholas, 'My earnest desire, which I am convinced you will share, is that at the conclusion of the war our two countries may come to a satisfactory settlement regarding many difficult matters between us, and that a lasting agreement may be arrived at similar to the one which we have lately concluded with France'.[38]

There remained a substantial anti-Russian party in Britain. Curzon and his followers favoured a policy based on strength, wishing to consolidate British influence in Afghanistan and China and to push forward in Persia and Tibet. Curzon's power reached its peak in 1904 when the Younghusband expedition was sent to Tibet and British posts in Persia were expanded. These vigorous gestures were not welcome to the Cabinet, which increasingly disliked Curzon's tendency to behave as a sovereign in his own right. Balfour even believed that if the Viceroy had his way he 'would raise India to the position of an independent and not always friendly Power'.[39] In 1904 Curzon returned to London for talks with the government. During the visit it became clear the apprehensions about British policy were justified. Lady Curzon wrote, 'I think it would be very grave if a crisis happened in India now, as they would tie your hands absolutely here and you would have to resign. Tibet has frightened the whole Cabinet, and they think it rash and are frightened to death'.[40] The forward policy was no longer acceptable to most Conservatives; the Liberals, despite their dislike of Tsarist autocracy, had long ago abandoned it. The reasoning behind the Anglo-Japanese treaty led inexorably to a defensive posture in Central Asia and the Persian Gulf. At the close of 1903 Balfour had put this plainly: 'There is really nothing in the way of territory which Russia possesses and we desire. In the Far East we are not an expansive power. We want no territory that we have not already got and our one object is to make that secure . . . our only permanent security seems to be to lay down, wherever possible, as regards all the essentials of our Eastern position, certain well-defined principles (e.g. the integrity of Afghanistan), which, if broken, we should regard as a *casus belli* . . . in Persia . . . perhaps it is not possible to find some definite ground of understanding at once so clear in itself, and of such obvious importance to our Imperial interests that the British people would consent to make its attempted infraction at once regarded as a sufficient ground for putting forward their whole strength in its defence.'[41]

Younghusband's adventures in Tibet, however, exacerbated relations and Lansdowne felt obliged to assure Benckendorff, the Russian Ambassador, that Britain wished neither 'to annex it, to establish a Protectorate over it, or in any way control its internal administrations'.[42] Japanese successes in the war produced an atmosphere of conciliation in London, but not in St Petersburg, where the military party became steadily more anti-British and turned to Germany for comfort. The Kaiser was only too happy to fish in troubled waters and Delcassé and Bompard began to fear for their alliance. The French dilemma was treated with sympathy by Lansdowne and a blind eye was turned to a French assistance to Russia. In Britain the anti-Russian party took comfort in the somewhat unexpected Japanese victories, while the friends of Russia realized that these triumphs made a belligerent posture unnecessary.

In autumn 1904 the French were placed in a still more embarrassing position. On 23 October the world was stunned by news that the Russian Baltic Fleet, on its way to its doom in Tsushima Strait, had sunk two Hull trawlers off the Dogger Bank, apparently mistaking them for Japanese torpedo boats. British opinion was outraged and there were widespread demands for war. The most pacific members of the Cabinet, including the Balfours, wanted immediate satisfaction. Edward VII proved belligerent in the early days of the crisis, accusing Russia of not treating 'the matter with that gravity of importance which it invites'.[43] Fortunately, the Russians changed their attitude quickly and full compensation was promised, though not before Fisher had noted on 1 November, 'I have been with the P.M. all day. It has very nearly been war again. Very near indeed, but the Russians have climbed down'.[44]

The incident helped convince reasonable men in both countries that Anglo-Russian relations must be put on a firmer footing. The part played by France in the crisis had been most important in helping preserve peace. Cambon, Bompard and Delcassé had worked hard to persuade Russia to admit the justice of the British gravamen. They reaped a rich reward of British goodwill. On 16 November, Edward VII told Cambon, 'I beg you to tell M. Loubet how grateful I am for the attitude of France and for the services rendered by her to the cause of peace'.[45] In Russia, German activities were increasingly seen as mischievous, much of the responsibility for the incident being attributed to a warning from Metternich, who, on 13 October, had advised Bülow, 'mines are to be laid in the Sound and Kattegat by agents in Japanese employment. I beg that this warning may be communicated to the Russian Government'.[46] By a strange chance it was Metternich who was soon after forced to admit 'The *Entente Cordiale*, however insignificant its services have doubtless been, has celebrated a new triumph here; it is given the main credit for the settlement of the dispute and will be strengthened by this incident'.[47]

The Tsar was still under the influence of the military party, which was largely pro-German in sentiment. The Kaiser encouraged Russian arrogance and reluctance to negotiate and Nicholas entirely failed to understand that defeats necessitated both increased loans from France and improved relations with Britain. During the crisis the Tsar had even suggested to the Kaiser, 'Germany, Russia and France should at once unite upon arrangements to abolish English and Japanese arrogance and insolence. Would you like . . . to frame the outlines of such a treaty?'[48] Pressure from France and revolt at home eventually compelled Russia to negotiate, though President Roosevelt was unimpressed by Russia's lack of realism: 'The Russian Government jumps from side to side. They have not been able to make war and now they cannot make peace; their representatives give me the worst impression; they are tricky and inefficient'.[49] On 5 September 1905 peace was signed.

The events of 1904–05 profoundly changed great power relationships. Russia was momentarily no longer a force in the Far East. Britain recognized this by concluding a new treaty with Japan on 12 August 1905. The new terms gave British recognition to Japanese preponderance in Korea and a Japanese guarantee of India and the adjoining territories. The treaty was to run for ten years, and the alliance was to operate in the event of attack by one power. It marked a serious reverse for both Russia and Germany—whose ambitions in China now had to be curtailed. The agreement was well received in Japan and inaugurated a period of close Anglo-Japanese understanding. From the start, however, British statesmen made it clear that they hoped to take advantage of Far Eastern stability to come to turns with Russia. Lansdowne did not wish to use the treaty as an instrument of blackmail to compel Russian acquiescence in expansionist plans. Writing to Hardinge in September 1905, he insisted, 'I can at any rate say with absolute conviction that this new arrangement must not be taken as an indication of unfriendliness on our part. I have . . . always desired . . . that we should live on neighbourly terms with Russia'.[50] A change of government in Britain in December 1905 made no difference to this policy. Morley told Minto, the new Viceroy, on 6 July 1906, 'you argue . . . as if the policy of *entente* with Russia were an open question. This is just what it is not. H.M.G. would almost unanimously support any agreement, public opinion having decided to make such an attempt as Russian circumstances may permit, to arrange an *entente*. The grounds for this I have often referred to when writing to you. Be they good or bad, be we right or wrong, that is our policy'.[51]

There thus existed in London and Paris strong sentiments of goodwill towards Russia. In St Petersburg the summer of 1905 saw the apogee of German influence. On 24 July the Kaiser induced the Tsar to sign the Treaty of Björkö, which would have bound Russia to Germany. Its intention was avowedly anti-British, as William II made clear in a letter: 'The Continental Combine . . . is the sole and only manner to effectively block the way to the whole world becoming John Bull's private property'.[52] The feeble Tsar did not reveal the contents of the treaty to Lamsdorff until the end of August, and was then advised by Witte, Lamsdorff and Grand Duke Nicholas to abandon the whole scheme. Failure to ratify the treaty marked the beginning of the end of German influence over Russian policy.

The financial advantages to be gained from working with the western powers were substantial. After 1905 Russia became credit-worthy in Britain and could resume industrial expansion. Balkan problems no longer proved a serious obstacle to co-operation, as events in Macedonia in 1903 had shown. The failure of the powers to agree on a reform package had led to serious unrest, to which Russia was hostile. Britain and France favoured introduction of a liberal constitution and persuaded Russia to support such an experiment. In October 1903 Russia and Austria jointly presented a limited reform programme to the Porte and in late 1905 a naval demonstration in the Aegean obliged Turkey to concede an international commission to supervise Macedonian finances. There was no complete agreement between Britain, France, and Russia, but, equally, no likelihood of confrontation.

Real improvement in Anglo-Russian relations dated from the Moroccan crisis of 1905–06, when both powers supported France against Germany. After April 1904 French influence in Morocco increased sharply, culminating in the presentation of a sweeping reform programme at the close of the year. Berlin was now thoroughly frightened by the prospect of Anglo-French amity and resolved to break the association by pressure at a vulnerable point. On 12 March 1905 Bülow announced that Germany would not watch idly while her Moroccan interests were destroyed. On 31 March the Kaiser landed at Tangiers where he told an amazed audience, 'The Empire has great and growing interests in Morocco. Commerce can only progress if all the Powers are considered to have equal rights under the sovereignty of the Sultan and respect the independence of the country. My visit is the recognition of this independence'.[53] The first Moroccan crisis was launched.

Britain recognized at once that Germany wished to wreck the *entente*. On 25 April Bertie assured Lansdowne that Bülow's aim was 'to show to the French people that an understanding with England is of little value to them and that they had much better come to an agreement with Germany'.[54] Even Lansdowne, who had always shown a partiality to Germany, argued that he could not see 'why any international complications should be created, unless German Govt. is determined to take advantage of what was at most a diplomatic oversight in order to make mischief or to disturb the *status quo*'.[55] German pressure on Delcassé confirmed this belief. A change of government in France in early 1905 had brought Rouvier, a supporter of concessions to Germany, into office. When the crisis broke, Delcassé became the target of criticism in the Chamber of Deputies. Receiving little support from his colleagues, apart from Loubet, he offered his resignation on 22 April, though it was soon afterwards withdrawn. Delcassé was seen in London as a symbol of the *entente* and the British were as anxious that he remain in office as the Germans were that he depart. On 3 May Cambon told Lansdowne, 'the conduct of the German Government . . . might be . . . an attempt to get rid of M. Delcassé'.[56] This was quite correct. In a memorandum of 2 May, Holstein had referred to 'the absolute mistrust of any French policy which is led by M. Delcassé. We believe that Delcassé does not stick to the truth and that he loses no opportunity of distorting German policy'.[57]

The precise details of a Moroccan settlement were largely unimportant to Britain. The matter of interest to Britain and Germany was the future of the *entente*. If strong British support enabled French control over Morocco to be consolidated then the association would become even closer, but if France were forced to retreat then the *entente* would seem useless to Paris. The weakness of Rouvier's government seemed as great a danger to the *entente* as German pressure, so the first concern of Lansdowne was to bolster Delcassé and the pro-British party. On 24 April it was agreed that Britain should concert with France to meet any German threat in Morocco. General fears about the *entente* were further reinforced by specific anxiety over German demands for a port, which raised strategic questions of major concern to the Admiralty.

In the case of Delcassé the Germans were not to be denied. German pressure for a conference on Morocco could not be resisted and Rouvier gave way. On 6 June Delcassé resigned, telling Bertie, 'his fall was brought about entirely by the intrigues of the German Government who have spent a good deal of money for the purpose... they regarded him as the obstacle to their schemes in having negotiated the Anglo-French understanding and in encouraging the idea of an understanding between England and Russia'.[58] If Germany had remained content with this victory it might have heralded the end of the *entente*, for there were already signs of distrust between London and Paris. Rouvier feared Britain would desert France in the event of conflict with Germany, and could not run this risk with Russia temporarily weak and useless. Similarly, British politicians feared a Franco-German bargain which would give Germany a free hand in a part of the world where British interests would be threatened. These uncertainties might not have been resolved if German demands for a conference had been dropped when Delcassé was forced to resign.

The Cabinet was depressed by French weakness. Balfour unflatteringly argued that 'France ... could not at present be counted on as an effective force in international politics. She could no longer be trusted not to yield to threats at the critical moment of a negotiation'.[59] Rouvier himself soon discovered that dealing with Germany was more difficult than at first sight appeared. Two weeks after Delcassé's fall he realized it was impossible to appease Germany save at prohibitive cost. He turned to Britain and by 22 July 1905 Metternich was arguing that 'In England the Morocco question has come to mean a fight for the friendship of France, and in order to keep this and also to prevent a predominant German hegemony over Europe, they would venture on a war'.[60] Two days earlier a secret sub-committee had been set up by the C.I.D. to examine the feasibility of an expeditionary force to Germany. During summer and autumn 1905 Anglo-German relations reached a new low point, with Kaiser and King exchanging frigidly courteous notes and the press striking bellicose positions. On 15 October *Le Matin*, Delcassé's mouthpiece, disclosed that Britain had offered armed aid to France against Germany. Lascelles found difficulty in calming the uproar in Berlin while Berlin observed a corresponding, and equally ill-founded, jubilation in Paris.

Revival of confidence between the western powers led to close co-operation before and during the projected Moroccan conference. It had been Holstein's contention that 'If the Conference is held, it will, whatever the result, definitely not hand Morocco over to the French'.[61] The Germans were confident of support from Morocco, Austria, Russia, Italy, Spain, the United States and some minor powers. German over-confidence and careful planning by Britain and France wrecked these calculations. By a mixture of persuasion and pressure the United States and Spain were induced to support France, while Russia had never intended otherwise. On 1 September a Franco-Spanish agreement ensured that Spanish claims could not be used as a lever against the *entente*; Spanish pretensions were still further flattered by the choice of Algeciras as the conference centre. Most importantly, Nicolson's instructions as British representative ordered him to 'cordially support the proposals which your French colleague may bring forward'.[62] The *entente* was in full working order.

The *entente*, which had begun as an adjustment of colonial grievances, was, under the impact of German pressure, beginning to take on the character of an anti-German front. By the close of

1905 public opinion in Britain was very hostile to Germany and policy-makers in Berlin began to have second thoughts. A year earlier Schulenburg, the military attaché in London, had warned, 'There need be no fear of an immediate war but little doubt . . . that war will eventually occur . . . it is altogether improbable that friendly relations will again be established'.[63] The events of 1905 had further damaged relations and on 23 December, Holstein changed tack, urging, 'We should hurry and improve our relations to England in the next few years while the new Russia is still busy at home'.[64] Metternich and Schulenburg were similarly worried. The ambassador reported that 'Here the Morocco question is generally regarded as a test of the Anglo-French *Entente*, and our Morocco policy as an attempt to smash it up'.[65] Schulenburg echoed Holstein's pessimism: 'If war breaks out between Germany and France, England will be all on France's side, and hatred of Germany will once again flame up brightly, with the probable result that England will take part in the war. Anything else is hardly conceivable'.[66]

While these warnings fell on deaf ears there were important developments in London. On 4 December the divided and discredited Balfour ministry resigned, to be replaced by a caretaker Liberal government under Campbell-Bannerman. At the ensuing General Election the new ministry was confirmed by a vast majority. Grey returned to the Foreign Office and held that post until 11 December 1916. The fall of the Conservatives created political uncertainty in the capitals of Europe. Berlin hoped that growing anti-German sentiment would be checked by the advent to power of Little Englanders like Campbell-Bannerman, Morley, Bryce and Lloyd George. This might have been the moment to correct the German course but the strong emphasis placed by Metternich on the Liberals' wish for peace deluded Bülow into believing that this meant pacifism. In Paris and St Petersburg there was a more accurate appraisal of the significance of a change of government. Cambon reported on 12 December that Grey had recently 'shown himself a stout supporter of the *entente*' and did not think 'we should worry that Grey has been given foreign affairs', despite the fact that 'above all the Liberals are peace-lovers', for 'the recent *entente* with France has their complete approval because it seems to them a guarantee of peace'.[67]

Grey certainly was a supporter of the *entente*. The anti-German party in the Foreign Office, strengthened by Sanderson's retirement in early 1906, was well pleased with the appointment. Hardinge, the new Permanent Under-Secretary, was supported by Mallet, Grey's private secretary, and Tyrrell, who replaced Mallet on his appointment as Assistant Under-Secretary in 1907. Other influential members of the anti-German group included Nicolson, who was shortly to become Ambassador to St Petersburg, and Eyre Crowe, the Head Clerk. This formidable alliance was further strengthened by Bertie, a favourite of Edward VII. It was not certain in 1906 that this group was going to dominate British policy—that it eventually did so owed as much to Liberal disunity as to persuasive argument or establishment power. Inside the party were many who wished to re-establish a link with Germany. Haldane, Rosebery and Loreburn sympathized with Germany and were given some support by Bryce, who publicly declared that 'nowhere are our political interests and Germany's antagonistic'.[68] Campbell-Bannerman's wish to avoid conflict effectively made him a member of this group too. Grey dissented, arguing that 'Rosebery is wrong about Germany and I feel it so strongly that if any government drags us back into the German net I will oppose it openly at all costs'.[69] Amid these disagreements it is hardly surprising that permanent officials had a major influence on policy-making.

It might be supposed that a Cabinet so divided on foreign policy would have discussed its direction. It proved quite otherwise. Grey was permitted a great deal of autonomy and his policy was largely unchecked, thus paving the way for the bitter recriminations of 1914. Events during the Algeciras Conference, which lasted from 16 January to 7 April 1906, confirmed this independence from Cabinet control. The conference itself was a major defeat for Germany and created acute tension in London and Paris. War seemed probable in early 1906 and France was eager to secure British support. On 10 January Cambon suggested military and naval conversations between the two countries, pointing out that informal consultations had already been held in Balfour's time. The permanent officials argued that such a gesture of solidarity would 'deter Germany from provoking a conflict'.[70] Grey reluctantly accepted an argument which Lansdowne had always rejected. Cambon feared the Prime Minister and the Little England party would not readily 'support such an understanding in case of eventual conflict'[71] and sought to convert the relationship into a full alliance. Grey discussed these matters with the premier and Ripon, the Lord Privy Seal, but no full Cabinet meeting was ever held. Grey believed that many ministers would have opposed military conversations and that a binding commitment would have been flatly rejected. It was more convenient to keep the Cabinet in blissful ignorance. The day he retired Sanderson put the reasons frankly to Cambon: 'Sir Edward Grey has told you all he can say, you may be sure of his intentions; but he cannot go further without consulting the Cabinet, and, in the present situation, such consultation would be dangerous, because no government whatsoever will bind itself in a hypothetical case'.[72] Indeed, it is doubtful if Grey told Ripon and Campbell-Bannerman the full story, for on 11 January Ripon assured Fitzmaurice: 'Our engagements with France are . . . confined to the promise of full diplomatic support . . . the French people and many of their public men are expecting support of another kind, if the Conference breaks down, and serious trouble with Germany arises. If that occurs and we decline, as I think we ought to decline, to go farther than diplomacy will reach, I cannot but fear a cry of "perfide Albion" and a destruction of the present friendship between the two nations. The situation requires great wariness, but we may trust Grey for that'.[73] This confidence in Grey was sadly misplaced.

The 1905–06 crisis damaged Anglo-German relations. It cemented the *entente* by encouraging Anglo-French co-operation at both diplomatic and military levels. Anti-German sentiment in Britain and anti-British feeling in Germany were promoted. Until Algeciras the *entente* had been worth little to France and had proved something of an embarrassment during the Russo-Japanese war. Its value was now displayed for all the world to see. Small wonder Cambon was authorized by Bourgeois to express 'great appreciation for the co-operation which had resulted from the Entente'.[74] Henceforth there was no real risk of a rift between the western powers; the development of naval and military conversations between the general staffs merely tightened existing bonds. But great harm had been done to Anglo-German relations. Britain was increasingly depicted as the leader of an anti-German coalition. In 1905 Bülow already believed 'The British are egging on Paris as much as they can, in order to bring about a Franco-German war, which all Englishmen desire'.[75] Nicolson's behaviour at Algeciras, when he repeatedly took the lead in resisting German pretensions, confirmed this opinion. Nicolson admitted his support for Révoil gave 'ground for the charge that the Germans are always bringing against me, that I am more French than the French'.[76] German suspicions were not far from the truth. In March 1905 Bertie had hoped that Morocco would 'be an open sore between France and Germany as Egypt was between France and ourselves'.[77] Few influential figures in Britain shared Bertie's extremism. The tragedy of German miscalculation over Morocco was that it gave anti-German views a weight and authority which otherwise were lacking.

By early 1906 it was generally accepted in Britain that some attempt should be made to improve relations with Russia. There were still powerful dissentient voices, but Grey favoured an understanding, arguing that 'An agreement with Russia was the natural complement of the agreement with France; it was also the only practical alternative to the old policy of drift, with its continual complaints, bickerings, and dangerous friction'.[78] Hardinge and Nicolson concurred, as did the French. Cambon pointed out that 'Lamsdorff, the ambassadors to London and Paris, and a wide section of Russian opinion favour rapprochement with England, though the Tsar, influenced by the Kaiser, is hesitant'.[79] Many influential Russians had been impressed by Anglo-French solidarity at Algeciras and this strengthened their resolve to break away from German patronage. There were still many obstacles, not least the chaotic internal condition of Russia. The struggle for a Duma created embarrassment among those Liberals who wished to treat with the Tsarist autocracy. Furthermore, Witte, the President of the Council of Ministers, was still under the Kaiser's spell and later admitted that 'It was owing to my opposition that the agreement was not concluded before 1907'.[80]

The basis of the British approach was the resolution of problems in Asia. It was never intended that an understanding would mean the abandonment of Japan, and Grey went out of his way to allay Japanese fears. On 28 May 1906 he told the *chargé d'affaires*, 'as soon as there was any question on our part of coming to an Agreement with Russia that affected matters within the scope of our Alliance with Japan I would take care to keep the Japanese Government informed'.[81] It was expected that the major problem would be Persia, which was in a state of acute internal unrest. Japan was deemed capable of containing any renewed Russian advance in China while Japanese support in Tibet had already been enlisted. Furthermore, on 27 April 1906 Britain and China concluded a treaty by which Tibet was to remain in a power vacuum. As Grey told Spring Rice, it was unlikely that Russia would want to upset this arrangement as it was 'one of the few places in the world where to leave things alone causes no inconvenience to anybody'.[82] In Persia matters were quite different. Local conditions favoured covert activity of the kind so regularly practised by Russia in the past. Grey insisted that an agreement with Russia must involve control of her agents in Persia and that 'enterprising Russian officers in Asia must not take advantage of the confusion at St. Petersburg to do things on their own account'.[83] Britain wished to solve local problems but realized this would prove a futile exercise unless a general atmosphere of goodwill existed.

Negotiation with Russia, however, was a different matter from negotiation with France. There were both political and institutional problems. As Spring Rice later observed, 'It was easy for two civil-ized and liberal nations like France and England to come to terms and act together, but common action between an English Liberal and a Russian bureaucrat is a pretty difficult thing to manage. A wild ass and a commissary mule make a rum team to drive'.[84] Grey also faced the problem that the Foreign Office was not the sole department interested in relations with Russia. He had to con-sider the Indian Government and the India Office, at this time under Morley. Grey was fortunate in that Morley behaved at the India Office like 'an autocrat and almost a martinet'[85] and hence over-ruled many of Minto's justifiable protestations about the abandon-ment of British interests on the Indian frontier. Morley's political heritage was Gladstonian in its love of peace and economy. His wish to diminish the scope of military involvement in India led him to support overtures to Russia. Indeed, a subcommittee over which Morley presided reported in May 1907 that a war with Russia for India would necessitate 'immense demands and vast sacrifices'.[86] For a government which was already heavily committed to expenditure on domestic reform and naval expansion this was a powerful argument for negotiation.

In early 1906 negotiations were impeded by Russian belief that Britain was 'dying to have an arrangement with them and would pay anything to have one'.[87] This judgment was erroneous, though Grey did tell Spring Rice he was 'impatient to see Russia re-established as a factor in European politics. Whether we shall get an arrangement with her about Asiatic questions remains to be seen; I will try when she desires it and is ready'.[88] Discussions eventually began on 29 May and detailed negotiations on 7 June. Russian preoccupation with internal affairs, however, held up progress until the autumn. Not only were the Russians not ready to negotiate but Edward VII and his advisers felt 'there could be no thought of an *entente* until a more stable state of affairs had been attained'.[89]

Developments in Persia decisively changed the course and tempo of the talks. Although both Britain and Russia had influential followings in Persia they feared the intervention of Germany. Ever since the completion of negotiations for the Baghdad Railway concession in 1903 Germany had shown increasing interest in the Persian Gulf. This interest was the object of suspicion in both London and St Petersburg and the collapse of order in Persia made the whole region a fertile field for commercial and diplomatic intrigue. On 29 July 1906 Nicolson advised Hardinge, 'I am anxious as to German movements and aims in Persia. . . . I think that we should endeavour, as soon as possible, to come to an arrangement as to Persia before Germany has any ostensible pretext for interference'.[90] In August there was news of German attempts to purchase a port from Persia at the mouth of the Shatt-el-Arab and at the end of the month Izvolsky revealed that when he refused a loan to Persia the Shah had threatened to turn to Germany for assistance. Izvolsky's proposal that 'as both Russia and Great Britain had large interests in Persia

it was desirable that they should work together without the intervention of third parties'[91] was accepted at once. Nicolson wryly
commented that Izvolsky 'would doubtless prefer a *ménage à deux*
to a *ménage à trois* in Persia, especially when the third party would
be such an exceedingly active partner as the Emperor William'.[92]

For the next few months negotiations revolved around the important issue of how to define Russian and British spheres of influence
in Persia. This was no easy task because of the weight of opinion
in Britain opposed to any extension of Russian power close to the
frontiers of India. In September Izvolsky put forward proposals
which effectively amounted to the partition of Persia. This move
provoked a reaction from the anti-Russian party. The most powerful
influence was that of Minto and Kitchener, neither of whom trusted
Russia. On 19 September Minto advised Morley to retain British
vantage posts on the Gulf and South Persia for he could 'put no
faith whatever on the honesty of Russian diplomacy or on the
reliability of Russian promises'.[93] Spring Rice, from his post in
Teheran, and Kitchener continued to oppose concessions to the
very end. As late as June 1907 the Indian Commander-in-Chief
wondered 'what effect your clear statement of the case has had on
the government at home. Will they be induced to pause in their
dangerous philandering with the bearded Cossack—or have they
already gone too far?'[94] Edward VII strongly advised his ministers
to 'act in unison with Viceroy . . . as Russian diplomacy never varies'.[95]
There was also opposition within the government and diplomatic
corps. Fitzmaurice, Parliamentary Under-Secretary to Grey,
favoured agreement with Germany and did not like the turn events
had taken. Lascelles, in Berlin, agreed. On 31 May Fitzmaurice had
told Lascelles that good relations with Russia ought not to exclude
amity with Germany and that although 'A loyal attempt has to be
made to improve our relations with Russia; but with the absolute
uncertainty of the future there, both in regard to institutions and
individuals, nobody can tell whether a *rapprochement* will be possible
or permanent'.[96] All these objections were ignored or overruled by
Grey and Hardinge.

Although Britain and Russia wished to exclude Germany from
Persia, neither country wished to offend Germany unnecessarily

so there was some manoeuvring in order to secure German consent
to any arrangement. Britain and Russia hoped to avoid a crisis
similar to that over Morocco. On 5 November Nicolson was able
to report that Germany desired to preserve only the 'open door'
for trading purposes in Persia and that there would be no German
objections to an Anglo-Russian agreement. Suspicions were still
harboured, however, well into 1907 when evidence came to light
of a possible revival of the Three Emperors' League in Europe.
These fears proved groundless and on 31 August 1907 the Anglo-
Russian Convention was signed.

The convention made arrangements for Persia, Tibet and Afghanistan. It contained no mention of a regulation of the Straits Convention for which Izvolsky had asked early in negotiations. Persia
was divided into a Russian sphere of influence in the north and a
British in the south-east. The central provinces were to form a
neutral zone. The Persian Gulf was not covered by the agreement
as Russia had previously accepted 'Britain's special interest in the
maintenance of the *status quo* in the Persian Gulf'.[97] In Tibet the
special interest of Britain was recognized but both powers agreed
neither to intervene nor to send representatives to Lhasa. There were
to be no scientific missions (which had sometimes been a cover for
intrigue) for three years. Britain engaged not to change the status
of Afghanistan, while Russia accepted that it lay outside her sphere
of interest. The Amir's consent was assumed, though it took an
expedition in 1908 to convince him of the desirability of these
arrangements.

Reception of the convention was mixed. There was no opposition
from Berlin or Vienna; Paris was warmly congratulatory. Press
reactions were much less favourable, particularly in Russian and
British nationalist organs. The German press was critical in tone,
unlike the official reaction. In both London and St Petersburg there
was much satisfaction. Edward VII told Nicolson that the convention
was 'a great triumph for British diplomacy'.[98] Most of the Cabinet
were pleased, though there were doubts among the Radical wing.
Opinion within the Foreign Office was favourable. The Tsar
believed a good bargain had been struck, though the military party
was displeased. In Persia opinion was very hostile and Spring Rice

reported widespread fear of a formal partition. There was a notable lack of enthusiasm at Simla.

British objections to the treaty took both a general and a particular form. The general objection had already been made during the course of negotiations and had as its central theme the dangers of entering into an agreement with Russia. Particular objections were made to the details of the convention and to the agreement's place in British arrangements for the Far East. Curzon led the attack, arguing that 'whatever may be the ultimate effects produced, we have thrown away to a large extent the efforts of our diplomacy and our trade for more than a century; and I do not feel at all sure that this treaty in its Persian aspect will conduce either to the security of India, to the independence of Persia or to the peace of Asia'.[99] Minto, Spring Rice and the vast majority of those concerned with Indian and Persian affairs concurred. Fitzmaurice, who put the case for the government in the House of Lords, and Grey, in the House of Commons, made a poor showing. It was left to Lansdowne and Sanderson, neither of whom were government spokesmen, to put the case satisfactorily. Lansdowne thought 'we are justified in regarding this as denoting a fundamental change in the Asiatic policy of Russia'.[100] Sanderson argued that 'It is an endeavour on the part of two Great Western Powers most interested in Asia to put aside small jealousies and suspicions, to come to an agreement on points on which there is danger of conflicting policies, and to work together in the cause of progress and civilization'.[101] These views were, perhaps, optimistic, but carried greater weight than those of the official spokesmen.

There was much greater criticism of the details of the convention, especially in regard to Persia. Many M.P.s, both Conservative and Radical, felt that the Persians had been sold into Russian bondage and that Britain would not profit from the deal as Russia would dishonour the agreement as soon as it suited her to do so. Spring Rice, a few weeks before the signature of the convention, had argued, 'If he [Grey] can get *real* agreement with Russia it is well worth sacrificing Persia—though I doubt whether a great country can afford to be mean even in the smallest things'.[102] Curzon was more positive in his estimate of the consequences: 'I do venture to say

that it ought to be one of the cardinal features of our policy . . . to
avoid any attitude or any policy which would be capable of arousing
the suspicion that we were in the least degree indifferent to the
interests of or careless about the future of Mahomedan countries or
institutions'.[103] The Radical group within the Liberal Party was
convinced that British policy would lead to the betrayal of the
constitutional party in Persia and, for once, found common ground
with the former Viceroy's view that 'I am almost astounded at the
coolness, I might even say the effrontery, with which the British
Government is in the habit of parcelling out the territory of Powers
whose independence and integrity it assures them at the same time
it has no other intention than to preserve'.[104] Grey could find no
reply to most of this criticism. Indeed, in a letter to Nicolson he
had already admitted that 'We shall have to keep the Russians up
to the spirit of the Agreement in dealing with their local agents'.[105]

Opinion amongst the Conservatives and Radicals that the agreements of 1904 and 1907 were not entirely comparable was correct.
It was true that the convention's value would largely depend upon
the spirit of interpretation, but there were far more important questions left unanswered in 1907 than in 1904. Despite Grey's claims,
it seems unlikely that the Conservatives would have signed a similar
instrument. Two key problems had been dodged. Russian recognition of British interests in the Gulf was not formally defined, so no
guarantee could be invoked in case of argument. Secondly, what
was to be Britain's attitude when Russia raised the matter of unfettered access to the Mediterranean? The readiness to consider that
'closing of [the] Straits is no longer [a] cardinal point of British
policy'[106] hardly coincided with the Admiralty's Mediterranean
strategy. Nor was it clear how Britain could avoid conflict with
Turkey if Russian demands were conceded. Grey certainly placed
a great deal of faith in the good intentions of Russia, thus giving
weight to the accusation that he had always wanted a Russian
alliance. Radical suspicions were so strong that perhaps they justified
Dilke's insistence in 1905 on staying 'outside the next Government
to kill . . . the deal with Russia'.[107] The failure of the opponents of
the convention was the result of the lack of options open to Britain
rather than the positive virtues of the bargain. Grey himself observed,

'People here do not think that the Convention, as an isolated bargain, is a good one; but they will be pleased if it leads to a generally friendly attitude of Russia towards us'.[108]

In the Far East the conclusion of the 1907 convention initiated a period of change in Anglo-Japanese relations. The price paid for the Japanese guarantee of India had been a free hand for Japan in Manchuria. After 1909, however, the interests of the two powers seemed increasingly divergent. British commercial interests began to complain about Japanese tariffs and Tokyo's monopolistic designs in an area in which Britain was committed to the principle of the 'open door'. Britain and the United States began to draw closer together, for there were no major points of incompatibility between them. British anxiety to conclude an arbitration treaty with the United States obliged her to support American claims to a right to trade in Manchuria and to become ever more hesitant in her support for Japanese policy, which now seemed to threaten the integrity of China.

To the Japanese the alliance of 1905 began to seem increasingly one-sided. Japanese expansionism, like that of Russia before, aimed at the break-up of China. Britain, on the other hand, favoured a conservative policy. It was inevitable that Russia and Japan should draw closer together and in early 1910 Izvolsky proposed 'maintenance of the *status quo* in Manchuria, the definite demarcation of the special Russian and Japanese interests and their protection against aggression on the part of a third power'.[109] On 4 July an agreement was signed: on 29 August Japan annexed Korea. British dependence on Japan to shoulder the burden of the defence of her Far Eastern interests inhibited protest. But within Britain there were growing doubts about the desirability of the alliance, particularly within the Foreign Office, the Admiralty and the China lobby. The two bases of Grey's policy—the preservation of the integrity of China and friendship with Japan—no longer seemed easily reconcilable.

By early 1911 criticism of the alliance had turned from a trickle into a torrent. Rumbold, then counsellor at the embassy in Tokyo, believed it had now served its purpose and should be abandoned, arguing 'The very argument used in our country in favour of the alliance, i.e. that we are able to withdraw our ships from the Far East to Home waters, is, to my mind, an argument against the alliance for we ought not to neglect our interests in the Far East, which are enormous. We ought to keep a strong fleet out here—alliance or no alliance'.[110] There was much support for this view, but it overlooked one essential fact—Britain no longer had sufficient resources to be powerful everywhere. Local interests admittedly were strong, but were they important enough to justify major sacrifices in security elsewhere? In the frenzied atmosphere of the naval scares Grey would have found it politically as well as financially impossible to convince his colleagues that Britain should either shift naval forces from home waters to the Far East or expand the naval building programme still further.

It was quite clear that the agreement of 1905 was no longer satisfactory and in 1911 negotiations for a revision began. Grey was confronted with a thorny task for, in addition to all his other problems, he had to face increasing pressure from the Dominions. Australia and New Zealand, giving advance warning of the robust nationalism which was afterwards to be such a prominent feature of their foreign policies, were particularly critical of three aspects of the existing alliance. The Pacific powers' objections were three-fold: the possible threat to their security from an expansionist Japan, dislike of Japanese immigration and the danger to their trade. Fisher too was opposed to the alliance, which he described as 'the very worst thing that England ever did for herself!'.[111] All these matters were discussed during the Imperial Conference in London in the summer of 1911, particularly at the C.I.D. meeting of 26 May. Grey contrived to overcome Dominion opposition, though only at the price of an agreement to differ, and a renewal of the alliance was reluctantly accepted as necessary.

A revised agreement was signed on 13 July 1911, to operate for ten years. The principal new features involved the removal of the anti-Russian clauses, thus greatly pleasing St Petersburg, and acceptance of the notion that neither Britain nor Japan would be obliged to go to war in support of its ally if conflict took place with a power with which either party had concluded an arbitration treaty. This provision greatly reassured Grey, who was trying to conclude such a treaty with the United States. The renewal was badly received in China, but was believed by Russia to help the interests of her European ally, France. Benckendorff, the Russian Ambassador, correctly assessed the importance of renewal: 'Since the coming into force of the Anglo-Japanese naval treaty, England has been able considerably to reduce her naval forces in the Far East and to strengthen her fleet in like measure in European waters. Through this England possessed an important guarantee for the maintenance of peace in the Far East, and has been enabled to strengthen her naval forces where they might eventually be needed'.[112]

Unfortunately, the years 1911–14 showed that the doubts felt about the alliance were well founded. The outbreak of revolution in China in October 1911 gave Tokyo an opportunity to promote Japanese interests in conditions of internal chaos. Japanese policy revived British fears as to her security in the Yangtze valley and relations grew more strained. In 1913 Grey was informed that 'We have no idea what the real intentions of the Japanese are with regard to China',[113] though these were by this time obvious enough. The following year Japanese pressure was so plainly detrimental to British interests that Grey was obliged to assert a claim to 'a privileged position in that part of the Yangtze Valley where [H.M.G.'s] interests are predominant' and resolved 'to assert [their] claim against all powers whose nationals may apply for concessions in that region'.[114] The wheel had turned full circle; it was now the Japanese who had taken up Russia's former rôle as bogeyman in China. With Europe now the main focus of Russian interest and attention the *raison d'être* of the alliance had gone and the outbreak of war merely postponed open diplomatic conflict between the allies of 1902.

In the Near East and in India the relief from Russian pressure was also a mixed blessing. The problem of Afghanistan still remained unsolved, though Tibet was quiet. In India itself attention was focused on internal political development. A government reshuffle in November 1910 brought Crewe to the India Office and Hardinge to Simla as Viceroy. Although Hardinge's term witnessed the apogee of British rule—the Coronation Durbar of 1911—it also marked the start of its decline. The old obsession of an external threat to Indian security was replaced by a new concern for internal stability. Riots, attempted assassinations and widespread political violence reinforced these fears. The inconsistencies of British policy could no longer be concealed and had a great impact upon British prestige. Internal security made it necessary for Hardinge to appease the Hindus, but wider imperial interests suggested concessions to the Muslims. Free from the Russian threat for the first time in fifty years divisions within Indian society suddenly threatened the security of the Raj. The opponents of the 1907 convention were not surprised.

In Persia the convention was a dead letter almost from the start. It was in British interests to promote stability in the whole area of the Gulf. This aim hardly coincided with that of the Russian Minister to Teheran, Hartwig, who was an expansionist of the old school. In conjunction with the Shah he endeavoured to overthrow the constitutional movement, thus inaugurating a period of unrest lasting from 1908 to 1912. Representations at St Petersburg had little effect except the transfer of Hartwig to Belgrade, where he promptly set about disturbing Balkan stability and encouraging Pan-Slav movements. His successor, Poklewsky, tried to advance Russian claims to Northern Persia and introduced Russian troops, thus violating the convention, opening the way for intervention by other powers and greatly embarrassing London. Nicolson, the new Permanent Under-Secretary, reacted feebly. Anxiety to remain on good terms with Russia led him to assert that criticism of her rôle was 'based on prejudices and false assumptions'.[115] This was a perfect description of his own attitude.

In an attempt to escape from these difficulties Britain suggested the appointment of an independent financial adviser to Persia. The choice fell on a young American, Morgan Shuster, who swiftly endeared himself to the Persians by denouncing the 1907 convention. British sympathy for the constitutional movement made Barclay, Minister to Teheran, reluctant to act against Shuster. Russia, however, immediately gave support to an attempted coup by the ex-Shah, whom Shuster described as 'the most perverted, cowardly and vice-sodden monster that has disgraced the throne of Persia in many generations'.[116] Russia demanded Shuster's expulsion, to which Britain was reluctantly compelled to agree; even Nicolson admitted 'it will be difficult for us to defend the Russian action in Parliament as the Russians . . . have not got a strong case'.[117] Sazonov, the Russia Foreign Minister, then laid claim to rights of occupation in Northern Persia. Grey was appalled, knowing that British public opinion would not tolerate such a concession. On 2 December 1911 he summoned Benckendorff and told him he could not defend this action without 'the whole question of Foreign Policy of both Govts'[118] being reviewed. In those circumstances he would leave revision 'to someone else'.[119] Sazonov gave way, realizing that the understanding was at risk. In early 1912 Shuster left Persia and the crisis passed. Damage to smooth relations had been serious; Grey observed that 'Recent events have made people here feel that Russian methods are not our methods'.[120] Nicolson took sick leave to recover from the strain and never regained his earlier faith in Russian benevolence.

In the decade preceding 1914 Persian and Mesopotamian affairs played a prominent part in exacerbating relations between Britain, Russia and Germany. Increasing German influence in the Ottoman Empire made Britain fear for her interests in the Gulf. The German-backed project of the Bagdad Railway encountered stiff opposition from London and St Petersburg. Russian opposition was based upon belief that improved communications in the region could only strengthen a traditional enemy. Izvolsky's definition of the problem in 1909 was unambiguous: 'The political, strategical, and economic meaning of the Bagdad Railroad . . . has already been carefully examined; our standpoint remains the same; the construction of the railroad will have unfortunate results for us, and we must take precautions to weaken their effects'.[121] The basis of British hostility was both economic and strategic. Discovery of oil fields at Mosul provided new trading opportunities for British commerce at a time when greater German competitiveness threatened established British positions throughout the Middle East. The Foreign Office did not intend to permit a successful penetration of the British sphere of influence and sought to mobilize Russia and France against Germany. Strategic considerations were also important. In 1911 George Lloyd, a Conservative M.P., asserted 'every nation that had lost its paramount position in the Persian Gulf had also very soon lost its paramount position in India'.[122] This belief was echoed in Germany where Jäckh, the eminent orientalist, considered 'Britain led and organized this opposition because she feared that India and Egypt were threatened by the Bagdad Railway'.[123]

At the turn of the century opinion was divided as to the danger to British hegemony in the Gulf. Curzon advocated annexation of most of the coastline and prohibition of foreign railroads: 'A Russian railway ending at Koweit would be in the highest degree injurious to British interests. A German railway to Koweit would be scarcely less so—even a Turkish railway to Koweit would be unwelcome. Any one of these would challenge our hitherto uncontested supremacy in the Gulf, and would turn those waters into a sort of mid-Asian Gulf of Pechili.'[124] Salisbury was as anxious to check Germany and Russia but did not support a 'forward' policy. However, on 23 January 1899 Britain concluded a treaty with Kuwait which irrevocably committed her to an active policy in the region, much to the distaste of Berlin and the Porte. There was still no official hostility towards German attempts to penetrate Turkey by economic means— in 1902, for example, Percy argued that 'Germany is doing for Turkey what we have been doing for Persia'.[125]

The change in tone came in 1903. Negotiations between the Anatolian Railway Company (a German-backed enterprise) and the Ottoman Empire gave the company major concessions, including rights to a railhead on the Persian border. The following decade witnessed a prolonged dispute between the three major powers interested in the region. Germany sought capital to build her railway, Russia continued attempts to exclude other powers and Britain took refuge in stalling tactics, inadvertently aided by the rusty machinery of Ottoman administration. A whole series of negotiations foundered on the powers' incompatible demands. The fall of Abdul Hamid II and the establishment of the Young Turk government, during 1908–09, at first injured but later increased German influence at Constantinople. British fears that the Turkish government was merely an agent of Berlin were intensified as she became increasingly involved in Gulf politics. In Britain criticism of the Anglo-Russian convention mounted. Ronaldshay picked on the convention's essential weakness: 'If the Government thought by this somewhat Machiavellian policy of "scotching" the ambition of

Germany by introducing Russia they were going to benefit Great
Britain they were grievously mistaken'.[126] Britain was on the
defensive in Persia, being unable to control Russia, and had incurred
German and Turkish enmity by her ill-starred manoeuvres there
and in Mesopotamia. So incensed was Turkey at British usurpations
in the Gulf that she even encouraged Kurdish raids on Persia.

In 1909 Bethmann Hollweg, the new Chancellor, sought to make
an arrangement with Britain which would encompass both Persia
and Mesopotamia. Grey was not averse to this plan and in early 1910
serious, but fruitless, discussions took place. The principal reasons
for the breakdown of talks lay outside their subject matter—in the
permanent officials' hostility to Germany and German refusal to
limit naval armaments—but British determination to press for full
internationalization of the Bagdad Railway or its sectionalization
into national areas of control did not smooth negotiations. British
demands for control over the Gulf section were unacceptable to
Berlin. As Britain was now in dispute with both Russia and Germany
it seemed sensible for them to come to terms. In November 1910
the Tsar paid an official visit to the Kaiser at Potsdam. In the
accompanying talks Germany accepted the 1907 convention and
agreed she had no political interests in Persia. In return Russia promised to withdraw objections to the Bagdad Railway and to promote
a link through Persia. A convention was ratified on 19 August 1911.
It was held in strong dislike in London and Paris. Hanotaux suggested
'the negotiations . . . oblige us to ask, now, if Russia has dissolved the
Triple Entente?'[127] A Liberal backbencher, Pickersgill, argued 'This
is a convenient opportunity for edging off from that close co-
operation which had been so mischievous not only in its effects in
Persia, but also in its effects upon European policy'.[128]

The risk of isolation in this region forced Britain to negotiate.
Great progress was made between 1911 and 1914. A complete
settlement of Persian and Mesopotamian questions was reached in
the convention of 15 June 1914. There seems little doubt this would
have contributed greatly to improved Anglo-German relations but
for events at Sarajevo. The convention was never ratified owing
to the outbreak of war and by 1918 the defeat of Turkey and
Germany had completely changed the nature of these questions.

The disputes of 1903–14 had, however, significantly damaged relations with Germany. Within the Foreign Office was an obsessive fear of German intentions. This distrust rubbed off on Grey. The result was that Russian breaches of faith were treated lightly, or even disregarded, while even mild attempts by Germany to promote her Mesopotamian interests were seen as direct threats to Britain's position. Until Russia and Germany reached a *modus vivendi* Britain refused to negotiate seriously; after 1910 she was compelled to do so. There were much better arguments against coming to terms with Germany than those used by Grey and his officials, but these had little impact. George Lloyd trenchantly observed in 1911, 'It cannot be supposed for a moment that a country so weighty in the councils of the world as England can perpetually add to the number of her *ententes* without either weakening them all or without disturbing the balance of power in Europe'.[129] If this argument had been fully discussed in Cabinet and Parliament by Grey, as its importance warranted, then much of the fatal ambiguity of 1914 could hardly have existed.

After 1906 the German problem dominated British foreign policy. Conflicts ranged over Middle Eastern, Mediterranean and colonial problems, as well as naval rivalry. Balkan affairs played little part in exacerbating relations before 1914. Numerous attempts were made to reconcile conflicting viewpoints but none was more than temporarily successful. Certainly one reason for these failures was attitudes prevalent in the Foreign Office and the Wilhelmstrasse. Hardinge, never as anti-German as a majority of his colleagues, pointed out in 1910: 'A general political understanding . . . is out of the question, and really never was feasible'.[130] Bethmann Hollweg, himself no Anglophobe, saw that 'The assimilation of the interests of humanity with those of the British Empire, which is peculiar to English thinkers is, of course, unacceptable to Germans'.[131] These were men who favoured peace and understanding, so it is clear how great was the gulf between the nations.

After the disastrous events at Algeciras a determined attempt to improve relations was made. Edward VII realized how serious was the situation and wrote to the Kaiser in friendly fashion, 'I am most desirous that the feeling between our two countries may be on the best footing'.[132] The Kaiser was pleased by this overture and a meeting was arranged for the summer. Hardinge lent his support to the visit, but Crowe was irreconcilable: 'We were never so badly treated by Germany as in the years when we were always making concessions in order to "gain their real friendship and good-will". They are essentially people whom it does not pay to "run after"'.[133] Haldane, the Secretary for War, supported the King's efforts, thus dealing a serious blow to the anti-German party. Much British resentment against Germany stemmed from naval programmes undertaken since 1898, so Haldane's decision undermined the arguments of those who opposed *détente*. Campbell-Bannerman, an inveterate lover of peace, was anxious to secure an Anglo-German *entente* to match the agreement of 1904. Pressure was put on Grey to urge France to improve relations with Germany, but the Foreign Secretary preferred to rely on his officials' advice. This obduracy rendered the visit of August 1906 sterile, despite Fitzmaurice's optimism that 'Things are certainly better than they were—nevertheless the anti-German current in the Office still flows, though it has been checked'.[134] The meeting itself went well and Hardinge came away convinced that Germany had abandoned the idea of destroying the *entente* and now wished to be part of a triple partnership of western powers. But Hardinge, despite his position, was not the strongest influence on Grey. Mallet, Bertie and Crowe were unconvinced. Bertie observed that he 'thought better of Hardinge's intelligence';[135] thus putting an end to their co-operation. There was thus an insufficiency of unity and purpose within the Foreign Office to push through a sensible programme of proposals which could form the basis of a serious negotiation with Germany. Grey's obsession with preserving French friendship at any cost was, therefore, the deciding factor which killed the initiative.

Dissension within the Foreign Office was complicated by anti-German pressures from outside the service. The press in both Britain and Germany was often rabidly nationalistic. In London it was known that governmental influence on the German press had been strong in Bismarck's day and it was assumed that this influence still existed, so any rabid outburst was viewed as an inspired leak emanating from the Wilhelmstrasse. Crowe put the point succinctly: 'If any importance . . . is to be attributed to the German press, it is only insofar as it is manipulated and influenced by the official Press Bureau, a branch of the Chancellor's office at Berlin'.[136] Lascelles disagreed, arguing, 'When I first came to Berlin eleven years ago, I was told that the attitude of an ordinary German in reading a newspaper was to ask whether the statements contained in it were official. If the answer was in the affirmative, he would read it with attention and respect; if in the negative, he would attach but little importance to what he read. Now, anything published by authority is received with suspicion and closely criticised, and constant attacks have been made in newspapers, which might be expected to support the authorities, not only against the action of the Government, but also against the person of the Emperor'.[137] In Germany there was similar suspicion that the attitudes of the British press were derived from the Foreign Office. The rôle of *The Times* was critical, particularly when its coverage was dominated by the anti-German reports of Chirol, Moberly Bell and Saunders. As has been shown by Zara Steiner, '*The Times*, of course, remained in a very special position. Despite repeated disclaimers from the Foreign Office, it was treated, both at home and abroad, as a semi-official newspaper'.[138]

Another problem which continued to vex Anglo-German relations was that of naval rivalry. In January 1906 the question was given a new twist by the decision to proceed with the Cawdor Programme of 1905, thus fundamentally altering British naval strategy. Pressure from the Radicals for a reduction in defence expenditure was later to produce a cut in the programme (and thus to make a major contribution to the naval scare of 1908–09) but did not invalidate the strategic assumptions behind the construction of big ships. If Fisher believed that 'Our present margin of superiority over Germany . . . is so great as to render it absurd in the extreme to talk of anything endangering our naval supremacy',[139] his views were not shared by the vigorous propagandists of the big ship programme. However, the change in naval building rendered much of the British fleet obsolete, so if Germany started a similar programme she might, theoretically, soon catch up. This fear was at the heart of most of the agitation of the next few years. In different ways both the Foreign Office and Admiralty put pressure on the government to maintain a large programme. Tweedmouth argued that 'All governments for the last 21 years have accepted and acted up to the Two-Power Standard and it is not to be lightly abandoned now'.[140] Hardinge's view was that 'supremacy at sea is a condition which must be regarded as an absolute *sine qua non*'.[141] In this atmosphere it was plain that a strong response to extension of the German naval programmes under the laws of 1906 and 1908 was inevitable.

Despite these unpromising circumstances a combination of factors pushed Britain and Germany towards further attempts to reconcile differences or, at least, produce a *détente*. The more radical elements within the Cabinet, notably Bryce, Loreburn, Morley and Campbell-Bannerman, favoured both reconciliation and a reduction in naval estimates; Asquith, as Chancellor of the Exchequer, was understandably anxious to save money. The year 1907 seemed propitious for agreement. During June–October the Second Hague Conference was in session and the government hoped that arms limitation might be discussed seriously with beneficial results for relations with Germany. Furthermore the overt truculence of the anti-German party had alarmed others within the Foreign Office and Cabinet. In his memorandum of 1 January 1907 Eyre Crowe had delivered a stinging broadside against Germany and her methods, likening her to 'a professional blackmailer, whose extortions are wrung from his victims by the threat of some vague and dreadful consequences in case of a refusal'.[142] Sanderson had produced a more balanced analysis, arguing that 'Germany is a helpful, though somewhat exacting, friend . . . a tight and tenacious bargainer, and a most disagreeable antagonist'.[143] Sanderson's attitude seemed in early 1907 the much more sensible.

In April 1907 Campbell-Bannerman visited France and had long and alarming discussions with Clemenceau. He was questioned in detail concerning British obligations to France in the event of war, and was pressed so hard that he told Clemenceau, 'The sentiments of the English people would be totally averse to any troops being landed by England on the continent under any circumstances'.[144] Clemenceau feared the *entente* was at an end and only the fullest assurances of Grey and Bertie that Campbell-Bannerman had not meant what he had said satisfied the French leader. But the Prime Minister was now at least partially aware of the danger of the naval and military conversations and consequently turned towards trying to improve Anglo-German relations. In this he was supported by Haldane who was influenced not only by his education but also by the success of his reorganization of defence. His emphasis on the necessity of flexibility thus made him hostile to Grey's notions of commitment to France.

It proved, however, quite difficult to improve relations with Germany. On 16 May 1907 Britain and France announced their preference for maintenance of the *status quo* in the Mediterranean and those parts of the littoral of Africa and Europe washed by the Atlantic. This agreement followed visits by Edward VII to the Kings of Spain and Italy the previous month and gave the impression of a calculated and well-organized snub to Germany's known pretensions in North Africa. The *Neue Freie Presse* even argued that Edward VII was campaigning against Germany and was engaged in a 'continual political labour, carried on with open recklessness, whose object is to put a close ring round Germany'.[145] Despite this unpromising start both Hardinge and Haldane continued to support in the teeth of Grey's opposition, the idea of a visit by the Kaiser during which some of the difficulties in Anglo-German relations could be discussed. His visit in November 1907 did lead to an agreement to discuss the Bagdad Railway *à quatre*. This success, however, paled into insignificance beside failure to resolve the questions of naval rivalry and arms limitation. At the Hague Conference the German delegation repeatedly threw cold water on the idea of arms limitation, thus earning their country much unfavourable comment in the world's press. Bülow was determined to play the rôle of the iron Chancellor: 'I had, of course, never any thought of sacrificing the safety of the country to the sanctimonious assurances of our enemies and of those who coveted our good fortune to the hollow phrasemongering of unsophisticated, and occasionally dishonest, fanatics'.[146] Many other politicians, including Roosevelt, Bourgeois and Grey, certainly agreed with Bülow, but were prudent enough to allow the burden of public disapproval to fall on Germany. Hope of a naval agreement was dashed by the German decision on 12 December 1907 to replace battleships after twenty instead of twenty-five years. This convinced the Admiralty that Germany was hoping to erode British naval superiority by effectively speeding up her building programme.

1908 witnessed the further strains in Anglo-German relations. At first prospects for agreement were good. In April Asquith replaced Campbell-Bannerman as Prime Minister and in the Cabinet re-shuffle which followed the radical elements significantly increased their influence. Lloyd George, Churchill and McKenna all favoured a limited naval programme and their views were echoed in the Liberal press. Following a visit to the Tsar at Reval, which had occasioned bitter murmurs of 'encirclement' in Berlin, Edward VII and Hardinge met the Kaiser at Cronberg in August. The visit was a disaster because William II refused to discuss seriously the vital question of naval limitation, taking refuge in generalities about Germany's sovereign right to build a large navy. Indeed in a comment made only a month before he had asserted 'I have no wish for good relations with England at the price of the development of the German navy. If England offers friendship on condition that we limit our navy it is unbounded impertinence and a gross insult . . . and must be rejected'.[147] Thereafter the British were reluctant to probe such an obviously sore point and the chances of understanding diminished with the passage of time. William II's conversation with Hardinge also damaged relations in a more subtle but equally significant fashion. The Permanent Under-Secretary was treated to an exhibition of the Kaiser at his hectoring worst and his earlier goodwill towards Germany decreased sharply. Characteristically, the Kaiser believed that his had been a personal triumph and a course of action to be recommended for future use.

William II's diplomatic forays proved ill-starred in even more spectacular fashion with the publication in *The Daily Telegraph* on 28 October of his interview with Stuart Wortley. The Kaiser hoped that some plain speaking might further 'the cause of good Anglo-German understanding'.[148] Instead, he contrived to enrage opinion in both countries. Bülow described his monarch's efforts as 'sad effusions which could scarcely have been surpassed in tactless stupidity'[149] and in Germany the nationalist press was incensed at the Kaiser's avowed English sympathies. In the British press, however, William II's *démarche* was widely regarded as a cunning subterfuge to conceal his country's anti-British machinations. Unfortunately, the only remark made to Wortley which was generally remembered was that the majority of the German people were very hostile to Britain, so good relations were hardly promoted. The Kaiser's observation that the greatest friends of Britain were in official circles was almost certainly false. In the opinion of Findlay, Minister at Dresden, 'the situation is exactly the contrary to what His Majesty believes it to be, i.e. the majority of the lower classes are well disposed towards Great Britain. The majority of the official educational and journalistic classes, together with a considerable contingent of commercial men and military officers are hostile'.[150] Bülow, however, deserved as much censure as the Kaiser; as Chancellor he failed signally to control this propensity to personal diplomacy. On occasions he seemed, for reasons of internal politics, almost to encourage his monarch. As long ago as 1906 Tyrrell had argued that 'The real cancer at Berlin is Bülow, who lacks all moral sense in no ordinary degree. I despair of decent relations with Germany as long as he has a finger in the pie'.[151] This was pertinent criticism indeed.

These events were, however, by no means the most critical in Anglo-German relations in 1908. One of the major problems was German fear of isolation and encirclement. There was certainly no 'Anglo-Franco-Russian agreement'[152] of the kind feared in Berlin, but belief in its existence led to some strange actions by Germany designed to break up the supposed alliance. Unfortunately for Germany these actions were seen in London, Paris and St Petersburg as part of a co-ordinated plan of attack on their *ententes*. The overall effect, therefore, as at Algeciras, was to strengthen understanding rather than weaken it. A typical example was provided by Bülow's provocative handling of a trivial dispute with France over an incident in Casablanca. The matter was easily settled in February 1909, but not before the diplomatic temperature had risen sharply. The Crown Prince of Germany asserted that 'The French are really trying to find out how far they can tax our patience, our love of peace'.[153] Grey even advised McKenna, 'I think the Admiralty should keep in readiness to make preparations in case Germany sent France an ultimatum and the Cabinet decided that we must assist France'.[154] Germany was the loser from these exchanges and even her ally, Austria, hoped that 'frictions between Berlin and London will not be allowed to affect the relations between Austria-Hungary and England'.[155]

The Balkan crisis of 1908–09 was even more serious in its effects. It was engineered by the fitful and erratic genius of the Foreign Ministers of Austria and Russia, Aehrenthal and Izvolsky. In January 1908 Aehrenthal secured permission from the Porte to build a railway through the Sanjak of Novi-Bazar. It was widely, though incorrectly, assumed that Germany was behind this move and that it was part of a larger scheme of strategic penetration of the Balkans. There was immediate reaction among Pan-Slav elements in St Petersburg and Izvolsky became anxious to obtain a compensation for Russia. He conceived the notion of obtaining Great Power agreement to the opening of the Straits to Russian warships, though this was bound to meet with a cool reception in London and Paris. In July Abdul Hamid II was overthrown and the Young Turks came to power, thus convincing London that Turkey was at last set on a liberal and constitutional path. Britain thus became very reluctant to entertain proposals which could only weaken the new régime. In despair Izvolsky sought Austrian support in return for acceptance of Austrian annexation of Bosnia-Herzegovina. Abdul Hamid's fall had created uncertainty in Aehrenthal's mind as to Austria's future position in the provinces, for it seemed possible that a reformed Turkey would resume the control surrendered in 1878. He therefore met Izvolsky in talks at Buchlau on 15 September. Quite what was decided has never been satisfactorily resolved, but on 6 October Austria annexed Bosnia-Herzegovina.

Izvolsky soon realized that the security of his agreement was illusory. Britain would agree only to a full opening of the Straits, a concession which would have endangered Russian security in the Black Sea. Furthermore, Austrian actions had excited bitter feelings in Russia and Izvolsky's domestic position was put under some strain.

He switched to a strongly anti-Austrian position, in which he had support from Paris and London, both of which were displeased with the revival of Balkan squabbles. Britain took a harsh line on the annexation, much to Aehrenthal's surprise, and this helped Germany formulate her position. Initially William II was very irritated with Austria's action, but Bülow persuaded him to support Aehrenthal no matter what the cost either to German influence in Turkey or to relations with Britain and Russia. For the Chancellor Austria had become the indispensable ally.

The first phase of the crisis thus had the effect of pushing Germany and Austria closer. There was no such unanimity among the *entente* powers. Grey would offer Izvolsky nothing of significance, telling him 'I positively desire to see an arrangement made, which will open the Straits on terms which would be acceptable to Russia and to the riverain States of the Black Sea, while not placing Turkey or outside Powers at an unfair disadvantage. Some such arrangement seems to me essential to the permanent establishment of goodwill between Russia and ourselves'.[156] This was elegantly phrased moonshine—of no use to a man fighting for his political life. Izvolsky then fell back on an international conference to ratify the annexation and to provide Russia with suitable compensation. Britain and France were ready to accept this; so too was Austria, for Aehrenthal realized that it would merely lead to acceptance of his *fait accompli*. Germany, however, killed the notion of a conference for reasons which had little, if anything, to do with Balkan politics. Indeed, Berlin had had little sympathy for Aehrenthal's adventure, but now sought to turn the crisis to her own advantage.

The second phase of the crisis witnessed an attempt by Germany to punish Russia for her temerity in coming to terms with Britain in 1907. More particularly the visit of Edward VII to Reval was resented and seen, as in the case of the more celebrated trip to Paris, as the beginning of a real Anglo-Russian understanding which would transcend the business arrangement of 1907. In effect German policy reverted to that of 1891 and the new course—of unquestioning support for Austria. But the aims of Bülow and Tirpitz were much larger—the destruction of Anglo-Russian understanding. Bülow made this crystal clear in his memorandum of 27 October: 'Ever

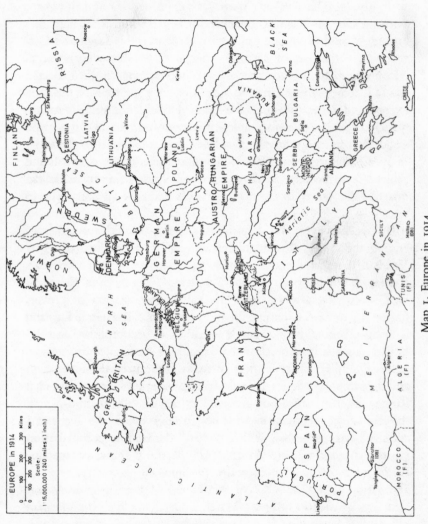

Map 1. Europe in 1914

since Russia became openly linked to England at Reval, we could not give up Austria. The European situation was so changed thereby that we were compelled to be more reserved to Russian wishes than formerly.'[157] The Russians were very depressed by and displeased with the German attitude. Benckendorff even asked what England's attitude would be 'supposing a crisis arose in the Balkans and Germany took the part of Austria as her ally'.[158] Grey was not at all encouraging, telling the ambassador 'it was not to be expected that a Cabinet would come to a decision on a question of this kind except under the pressure of a crisis. I could not submit such a question to my colleagues unless it became urgent: and it was no good for me to say anything unless I was authorized to do so by them.'[159] Reports from Paris told Izvolsky the same tale—a profound reluctance to become involved in war because of a trivial Balkan quarrel. The falsity of German fears was plain for all but Berlin to see.

Bülow, however, was determined to press on with the policy of ending the Anglo-Russian understanding. In a letter to the Tsar William II referred to 'the patent fact that for the last two years Russian policy has been gradually drawing away from us more and more; evolving always closer towards a combination of powers unfriendly to us. A triple entente between France, Russia and England is being talked of by the whole world as an accomplished fact'.[160] In early 1909 it became clear that Izvolsky's conference project had failed. On 26 February Turkey formally recognized the annexation and the same day the French told Izvolsky that in their opinion vital Russian interests were not involved in the dispute. In mid-March the Russian government decided not to intervene in the event of a conflict between Serbia, which was still demanding compensation for the annexation, and Austria. All that now remained was for Russia to acknowledge formally the annexation and accept the abrogation of Article XXV of the Treaty of Berlin. Izvolsky was reluctant so to do but on 21 March Pourtalès delivered a German ultimatum demanding 'a precise answer—yes or no—any evasive, complicated or unclear answer will be regarded as a refusal'.[161] Izvolsky was forced to surrender. Kiderlen Wächter, who had replaced Holstein, had obtained a signal victory. But, as in the case of Holstein's victory over Delcassé, this triumph was to have far-reaching consequences.

The hard line taken by Germany during the crisis of 1908–09 sounded a tocsin in the Foreign Office, where feeling grew that Germany was making a bid for control of Europe and that to resist these ambitions Britain would need to combine with other powers. Nicolson was soon committed to an anti-German policy. On 24 March he wrote to Grey urging him to seek a firm alliance with Russia and France: 'When we have passed through the present "Sturm und Drang" period, I should not be surprised if we were to find both France and Russia gravitating rapidly towards the Central Powers, as neither of the former, distrustful of each other, feels that she can stand alone against the power of the central combination. Our Entente, I much fear, will languish and possibly die. If it were possible to extend and strengthen it by bringing it nearer to the nature of an alliance, it would then be possible to deter Russia from moving towards Berlin'.[162] Grey was much less enthusiastic, replying, 'the feeling here about definite commitments to a continental war on unforeseeable conditions would be too dubious to permit us to make an alliance'.[163] Politicians and officials were no longer in step. Within the Liberal Party a strong group opposed any further extension of British commitments, particularly to Tsarist Russia. The views of Dilke were not unrepresentative of this group; on 22 July 1909 he told the House, 'the policy into which we had been drawn by M. Izvolski had been damaging to our interests, not only because it had strengthened the ties between the members of the Triple Alliance, but because it assisted the popularity in Germany of a naval rivalry, which oppressed us with the cost of ever-increased armaments at sea'.[164] Grey was obliged to take note of these and similar opinions and the alliance project fell into disfavour.

One outcome of the Balkan crisis was increased Anglo-German naval rivalry. Despite a visit by Edward VII to Berlin in February 1909, during which it was announced that all difficulties between Germany and Britain had been solved, matters were too serious to be settled by talks between monarchs. Indeed 1909 witnessed a further deterioration in relations. During the years since 1906

Campbell-Bannerman and then Asquith had reduced the government's commitment to the Cawdor Programme, but in late 1908 news of German naval construction created panic in the Admiralty. German actions in the Balkan crisis had created an atmosphere of suspicion which was turned to advantage by those who favoured British naval expansion. Grey was instructed to broach the subject with Metternich, and in a singularly unsuccessful interview it was made plain that Germany had no intention of limiting her construction programme. McKenna, Grey and the other ministers favouring increased naval expenditure were thus able to carry a reluctant Cabinet with them. On 14 March the naval estimates were published, allowing for four new dreadnoughts and the possibility of four more by the end of 1909. Agitation for immediate construction of all eight began and, in the face of overwhelming pressure from the Admiralty, the Conservative Opposition, the press, some members of the Cabinet, and the public, Asquith's government agreed on 16 July to the full programme. What was particularly injurious to Anglo-German relations was British justification of the new programme in terms which openly accepted that the government's major concern was to keep ahead of German naval construction. Henceforth this assumption was to be the guiding principle of naval policy. It was bound to have, and did have, serious diplomatic repercussions.

Bülow, belatedly, was greatly alarmed. He was anxious to assuage British feelings and readily accepted Kiderlen Wächter's argument that there should be talks between the powers. Goschen, the new Ambassador to Berlin, believed there was much more to German proposals than first met the eye. In a letter of 16 April he told Grey 'it is my impression that the only kind of understanding really wished for by Germany is one which would clear the way to her becoming the sole arbiter of the destinies of Europe and relieve her from all anxiety with regard to her only vulnerable side—the sea'.[165] Comments on Goschen's despatch (by Grey, Hardinge, Campbell, Crowe and Spicer), showed how widely these fears were shared. Nevertheless, it was decided that a frank exchange of views on naval questions could hardly harm Anglo-German relations. However, negotiations were never started. Powerful groups in Germany were hostile to any notion of concession. Indeed Bülow's and Metternich's pleas for negotiation led to resignation of the one and eclipse of the other's influence. Tirpitz and his party won the day. The Kaiser obstinately refused to recognize the risks attached to this policy, arguing that 'England ... has made no single honest suggestion for binding negotiations between equals, but has tried, in an informal and underhand fashion, to corner us and prevent us from building'.[166] No compromise between the German and British viewpoints was possible.

In the summer of 1909 Bülow was replaced as Chancellor by Bethmann Hollweg. The new Chancellor was peace-loving by temperament and fearful of the consequences of allowing Tirpitz to dictate German policy towards Britain. But he was also reluctant to take the initiative in controlling the anti-British group. In 1912 he wrote that 'The whole policy is of a sort that I cannot co-operate with it. But I ask myself again and again whether the situation will not develop even more dangerously if I go and then probably not alone'.[167] Bethmann Hollweg never succeeded in escaping from the chains with which he bound himself at the moment of acceptance of office. His goodwill and pacific intentions availed little.

The years 1909–14 witnessed a deadlock in Anglo-German relations, for the question of naval rivalry was never satisfactorily answered. Negotiations continued in desultory fashion. In October 1909 Berlin suggested that a delay in the tempo of naval construction might be conceded in return for a political bargain. This was rejected on the grounds that the German proposals effectively involved the destruction of the *entente*. The Germans could not understand Grey's view that 'a general understanding would have no beneficial effect whatever on public opinion, and would indeed be an object of criticism, so long as naval expenditure remained undiminished'.[168] The German quest for general agreement and British anxiety for a detailed naval settlement remained irreconcilable aims. In 1910 Grey responded to further overtures from Bethmann Hollweg but was obliged to tell him 'there would be difficulty in accepting any formula which would give the impression of an understanding different in kind from that which exists between

His Majesty's Government and any other European Power'.[169] Any anti-German views held by Grey were certainly reinforced by those of Nicolson, who succeeded Hardinge as Permanent Under-Secretary in October 1910. Thus at the heart of policy-making in both Berlin and London there existed powerful cabals unwilling to show flexibility in attitudes towards a suspected and feared rival power.

During 1911 anti-German feeling mounted in Britain, fanned by press campaigns in the *Daily Mail* and Blatchford's *Clarion*. The atmosphere was frenzied. There were rumours of secret weapons possessed by Germany, invasion plans, mass espionage and corruption of those in high places. Even a visit by the Crown Prince at the time of the coronation of George V did not seriously diminish the flood of anti-German propaganda. When it was suggested to Nicolson that the visit might be an opportunity for mending a few fences he is reported to have 'emphatically declared that as long as he was at the head of the Foreign Office, England should never, never be friends with Germany'.[170] Realizing in 1911 that naval estimates were becoming a serious drain on the Exchequer and that a possible amendment of the German Navy Law scheduled for 1912 would put still further strain on the government's budgeting, Asquith was compelled to take a serious view of Anglo-German relations. At this moment two private citizens, Sir Ernest Cassel and Albert Ballin, decided to try to act as intermediaries in an attempt to improve relations. The atmosphere was thus conducive to a renewal of negotiations and in February 1912 Haldane set off for Berlin. Both he and Bethmann Hollweg were anxious for peace and at first discussions went well. Talks with Tirpitz and Kiderlen Wächter were not so fruitful and when Haldane brought back details of the proposed new German Navy Law the Admiralty was horrified by its scope. Despite valiant attempts by Haldane and Metternich discussions first faltered and in the end were halted by German demands which would have led not to a *détente*, which Britain wanted, but fragmentation of the *ententes*, a long-desired aim in Berlin. The Haldane mission proved as abortive as all previous negotiations, though it did lead to an important strategic decision; in February 1913 British and French naval forces were redistributed in such a way as to leave the principal burden of defence in the Channel and North Sea to the Home Fleet. This in turn involved abandoning British control in the Mediterranean and hence made France an essential ally. In practical terms the failure of Haldane's mission strengthened the *entente*.

Naval rivalry was not the only barrier to good relations. Opinion in Britain became increasingly irritated by German ventures in Morocco, a particularly sensitive area after the events of 1905-06 and 1908. The Franco–German agreement of February 1909 proved to be insufficient to restrain the ambitions of those who believed in *Weltpolitik*, especially the advocates of *Mittelafrika* who expected that by putting pressure on France in Morocco gains for Germany could be secured elsewhere in Africa. Despite the miserable economic position of Morocco occasioned by the Sultan's maladministration, it was generally believed in Germany that the *entente* of 1904 and the conference at Algeciras in 1906 had handed a rich prize to France. In April 1911 internal unrest in Morocco compelled France to take action, despite Kiderlen Wächter's warning that occupation of Fez would be deemed a violation of the Algeciras settlement. Both William II and the Chancellor were opposed to a forward policy in Morocco but, as usual, succumbed in the face of pressure by Kiderlen Wächter. On 1 July it was announced that the *Panther* had been sent to Agadir to protect German interests. The rest of the world was amazed, as it was obvious that there were no significant interests to protect. It soon became clear that Germany would relinquish her claims in return for most of the French Congo. The *Panther*'s 'spring' was thus plainly exposed as an exercise in political blackmail.

Opinion in France and Britain was outraged. Initially Grey suggested sending a British warship to support France but was over-ruled in a Cabinet meeting. On 21 July, at the Mansion House, Lloyd George argued that if Britain were treated 'where her interests were vitally affected, as if she were of no account in the Cabinet of Nations: then I say emphatically that peace at that price would be intolerable for a great country like ours to endure'.[171] Germany chose to ignore this plain warning; though Goschen reported that 'German public opinion is beginning to realise that Agadir was a mistake'[172] his judgment was erroneous. Britain, compelled to support France, came close to war in September 1911. It was not until 22 September that readiness of war was deemed unnecessary. Eventually, on 4 November, France and Germany signed an agreement. But Anglo-German relations had been seriously damaged. On 17 September Grey suggested 'Our fleets should, therefore, always be in such a condition and position that they would welcome a German attack, if the Germans should decide on that suddenly'.[173] On 14 September Nicolson had told Hardinge 'It really amounts to a question as to whether we ought to submit to any dictation by Germany, whenever she considers it necessary to raise her voice'.[174] Increasingly Germany was seen as the enemy.

Kiderlen Wächter's reversion to Holstein's diplomatic style created numerous problems. France was much emboldened by Germany's ultimate capitulation; Italy was inclined to seek compensation in North Africa and, indeed, seized Cyrenaica and Tripolitania in the autumn of 1911. In Germany failure of the Agadir gamble further strengthened anti-British feeling. In the Reichstag debates of autumn 1911, following the resignation of Lindequist (the Colonial Secretary), both Conservatives and Centrists described England as the foe. Heydebrand, the Conservatives' leader, in reference to Lloyd George's speech observed, 'Such incidents like a flash in the dark show the German people where is the foe. The German people now knows, when it seeks foreign expansion and a place in the sun, such as is its right and destiny, where it has to look for permission. We Germans are not accustomed to that and cannot allow it and we shall know how to answer'.[175] These pressures made it inevitable that the Navy League and Tirpitz would obtain their cherished naval increases, thus further exacerbating relations with Britain. Relations during 1911-12 were worse than at any point in the history of the Empire and, although there was some improvement during 1913-14, the old basis of trust was never renewed—with incalculable consequences for the crisis of summer 1914.

Despite the deterioration of relations with Germany the *entente* with France did not develop as far and as fast as Nicolson and Bertie hoped. The Russians consistently dishonoured the spirit of their

1907 agreement with Britain, and France did little to control her ally. Indeed, had Germany behaved at all cautiously in the period 1906–11 then the 'triple entente' which she so feared would have been totally insubstantial. Grey, despite his pro-French stances in the crisis of 1906 and 1911, was not anxious to commit Britain to an alliance with France. He rejected Nicolson's pleas and was sufficiently alert to instruct Nicolson not to use the term 'triple entente', lest it be supposed that Britain was committed to an alliance system.[176] Political problems inside the Liberal Party made it hard for Grey, even if he had so wished, to make an alliance with France. Haldane was very sympathetic to Germany; Lloyd George, Churchill and the bulk of the radical group did not want confrontation with Germany, were suspicious of Russian good faith and hence did not value highly an alliance with France. On the back benches opinion was strongly against heavy naval expenditure, which it was feared would injure the programme of domestic reform.

The years 1906–11 saw, therefore, little progress in the development of an Anglo-French alliance, though semi-official military and naval contacts remained close. Inevitably, a party arose in France which favoured compromise within Germany. In 1905 this group, dominated by Schneider-Creusot and other heavy industrial interests, was led by Rouvier; later the leadership passed to Caillaux, who had some responsibility for the 1909 Morocco agreement. The events of 1911 initiated a process of change. By an unhappy chance Caillaux became French premier at the time of the Agadir crisis and so had a baptism of fire at a time when he was looking for reconciliation. Caillaux sought to come to terms with Germany for he realized that Russia could not be counted on to back French resistance and he had no faith in British support. The Agadir crisis showed how flimsy was the political side of the *entente*. Grey's general principle of giving 'France such support as would prevent her from falling under the virtual control of Germany and estrangement from us'[177] was neither understood in Paris nor accepted in London. Caillaux and his Foreign Minister, de Selves, operated upon different principles. Caillaux exaggerated German demands in order to persuade Britain that the crisis was too serious to intervene (as it would carry a high risk of war) while de Selves expected that such exaggeration would persuade Britain to come to the rescue. In the confusion it is hardly surprising that Kiderlen Wächter, who at least knew what he wanted—the French Congo—had some initial success. As in 1905–06 the real dispute soon became Anglo-German rather than Franco-German, with France being dragged along in the wake of Britain. The result was a strengthening of Franco-British ties. The crisis of July–September 1911 brought representatives of the armed forces into close contact and ultimately also secured Caillaux's fall. The ascendancy of Poincaré which followed, first as premier in 1912 and then as President from 1913, placed at the head of affairs a man whose hostility to Germany was implacable. Concurrent political developments in Britain helped cement a new understanding with France.

The events of 1911 had persuaded many Liberals that Germany was not to be trusted and that salvation must be sought in association with France. Those strongly opposed to co-operation with France were reduced to a rump: Crewe, Esher, Harcourt, Loreburn and Morley. Even those, like Asquith, who distrusted the notion of Anglo-French military conversations were ready to accept them as a necessary evil in the autumn of 1911. Although there was a reaction later in the year against what seemed to have been an unnecessarily belligerent attitude, the failure of the Haldane mission in early 1912 seemed to confirm that agreement with Germany was impossible. Nicolson was delighted at Haldane's failure and was congratulated by Goschen for his efforts in bringing about the collapse of discussions—'You have been foremost in this good work'.[178] The truth was Nicolson wanted an alliance with France and no engagement of any kind with Germany. In 1912 he told Bertie, 'I do not myself see why we should abandon the excellent position in which we have been placed, and step down to be involved in endeavours to entangle us in some so-called "understandings" which would undoubtedly . . . impair our relations with France and Russia'.[179] Yet Nicolson was well aware of the limits to his influence and Grey's power. In April 1912 he minuted that 'If at this moment France were to come forward with proposals so to reshape our understanding as to give it more or less the character of an alliance, I felt sure that neither the Government as a whole nor large sections of

British public opinion would be disposed to welcome such proposals'.[180] An overt alliance was impossible.

The naval arrangements of 1912 and 1913, however, went a long way towards creating a relationship not far removed from an alliance. The concentration of British ships in home waters and at Gibraltar obliged Britain to rely on France to protect her interests in the Mediterranean against all possible threats. Despite attempts by Cambon and Poincaré to turn this understanding into an alliance, the Cabinet refused to commit itself to France in the event of a German attack. Yet in the summer of 1912 Poincaré assured Sazonov, the Russian Foreign Minister, there existed a 'verbal agreement, by virtue of which England has declared herself ready to aid France with her military and naval forces in case of an attack by Germany'.[181] But this was untrue, though no doubt it suited Poincaré well enough to pretend to Russia that he had another ally in reserve. What was perhaps most significant in the long run was that high-ranking military and naval officers in the Western countries came to look on each other as allies in a common cause. This bond of comradeship was not without influence in 1914.

Trust between Britain and France was not strong. Nicolson and Crowe suspected that Caillaux and his allies were anxious to come to terms with Germany. At one point Crowe even believed that the Agadir crisis had been contrived by Caillaux and Kiderlen Wächter. On the French side there was rather more cause for suspicion.

Britain continued to look for an accord with Germany even after 1912. The Haldane mission, negotiations over the Bagdad Railway and the Portuguese colonies were examples which sprang readily to mind. In 1914 agreements on the Bagdad Railway and the Portuguese colonies were reached between Britain and Germany, so there was some evidence for French apprehension. France, too, had the problem of two associates (Britain and Russia) that were not easy horses to run in the same shafts. Only the personal contacts of men like Cambon and Bertie prevented latent suspicions becoming overt and a serious danger to the *entente*.

In 1912 a fresh outbreak of violence in the Balkans dragged the powers to the brink of war. The crisis was precipitated by a revival of Russian interest in the area, following Izvolsky's decision in 1909 to try to form a pro-Russian league of Balkan states. Hartwig, transferred from Teheran, was the principal agent and soon gained complete ascendancy over the policy of Serbia. During the course of 1912 treaties were signed between a number of Balkan states with the obvious intention of launching an attack on Turkey. Poincaré, who visited Russia in 1912, did nothing to discourage Russia from supporting this venture. France could hope to be a gainer in any conflict which damaged Austrian security for this would bring Russia and Germany into opposition. Germany and Austria looked on nervously, for they feared the consequences of Turkish collapse. In the summer of 1912 William II and Nicholas II met at Port Baltic and discussions there suggested that Russia too was fearful of the collapse of the Ottoman Empire. But matters had passed out of the control of the sick and feeble Sazonov, described by Nicolson in 1913 as a man 'impossible to foresee from one day to another what [he] will do'.[182] The decisions were being taken by ambitious Russian agents such as Hartwig and Romanovski, supported by the Pan-Slavs and *Novoye Vremya* at home. In early October, Montenegro, Greece, Bulgaria and Serbia declared war on Turkey and a month later the Turks had been driven out of Europe, apart from Constantinople and a few fortresses.

The outcome of the war, though foreseen by the more prescient military experts in Germany and Austria, was disastrous for the Central Powers. The destruction of Turkey now put Austria in the front line against growing Balkan nationalism. The rapid rout of the Turks also created some apprehension in St Petersburg, for the Tsar had no wish to see Bulgaria occupy Constantinople. However, the military effort of the Balkan states faded and in early December an armistice was signed. As in 1878, the task now became one of recreating a political settlement. The conference assembled at London, for Britain alone of the major powers had little direct interest in the details of territorial adjustments. The most important question to be resolved was that of Serbian access to the sea, to which Austria had declared herself opposed. Berchtold's demands were conceded and a new independent state of Albania was created.

Despite a brief resumption of the war, by May 1913 the Balkans seemed to have been pacified.

Much of the credit for the pacification must be allotted to Britain and Germany. Grey and Jagow, who had succeeded Kiderlen Wächter, wanted peace. Berchtold was too anxious to avoid the consequences for Austria of his own disastrous misjudgments to argue with his ally, while Sazonov had been greatly alarmed by the strength of the Pan-Slav party and its clamour for war with Germany and Austria unless those powers gave way on all significant points. *Novoye Vremya*'s references to the London Conference as a 'diplomatic Mukden' served only to irritate the Russian Foreign Minister. Poincaré took a belligerent line but knew that he could not rely on British support if he provoked Russia into war with Germany and Austria. German attitudes proved decisive, Bethmann Hollweg informing the Reichstag on 2 December, 'If our allies, in the maintenance of their interests, are, against all expectation, assailed from a third quarter, we shall have resolutely to take our place beside them, in fulfilment of our allied pledge'.[183] The clear but unprovocative nature of the Chancellor's warning was crucial in the preservation of peace and laid the foundation for Anglo-German co-operation in the conference which followed.

Grey found it easy to work with Lichnowsky, the new German Ambassador, and relations with Germany were more amiable in 1913 than for many years. Bethmann Hollweg, freed of Kiderlen Wächter, was well aware of the advantages of this change, telling Berchtold, 'we may look for a new orientation of British policy if we can get through the present crisis without any quarrels. . . . I think it would be a mistake of immeasurable consequence if we attempt a solution by force . . . at a moment when there is even the remotest prospect of entering this conflict under conditions more favourable to ourselves'.[184] In Britain the influence of Tyrrell, Grey's private secretary, was in the ascendant and by 1913 he was ready to approach the German problem with more flexibility than Nicolson or Crowe. Tyrrell distrusted Russian policy and realized the impossibility of being on bad terms with both Russia and Germany. By 1914 the Germanophobes were in high alarm about Tyrrell, Austin Lee telling Bertie, 'I am told [Tyrrell] is in high favour and is everything to Grey. Both are now very Germanophile'.[185] The agreements of 1914 stemmed directly from this improvement in relations and leading figures in both countries hoped that these would be the prelude to a real elimination of differences.

Despite these encouraging signs 1913 brought more trouble to Europe. France, Germany and Russia all embarked upon massive new programmes of military expenditure. In June the Balkan states quarrelled amongst themselves and Bulgaria was severely defeated by a combination of her neighbours. The result of Bulgaria's defeat was the creation of a much larger Serbia by the Treaty of Bucharest of 10 August 1913. In Berlin these developments were seen as satisfactory; the Balkan League had been split and Russia could no longer act as the co-adjutor of all the Slav states. In Vienna and Budapest, however, the reaction was very different. Berchtold was obsessed by fear of Serbia and was anxious for a diplomatic triumph. This was provided for him in October by provocative action by Serbia against Albania. An Austrian ultimatum, backed by Germany, was accepted by Serbia—which had received no support from France or Russia. The October crisis, however, was to have an important impact on the crisis of July 1914, for it convinced many influential figures in the Hapsburg Empire that a belligerent policy towards Serbia was the best, that German backing could be relied upon and that the Dual Alliance would not necessarily back Serbia. While there was some truth in all these assumptions they could not be dealt in as certainties as their supporters supposed.

Britain remained aloof from all these troubles, preoccupied as she was with the problems of Ulster. During 1913–14 Britain played little part in the diplomatic prelude to war. Grey showed little interest in the Liman von Sanders affair, and such attention as he did pay was scarcely favourable to Russian wishes. Britain opened negotiations with Russia for a naval convention in May 1914, but this could hardly be construed as a major departure in policy. How far removed Britain was from any interest in a continental conflict can be gauged from Grey's instructions to Bertie in May: 'If there were a really aggressive and menacing attack made by Germany on France, it was possible that public feeling in Britain would justify . . . helping France. But it was not likely that Germany would make an aggressive and menacing attack on Russia; and, even if she did, people in Great Britain would be inclined to say that . . . Russia's resources were so great that, in the long run, Germany would be exhausted without our helping Russia. Besides this, the French Government were a free Government, while the Russian Government were not; and this affected the sympathy of public opinion in Great Britain'.[186] There was thus no firm commitment to France in the early summer of 1914, still less assurance of any help for Russia in the event of war.

The murder of the Archduke at Sarajevo on 28 June stunned the world. Diplomats everywhere realized that Austria would press for stern measures against Serbia but few had any notion of the extent to which Austrian policy was now dominated by the anti-Serb party. Even those who feared that there would be war were uncertain as to its scope. Knowledgeable men could not predict the British attitude. Benckendorff told his son to pack and return home, but added: 'I think this time we are in for it. And I really don't know what the English will do'.[187] Bethmann Hollweg was more pessimistic, telling Bassermann, 'If there is war with France, England will march against us to the last man'.[188] Both men were, in the final analysis, proved correct. British policy was resolved only at the last minute, but then followed the course predicted by the Chancellor. During July it gradually became clear that 'something very strong was being cooked, and one could smell it'.[189] On 23 July, Austria delivered her ultimatum to Serbia, but as she was determined on war, acceptance or rejection of its terms were an irrelevancy except in so far as it affected the attitude of other powers. Crowe's reaction was predictable: 'Our interests are tied up with those of France and Russia in this struggle, which is not for the possession of Serbia, but one between Germany aiming at a political dictatorship in Europe and the Powers who desire to retain individual freedom. If we can help to avoid the conflict by showing our naval strength . . . it would be wrong not to make the effort'.[190] After a period of thinking that the crisis could be solved through the usual diplomatic channels, opinion in Britain veered towards recognition that action might be necessary to preserve peace. This necessarily involved discussion at the highest level, and on 24 July the whole question was first aired at a Cabinet meeting.

Opinion within the Cabinet was divided. One group was implacably opposed to any possibility of involvement. This included Burns, Morley, Simon and Beauchamp—the four who were to resign when Britain declared war on 4 August. In late July, however, the group opposing war was stronger. On 29 July Grey was quite unable to persuade his colleagues to agree to a declaration of support for France. On 31 July another meeting, which discussed the matter of Belgian neutrality, showed how far away war still seemed: 'We had a Cabinet at 11 and a very interesting discussion, especially about the neutrality of Belgium. . . . Of course, everybody longs to stand aside . . . Grey had to tell Cambon, for we are under no obligation, that we could give no pledges and that our actions must depend upon the course of events, including the Belgian question and the direction of public opinion here'.[191] On 1 August Grey and Churchill agitated for mobilization, but Lloyd George and others favoured an uncommitted position. Even on 2 August when it was clear what Germany was doing, Asquith could only record: 'We had a long Cabinet from 11 till nearly 2, which very soon revealed that we are on the brink of a split. We agreed at last with some difficulty that Grey should be authorized to tell Cambon that our fleet would not allow the German fleet to make the Channel a base of hostile operations. John Burns at once resigned, but was persuaded to hold on at any rate till the evening, when we meet again. There is a strong party against any kind of intervention in any event. Grey, of course, will never consent to this and I shall not separate myself from him. Crewe, McKenna and Samuel are a moderating intermediate body. Bonar Law writes that the Opposition will back us up in any measure we may take for the support of France and Russia'.[192] On 3 August the German ultimatum to Belgium tipped the scales and on 4 August Britain found herself at war with Germany. The basis of British policy was as uncertain and as little agreed in 1914 as it had been when the Liberals entered office in 1905.

The British involvement in war came later than that of any other major power, save Italy. Unlike the other nations, Britain was not bound by formal alliances, so in one sense the importance of short-term factors stands out. Two in particular helped convince the politicians that Germany must be resisted. The Central Powers did not treat seriously the British notion of a conference of the Powers and this gained them a bad press. The fact that Russia and France only paid lip-service to the proposal was generally overlooked in the hubbub following Austria's declaration of war on 28 July. In that sense Nicolson's comment of 29 July that 'the resources of diplomacy are, for the present, exhausted'[193] was quite correct. The other influential factor was clearly the German threat to Belgian neutrality, a matter of interest to Britain for many years. Again, the fact that France also had contingency plans for the invasion of Belgium was discreetly ignored. Yet this emphasis on short-term factors is illusory. In reality Britain was bound by informal links to France which were in their own way as strong as any treaty. These connexions had their roots in the diplomatic and political developments of the previous two decades, and in that sense the declaration of war on Germany was the fulfilment of a destined course.

The immediate factors were not, then, the most significant; important though they were. Britain might claim that war was declared in 1914 to protect freedom (though this did not prevent conscription and censorship during the war) and the rights of small nations (to whom little regard was paid in the post-war settlement), but the truth was that Britain became involved because it was the consensus of opinion that her interests and the balance of power were threatened by Germany. In fact, German power was probably over-estimated, but the reasons for this misjudgment stemmed too from the errors of the past. For two decades public opinion had been moving in a direction hostile to Germany, fanned by a generally Germanophobe press. It was widely believed that Germany would easily defeat France and Russia and then impose a new hegemony on Europe. The public had become imbued with Social Darwinist theories about vigorous and decaying nations and it was believed that the choice lay between third-rate obscurity and fighting Germany.

Germany had, of course, contributed handsomely to the alienation of opinion in Britain. Ill-starred forays into public affairs by the Kaiser, the clumsy interventions in Morocco, the use of blackmail at times of crisis for Britain and the building of a large and unnecessary navy had played important parts in sounding the tocsin. There was, too, a great deal of misunderstanding of intention on both sides. Some of those best placed to clear up misconceptions had no wish to do so. In that sense the war of 1914 was the creation of Nicolson, Crowe, Holstein and Bülow. Nicolson, for example, showed great restraint in dealing with Russia, even when her conduct was treacherous, but never showed consideration of the same kind in dealing with Germany. The diplomats and politicians were not alone in their responsibility. The bulk of the educated classes in both Britain and Germany suspected and distrusted their opposite numbers. The military in Britain favoured France, as did business and trading interests. In universities there were many examples of nationalist bigotry at its strongest—and best argued.

In the end, however, the major share of the responsibility must fall on the politicians and the diplomats. It is all very well to seek an explanation in 'the internal dynamism that had accumulated in forty years of peace and now sought violent release', or, 'that mysterious frenzy of the millions which can hardly be described in words, but which, for a moment, gave a wild and almost rapturous impetus to the greatest crime of our time'.[194] But the responsibility may be pinned down more closely than such general statements suggest. There were fundamental misconceptions among the diplomats and the politicians which, when accumulated, produced the July crisis. Even otherwise competent diplomats suffered from the most amazing blind spots. De Bunsen, Ambassador in Vienna, was told by Nicolson in 1913, 'The whole of this Albanian question seems to me such a fiction and unreality that I really cannot take any intense interest in it'.[195] Albania was not, of course, a major concern of Britain, but it was symbolically very important for Austria and therefore necessarily of interest to Britain. Similar to this was the bland disclaimer of interest in the fate of the Yangtze interests of Britain by Germany in the early 1900s, at a time when Germany was seeking an understanding. The examples are legion and, *in toto*, were very damaging to relations.

The politicians were too often swayed by rhetoric and too rarely by common sense. Unfortunately, in 1914 the radical and pacifist wings of the Labour and Liberal parties were weak, just as their opposite numbers in Germany were. The Conservatives in both countries had become committed to strong nationalist doctrines intolerant of *entente*. Furthermore, politicians had clouded the issues by creating a state of uncertainty. In Britain no one, except perhaps Grey, knew how far Britain was committed to France. In Germany the anodyne reports of Lichnowsky were preferred to the sharp prescience of his predecessor, Metternich. The Chancellor knew well what the situation was, but preferred to pretend that unreality was reality.

All these factors then contributed to that dissolution of the old link between London and Berlin, the final snapping of which was to precipitate the involvement of Britain in war in 1914. When the crisis came, Grey and Bethmann Hollweg were both prisoners of the past, of the actions of others and even themselves. Bethmann Hollweg was aked by Bülow how the war came about and could only reply: 'Oh—if I only knew'.[196] Grey, while pushing through the Cabinet by threat of resignation a policy which could only lead to British involvement, declared, 'I hate war, I hate war'.[197] Both men, unlike most of their contemporaries, did foresee the destruction of society which the war was to wreak, but both felt powerless in the crisis, suffocated by the grip of forces too strong and too determined for them. Neither man accepted the validity of the arguments put forward by those who just wanted to fight. They saw that a war between Britain and Germany would be a disaster for both nations and for Europe. As Bethmann Hollweg later wrote, 'Thus we find the Anglo-German conflict to be the ultimate origin of the war'.[198] But though both men recognized that the end of an era had come, a tribute to their perception, their failure to clear the routes of communication either internally or externally is an equal testament to their fallibility. Even in 1914 'the men of goodwill' were 'on the whole the more impressive team'[199] but goodwill was not enough when 'Death looks gigantically down'.[200]

REFERENCES

1 *Memories and Reflections* by the Earl of Oxford and Asquith. Vol. II. p. 7.
2 Curzon to Hamilton, 25 September 1901. Hamilton MSS. Vol. III.
3 *The End of Isolation* by G. W. Monger. p. 69. Lascelles to Lansdowne, 26 April 1902.
4 *German Diplomatic Documents, 1871–1914* ed. E. T. S. Dugdale. Vol. III. No. XXIV/30. Metternich to Bülow, 3 February 1908. (Henceforward referred to as *GDD.*)
5 *British Documents on the Origins of the War, 1898–1914.* Vol. II. No. 131. Lansdowne to Monson, 12 February 1902. (Henceforward referred to as *BD.*)
6 Monger, op. cit., p. 72. Lansdowne to Cromer, 26 December 1901.
7 *Life of Joseph Chamberlain* by J. Amery. Vol. IV. p. 180. Metternich to Bülow, 30 January 1902.
8 *King Edward VII. A biography* by Sir S. Lee. Vol. II. p. 144. Conversation with Eckardstein, 8 February 1902.
9 Monger, op. cit., p. 128. Cromer to Lansdowne, 29 May 1903.
10 *Théophile Delcassé and the making of the Entente Cordiale* by C. Andrew. p. 181.
11 ibid., p. 185. Monson to Lansdowne, 31 December 1902.
12 Lansdowne to Monson, 30 April 1902. F.O. West Africa 7996/18.
13 Amery, op. cit., Vol. IV. p. 163. Chamberlain to Lansdowne, 17 March 1901.
14 Lansdowne to Monson, 20 March 1901. F.O. Newfoundland 7817/36.
15 *BD.* Vol. II. No. 325. Lansdowne to Monson, 15 October 1902.
16 Amery, op. cit., Vol. IV. p. 203. Lecomte to Delcassé, 12 December 1902.
17 ibid., Vol. IV. p. 206. Chamberlain to Austen Chamberlain, 9 January 1903.
18 *Correspondance de Paul Cambon, 1870–1924* ed. H. Cambon. Vol. II. p. 89. Cambon to Henri Cambon, 3 February 1903.
19 *Lord Lansdowne* by Lord Newton. p. 275. Monson to Lansdowne, 13 March 1903.
20 *Documents diplomatiques français.* Second Series. Vol. III. No. 229. Geoffray to Delcassé, 9 May 1903. (Henceforward referred to as *DDF.*)
21 *DDF.* Second Series. Vol. III. No. 317. Bihourd to Delcassé, 20 June 1903.
22 *DDF.* Second Series. Vol. III. No. 229. Geoffray to Delcassé, 9 May 1903.
23 *BD.* Vol. II. No. 357. Lansdowne to Monson, 7 July 1903.
24 *DDF.* Second Series. Vol. III. No. 362. Delcassé to Cambon, 21 July 1903.
25 *DDF.* Second Series. Vol. IV. No. 7. Cambon to Delcassé, 11 October 1903.
26 *DDF.* Second Series. Vol. III. No. 392. Cambon to Delcassé, 6 August 1903.
27 *DDF.* Second Series. Vol. IV. No. 36. Delcassé to Cambon, 24 October 1903.
28 *BD.* Vol. II. No. 308. Salisbury to Drummond Wolff, 7 June 1899.
29 *DDF.* Second Series. Vol. IV. No. 89. Cambon to Cogordan, 18 November 1903.
30 *BD.* Vol. II. No. 387. Cromer to Lansdowne, 21 January 1904.
31 *DDF.* Second Series. Vol. IV. No. 201. De la Boulinière to Delcassé, 20 January 1904.
32 *DDF.* Second Series. Vol. IV. No. 46. Cambon to Delcassé, 28 October 1903.
33 *From the Dreadnought to Scapa Flow* by A. J. Marder. Vol. I. p. 115. Fisher to Lansdowne, 22 April 1905.
34 *DDF.* Second Series. Vol. III. No. 381. Cambon to Delcassé, 31 July 1903.
35 *BD.* Vol. II. No. 259. Lansdowne to Monson, 11 December 1903.
36 Andrew, op. cit., p. 230. Bompard to Delcassé, 2 April 1904.

37 Monger, op. cit., pp. 97–8. Balfour to Selborne, 6 April 1904.
38 Lee, op. cit., Vol. II. p. 289. Edward VII to Nicholas II, 12 May 1904.
39 *Records and Reactions, 1856–1939* by the Earl of Midleton. p. 198.
40 *Life of Lord Curzon* by the Earl of Ronaldshay. Vol. II. p. 344. Lady Curzon to Curzon, 4 March 1904.
41 Monger, op. cit., pp. 98–9. Balfour to Lansdowne, 21 December 1903.
42 *BD.* Vol. IV. No. 291. Lansdowne's Memorandum, 10 May 1904.
43 Lee, op. cit., Vol. II. p. 302. Edward VII to Nicholas II, 26 October 1904.
44 *Fear God and Dread Nought* by A. J. Marder. Vol. II. p. 47. Fisher to Lady Fisher, 1 November 1904.
45 *DDF.* Second Series. Vol. V. No. 449. Cambon to Delcassé, 17 November 1904.
46 *Die grosse Politik der europäischen Kabinette, 1871–1914.* Vol. XIX. No. 6100. Metternich to Bülow, 13 October 1904. (Henceforward referred to as *GP.*)
47 *GP.* Vol. XIX. No. 6111. Metternich to Bülow, 1 November 1904.
48 *Briefe Wilhelms II an den Zaren* ed. W. Goetz. 28 October 1904.
49 Newton, op. cit., p. 325.
50 ibid., p. 328. Lansdowne to Hardinge, 4 September 1905.
51 *Servant of India* by M. Gilbert. p. 25. Morley to Minto, 6 July 1906.
52 Lee, op. cit., p. 357. William II to Nicholas II, 27 July 1905.
53 ibid., pp. 339–40.
54 *BD.* Vol. III. No. 93. Bertie to Lansdowne, 25 April 1905.
55 *BD.* Vol. III. No. 83. Lansdowne to Durand, 27 April 1905.
56 *BD.* Vol. III. No. 86. Lansdowne to Bertie, 3 May 1905.
57 *GDD.* Vol. III. No. XX/358. Holstein's Memorandum, 2 May 1905.
58 *BD.* Vol. III. No. 96. Bertie to Lansdowne, 10 June 1905.
59 Lee, op. cit., p. 344. Balfour to Edward VII, 8 June 1905.
60 *GDD.* Vol. III. No. XX/647. Metternich to Bülow, 22 July 1905.
61 *The Holstein Papers* ed. N. Rich and M. H. Fisher. Vol. IV. p. 329. Holstein to Bülow, 5 April 1905.
62 *BD.* Vol. III. No. 193. Grey to Nicolson, 14 December 1905.
63 *GP.* Vol. XIX. No. 6154. Schulenburg to Bülow, 13 December 1904.
64 Rich and Fisher, op. cit., Vol. IV. p. 377. Holstein to Brandt, 23 December 1905.
65 *GDD.* Vol. III. No. XXI/52. Metternich to Bülow, 4 January 1906.
66 *GDD.* Vol. III. No. XXI/83. Schulenburg to Bülow, 31 January 1906.
67 *DDF.* Second Series. Vol. VIII. No. 219. Cambon to Rouvier, 12 December 1905.
68 Monger, op. cit., p. 261. *The Times,* 17 October 1905.
69 *Grey of Fallodon* by G. M. Trevelyan. p. 84. Grey to Ferguson, 13 August 1905.
70 *BD.* Vol. III. No. 299. Hardinge's note on Grey's Memorandum, 23 February 1906.
71 *DDF.* Second Series. Vol. VIII. No. 55. Cambon to Rouvier, 25 January 1906.
72 *DDF.* Second Series. Vol. VIII. No. 106. Cambon to Rouvier, 31 January 1906.
73 *Life of Lord Ripon* by L. Wolf. Vol. II. pp. 292–3. Ripon to Fitzmaurice, 11 January 1906.
74 *BD.* Vol. III. No. 396. Grey to Bertie, 4 April 1906.
75 *GDD.* Vol. III. No. XX/368. Bülow to Holstein, 5 May 1905.
76 *Sir Arthur Nicolson, Bart. First Lord Carnock: A study in the Old Diplomacy* by Sir H. Nicolson. p. 192.

77 Monger, op. cit., p. 285. Bertie to Mallet, 31 March 1905.
78 *Twenty-five Years, 1892–1916* by Lord Grey of Fallodon. Vol. I. p. 153.
79 *DDF*. Second Series. Vol. VIII. No. 87. Cambon to Rouvier, 27 October 1905.
80 Lee, op. cit., Vol. II. p. 308.
81 *BD*. Vol. IV. No. 220. Grey to MacDonald, 28 May 1906.
82 *The Letters and Friendships of Sir Cecil Spring Rice* ed. S. Gwynn. Vol. II. p. 72. Grey to Spring Rice, 16 April 1906.
83 ibid., Vol. II. p. 54. Grey to Spring Rice, 22 December 1905.
84 ibid., Vol. II. p. 95. Spring Rice to Cranley, 28 March 1907.
85 *Great Contemporaries* by W. S. Churchill. p. 74.
86 Monger, op. cit., p. 285.
87 Gwynn, op. cit., Vol. II. p. 61. Spring Rice to Mallet, 31 January 1906.
88 ibid., Vol. II. p. 65. Grey to Spring Rice, 19 February 1906.
89 Lee, op. cit., Vol. II. p. 568.
90 Monger, op. cit., p. 288. Nicolson to Hardinge, 29 July 1906.
91 *BD*. Vol. IV. No. 336. Nicolson to Grey, 1 September 1906.
92 *BD*. Vol. IV. No. 228. Nicolson to Grey, 12 September 1906.
93 Monger, op. cit., p. 291. Minto to Morley, 19 September 1906.
94 Gwynn, op. cit., Vol. II. p. 101. Kitchener to Spring Rice, 19 June 1907.
95 Lee, op. cit., Vol. II. p. 569. Edward VII to Hardinge, 22 September 1906.
96 Monger, op. cit., p. 290. Fitzmaurice to Lascelles, 31 May 1906.
97 *BD*. Vol. IV. No. 448 (Enclosure 2 relating to No. 492). Grey to Nicolson, 8 August 1907.
98 *BD*. Vol. IV. No. 535. Edward VII to Nicolson, 17 September 1907.
99 *Hansard*. House of Lords. 6 February 1908.
100 *Hansard*. House of Lords. 10 February 1908
101 *Hansard*. House of Lords. 10 February 1908.
102 Gwynn, op. cit., Vol. II. p. 102. Spring Rice to Ferguson, 18 July 1907.
103 *Hansard*. House of Lords. 6 February 1908.
104 *Hansard*. House of Lords. 6 February 1908.
105 *BD*. Vol. IV. No. 537. Grey to Nicolson, 18 September 1907.
106 *BD*. Vol. IV. No. 264. Nicolson to Grey, 14 April 1907.
107 *The Life of Sir Charles Dilke* by S. Gwynn and G. Tuckwell. Vol. II. p. 502.
108 *BD*. Vol. IV. No. 550. Grey to Nicolson, 24 February 1908.
109 *Diplomatische Aktenstücke zur Geschichte der Ententepolitik der Vorkriegsjahre* ed. B. von Siebert. p. 262. Malevsky–Malevitch to Izvolsky, 8 March 1910.
110 *Great Britain and Japan, 1911–15* by P. Lowe, p. 41. Rumbold's Diary, 18 March 1911.
111 *From the Dreadnought to Scapa Flow* by A. J. Marder. Vol. I. p. 235.
112 Siebert, op. cit., p. 33. Benckendorff to Neratov, 17 July 1911.
113 Lowe, op. cit., p. 156. Gregory to Grey, 21 September 1913.
114 Lowe, op. cit., p. 166. Grey to Greene, 21 February 1914.
115 Nicolson, op. cit., p. 354.
116 *The strangling of Persia* by M. Shuster. p. xxi.
117 Nicolson, op. cit., p. 355. Nicolson to Stamfordham, 13 November 1911.
118 *BD*. Vol. X (i). No. 885. Grey to Buchanan, 2 December 1911.
119 Grey, op. cit., Vol. I. p. 170.

120 *BD.* Vol. X (i). No. 912. Grey to Buchanan, 2 January 1912.
121 Siebert, op. cit., pp. 327–8. Izvolsky to Tscharykov, 26 November 1909.
122 *Hansard.* House of Commons. 7 February 1911.
123 *Die deutsch–türkische Waffenbrüderschaft* by E. Jäckh. p. 18.
124 Political and Secret Home Correspondence. F.O. Vol. CLXXX. Curzon's Memorandum, 19 November 1898.
125 *Hansard.* House of Commons. 22 January 1902.
126 *Hansard.* House of Commons. 17 February 1908.
127 *Problems of Power* by W. M. Fullerton. p. 171.
128 *Hansard.* House of Commons. 21 March 1911.
129 *Hansard.* House of Commons. 7 February 1911.
130 *BD.* Vol. VI. No. 343. Hardinge's Minute, 11 April 1910.
131 *Reflections on the World War* by T. von Bethmann Hollweg. p. 167.
132 Lee, op. cit., Vol. II. p. 525. Edward VII to William II, 27 January 1906.
133 *BD.* Vol. III. No. 419. Crowe's Minute, 26 June 1906.
134 Monger, op. cit., p. 303. Fitzmaurice to Lascelles, 21 September 1906.
135 Monger, op. cit., p. 303. Bertie to Mallet, 25 August 1906.
136 *BD.* Vol. III. Appendix A. Crowe's Memorandum, 1 January 1907.
137 *BD.* Vol. III. Appendix C. Lascelles' General Report for 1906, 24 May 1907.
138 *The Foreign Office and Foreign Policy, 1898–1914* by Z. S. Steiner. p. 190.
139 *Fisher of Kilverstone* by R. F. Mackay. p. 358. Fisher to Tweedmouth, 26 September 1906.
140 Monger, op. cit., p. 311. Tweedmouth to Campbell–Bannerman, 21 November 1906.
141 Steiner, op. cit., p. 98. Hardinge to Bryce, 4 June 1909.
142 *BD.* Vol. III. Crowe's Memorandum, 1 January 1907.
143 *BD.* Vol. III. Sanderson's Comments in Appendix B, 21 February 1907.
144 *A life of Sir Henry Campbell–Bannerman* by J. Wilson. p. 542. Note by Lady Cecil, 10 April 1907.
145 Lee, op. cit., Vol. II. p. 542. Leader of 15 April 1907.
146 *Memoirs of Prince von Bülow.* Vol. II. p. 329.
147 *GP.* Vol. XXIV. No. 8217. Metternich to Bülow, 16 July 1908.
148 *Fifty Years of Europe* by S. Spender. p. 318.
149 Bülow, op. cit., Vol. II. p. 392.
150 *BD.* Vol. VI. No. 133. Findlay to Grey, 12 November 1908.
151 Steiner, op. cit., p. 119. Tyrrell to Spring Rice, 1 May 1906.
152 *DDF.* Second Series. Vol. XI. No. 441. Clemenceau to Pichon, 2 September 1908.
153 *Bülow*, op. cit., Vol. II. Crown Prince William to Bülow, 2 October 1908.
154 *BD.* Vol. VII. No. 132. Grey to McKenna, 5 November 1908.
155 *The Fall of the House of Habsburg* by E. Crankshaw. p. 341.
156 *BD.* Vol. V. No. 387. Grey to Izvolsky, 15 October 1908.
157 *GP.* Vol. XXVI (i). No. 9074. Bülow's Memorandum, 27 October 1908.
158 Nicolson, op. cit., p.284. Grey to Nicolson, 10 November 1908.
159 ibid., p. 286. Grey to Nicolson, 10 November 1908.
160 *GP.* Vol. XXVI (ii). No. 9188. William II to Nicholas II, 5 January 1909.
161 *GP.* Vol. XXVI (ii). No. 9460. Bülow to Pourtalès, 21 March 1909.

162 Nicolson, op. cit., p. 305. Nicolson to Grey, 24 March 1909.
163 ibid., p. 307. Grey to Nicolson, 2 April 1909.
164 Gwynn and Tuckwell, op. cit., Vol. II. p. 512.
165 *BD*. Vol. VI. No. 174. Goschen to Grey, 16 April 1909.
166 *Bülow*, op. cit., Vol. II. p. 480.
167 *The Struggle for Mastery in Europe, 1848–1918* by A. J. P. Taylor. p. 460.
168 *BD*. Vol. VI. No. 202. Grey to Goschen, 28 October 1909.
169 *BD*. Vol. VI. No. 387. Grey's Memorandum, 26 July 1910.
170 *The Life and Letters of Lord Wester Wemyss* by Lady Wemyss. pp. 127–8.
171 *The Times*, 22 July 1911.
172 Nicolson, op. cit., p. 344. Goschen to Nicolson, 26 August 1911.
173 ibid., p. 346. Grey to Nicolson, 17 September 1911.
174 ibid., p. 347. Nicolson to Hardinge, 14 September 1911.
175 *Origins of the First World War* by L. C. F. Turner. p. 22.
176 Steiner, op. cit., p. 124.
177 *C. P. Scott of the Manchester Guardian* by J. L. Hammond. p. 161. Conversation between Grey and Scott, 25 July 1911.
178 Steiner, op. cit., p. 127. Goschen to Nicolson, 20 April 1912.
179 ibid., p. 127. Nicolson to Bertie, 8 February 1912.
180 *BD*. Vol. VI. No. 576. Nicolson's Minute, 15 April 1912.
181 Taylor, op. cit., p. 481. Sazonov to Nicholas II. 17 August 1912.
182 Turner, op. cit., p. 34. Nicolson's comment, 19 August 1913.
183 *Colonial Zeitung*, 3 December 1912.
184 Taylor, op. cit., p. 495. Bethmann Hollweg to Berchtold, 10 February 1913.
185 Steiner, op. cit., p. 152. Austin Lee to Bertie, 14 April 1914.
186 *BD*. Vol. X (ii). No. 541. Grey to Bertie, 1 May 1914.
187 *The Twelve Days* by G. M. Thomson. p. 56.
188 Turner, op. cit., p. 73.
189 *The Mist Procession* by Lord Vansittart. p. 122.
190 *BD*. Vol. XI. No. 101. Buchanan to Grey, 24 July 1914. Minute by Crowe, 25 July 1914.
191 Asquith, op. cit., Vol. II. p. 7.
192 ibid., Vol. II. p. 8.
193 *BD*. Vol. XI. No. 252. Rodd to Grey, 29 July 1914. Minute by Nicolson.
194 *The World of Yesterday* by S. Zweig.
195 *Maurice de Bunsen. Diplomat and Friend* by E. T. S. Dugdale. p. 279. Nicolson to de Bunsen, 31 December 1913.
196 Turner, op. cit., p. 112.
197 Nicolson, op. cit., p. 422.
198 Bethmann Hollweg, op. cit., p. 160.
199 Thomson, op. cit., p. 207.
200 From the poem 'The City in the Sea' by E. A. Poe.

5 The War and the Peace, 1914–22

Grimed with smears
I stand amid the dust o' the moulded years.
My mangled youth lies dead beneath the heap.
Francis Thompson, *The Hound of Heaven*

During and after the war of 1914–18 it was fashionable to blame 'the old diplomacy' for the catastrophe of 1914 and subsequent disasters. Woodrow Wilson set the fashion for criticism by referring in his Fourteen Points to the need for 'Open covenants of peace openly arrived at, after which there shall be no private understandings of any kind, but diplomacy shall proceed always frankly and in the public view'.[1] Leaving aside the accuracy of his implied criticism, it is evident that new methods were not applied either during the war or in peace negotiations. Diplomacy continued to be conducted by the same or similar men who had managed affairs before 1914. In Britain, reluctantly involved in 1914 and victorious in 1918, there seemed little reason to abandon well-tried methods. British diplomacy followed predictable lines, developing in wartime those characteristics already discernible before 1914. During the peace conferences there were important changes in style—usually made to meet the wishes of other parties—but few alterations in basic aims. There was little evidence of British enthusiasm for creating a new world order or democratic nation-states. The motives for entering the war, for continuing it, and for constructing a peace were based upon consideration of traditional interests or concepts— in fact the pursuit of ends such as Belgian neutrality or a European balance of power.

It would be inaccurate to suggest British unanimity as to the

References are printed on p. 219.

aims of foreign policy in wartime. However, there were certain principles to which the broad mass of the electorate, diplomats and politicians assented. These may be summarized as follows: the defeat of Germany, protection of France and Belgium, maintenance of good relations with the United States, strengthening ties with the Empire and with Russia, sensible territorial reconstruction after the war, and creation of a lasting peace. As the war dragged on some of these aims were modified. Relations with the United States and Russia changed in 1917. In 1918, when German power had received a serious check, attitudes towards former allies and opponents underwent subtle metamorphosis. Furthermore, there had always been a vocal party in Britain which had dissented from the aims and methods of policy. The making of foreign policy was thus not an entirely smooth and untroubled process.

Reasons cited in 1914 for Britain's entry into the war compare instructively with the war aims defined above. Asquith declared on 6 August that Britain was fighting 'to fulfil a solemn international obligation—an obligation which, if it had been entered into between private persons in the ordinary concerns of life, would have been regarded as an obligation not only of law, but of honour, which no self-respecting man could possibly have repudiated. I say, secondly, we are fighting to vindicate the principle . . . that small nationalities are not to be crushed, in defiance of international good faith, by the arbitrary will of a strong and overmastering Power'.[2] It was a long time before Asquith abandoned this definition of war aims. Morley saw matters differently, believing, 'The precipitate and peremptory blaze about Belgium was due less to indignation at the violation of a Treaty than to natural perception of the plea that it would furnish for intervention on behalf of France, for expeditionary force and all the rest. Belgium was to take the place that had been taken before, as pleas for war, by Morocco and Agadir'.[3] Morley saw that British war aims involved defending France and subjugating Germany rather than protecting decency and honour in international affairs. Events during 1914–18 vindicated his judgment rather than that of Asquith.

The most important goal was the defeat of Germany. Germany was the main target of popular hatred and the focus of diplomatic and political distrust. The wish to defeat her bound together different groups: the naval lobby, commercial men fearing competition, advocates of imperial expansion, Russophiles, Francophiles, and those who wanted to create independent nation-states in Eastern Europe. Apostles of a new international order accepted the same priority as those who wanted a return to the old system. Those who believed Britain had been driven into war were at one with those who had favoured preventive war. Germany had stood for so long in the path of so many ambitions and aspirations that her defeat was the *conditio sine qua non* of a return to peace and stability.

Floods of propaganda justified this position. It was necessary to tell the public why German peace offers were rejected; the simple explanation was that Germany had behaved in unforgivable fashion. In 1917 Paget told a Danish peace envoy, 'one could not treat with the Germans on the same footing as one would another enemy. They had placed themselves beyond the pale and could only be treated as criminals'.[4] Germany's initial successes had intensified fear and hostility and Asquith succumbed at an early stage to the temptation of moralizing. On 2 October 1914 he referred to 'hordes who leave behind them at every stage of their progress a dismal trail of savagery, of devastation and desecration worthy of the blackest annals in the history of barbarism'.[5] Germany was thus a country of different type, inhabited by savages and guided by non-European instincts. Britain's allies were equally vehement: Clemenceau believed 'The barbaric methods of German warfare . . . were no less a crime than the original aggression'.[6] Others saw further: Llewellyn Woodward understood 'The war had to be won, and as it would have to be won by those who were directing it or by other professionals of the same plodding type, the end would be one of mutual exhaustion in which the moral standards of the victors as well as the defeated would be dangerously lowered'.[7] An anti-war pamphlet asked pertinently, 'Which is the greater peril to this country, 65 million civilized Germans, of our own race and blood, mainly engaged in trade and industry and peaceful occupations, or 140 million Russians, the slaves of a corrupt autocracy, and trained to the use of force alone?'[8] But these voices did not determine policy.

The effects of adopting this line of propaganda had serious consequences when the time came to make peace. In the meantime it also affected diplomacy. Determination to defeat Germany ruled out the possibility of negotiated peace, thus counteracting the revulsion from the carnage of 1914–16. It was also feared that without military victory a compromise peace would mean a return to the position of 1914. Bethmann Hollweg[9] and Nicolson[10] both rejected this solution out of hand. The temptation to negotiate remained among the Allies only because of Russian incapacity. Prior to American entry into the war in 1917 nothing looked less likely than Allied victory. Britain might be committed to Germany's defeat and would not make overtures to her, but this did not prevent consideration of offers made directly by Germany, or through neutrals, or proposals of mediation by neutrals themselves.

On several occasions German peace overtures interested the Cabinet—most importantly in September 1914, December 1916 and August 1917. These offers were not made in desperation. Indeed, German optimism remained high to the very end. On 27 September 1918 Hindenburg was still demanding annexation of the Briey-Longwy ironfields as a precondition of armistice.[11] German offers had not been made as a suppliant. In September 1914, following stabilization of the Western Front at the Marne, it became clear that an immediate German victory was impossible. Bethmann Hollweg, who had already formulated sweeping demands in expectation of victory, now argued for negotiation. His readiness to abandon probably chimerical gains for a solid peace divided him from most of his colleagues and made him a focal point of unpopularity. He understood it was enough for Germany to withstand her enemies and that total victory was unnecessary. He was unable to convince his colleagues of this simple fact, partly because of their *idées fixes* and partly because it was not in his nature to force his opinions on them. The Chancellor's proposals to Britain were rejected without serious discussion—neither Lloyd George nor Grey felt them worthy of mention in their memoirs, while Asquith merely noted that at Washington 'both the German and Austrian Ambassadors . . . are working for peace . . . the Germans would gladly agree to evacuate Belgium and give full compensation and securities against future attack'.[12] This was a rather inaccurate description of German proposals. Curzon was probably more representative of public opinion and more accurate in his pessimistic estimate of likely peace terms when he argued, 'It is impertinent . . . to talk about peace now'.[13] Haldane, supposedly pro-German, took the toughest line. In a Cabinet memorandum of 8 April 1915 he argued, 'The conclusion of the present war . . . is likely to be attended with a new set of problems . . . this war, unlike some others, cannot be allowed to terminate as a drawn battle, or even as a victory evidenced by mere cession of territory or payment of indemnities. It is conflict with a power which threatens, should it win, to dominate ruthlessly a large part of the civilized world. It is therefore essential that it shall not in the future be likely to succeed in a second attempt at armed supremacy. To insure this it is desirable that military hierarchy in Germany should be dethroned'.[14] The Lord Chancellor realized that to depose the military required Germany's defeat—an assessment with which Bethmann Hollweg would have concurred—thus making negotiated peace unthinkable.

The most important peace initiative was that of 12 December 1916. All belligerents were weary. In Eastern Europe the mood was very much for peace. The Tsarist régime, while still outwardly bellicose, was in grave danger following the failure of Brusilov's offensive. Britain was half-starved; France and Germany were exhausted by the blood-letting at Verdun. Falkenheyn's dismissal on 28 August opened the way for those favouring a political solution. The alternative was, as Bethmann Hollweg knew, 'unrestricted U-boat war . . . carried out in dead earnest'.[15] In October 1916 Burian, Austria's Foreign Minister, visited Germany to discuss a possible peace offer. The terms formulated in the next few weeks were strongly influenced by military and conservative circles. In particular, industrial interests pressed for annexations and special concessions in Western Europe, so the terms differed little from those of 1914. Major items included guarantees from Belgium (or, alternatively, the cession of Liège), return of most German colonies, annexation of Courland, Lithuania and Luxemburg, and favourable territorial adjustments in the Congo, Alsace-Lorraine and the Briey-Longwy basin. This was a package unlikely to appeal to the Allies.

Germany's offer met with a poor reception. Briand, the French premier, accused Germany of trying to destroy Allied unity; his theme was echoed by Sonnino in Italy and Pokrovsky in Russia. In Britain the situation was rather different for on 13 November Lansdowne, the influential Minister without Portfolio, presented a memorandum discussing peace proposals. It was highly critical of Britain's allies and of the military advice to the government. Lansdowne argued it was time to look at old problems again. 'Many of us', he wrote, 'must of late have asked ourselves how this war is ever to be brought to an end. If we are told that the deliberate conclusion of the Government is that it must be fought until Germany has been beaten to the ground and sues for peace on any terms which we are pleased to accord to her, my only observation would be that we ought to know something of the data upon which this conclusion has been reached. To many of us it seems as if the prospect of a "knock-out" was, to say the least of it, remote. . . . I may be asked whether I have any practical suggestion to offer, and I admit the difficulty of replying. But is it not true that, unless the apprehensions which I have sketched can be shown, after such an investigation as I have suggested, to be groundless, we ought at any rate not to discourage any movement, no matter where originating, in favour of an interchange of views as to the possibility of a settlement?'[16] This remarkable paper produced confusion and uncertainty within the rickety coalition government. Indeed, according to Crewe, 'the veritable *causa causans* of the final break-up is to be traced to Lord Lansdowne's striking paper'.[17] It certainly accelerated the collapse of Asquith's administration and its replacement on 7 December 1916 by a new coalition under Lloyd George.

It was inconceivable that the new government, composed as it was of old hands, would adopt a new policy on negotiations. The military (with the possible exception of Robertson) were dead against discussions. Lord Robert Cecil spoke for the Tories when in his memorandum of 27 November he argued, 'A peace now could only be disastrous. At the best we could not hope for more than the *status quo* with a great increase in the German power in Eastern Europe'.[18] Cecil was in the new coalition, Lansdowne was out; it seemed likely that the reshuffle would lead merely to delay in replying to peace overtures rather than a policy change.

So it proved. Lloyd George soon endorsed his allies' views, as 'Nothing had . . . happened to alter the situation since the Asquith Cabinet decided in November not to encourage or countenance peace negotiations'.[19] On 18 December the Cabinet decided it would be tactically best to concert a joint reply to Germany and for France to deliver it *via* Washington. On 30 December the Allied Note was delivered, describing German proposals as 'lacking all substance and precision . . . less an offer of peace than a war manoeuvre . . . empty and insincere'.[20] This was meaningless rhetoric, designed to gull the public. German proposals were unacceptable but hardly imprecise. Germany's note was a manoeuvre but so too was the Allies' blatant attempt to ingratiate themselves with the neutrals.

The real objections to coming to terms were much less flimsy. There was a deep fear lest peace leave Germany strong enough to break an agreement at a convenient time. The awesome industrial might of Germany would not be weakened by any peace treaty acceptable to the *Deutscher Industrierat*, and there was nothing in German proposals to suggest a more acceptable colonial or naval policy. Dwarfing all other considerations, however, was fear of disunity—that the real differences between the Allies would be exposed to Germany's advantage during negotiations. The Foreign Office argued, therefore, that it would be safer not to negotiate. Rumbold, from his vantage point in neutral Berne, reiterated that Germany's will to fight was being eroded and that victory was but a short time away: 'The Rhine-whine is very audible now, but I hope that nobody in any of the countries of the Entente will listen to it',[21] he wrote on 19 December. De Bunsen too was hostile, considering the German overture 'very unpromising—overbearing, arrogant and sanctimonious'.[22] Hardinge, once more permanent Under-Secretary, argued against negotiation on the grounds that 'We never knew what the terms of peace were, the Germans having refused to give them until we declared ourselves ready to discuss them'.[23] In one sense this was accurate in that Germany had not enunciated precise demands, but she had judiciously leaked her terms. In fact the overture was rejected because negotiation was regarded as inconsistent with both British war aims and the paramount necessity of preserving Allied unity.

These basic objections were maintained during the overtures of 1917, though by then political and military conditions had changed radically. In 1917 Germany was in a state of political confusion which culminated in the forced resignation of Bethmann Hollweg on 13 July. The temper of the Reichstag was such that Chancellor Michaelis, a political nonentity, was obliged to accept the Peace Resolution of 19 July (passed by 212 to 126 votes, with 17 abstentions) which called for 'a peace of understanding and the permanent reconciliation of peoples. Forced territorial acquisitions and political, economic, or financial oppressions are irreconcilable with such a peace'.[24] Groups favouring an annexationist peace, however, soon regained influence, as their actions in the autumn were to show. In September Michaelis and Kühlmann pressed a special meeting of the Crown Council for authority to announce readiness to restore 'the territorial integrity and sovereignty of Belgium'.[25] It was generally supposed that concessions on Belgium would be the surest way of attracting Britain to the negotiating table. This was entirely correct, for Lloyd George had stated on 21 July that 'The determination of the Allies is this, that Belgium must be restored as a free and an independent people. . . . We must not have a Belgian scabbard for the Prussian sword'.[26] The Crown Council's readiness to give assurances was rendered futile by the imposition of extra conditions by the annexationists. Britain was therefore put under no pressure to consider the offer seriously.

None the less, the offer produced mixed reactions. Briand favoured talks while Ribot and Painlevé were firmly opposed. Opinion in Britain was also divided. Bryce, who had consistently favoured negotiation, opined, 'no good could come of such a *démarche*'.[27] Balfour, who by contrast had opposed talks, now believed 'We cannot ignore Kühlmann's proposal. To do so would greatly help the Pan-German forces at Berlin. It would also, I think, weaken the Government in Britain. It would tend to unite Germany in favour of the War and to disunite public opinion at home, which is quite ready vigorously to support the War, if war be necessary, but would shrink from anything which looked like an unreasonable determination to fight for fighting's sake'.[28] This view prevailed; Hankey (Secretary of the War Cabinet) reported, 'The . . . War

Cabinet was in favour of seeing the proposals and deciding whether the Germans meant business or not'.[29] Failure to announce the intention of restoring an independent Belgium relieved the Allies of responsibility to consider the proposals in detail. As Lloyd George perceived, the reasons for this omission were internal: 'Kühlmann knew that the moment he gave a categorical and unambiguous answer satisfactory to the Allies, Junkerdom would be in arms, and "the place he knew would know him no more".'[30]

In 1918 German collapse, following the 'black day' of 8 August, was so rapid that negotiations never started in earnest. In the spring, despite the arrival of American troops in large numbers, the Russian surrender at Brest-Litovsk on 3 March had pointed to a negotiated peace as the alternative to unending trench warfare. Even the most resolute anti-Germans had wavered. On 4 March Bertie wrote gloomily, 'I don't think that we have, throughout this war, had so black a situation as the present one, except when the Germans were close to Paris at the beginning of September 1914'.[31] The peace party had grown in strength in 1917 and Lansdowne's letter of 29 November, published in *The Daily Telegraph*, had argued that prolongation of the war 'will spell ruin for the civilised world, and an infinite addition to the load of human suffering which already weighs upon it'.[32] Germany's decision to launch a series of offensives sealed the fate of the peace movement, however, as well as signalling the end of her war effort when they failed. At last the view that the German people would accept any peace, assiduously peddled by Rumbold ever since 1916,[33] bore some resemblance to the truth. In these circumstances any notion of negotiation was superfluous.

Wartime 'negotiations' thus never acquired formal status. The world knew the outlines of peace proposals, and sometimes details, but conferences never started. The precise effect of years of 'victory' propaganda, of calls for sacrifices and for unity, was, though uncertain, strong enough to prevent a will to peace in Britain— especially in the absence of assurances on Belgium. Nevertheless attempts to promote talks continued. Even the neutrals were not disheartened. In 1917 Pope Benedict XVI circulated a Peace Note which proposed a return to the *status quo* of 1914 and the creation of international bodies to arbitrate and to supervise disarmament.

The British press, regarding these proposals as in the German interest, received the note badly. On behalf of the Allies Britain replied that the matter could be taken no further unless there was a German statement as to war aims. German clumsiness now came to the rescue for, on 21 September, Berlin's reply made no mention of Belgium— which the Note of 1 August had identified as the central issue.

In fact clumsy German diplomacy missed several opportunities of putting pressure on Britain to bow out of the contest by giving firm guarantees of Belgian independence. The demands of industrialists and annexationists were too strident to be stifled. Their opponents knew the importance of the Belgian issue; Bethmann Hollweg and Bernstorff even argued that unless it was solved it might bring the United States into the war as well as keeping Britain in.[34] These were voices crying in the wilderness. Ultimately Germany's internal political weaknesses cost her more than military blunders. In Berlin British war weariness and exasperation with feeble allies was used as an argument for continuing rather than ending the war. The inevitable British response was a determination to fight on, not to pay an impossible political price for peace. British policy towards talks was thus made as much in Berlin as London.

After 1900 Anglo-American relations had improved greatly. The wish to remain on good terms with Washington was closely linked to Britain's interest in peace talks. Roosevelt, the most influential figure in American politics, was a confirmed Anglophile and during his presidency many misunderstandings had been cleared away. In 1914 Woodrow Wilson was President but his knowledge of foreign affairs was small. Opinion in the United States was startled by the outbreak of war and there was a tendency to regard it as a typical European folly: 'Blood-mad monarchs prepare dread sacrifice. Fifteen millions facing death. Royalty forces wreck and ruin on fated lands. Stubborn rulers play subjects as pawns',[35] shrieked the Cedar Rapids *Gazette*. This reaction was not unusual, for there was an amazing ignorance of Europe in a land largely populated by those of European descent. American anxiety to avoid involvement extended throughout society. Spring Rice, the British Ambassador, pointed out, 'He [Wilson] and the Secretary of State [Bryan] are quite determined to take no action which would lose him sympathy of either of the contending parties'.[36] There was, fortunately, in Britain an awareness of the necessity of retaining the goodwill of the United States. The potential strength of the republic was recognized from the earliest days of the war, as Vansittart recalled: 'We could not afford to offend the Americans who supplied us with the munitions which we had omitted to make. . . . The two greatest English-speaking countries were always within reach of misunderstanding, and we had dire need of dollars . . . and of raw materials which Congress might refuse'.[37] It was fully understood in Britain that the rôle of the United States might be critical if war lasted more than a few months, so there was greater readiness to fall in with Washington's wishes in London than in Berlin.

Certainly the United States was never seen as a possible enemy. Walter Page, the American Ambassador, was known to be pro-British and, according to Grey, 'From the first he considered that the United States could be brought into the war early on the side of the Allies if the issue were rightly presented. . . . The comfort, support, and encouragement that his presence was . . . may be imagined, but cannot be over-estimated'.[38] Page's letters confirm Grey's view. On 22 September 1914 he told House, 'If sheer brute force is to rule the world, it will not be worth living in. If German bureaucratic brute force could conquer Europe, presently it would try to conquer the United States'.[39] But it was a delicate task to avoid offending opinion in the United States where there was still an influential anti-British party. German and Irish ethnic groups were loud in their condemnation of the Allies. Pro-German elements were particularly strong in financial and banking circles; according to Spring Rice 'the influence of the Germans and especially the German Jews is very great, and in parts of the country is supreme. We must not count on American sympathy as assured to us'.[40] The danger, then, lay in an attitude of hostile neutrality by the United States and it was this which British diplomacy sought to avert.

British policy was characterized by a wish to fall in with reasonable American proposals. This was evident in 1914, though neither Nicolson nor Hardinge held the United States in high regard.[41]

In the late summer of 1914 it became evident that, prompted by Bryan, Wilson wished to mediate between the belligerents. His proposals came to nothing, however, save that Britain accepted Bryan's arbitration treaty—though a more important proposal that she ratify the London Declaration of 1909 (which would have made impossible the strategy of naval blockade against Germany) was rejected. The question of neutrals' naval rights loomed large in Anglo-American relations, for British interests cut across both German strategy and the neutrals' commercial enterprise. As Grey admitted, 'The object of diplomacy, therefore, was to secure the maximum of blockade that could be enforced without a rupture with the United States'.[42] With Page's help many of the more awkward incidents were smoothed over and American opinion was not unduly antagonized.[43]

The importance of good relations was evident when, in January 1915, Wilson sent his confidant, House, to Europe on a peace mission. He went first to London and was received by Grey, who seems almost to have encouraged the belief that Britain would welcome mediation. This was very misleading and Hankey subsequently argued strongly against any proposal which would inhibit British naval strategy, for such was the price of American mediation.[44] Grey, however, did perceive the weak point of Wilson's initiative and asked whether the United States would be willing to support and participate in the international body which was to be set up to reduce the conflict to manageable proportions and ultimately to regulate world affairs. House was only able to reply that it was American policy 'not to become involved in European affairs'.[45] Thus the Allies were able to dodge the unwanted proposals for mediation and peace without incurring Wilson's displeasure. This contrasted strongly with Germany's overt hostility. The sinking of the *Lusitania* on 7 May 1915 then further reinforced anti-German feeling in the United States.

Anglo-American relations remained good in 1915, despite a personal antipathy between Spring Rice and Wilson. In June 1915 Bryan resigned as Secretary of State, following disagreement with Wilson concerning the tone of American Notes to Germany on submarine warfare. Bryan had strongly influenced the formulation of a neutralist policy, despite knowing even less about world affairs than Wilson. Indeed, the perception of his speeches on domestic issues contrasted sadly with the triviality and irrelevance of those on foreign affairs, where he resembled J. K. Stephen's 'old half-witted sheep which bleats articulate monotony'.[46] Lansing, his successor, while anxious to keep out of the war, had always believed that Germany posed a threat to his country. On 11 July he noted in his diary, 'Germany must not be permitted to win this war and to break even, though to prevent it this country is forced to take an active part. This ultimate necessity must be constantly in our minds in all our controversies with the belligerents'.[47] Lansing did not hesitate to warn Berlin in strong terms both privately and publicly that she was running the risk of war with the United States. Lansing pressed Wilson not to shrink from conflict if Germany's submarine warfare continued to alienate American opinion. As early as 24 August he had argued, 'it would appear that our usefulness in the restoration of peace would certainly not be lessened by a state of war between this country and Germany, and it might even be increased'.[48] On 22 September House recorded that Wilson had told him 'he had never been sure that we ought not to take part in the conflict, and if it seemed evident that Germany and her militaristic ideas were to win, the obligation on us was greater than ever'.[49] The skill with which Grey and Spring Rice handled relations, though greatly aided by the pro-Ally views of Page, Lansing and House, contrasted strongly with Berlin's ponderous diplomacy.

In 1916 Wilson and House made another attempt to secure peace. At the close of 1915 House persuaded the President that omens for a negotiated peace were favourable. In this he was quite wrong. Germany could never agree to the terms House had in mind, while Britain was non-committal. On 6 January 1916 House began his round of talks in London. The government was most anxious to keep him in good humour as naval measures were having a serious effect on American trade, so he met almost all leading British politicians and was fêted wherever he went. According to Hankey the motive was 'to discuss peace before we have passed our zenith or to get the U.S.A. behind us, in which case we could go on for ever'.[50] On 14 February House dined at Lord Reading's home with Asquith,

Balfour, Grey and Lloyd George. During the evening a plan for a possible peace conference was thrashed out.[51] The terms of the draft were recorded in Grey's memorandum of 22 February, though they were only of transient importance as the whole scheme soon collapsed. One section was of real significance, however: 'House told me that President Wilson was ready, on hearing from France and England that the moment was opportune, to propose that a Conference should be summoned to put an end to the war. Should the Allies accept this proposal, and should Germany refuse it, the United States would probably enter the war against Germany'.[52] Had this plan been acted upon it seems probable that the United States would have entered the war in 1916 but, as Lloyd George acidly observed, 'President Wilson was afraid of public opinion in the U.S.A. and Sir Edward Grey was frightened of our Allies'.[53] Yet another peace overture had failed, though once more British relations with Washington remained unimpaired.

Britain was relieved from further pressure by the exigencies of a Presidential campaign in which both candidates reiterated their determination to maintain American neutrality. After his narrow victory Wilson promptly revived mediation plans, though both Lansing and House argued that they would be against Allied interests. Wilson was unmoved and on 18 December circulated a Note asking for statements of war aims from all belligerents. The project was misconceived and hurtful in that it appeared to equate Allied to German motives for involvement in the war. Opinion in Britain was outraged. Samuel described the Note as 'monstrous'.[54] Northcliffe told Page 'everybody is as angry as hell', Page himself spoke of Wilson's 'insulting words', Lord Robert Cecil was 'deeply hurt',[55] while Bonar Law cynically observed, 'What President Wilson is longing for, we are fighting for'.[56] Balfour, the new Foreign Secretary, made it clear in his reply that war aims necessarily involved the defeat of Germany, though he did not exclude the possibility of a peace conference. On 22 January 1917 Wilson, addressing the Senate, made a last desperate plea to the world, but Germany's reply to his December circular showed that annexationist demands were incompatible with American proposals. Mediation was dead.

On 1 February 1917 Germany resumed unrestricted submarine

warfare; two days later the United States broke off relations with her. The sinking of American vessels and the affair of the Zimmermann telegram finally forced Wilson on 2 April to declare war on Germany. Opinion in Britain was delighted. 'It's a great day for the world'[57] Balfour told Page; he had yet to experience working with Wilson. On 10 April the Cabinet decided to send Balfour to Washington to formulate a joint policy. The visit was a diplomatic success but led to no full agreement on policy. The structure of American government made it hard for Washington to adjust to the military, diplomatic and financial demands of wartime, so initially the main benefit from American entry into the war was a rise in Allied morale. Not until 24 August 1917 were financial relations between Britain and the United States put on a sensible footing and only in 1918 did large numbers of American troops arrive in Europe. But the Allies no longer believed the war could not be won.

From April 1917 to the Armistice Anglo-American relations were dominated by the fact of alliance. Instead of being a powerful bystander the United States became yet another ally whose opinions had to be heard, whose advice had to be sought, and whose demands had to be reconciled with those of other allies. Britain was never entirely happy with her allies and the United States proved no exception to the rule. However, apart from a certain lack of realism, most problems with the United States preceded April 1917 or dated from after November 1918. In the cases of her other major allies— France, Italy and Russia—Britain had serious problems throughout the war.

Anglo-Italian relations were dominated by the fact that Italy declared war on 23 May 1915 in return for territorial concessions promised in the secret Treaty of London of 26 April. The romantic lure of an Adriatic empire and recovery of all the *terre irredente*, popular among widely different political movements, proved too strong for Italian links with the Central Powers. Vansittart observed, 'Sonnino . . . gave Austria first chance to buy her. He asked for the Isonzo valley, some Dalmatian islands, a free hand in Albania, all the Trentino, and the carving of an independent state out of Trieste and north-western Istria. When the Austrians winced he turned to the Allies, like a good business man asked for more, and got it'.[58] This unkind accuracy failed to understand the attraction of the semi-Italian provinces among all ranks of society. Even Varè, a seasoned diplomat, recorded in 1918, 'Trent and Trieste are redeemed. It meant not only the realization of my own fondest hopes, but those of my father before me. From one generation to another, this had been our aim in life. This had been our dream'.[59] Consequently attempts to vary the terms by which Italy had entered the war were met with stubborn hostility.

Italy posed Britain two separate but linked problems. The Italian alliance created difficulty with other associates—during 1915-18 with those Balkan states upon whose lands Italy cast covetous eyes, and after 1917 with the United States, whose commitment to national self-determination hardly accorded with the arbitrary distribution of territory envisaged in 1915. The second problem was that of trying to determine the usefulness of the Italians in drawing off Austrian and German forces. Neither of these matters was satisfactorily settled despite British spokesmen maintaining a pose of supreme confidence in their ally's intentions and capacity. Privately there was no enthusiasm. Rumbold was frankly contemptuous, saying, 'it is very disagreeable to think that so many lives should have been lost for the sake of people like the Russians and the Italians. . . . As for the Italians, what can you expect from a nation the majority of which would be better employed selling ice-cream?'[60] Bertie held no better opinion, while Newton hoped that 'we shall not allow our men to be sacrificed because the Italians won't fight for their own country'.[61] After the disaster at Caporetto in autumn 1917 Lloyd George 'spoke as though Italy were a spent force'.[62] Even the recovery of military prestige at Vittorio Veneto a year later failed to convince most British diplomats that Italy had been worth the bribes promised in 1915.

Italy's military failures, which included eleven battles on the Isonzo before attaining a limited victory, affected Allied attitudes. France had never enthusiastically supported major concessions to Italy, while Russia had assented to the Treaty of London with ill grace. Russian objections were founded on dislike of territorial concessions which Balkan Slavs were bound to claim. Serbia and

Montenegro had the same opinion and the promises made to Italy at the probable expense of an enlarged Serbia made that state still less willing to accommodate Greece and Bulgaria. In terms of Balkan politics an Italian alliance was a poisoned chalice. France, as Russia's ally, tended to endorse these objections but was additionally indignant in that Italy conspicuously failed to declare war on Germany. Old rivalries in North Africa and the Mediterranean hardly proved an ideal basis for wartime co-operation and France frequently pressed for a reduction in concessions to Italy. All these factors worked against a full and frank Anglo-Italian relationship and matters were made worse by Britain's wish to detach Austria from her alliance with Germany by making a generous peace. This recurrent theme of British diplomacy found the commitment to Italy an awkward obstacle.

The impending defeat of Russia made Italian aid more important in 1917. On 6 May Ribot wrote, 'Lloyd George told me yesterday that if Russia defaulted it would be necessary to make peace with Austria and compel Italy to content herself with less'.[63] Ribot and Lloyd George wanted to keep the three Western Powers in step lest Italian failures cause her to seek a separate peace with Austria.[64] Italy was suspicious of British sympathy for Austria and had never trusted French intentions. Attempts by France to put pressure on Italy were unsuccessful and created an atmosphere of distrust which was to influence profoundly the diplomacy of 1918–19. As Ribot lamented, 'It must never be forgotten that, because of our geographic situation . . . we find ourselves in a much less advantageous situation than England'.[65] Quite simply, the bargain of 1915 had been based upon self-interest and all three parties were constantly looking for ways to improve the benefits which were to accrue.

Anglo-French relations were not harmonious, despite general agreement as to war aims. Many difficulties arose from the incompatibility of two military establishments, which were not only reluctant to co-operate at the highest level but unwilling to learn from the blunders of each other. Thus the Somme (a joint offensive) was followed by the Second Aisne (Nivelle's brainchild) and then Passchendaele (Haig's offensive). Not until Foch was appointed to the supreme Allied command on 14 April 1918 was there full integration. This haphazard fashion of managing the war not only gave opportunities for almost limitless politicking among the generals but adversely affected relations between the politicians; on both sides they were compelled, for reasons of national prestige, to proclaim faith in generals for whom privately they felt only contempt.

In the long term political sources of discord were more important. Differences of opinion concerning the future of the European power structure were fundamental and irreconcilable. At Versailles they had dire results. Above all else France wanted security against German attack. Various methods of attaining such security were debated hotly but the most popular proposed annexation of German territory up to the Rhine and, preferably, dismemberment of Imperial Germany. This scheme did not commend itself to British policy-makers, who feared French domination of Europe. Cambon had observed that 'France victorious must grow accustomed to being a lesser power than France vanquished',[66] but his advice was not heeded and suspicions in London and Washington multiplied. Vansittart recognized 'She [France] was as rightly convinced that only control of the Rhine's left bank would ensure her safety as the British and Americans were rightly convinced that such a mutilation of Germany would only increase France's danger'.[67] Balfour told the Commons in 1919, 'Never did we desire, and never did we encourage the idea that a bit of Germany should be cut off from the parent state . . . so as to make a new buffer state'.[68] Nor did Lloyd George give France much hope that Britain would support a French-dominated power structure. In a broad survey of war aims on 5 January 1918 the premier revealed how wide was the gulf between British and French aspirations;[69] during the peace negotiations it widened further.

Differences of opinion over the future of the Ottoman Empire were deep-rooted and plagued relations. In anxiety to relieve Turkish pressure Britain entered into far-reaching commitments to the Arabs in autumn 1915. These promises conflicted with French interest in the reversion of Syria. In October Sykes, a Foreign Office representative, was commissioned to negotiate with Picot of the

Quai d'Orsay. On 4 February 1916 the Sykes–Picot agreement was approved and Russian consent to an amended version was obtained on 23 March. An Arab rising in Hejaz in June created an impossible situation for Britain, now committed to two opposed courses of action. This muddle, however, paled into insignificance beside that of the Balfour Declaration of 2 November 1917. The Foreign Secretary told Lord Rothschild that the government viewed 'with favour the establishment in Palestine of a national home 'for the Jewish people, and will use their best endeavours to facilitate the achievement of this object'.[70] In two years Britain had promised most of the Holy Land to Hejaz, to divide it with France and to give control of it to the Jews. Not unnaturally, Paris was anxious about these conflicting claims—particularly because of 'growing apprehension as it became clear that when the war ended British forces would probably be in control of a large part of the territory and the sphere of influence allotted to France'.[71] Suspicion increased apace, and not only between London and Paris. The crowning folly was an Anglo-French Declaration of 9 November 1918 in favour of Arab independence and contrary to the Sykes–Picot agreement. By the close of 1918 all parties to the Palestine dispute had good cause for mutual distrust.

Anglo-Russian relations posed even more of a problem, for Britain had little sympathy for Russia in her historic conflict with Austria and still less for her autocracy. Ancient rivalries had not been stilled by the convention of 1907; under the pressure of war old suspicions re-emerged. There was relief when the Tsar's régime fell, though this hardly warranted the optimism of Lloyd George who 'actually congratulated the poor Provisional Government on the revolution as "the greatest service the Russian people have yet made to the cause for which the Allies are fighting" '.[72] The Foreign Office view favoured 'a permanent Anglo-Russian alliance to guarantee peace'[73] but Bertie was less enthusiastic about this notion than Hardinge or Nicolson, observing in August 1914, 'The German Military Power has been a curse to the world: may it come to an end and not be replaced by that of another Power such as Russia'.[74]

Early in the war the pro-Russian faction held the upper hand and St Petersburg received generous treatment, such as the decision to promise Russia Constantinople. The involvement of Turkey on the other side of the Central Powers had weakened the British preference for Ottoman unity—a preference which had been waning ever since 1878. In September 1914 Sazonov put forward claims for territorial concessions after the war, though these did not include the Straits. Russian support, even after the miracle of the Marne, was essential in autumn 1914 but the Western Powers did not like Sazonov's proposed reconstruction of Eastern and Southern Europe. The Turkish involvement in war on 5 November was a godsend, as the Straits, long the dream of many Russians, could be ceded in return for reduced Russian demands elsewhere. As early as 13 November George V told Benckendorff, 'as far as Constantinople is concerned it is clear that this city must be yours'.[75] This decision, made formally in the War Councils of 6 and 10 March 1915,[76] was a serious error of judgment. Asquith's view that 'Britain must finally abandon the formula of Ottoman Integrity'[77] was backed by the military and naval establishments, who professed to see no threat to strategic interests in Russian occupation of the Straits. Simultaneously these 'experts' argued for retention of Alexandretta as a counterpoise.[78] This muddled thinking, viewed with dismay by Russophobes such as Curzon,[79] formed part of that general misjudgment of Russian capabilities and acceptance of an intolerable régime which had for so long characterized Republican France and the British Foreign Office. Under the stress of war it now penetrated the whole political establishment.

As the war progressed Russian military capacity was revealed. Scales fell from the eyes of politicians and diplomats. Russian opposition to peace with Austria became increasingly irksome, though the Western Powers were bound by the agreement of 4 September 1914: 'The three allies should not separate when it comes to a question of making peace . . . no one of the allies will demand or propose terms of peace without the consent of the others'.[80] Also, instead of Russia being a prop to the alliance, it became customary to launch offensives in the West to relieve pressure in the East. Operations in Eastern Europe were conducted on a heroic scale but had

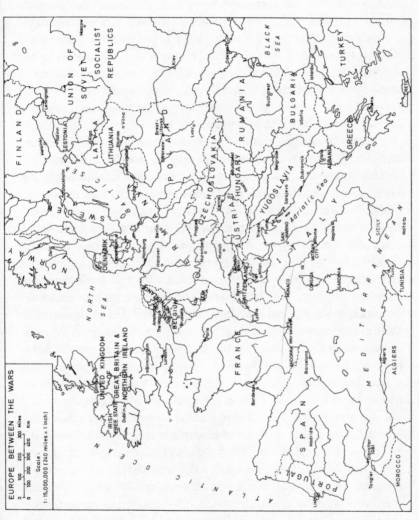

Map 2. Europe in 1920

little else to recommend them. The seizure of Przemsyl in March 1915 hardly relieved German pressure on the Western Front, but the fall of Pinsk and Novogeorgievsk to the Germans forced Franco-British attacks at Loos and in Champagne which set back Western military prospects by many months. In Britain there was fear lest Russia make peace separately, for in St Petersburg one faction had always sympathized with Germany and had been hostile to the democracies. In London it was argued that this influence could be minimized only by concessions. This opinion was mistaken, for there was little chance of Germany and Russia reaching agreement on the future rôle of Austria in Eastern Europe.

During the winter of 1916–17 Russia's plight became desperate and British pressure for peace with Austria increased. Drummond drafted a memorandum, subsequently endorsed by Hardinge and Lord Robert Cecil,[81] which envisaged a settlement unlikely to please Russia. However, before it was discussed Nicholas II was replaced by the Provisional Government, whose commitment to both democracy and the war was warmly welcomed. Talks were abandoned, though soon the good faith of Russia once more came into question as Kerensky was faced with fresh demands for peace. Newton told Rumbold bitterly, 'it is lamentable when people in high places are deficient in brains: and war finds them out'.[82] He elaborated this theme in his memoirs, recalling, 'when the Czar's Government came to an end, we at once constructed a fool's paradise in which we luxuriated for a brief period. We fondly imagined that the real reason for Russian inefficiency was treason and stupidity in high places, and airily assumed that the new constitutional administration would put out all its strength into a real effort to win the war. What we had failed to realise was that the Russians had never been whole-hearted and were now only too glad to find an excuse for retreat and eventual collapse. The awakening was bitter, and worse still the discovery that Russia, our former Ally, would in all probability shortly become an open enemy'.[83] The prophets of gloom were soon justified. In August Rumbold minuted, 'The Russians have let us down badly again, they are dreadful allies . . . because one can never tell what to expect from them. We have poured out money and munitions for them. . . . It is very disgusting, and if only they had played up properly the war would have been over this autumn'.[84] Russian withdrawal from the war in March 1918 eased British difficulties in reconciling conflicting aspirations in Eastern Europe but left the problem of choosing between the rival Bolshevik and White régimes. It was a sad dilemma. Vansittart argued for intervention on the basis that 'We might have got from Kolchak and Denikin a decent democratic government, coupled with a federalism which would have obviated another centralized tyranny. . . . From the start neither good faith nor human life was of the least account to the Bolsheviks'.[85] A fatal capacity for inaction decided the issue by default and after March 1918 Russia was almost completely omitted from policy calculations; this was to produce dire results.

In 1914 the Dominions had rallied with alacrity to the call to arms and had provided considerable support in the European theatre. Preparations for Imperial co-operation in wartime had existed in some form ever since creation of the Committee of Imperial Defence in 1902. However, what mattered in 1914 was not the plans but the readiness to implement them. Canada, New Zealand and Australia all produced larger contingents than they had promised. The strain on British manpower which led to conscription in 1916 would have become apparent sooner but for Imperial contributions. The consequences of Imperial assistance were far-reaching. In March 1917 the Imperial War Cabinet was created to resolve strategic problems, for none of the Dominion war leaders had much enthusiasm for frontal assaults in the West. Furthermore, Borden (Canada), Smuts (South Africa), Massey (New Zealand) and Hughes (Australia) regarded themselves as equals of Lloyd George rather than as auxiliaries and thus showed little inclination to bow to his will. On the one hand there was, according to Roskill, 'a growing sense of "nationhood", and of the need to show complete political independence, among most of the Dominion statesmen—especially those from Canada and South Africa'.[86] At the same time there were real differences of interest. Rothwell pointed out that 'In view of the immense contribution which the Empire . . . was making to the war effort, its leaders had the moral and political right to make their influence felt wherever they chose. They were always concerned that the German colonies, especially those occupied by South Africa, Australia and New Zealand, should remain in Allied hands. In this way they betrayed, to Lloyd George's mind, a narrow and mistaken conception of war aims. In 1918, most of them, especially the Canadians, added their voices to those which called for the abandonment of the western strategy, a development highly relevant to war aims'.[87]

Dominion fears regarding the future of German colonies were to play a major part in the Versailles debates; they stemmed primarily from a belief that in the long term European strategic interests would dominate London's decisions. Dominion wishes had been regarded as secondary even by 1914, for objections to Japanese expansion had been brushed aside by Grey. Now that Britain needed aid Dominion statesmen intended to ensure their interests were not overlooked. American suspicions of Japan reinforced the bargaining position of Australia and New Zealand and, by forcing a change in British attitudes, modified the Anglo-Japanese relationship. Wartime pressures made it plain that the 'Britain knows best' attitude was no longer acceptable. Smuts put it clearly in May 1917: 'You cannot settle a common foreign policy for the whole of the British Empire without changing that policy very much from what it has been in the past, because the policy will have to be, for one thing, far simpler. In the other parts of the Empire we do not understand diplomatic finesse'.[88] Although emotional ties between Britain and the Dominions remained strong, the old relationship of tutelage, weakened by 1914, was destroyed by war.

British policy in Asia was forced to change, though the magnitude of the change was not seen until after 1918. In 1914 the Under-Secretary of State for India observed, 'India's partnership with us in spirit and on battlefields cannot but alter the angle from which we shall henceforward look at the problems of the government of India'.[89] Prescience indeed—by 1917 some Indians were included in the Imperial War Cabinet. A strong group still favoured the *status quo* but a growing party, led by Montagu, preferred autonomy on Dominion lines. What was suitable for Australia was believed to be appropriate for India. Japan's example showed that the days of colonial rule in Asia were numbered. In 1914 she declared war on

Germany and promptly seized Kiaochow and Shantung. In 1915 Tokyo shackled Chinese economic and political development by making her Twenty-one demands in the face of British hostility. The moves against Germany were irrelevant to the main war effort and, as Vansittart argued, 'While the Japanese gave to us negligible help, they helped themselves to our trade and a fair amount of booty'.[90] By 1918 'British officials . . . attributed to Japan the worst characteristics of their European neighbours: the militarism of Germany and the commerical monopolism of France'.[91] Pressure from the Dominions and the United States had obliged Britain to loosen her ties with Japan; now Japanese independence acted as a beacon to the rest of Asia.

Despite difficulties with her allies, Britain had assumed peacetime co-operation. Even after Brest-Litovsk, the publication of secret treaties, and the Tsar's execution, few argued that obligations previously entered into could be discarded. The fact remains that Britain had made promises which were not wholly reconcilable. Anxiety to sustain flagging efforts, particularly in Eastern Europe, had led to a policy of acquiring allies at almost any cost. But for Russia's collapse Britain could not have honourably discharged her obligations to Greece, Serbia, Roumania and a number of Eastern European nationalities and simultaneously have preserved Austria and Turkey in some recognizable form. Perhaps the intention was always to deal with the situation on an *ad hoc* basis. Hardinge, for example, said of the promises made to the Poles: 'So long as it [a free and united Poland] is only a pious aspiration it does not much matter what is said'.[92] This was British *Realpolitik* on a Bismarckian scale.

It seems that British policy in Eastern Europe was, on the whole, confused rather than Machiavellian. There was more than a hint of 'a far-away country . . .'[93] in the policies of 1914–18 as well as those of the 1930s. Indeed there was much confusion, often stemming from unresolved and conflicting policies. Vansittart even recorded that 'Lloyd George . . . let on or out that he thought Kharkov a general'.[94] To Britain, an Eastern Europe dominated by Russia was never as attractive as some revival of the pre-1914 structure. The

inconsistent and ambiguous attitudes of Greece, Bulgaria and
Roumania added to the prevailing confusion. Sir Almeric Fitzroy
noted in 1916 how elliptic British policy seemed: 'Troubridge
[head of the naval mission to Serbia] spoke in strong condemnation
of British diplomacy, which appeared incapable of realising the
simple faith of such a people or understanding how lost they were to
refinements of policy and intricate calculations. . . . After the destruction of the Austrian invader the Serbians desired, with the keen
insight of untutored minds, to attack the Bulgarians before they
were mobilised, when Bulgaria could easily have been overrun;
but our agents were fatuous enough to suppose they could hold
the Bulgars in leash, and refused the Serbs the desired permission.
Evidence of Ferdinand's coming perjury was under their noses,
but they preferred to rely upon the infallibility of their convictions'.[95]
Later in the war the experts on Eastern Europe within the Foreign
Office, Namier and Seton-Watson, showed hostility to the continued
existence of a Danubian state and pressed for the recognition of
national states. This further complicated the British position and
provided fertile ground for the inconsistencies of 1919–22.

The collapse of Germany in autumn 1918 ended the war and
ushered in a period of intense diplomatic activity. The shape of
a settlement could be but dimly seen in November 1918, not least
because of the chaos in Central Europe. Germany was in the throes
of revolution and new governments were being proclaimed in
Prague, Warsaw, Helsinki and the Baltic lands. Almost as much
confusion existed amongst the Allies. Having secured Germany's
defeat, the Allies could now settle down to leisurely consideration
of a detailed settlement, though this required basic agreement on
general principles. No such consensus existed.

The major participants in the peace conference were Britain,
France and the United States. Russia, Japan and Italy all played
important parts both at and away from deliberations but hardly
shaped the settlement in the same way as the Big Three. In early
1918 Wilson had enunciated Fourteen Points as the basis for a possible
settlement. On 11 February he had called for peace based upon
Four Principles and on 27 September had added his Five Particulars.
These lofty guidelines concealed the weakness that, according to

Keynes, 'the President had thought out nothing; when it came to practice his ideas were nebulous and incomplete. He had no plan, no scheme, no constructive ideas whatever for clothing with the flesh of life the commandments which he had thundered from the White House'.[96] A few days before Wilson's original address, Lloyd George had called at Caxton Hall for an international organization to promote collective security and had promised a just peace. The premier's speech had merely anticipated the President's proposals; apparently there was no unbridgeable chasm between Wilson and Lloyd George. The French position was very different. Early in 1918 it was obviously untimely for Clemenceau to speak out against Wilson's idealism, but his government never subscribed at any stage to these proposals.

Evidence of the incompatibility of Allied aims was plain for those who wished to see. Quite apart from the certainty of French intransigence, publicly confirmed by Clemenceau on 29 December 1918, the territorial ambitions of Japan, Italy and the Dominions made it unlikely that Wilson's ideals could be achieved. Almost before the Armistice had taken effect the peacemakers were bombarded with conflicting proposals. On the one hand Lord Robert Cecil called for the creation of 'a League of Nations . . . to insure the fulfillment of accepted international obligations and to provide safeguards against war'.[97] At the opposite extreme Foch and Weygand demanded in a memorandum of 10 January 1919, 'the Rhine. . . . Unless the Rhine is taken from German control, the peaceful, industrial countries of the North-west of Europe will be submerged'.[98] The alternative of a conciliatory or a punitive peace was never more plainly stated.

British policy lay at neither extreme. Commitments had been made, but these were usually vague. Lloyd George had promised in the election campaign to make Germany pay 'to the limit of her capacity',[99] but had already told Riddell, 'the question is how they can be made to pay beyond a certain point. . . . We do not mean to take their goods, because that would prejudice our trade'.[100] In similar fashion the War Cabinet had agreed to Curzon's motion that 'the armistice should represent the admission of German defeat by sea', and hence the surrender of much of the German Fleet, but

Lloyd George went to the conference inveighing against 'our stupid admirals'.[101] Nicolson's son, a British delegate, believed 'We were journeying to Paris, not merely to liquidate the war, but to found a new order in Europe. We were preparing not Peace only, but Eternal Peace. There was about us the halo of some divine mission. We must be alert, stern, righteous and ascetic. For we were bent on doing great, permanent and noble things'.[102] Rumbold, by contrast, hoped 'the new armistice terms will be really stiff'.[103] By a strange paradox the British Government was committed to very little of substance but, because of public expressions of opinion, had little room for manoeuvre. Such flexibility as existed was further constrained by the definite positions of Britain's allies.

Indeed, British policy at Versailles became less a fulfilment of aims than an avoidance of potentially disastrous solutions. The conflicting personalities of Lloyd George, Clemenceau and Wilson, combined with different national interests, pushed them towards conflict not co-operation. Anatole France was savagely critical of both Wilson and Lloyd George, remarking of the President: 'The most comic of all the delegates is Wilson. He knows nothing of Europe or its history, and he comes here to weigh the rights of nations in a chemist's balance. He hands out justice by the milligramme. These Protestants are terrible. They mingle the principles of the Bible with the interests of finance: the result is odious'.[104] He was scarcely more complimentary about the Briton: 'He speaks the same language as Wilson, but he is utterly different. The other is a naïf. Lloyd George is a clever fellow. He reads the Bible and sings his psalms, but he serves his country and himself. He is a great Englishman. He will abandon us before long, for at bottom he detests us'.[105] This view of Lloyd George as a deceiver was echoed by Keynes—'this extraordinary figure of our time, this syren, this goat-footed bard, this half-human visitor to our age from the hag-ridden, magic and enchanted woods of Celtic antiquity. . . . Lloyd George is rooted in nothing; he is void and without content'.[106] The same observer also painted a vivid portrait of Clemenceau: 'His age, his character, his wit, and his appearance joined to give him objectivity and a defined outline in an environment of confusion. One could not despise Clemenceau or dislike him, but only take a different view as to the nature of civilised man, or indulge, at least, a different hope . . . he closed his eyes often and sat back in his chair with an impassive face of parchment, his grey gloved hands clasped in front of him . . . dry in soul and empty of hope . . . he had one illusion —France; and one disillusion—mankind'.[107] Real understanding between Wilson and Clemenceau was impossible; Lloyd George was expected to bridge the gulf. In the attempt strange policies were adopted which in sum represented neither the short nor long term interests of any party to the settlement.

The Treaty of Versailles, signed on 28 June 1919, was highly unsatisfactory. British interests in essence involved equitable territorial redistribution, modest reparations, creation of a new security system, destruction of the German Navy, and a *modus vivendi* with the defeated nations. On the whole Lloyd George and his delegation recognized and tried to secure these interests, though allowance has to be made for election promises and a Tory-dominated coalition. It was, for example, quite impossible to hang the Kaiser or even to try him, as he was a refugee in neutral Holland. While Lloyd George claimed an anxiety to bring war criminals to justice there is reason to think he was not sorry to evade the issue: Vansittart commented, 'His flight [the Kaiser's] . . . relieved us from the nuisance of not knowing what to do with him. . . . It was idiotic even to think of hanging him in compliance with irresolute clamour, but I was among the unwise who wished some evil to befall him. He deserved ill of the world . . .'.[108] However, the major obstacle to fulfilment of British aims was not this kind of reality, nor even French obstinacy and American idealism, but British irresolution. Britain found herself in sympathy with French and Eastern European demands for compensation (which at times amounted to revenge) and also with American notions of an ideally just peace. In neither situation could Germany play the part Britain desired for her—that of commercial partner and bulwark against Bolshevism—and Britain could not prevail on Wilson and Clemenceau to abandon their illusions. Lloyd George soon gave up the struggle to produce an integrated policy and confined his efforts to salvaging individual interests. The logic of British arguments at Versailles was thus obscured and the whole policy opened to charges of inconsistency, malevolence and stupidity.

It is of interest to see how British aims were frustrated. The most significant defeat was that over the territorial clauses. Opinion was well aware of the potential danger of fragmentation of Central and Eastern Europe into small, jealous nation states. Sir Eric Geddes had argued on 17 September 1918, 'For post-war purposes I suggest that we want a strong united Austria and not a disintegrated collection of German vassal states'.[109] This argument was entirely consistent with the general trend of wartime policy, for Britain had not sought Austrian destruction but merely separation from German influence. Only a few officials had shown enthusiasm for the subject nationalities. The creation of the successor states was the result of Wilson's commitment to self-determination and Clemenceau's opportunist transfers of territory to weaken Germany. Wilson was convinced that the nationalities had been oppressed and that independence would eliminate injustice. It was hard to argue against such naiviety, especially when Americans of Eastern European descent had been overwhelmingly pro-Ally after 1917. Furthermore, the bandwagon of self-determination as democracy's answer to Bolshevism soon gathered pace. The position of Poland shows how unreal was the rôle assigned to these states. Poland was, in France's view, to contain Germany; in American eyes she was to be a bulwark against Bolshevism. Each task was uniquely different, together quite impossible.

Comments on the territorial settlement were largely adverse, though the criticism was often inconsistent. Objections tended to fall into one of three categories—that the settlement made no economic sense, that it was ethnically inaccurate, or that it was generally inadvisable in terms of politics and strategy. These faults were exaggerated; no settlement could have done justice to the conflicting aspirations of polyglot Eastern Europe, though the inconsistency of the territorial adjustments deservedly attracted much unfavourable comment. If the settlement was intended to reflect the principle of self-determination it was hard to explain the transfer of millions of Magyars to Roumania and of Germans to Czechoslovakia. Equally, if the settlement was supposed to provide new states with sound economic and strategic positions, how were these aims advanced by creating the monstrous city-states of Fiume, Memel and Danzig? If the intention was punitive, why were plebiscites held in East Prussia, Silesia and Schleswig-Holstein? The failure to 'agree as to the means by which these aims shall be secured'[110] created confusion immediately and stored up regrets and resentment for the future.

Contemporary ciriticism of the territorial settlement was ferocious. Keynes, who reserved most of his spleen for the economic clauses, was contemptuous in his view of Poland: 'unless her great neighbours are prosperous and orderly, Poland is an economic impossibility with no industry but Jew-baiting . . . when she finds that the seductive policy of France is pure rhodomontade . . . she will fall, as promptly as possible, into the arms of somebody else'.[111] Eastern European politics now seemed Ruritanian, but without the romance. Sir Percy Loraine remarked that the new states reminded him 'of children saying to each other: "You broke my toy long ago, so now I'll break yours".'[112] Even Hardinge, who believed it was necessary to punish Germany, was unhappy: 'The Treaties of Versailles and of St Germain both contained provisions which anybody with any knowledge of foreign politics or of European affairs would have realized as being opposed to every principle of national life and existence. In Central Europe, States were created which could not be self-supporting and economic barriers were raised which could not fail to strangle their development'.[113] Nor were the Eastern Europeans themselves satisfied. Poland quarrelled with Czechoslovakia over Teschen and with Lithuania over Vilna. Twenty years after Roumania had absorbed most of Transylvania, Bratianu's son still lamented that Trianon 'had denied them their rightful frontier on the Tisza'.[114] The settlement's failure was summed up by Churchill: 'No peace had been made acceptable to Germany or giving security to France. Central and Southern Europe had broken into intensely nationalistic fragments sundered from each other by enmities and jealousies'.[115]

The decision to ignore Russia was a particularly strange feature of the settlement, though the Allies somewhat halfheartedly supported intervention. The likely reaction of any future Russian government, whatever its political complexion, made this unwise. Smuts was critical, telling Lloyd George, 'It is reasonably certain that Germany and Russia will again be great Powers. . . . I think that we are building a house of sand'.[116] Keynes similarly referred to 'crazy dreams and childish intrigue in Russia'.[117] The problem was that Wilson's dreams of self-determination could not be reconciled with preservation of the 1914 Empire or inflated claims made by the Tsarist government after the outbreak of war. The peacemakers took advantage of a weak and much disliked régime to impose a settlement which was bound to be challenged as soon as a strong Russian government emerged. Lloyd George himself admitted that 'Denikin is opposed to the new states so that in protecting them you are fighting Denikin'.[118] An enemy had been created without compensating advantage elsewhere. Versailles was in this sense less realistic than Brest-Litovsk.

Britain also sustained a defeat over reparations. Although Lloyd George was under pressure to demand enormous sums from Germany, Britain had not fought on in 1918 in order to secure reparations and it seems unlikely that policy-makers ever did consider compensation as the central issue. However, Belgian and French politicians led the way, closely followed by Hughes. Within the Coalition was strong anti-German feeling and on 9 December Sir Eric Geddes, who had previously been suspected of being unwilling to press Germany hard, argued for mass confiscation of German resources, art treasures and manuscripts: Germany 'is going to pay restitution, reparation, and indemnity, and I have personally no doubt we will get everything out of her that you can squeeze out of a lemon and a bit more'.[119] Northcliffe, supported by Churchill and the Tory hard-liners, ran a sustained campaign in the press. Within the Foreign Office there were doubts as to the practicability of these demands, though some, like Rumbold, did support a punitive peace.

The essential problem was that Britain needed a quick German recovery so that traditional trading patterns could resume. Economic interest stood opposed to election promises. Lloyd George was incapable of resisting French demands for huge reparations without Wilson's support, but the President was aware of the domestic necessity of securing repayment of American loans and took the line of least resistance. In fact, Wilson favoured only a small levy as he did not wish to precipitate Germany into the arms of the Bolsheviks. He failed to understand that the basis of French demands was not a wish for justice but determination to reduce Germany to a weak unit. In France there was almost total incomprehension of the connexion between British and German prosperity. At home the figures provided by Cunliffe and the blue-ribbon committee, set up in November 1918 to determine German capacity to pay, were widely accepted as a basis for British policy. Little attention was paid to the very different analysis of Keynes. Indeed, there was little to choose between the vengeful attitudes of the French and British Right. Lloyd George was saddled with a powerful group of intransigents—the Geddes brothers, Churchill and Long—while Clemenceau's realism was restricted by the activities of Poincaré, Foch and Finance Minister Klotz, of whom Clemenceau wryly observed, 'he was the only Jew who could not count'.[120] Political expediency thus dictated Allied conduct.

Those who were well placed to judge thought proceedings disastrous. Harold Nicolson believed 'The great crime is in the reparation clauses, which were drawn up solely to please the House of Commons, and which are quite impossible to execute. If I were the Germans I shouldn't sign for a moment. You see it gives them no hope whatsoever, either now or in the future'.[121] The Germans argued, 'We do not know, and indeed we doubt, whether the Delegates of the Allied and Associated Powers realise the inevitable consequences which will take place if Germany . . . suddenly finds herself pushed back to the phase of her development which corresponds to her economic condition and the numbers of her population as they were half a century ago. Those who sign this Treaty will sign the death sentence of many millions'—Keynes' comment was 'I know of no adequate answer to these words'.[122] British interest was not served by the economic settlement but badly damaged.

British policy was successful in that the League of Nations was created in order to provide a security system. Lord Robert Cecil's fear that 'All the European bureaucracies will be against the idea, including probably the bureaucracy of this country'[123] was not borne out in practice. The Foreign Office favoured the League as a means to restore Germany to respectability while providing security for her former enemies. The League was seen as the alternative to continuation of the wartime alliances, already becoming unpopular with the public. There was little more that Britain could have done to make the League work better, for success hinged on the attitude of the United States. In March 1920 the appropriate instruments were not ratified by the Senate; thereafter the League was doomed to impotence. Without full American participation the League could not enforce its collective will on recalcitrant states. The whole framework for collective security had been designed in accordance with an American membership now denied. Britain and France were not strong enough to act as arbiters of the world, while Italy and Japan soon appeared as revisionist as the defeated nations. France had never been an enthusiast for the League, preferring an alliance with Britain and the United States—or at least an Anglo-American guarantee. Having given up many claims in return for promises that the League would provide all the security the French could reasonably require, Clemenceau and Poincaré were understandably nettled by American refusal to ratify arrangements made specifically to ensure American participation. Many Britons sympathized with France's feelings, though not her demands, but nothing could be done. Perforce France turned to Eastern Europe for allies, so opening a wide breach with Britain. Thus, even in the case of the League, British aspirations were not fulfilled.

The scuttling of the German Navy at Scapa Flow removed another British anxiety, though the evidence of German bad faith caused a furore in Paris. A hardening of Allied attitudes was the inevitable consequence and Germany was deemed trustworthy only if under strict surveillance. The German colonies were divided amongst the victorious powers, including the Dominions, for the most part to British satisfaction. The two principal strategic threats of the years before 1914 had, therefore, been eliminated and the Empire seemed more secure than at any point since the 1880s.

The most difficult task which faced Britain was to reach a *modus vivendi* with the defeated nations. Anti-German propaganda prevalent since 1900, outrage at the violation of Belgian neutrality, casualty lists of 1914–18, economic hardship in wartime and poor prospects thereafter, had created a vast accumulation of resentments. In Germany there were many parallels and the inconsistencies of the peace settlement added to the problem. In both Britain and Germany it was argued that the settlement had delayed rather than promoted agreement. Von Papen drew attention to the totality of peace terms, arguing, 'The question may well be asked whether this totality in the name of democracy did not plant the seed of later totalitarian political developments'.[124] The fact that the settlement was widely expected to provide a cure for all European ills made its inadequacy all the more unacceptable. The peace was disliked and despised by both the Allies and the Central Powers and contributed little, if anything, to the establishment of any long-term balance of interests. Neither France nor the United States showed much interest in promoting European amity, so problems engendered by German distaste for *Diktat* concerned them only indirectly; on Britain they had an immediate and critical impact. Indeed, as early as 1920 British policy began to be shaped by anxiety to avoid further offending Germany. Under Lloyd George the drift towards appeasement was not extensive, but gathered pace later in the decade.

Concerted action from the major guarantors of the peace settlement was needed to find solutions to the very serious problems which faced the post-war world. Yet there existed neither unanimity among the victors nor conciliatory spirit amongst the vanquished. The settlement had been shaped largely by statesmen pursuing national interests; it seemed logical after 1919 to base policy on the same considerations—many of which markedly resembled those of the pre-1914 era. The selfish attitude of France and the rapacious greed of Italy and Japan were as apparent to contemporaries as to subsequent generations, but it was little realized—in Britain at least—how narrowly nationalist was British policy. In 1935 King-Hall commented that 'British policy was—as it always has been—extremely flexible in detail and wider in its scope than that of France. It was the policy of a World Power in contrast to that of a continental power'.[125] He also asserted that Britain tried harder than other

nations to make collective security work. These pertinent obser-
vations, however, obscure the fact that Britain seems to have believed
that, as a non-continental power, she could in the end opt out of
difficult situations and embarrassing commitments. These reservations,
based on an erroneous view of Britain's situation, greatly affected
the attitudes of the two major continental powers. Suspicions concerning British reliability haunted the Quai d'Orsay and drove
France into Shylock-like postures. The Wilhelmstrasse pinned its
hopes on British reluctance to endorse further punitive action.
Germany thus adopted a policy of procrastination, believing that
Britain would rather make concessions to her than fight for France.
The years 1920–22 witnessed hesitant steps towards appeasement.
Dissolution of the wartime alliance was followed by the break-
down of the *entente*.

British policy during 1920–22 was pragmatic in concept if
unrealistic in execution, being an attempt to match the commitments
of 1919 to the facts of the post-war world. British policy-makers
were thus concerned with a number of familiar and new problems.
Recurrent themes included a desire for good relations with the
United States and France, growing fears of Japan and Italy, suspicion
of Russia and a deep reluctance to use force to solve problems. New
points of concern involved the territorial settlement in Europe and
the Levant, a search for good relations with Germany, reparations
and disarmament. All these problems had to be tackled when Britain
had lost most of that self-confidence which had previously so irritated
her rivals. A General Staff minute of 1921 bewailed, 'our liabilities
are so vast . . . that to assess them must be largely a matter of
conjecture'.[126] There was little realism to match the prevailing gloom
concerning the future. As Professor Howard pointed out, 'There
was . . . a quite terrifying contrast between the state of the post-war
world as British governments perceived it, and as the British people
wished it to be'.[127] It is hardly surprising, then, that the Foreign
Office proved such a bed of nails in the inter-war period. Viscount
Templewood, writing in 1954, observed, 'Since the end of the
First World War, no Foreign Secretary, with the possible exception
of MacDonald, could claim to have made a success of his period of
office. . . . Was it that the problem of satisfying at one and the same

time both the British public and many foreign governments was insoluble?'[128] Problems were vast and lack of confidence increased their scope.

Relations with former allies were particularly difficult. After the end of the war the special links between Britain, Japan and the United States were broken. Since 1911 Britain had not played a primary rôle in the Far East but had assigned protection of her interests to an ally, Japan, and a friendly power, the United States. These nations had increasingly shown an inability to co-operate, thus causing London grave embarrassment. The events of 1914–18 had provided no relief and it was with some trepidation that in 1919 the Foreign Office suggested conclusion of an *entente* between the three countries. Britain needed local support in the Far East and diplomatic help at Versailles, so could not afford an American–Japanese quarrel. In dealing with some European problems, such as Silesia, Japan was more reliable than the United States, so Britain was not anxious to abandon her ally. The principal obstacle to smooth Anglo-Japanese relations was Japanese expansion in China, heartily disapproved of by both Britain and the United States. In 1920, therefore, a Foreign Office committee was appointed to examine the desirability of renewing the alliance of 1911.

Debate continued well into 1921, particularly during the Imperial Conference at which Australia and New Zealand strongly supported renewal and Canada, equally vigorously, argued for co-operation with the United States and jettisoning the alliance. Opinion among experts and politicians was also divided, but on balance favoured renewal. Curzon, the Foreign Secretary, Balfour and Lloyd George were among the majority. Churchill, the Colonial Secretary, had substantial reservations. He believed that renewal would revive problems with the United States, particularly with regard to naval building: 'It would be a ghastly state of affairs', he wrote 'if we were to drift into direct naval rivalry with the United States'.[129] Curzon's allies, better acquainted with American unreliability, were less concerned to curry favour with Washington. At the Imperial Conference, however, Lloyd George was badly frightened by Hughes' anti-American outbursts and declaimed that 'Friendly co-operation with the United States is for us a cardinal principle'.[130] It was plainly impossible to renew the alliance and remain on close terms with Washington. Britain was saved from this dilemma on 11 July by President Harding's call for a Pacific Conference to discuss the Far East, the naval race and associated problems. All parties eagerly accepted the Conference as a solution to their problems.

The Washington Naval Conference opened on 12 November 1921 and ended on 6 February 1922. The chief British delegate was Balfour, whose masterly handling of contentious issues enabled Britain to avoid too many embarrassing decisions. But even he could not avoid ending the Japanese Alliance. On 13 December the alliance was terminated and the new agreements substituted. An observer commented: 'As the last sentence sounded and the Anglo-Japanese alliance publicly perished, his head fell forward on his chest exactly as if the spinal chord had been severed. It was an amazing revelation of what the Japanese Treaty had meant to the men of a vanished age'.[131] Replacing the Treaty was the new Five Power Treaty, which fixed a 5:5:3:1·75:1·75 ratio in capital ships and aircraft carriers for Britain, the U.S.A., Japan, France and Italy respectively. There were also limitations on tonnage, a ten-year holiday in naval building and a moratorium on further fortification of various potential bases in the West Pacific. The conference significantly failed to agree on the future of China. By simultaneously abandoning China to her fate and failing to renew the Anglo-Japanese Alliance Britain lost all control over Japanese actions. Nor had active American participation been secured in compensation. The effect of these events, however, was not fully apparent until the end of the decade.

The Anglo-Italian alliance also collapsed. The democratic parties in Italy were gravely weakened by Orlando's failure at Versailles. Italy's complaint that she had been promised much and given little helped pave the way for Mussolini's advent to power in October 1922. National sentiment was more hostile towards former allies than to the nations whom Italy had hoped to plunder. On 12 September 1919 D'Annunzio seized Fiume, then under direct Allied military control, without French or British troops firing a shot, and held the city until 26 December 1920. His defiance showed that Italian governments found it easier to tolerate than to resist irredentism. The

British failed to learn from this that Italy had effectively become a revisionist power, and initiated a policy of appeasement. The more D'Annunzio insulted Britain the readier London was to please Rome. The lyric dictator attacked Britain's 'spiritual murder of struggling Ireland, black-jacked Egypt and downtrodden India' and referred to the League as 'another instrument of Great Britain for oppression'.[132] The response was to offer Italy concessions. On 12 January 1920 Lloyd George told Nitti, 'As regards Albania, no one seemed to want it. If, therefore, the Italians were willing to take it, they would not find anyone else desired to have it'.[133]

Italian friendship was consistently over-valued and repeatedly bought, only for Britain to discover that when Italian assistance was required it could not be obtained. Growing Franco-Italian rivalry in Central and Eastern Europe pinpointed the strategic weakness of British policy. As Petrie pointed out, 'the two powers intrigued against one another in every capital in Europe, and this rendered most difficult the position of Great Britain, which had no other ambition than to keep on the best of terms with both'.[134] The notion that Italy could be persuaded to co-operate enthusiastically in the development of a system of collective security was a fundamental misapprehension of British foreign policy. This error of judgment was not finally corrected until 1940.

Franco-Italian rivalry made British attempts to work with France much more hazardous, though there already existed a wide range of disputes between London and Paris. Some of these (reparations, the Rhineland, Silesia, collective security) had been apparent at Versailles. But fresh problems arose to exacerbate Anglo-French relations. The two views on policy towards Arab countries were incompatible and led both to local complications in Palestine and more general problems for the Allies. Indeed, the resentments caused by disagreement in the Middle East were to play a central part in the hostility shown by the French Right towards Britain in 1939–40. British strategy in these areas was dictated by two considerations: how best to escape from the contradictory promises of 1915–18, and how to preserve oil interests and other commercial ventures without unduly high expenditure. Good relations with the Arabs were an obvious *sine qua non*. In 1922 Egypt was granted 'independence' which did little to ease Britain's position and a great deal to annoy France. The French riposted by handing over control of Syria first to Weygand and then Sarrail, neither of whom were trusted in Britain. The two nations drifted further apart. The real rift in the alliance was fully exposed by events in Turkey. In the course of the war schemes for the dismemberment of the Ottoman Empire had proliferated. The most infamous was that of St Jean de Maurienne, signed on 17 April 1917, by which Italy was offered large areas of Asia Minor. Although the Empire was destroyed it proved not at all easy to dispose of its parts in the intended fashion. Allied policy was self-contradictory and, in any event, depended on power which was no longer available. In Arabia the India Office backed Ibn Saud while the Foreign Office supported Hussein, thus making British policy even more incomprehensible. In 1919 the Greek Government offered to come to the rescue in Asia Minor by taking over the duties of policeman. This offer was eagerly accepted by the Allies and on 24 April 1920 at San Remo the terms of the Treaty of Sèvres were published. This treaty imposed humiliating concessions on Turkey and was at once denounced by Kemal Ataturk and the Nationalists. Britain became the patron of expansionist Venizelist Greece, thus simultaneously antagonizing the Turks, France and Italy. Both of the European powers believed that Britain was using Greece as a stalking horse for her own ambitions, and thus preferred an independent Turkey to one controlled from Athens and London—which would remove all scope for further intervention.

In fact, British policy towards Turkey was largely the creation of one man—Lloyd George. Unlike both his Cabinet colleagues and his French and Italian allies, the Prime Minister was fervently phil-Hellene. At the London Conference, held in early 1921, Curzon found it impossible to balance between these divergent interests. From this time Tory confidence in Lloyd George's leadership waned. In the summer a renewal of Turco-Greek hostilities was followed in October by the Franklin–Bouillon Agreement. In April 1922 Italy concluded a similar treaty renouncing all claims in Asia Minor. The last rags concealing Allied disunity had been stripped away. Kemal now seized his opportunity and late in the summer of 1922 drove the Greeks out of Asia Minor. Frightful scenes at Smyrna led to vigorous pleas by Athens for Allied intervention, particularly as the Turks now menaced the neutral zones occupied by Allied forces. Lloyd George insisted in Cabinet that a stern *communiqué* be sent to Ankara, but its effect was spoiled by the fact that Curzon's dissent was only thinly veiled while France, Italy and most of the Dominions made it plain that they saw no reason for war.

Under great pressure Lloyd George agreed to the withdrawal of British troops from Chanak and the calling of an international conference. But his position had been gravely weakened, for the Chanak humiliation had brought to a head the grumbling disaffection within the Tory majority of his adherents. On 20 October 1922 the premier resigned. In the meantime political changes had given Kemal the upper hand. Constantine I had abdicated, leaving Greece in political chaos. In Turkey, Mehemet VI had fled, leaving Kemal's Nationalists unchallenged. By the Treaty of Lausanne, 23 August 1923, Turkey recovered Eastern Thrace and secured the withdrawal of Allied forces from the Straits, though demilitarization of the latter had to be accepted. The long-term implications of Kemal's victory were very serious. Other national movements in the Middle East were encouraged while the rifts between Britain and her allies made the possibility of sustained resistance to these movements less likely. Furthermore, as in the case of Palestine, Franco-British quarrels in Asia Minor continued to make co-operation in Europe more and more difficult.

By 1922 Anglo-French co-operation in European affairs was almost a fiction. Admittedly both countries feared a resurgence of German power but their methods of coping with this problem were entirely different. France soon reverted to the pre-1914 pattern, making an alliance with Poland in 1921 and encouraging the formation of the Little Entente in 1922. Those who were believed, rightly or wrongly, to be willing to make concessions to Germany to preserve the British alliance were frequently subjected to public humiliation. Clemenceau was beaten by Deschanel in the Presidential Election of January 1920; Briand was forced out of office two years later. It was over the military clauses that the first major clash occurred. In March 1920 the German government sent troops into the Ruhr to put down a left-wing rising. The French reaction was to seize Frankfurt and four other towns, despite the objections of Britain. A year later the two countries fell out over the issue of the Silesian plebiscite. The voting showed a clear preference for incorporation into Germany but Poland and France refused to accept the verdict of the polls. In the end a League commission partitioned Silesia between Poland and Germany.

By the spring of 1921, therefore, it was plain that France wished to impede German recovery by any means possible. Briand's attempts later that year to secure a British guarantee to France in the event of German attack met with failure. Britain was willing to guarantee the French frontier but not the settlement in the East. Furthermore, Lloyd George was unwilling to help Poland, France's *protégé*, against Bolshevik Russia. The *entente* now existed only in name. A further blow was dealt to good relations between the powers by the issue of reparations. In December 1920 Hardinge told Leygues, the Minister for Foreign Affairs, 'it would be absolutely impossible to carry out the intention . . . to extract from Germany payment of the whole cost of the war'.[135] France refused to accept this view and the Reparations Commission, on which France and Belgium commanded a majority, continued to insist on vast reparations. By 1921 Britain was ready to resume good relations with Germany. The financial, economic and monetary instability promoted by the uncertainty over reparations was as damaging to Britain as Germany and in November 1922 led to open conflict between Bonar Law and Poincaré. The views of British politicians, whether of the Left or Right, were overwhelmingly in favour of negotiating payment of a smaller and more reasonable sum by Germany. A similar majority in France wished to threaten a repeat of the Ruhr invasion. The Reparations Commission and the conference being held in London reached deadlock, then broke up in open dispute.

Thus, by the end of 1922, it was evident that important decisions had to be made by British policy-makers. The old system had collapsed. The United States was preoccupied with internal and American issues. The alliance with Japan had been terminated. Italy, under Mussolini, was now an unknown quantity in European affairs.

The *entente*, under pressure of disputes in the Middle East, over reparations and over Russia, was no longer an effective instrument. Russia, after a long period of turmoil, was beginning to emerge as a new force in Europe. The League of Nations was already, in the eyes of the realists, more important as a symbol than as a guardian of peace and security. In these changed circumstances, with British resources sadly diminished and economic pressure mounting, it was essential for Britain to take a new course. But it was not clear what direction policy would take in these changed circumstances and with new men at the head of government in Britain. Politicians and diplomats can hardly ever in British history have been as poorly prepared and as badly informed as they were at the close of 1922. It was, perhaps, a sign of how rapidly events moved in the post-war world and how the British diplomatic system, accustomed to more sedate times, was unable to adjust to the new demands of a different world.

REFERENCES

1 *Peacemaking 1919* by H. Nicolson. p. 39. Wilson's Speech, 8 January 1918.
2 Quoted in *Life of Lord Oxford and Asquith* by J. A. Spender and C. Asquith. Vol. II. p. 114. Asquith's Speech, 6 August 1914.
3 *Memorandum on Resignation* by Lord Morley. p. 14. See also Spender and Asquith, op. cit., Vol. II. p. 99.
4 *British War Aims and Peace Diplomacy, 1914–18* by V. H. Rothwell. p. 66. Undated.
5 Rothwell, op. cit., pp. 18–19. Asquith's Speech, 2 October 1914.
6 *Grandeurs et misères d'une victoire* by G. Clemenceau. p. 244.
7 *Great Britain and the War of 1914–1918* by Sir Llewellyn Woodward. p. xx.
8 Quoted in *The Roots of Appeasement* by M. Gilbert. p. 13.
9 *Germany's Drive to the West* by H. W. Gatzke. pp. 16–17.
10 Rothwell, op. cit., p. 33.
11 Gatzke, op. cit., p. 286.
12 *Memories and Reflections* by Earl of Oxford and Asquith. Vol. II. pp. 50–1. Entry for 25 December 1914.
13 Rothwell, op. cit., p. 20. Curzon's Speech, 14 October 1914.
14 *Haldane* by Sir Frederick Maurice. Vol. II. p. 15. See also Woodward, op. cit., p. 216.
15 Gatzke, op. cit., p. 140.

16 Oxford and Asquith, op. cit., Vol. II. pp. 143, 145. Memorandum of 13 November 1916.
17 ibid., Vol. II. p. 128. Memorandum of 20 December 1916.
18 ibid., Vol. II. p. 148. Memorandum of 27 November 1916.
19 *War Memoirs* by David Lloyd George. Vol. III. pp. 1096–7.
20 ibid., Vol. III. p. 1110.
21 *Sir Horace Rumbold* by M. Gilbert. p. 139. Rumbold to Newton, 19 December 1916.
22 *Maurice de Bunsen* by E. T. S. Dugdale. p. 314. Bunsen to his wife, 12 December 1916.
23 *Old Diplomacy* by Lord Hardinge. p. 206.
24 Gatzke, op. cit., p. 199.
25 *Germany's Aims in the First World War* by F. Fischer. p. 424.
26 Lloyd George, op. cit., Vol. IV. p. 2049.
27 *James Bryce* by H. A. L. Fisher. Vol. II. p. 141.
28 Lloyd George, op. cit., Vol. IV. p. 2095. Balfour's Memorandum, 20 September 1917.
29 Hankey. *Man of Secrets* by S. W. Roskill. Vol. I. p. 438. Diary, 24 September 1917.
30 Lloyd George, op. cit., Vol. IV. p. 2107.
31 *The Diary of Lord Bertie, 1914–18* ed. Lady Lennox. Vol. II. p. 276. 4 March 1918.
32 *Lord Lansdowne* by Lord Newton. p. 467.
33 *Sir Horace Rumbold* by M. Gilbert. pp. 137–80 *passim*.
34 *Erinnerungen* by Count Bernstorff. pp. 126–284 *passim*. See also Fischer, op. cit., pp. 284–300.
35 *The Good Years* by W. Lord. p. 339.
36 *The Letters and Friendships of Sir Cecil Spring Rice* ed. S. Gwynn. Vol. II. p. 256. Spring Rice to Grey, 26 February 1915.
37 *The Mist Procession* by Lord Vansittart. pp. 138–40.
38 *Twenty-five Years* by Lord Grey of Fallodon. Vol. II. p. 98.
39 *The Life and Letters of Walter H. Page* ed. B. J. Hendrick. Vol. I. p. 327. Page to House, 22 September 1914.
40 Gwynn, op. cit., Vol. II. p. 219. Spring Rice to Grey, 25 August 1914.
41 Rothwell, op. cit., pp. 21–3.
42 Grey, op. cit., Vol. II. p. 103.
43 ibid., Vol. II. pp. 106–7.
44 Roskill, op. cit., Vol. I. p. 158. Hankey to Asquith, 25 February 1915.
45 Woodward, op. cit., p. 212.
46 *Lapsus Calami* by J. K. Stephen.
47 *The Great Departure* by D. M. Smith. p. 19.
48 ibid., p. 61. Lansing to Wilson, 24 August 1915.
49 Woodward, op. cit., p. 209 fn. 1. 22 September 1915.
50 Roskill, op. cit., Vol. I. p. 248. Diary, 14 March 1916.
51 Lloyd George, op. cit., Vol. II. p. 686.
52 Grey, op. cit., Vol. II. p. 123. Grey's Memorandum, 22 February 1916.
53 Lloyd George, op. cit., Vol. II. p. 688.
54 Rothwell, op. cit., p. 62. Samuel to his mother, 22 December 1916.
55 Hendrick, op. cit., Vol. II. pp. 207–9.
56 Woodward, op. cit., p. 210.

57 *A. J. Balfour* by B. E. C. Dugdale. Vol. II. p. 193.

58 Vansittart, op. cit., p. 141.

59 *Laughing Diplomat* by D. Varè. p. 146.

60 *Sir Horace Rumbold* by M. Gilbert. p. 165. Rumbold to Campbell and Rumbold to Newton, 10 November 1917.

61 ibid., p. 165. Newton to Rumbold, 16 November 1917.

62 Rothwell, op. cit., p. 158. Anglo-American Conference, 20 November 1917.

63 *Journal de Alexandre Ribot et correspondances inedites, 1914–22* ed. A. Ribot. p. 88. 6 May 1917.

64 See Ribot, op. cit., pp. 103–25 *passim.*

65 Ribot, op. cit., pp. 110–11. 25 May 1917.

66 *The Collapse of the Third Republic* by W. Shirer. p. 132.

67 Vansittart, op. cit., p. 212.

68 *Portrait of a Decision* by H. Elcock. p. 10. *Hansard.* House of Commons. 19 December 1919.

69 Lloyd George, op. cit., Vol. V. pp. 2515–27.

70 Dugdale, op. cit., Vol. II. p. 233.

71 *The Eastern Question, 1774–1923* by M. S. Anderson. p. 341.

72 Vansittart, op. cit., p. 169.

73 Rothwell, op. cit., p. 22.

74 Lennox, op. cit., Vol. I. 7 August 1914.

75 *Great Britain and the 1914–15 Straits Agreement with Russia: The British promise of November 1914* by C. Jay Smith. American Historical Review. Vol. LXX. p. 1031. This article discusses the whole question in some detail and propounds a novel theory. pp. 1015–34.

76 Oxford and Asquith, op. cit., Vol. II. p. 65.

77 Spender and Asquith, op. cit., Vol. II. p. 129. Asquith's report, 20 October 1914.

78 Jay Smith, op. cit., pp. 1023–9.

79 For his opposition to any major power being established at Constantinople see *Life of Lord Curzon* by Earl Ronaldshay. Vol. III. pp. 262–4.

80 Jay Smith, op. cit., p. 1021. Asquith to George V, 5 September 1914.

81 Rothwell, op. cit., p. 81.

82 *Sir Horace Rumbold* by M. Gilbert. p. 147. Newton to Rumbold, 17 March 1917.

83 *Retrospection* by Lord Newton. p. 233.

84 *Sir Horace Rumbold* by M. Gilbert. p. 158. Rumbold to his stepmother, 7 August 1917.

85 Vansittart, op. cit., p. 180.

86 Roskill, op. cit., Vol. I. p. 372.

87 Rothwell, op. cit., p. 6.

88 *Jan Christian Smuts* by J. C. Smuts. p. 191. Speech of 15 May 1917.

89 *Liberalism and Indian Politics, 1872–1922* by R. J. Moore. p. 112.

90 Vansittart, op. cit., p. 138.

91 *British Strategy in the Far East, 1919–39* by W. R. Louis. p. 17.

92 Rothwell, op. cit., p. 2.

93 Speech of Neville Chamberlain, 27 September 1938.

94 Vansittart, op. cit., p. 212.

95 *Memoirs* by Sir Almeric Fitzroy. Vol. II. p. 618. 7 February 1916.

96 *The Economic Consequences of the Peace* by J. M. Keynes. p. 39.

97 *A Great Experiment* by Lord Robert Cecil. p. 67.

98 Elcock, op. cit., pp. 60–1.

99 *Tempestuous Journey* by F. Owen. p. 501.

100 *Lord Riddell's Intimate Diary of the Peace Conference and After* by Lord Riddell. p. 3. 30 November 1918.

101 Rothwell, op. cit., p. 260.

102 *Peacemaking, 1919* by H. Nicolson. pp. 31–2.

103 *Sir Horace Rumbold* by M. Gilbert. p. 180. Rumbold to Graham, 17 February 1919.

104 *A Mirror to Geneva* by G. Slocombe. p. 41.

105 ibid., p. 41.

106 Elcock, op. cit., p. 2.

107 Keynes, op. cit., pp. 26–9.

108 Vansittart, op. cit., p. 192.

109 Elcock, op. cit., pp. 22–3.

110 *Peacemaking, 1919* by H. Nicolson. p. xii.

111 Keynes, op. cit., p. 273.

112 Vansittart, op. cit., p. 210.

113 Hardinge, op. cit., p. 240.

114 *Eastern Europe between the Wars* by H. Seton-Watson. p. 199 fn.

115 *The Roots of Appeasement* by M. Gilbert. p. 82.

116 *Politics and Diplomacy of Peacemaking* by A. J. Mayer. p. 797 fn. Smuts to Lloyd George, 22 May 1919.

117 Keynes, op. cit., p. 273.

118 Riddell, op. cit., p. 163. 24 January 1920.

119 *The Times*, 10 December 1918.

120 Vansittart, op. cit., p. 223.

121 *Peacemaking, 1919* by H. Nicolson. p. 350. Nicolson to Sackville West, 28 May 1919.

122 Keynes, op. cit., p. 125. Keynes was quoting Brockdorff-Rantzau's report.

123 *All the way* by Viscount Cecil. p. 143. Cecil to Wiseman, 19 August 1918.

124 *Memoirs* by F. von Papen. p. 94.

125 *Our Own Times* by S. King-Hall. p. 115.

126 C.I.D. Papers, 133-C, CAB 4/2. 23 February 1921. See *The Continental Commitment* by M. Howard. p. 77.

127 Howard, op. cit., p. 80.

128 *Nine Troubled Years* by Viscount Templewood. p. 109.

129 Louis, op. cit., p. 47. Cabinet Minutes, 30 May 1921.

130 ibid., p. 58. Lloyd George's Speech, 20 June 1921.

131 ibid., pp. 107–8. See *An Indiscreet Chronicle from the Pacific* by Putnam Weale. pp. 186–7.

132 *The Poet as Superman. D'Annunzio* by A. Rhodes. p. 183.

133 *Documents on British Foreign Policy, 1919–39*. First Series. Vol. II. p. 825. 12 January 1920. (Henceforward referred to as *DBFP*.)

134 *Life and Letters of Austen Chamberlain* by Sir C. Petrie. Vol. II. p. 315.

135 *DBFP*. First Series. Vol. X. p. 558. 2 December 1920.

6   A Decade of Uncertainty, 1923–33

And year by year as we go round and round
The mulberry bush.

Lord Vansittart: *Homo Sapiens*

Relations with Germany continued to dominate British foreign
policy problems throughout the decade. There was a certain consistency of attitude by British governments whatever their political
complexion, for by 1923 Britain was committed to a policy of
conciliation. Increasingly her ally, France, came to be regarded as
the more dangerous threat to European peace and stability. Until
the close of the 1920s Germany was able to take full advantage of
the British position. In this she was aided by the diplomatic skill of
Stresemann and Briand's gradual acceptance of the wisdom of the
British solution.

In early 1923 this all seemed far distant. On 11 January French and
Belgian troops occupied the Ruhr, provoking a policy of passive
resistance which lasted until 26 September. Britain was isolated.
Most of the Eastern European states sympathized with France, the
Scandinavian countries remained discreetly aloof and Italy initially
lent support to the invaders. The French move was intended to
expedite the collection of reparations and at first enjoyed some
success. The combination of industrial paralysis, a sharp rise in
imports and massive printing of bank-notes soon, however, led to
German economic collapse. From the first France had been warned
against such precipitate action. On 12 December 1922 Bonar Law
had made it clear to Poincaré that 'no British Government could
agree to the occupation of the Ruhr to enforce demands which

References are printed on p. 259.

everyone recognised as impossible'.[1] Political repercussions were very serious. As D'Abernon, Ambassador to Berlin, observed on 21 January: 'The French . . . have done more to bring together all parties and all classes in Germany than it was possible to effect by any other means'.[2] Hostility to France was scarcely less vehement in Britain. Lady Violet Bonham Carter found it hard to imagine 'a more futile and frivolously dangerous adventure'.[3] Curzon, who was struggling to pursue a policy of neutrality in a situation which did not permit compromise, admitted on 18 March, 'Public opinion here is getting more restive and will not stand benevolent neutrality *ad infinitum*'.[4]

Opinion in France was solidly behind Poincaré. A complete breakdown in Anglo-French relations seemed probable, particularly when Curzon and Poincaré showed equal intransigence. The French premier insisted that troops would only be withdrawn when effective payment of reparations began. However, as the summer of 1923 went by British influence increased. The French economy became strained as the costs of occupation rose. Fear of losing all British sympathy began to dominate the thinking of parties of the Centre and Left. The Italians announced on 16 November that they now favoured a moratorium and a reduction of the reparations debt. Poincaré's last desperate throw was to try to set up an autonomous government in the Palatinate, but in the face of unrelenting British and German opposition this gamble failed too. In May 1924 Poincaré was defeated at the polls and harmonization of British and French policy once more became possible.

Even before Poincaré's defeat there had been signs of a relaxation in French policy. In late 1923 it was agreed that a committee of experts, of whom the most formidable was the American Owen Young, should look into the whole question of reparations. Young and another American, Charles Dawes, dominated the committee's deliberations and its report, presented in April, was favourable to German interests. The Dawes plan envisaged comprehensive control of German economic and fiscal affairs, but reduced reparations and specifically forbade measures such as the occupation of the Ruhr save with the consent of all Germany's creditors. The plan was accepted by all parties at a conference held in London in the summer of 1924. But there were ominous signs for the future. Though France was now governed by Herriot, at the head of a Centre–Left coalition, there was little sympathy for his country in the new Labour Government. The prejudices of Snowden were typical: 'The French are the most pleasant people in the world to get along with provided they get all their own way; but cross them, oppose them, criticise them and the French Press will burst out into unrestrained vituperation'.[5]

Britain was now firmly set on a course of appeasement. To the British appeasement meant co-operation between the four great Western European powers to preserve peace. The advent of Stresemann to power in Germany and Briand's arrival at the Quai d'Orsay in 1925 gave great encouragement to those in Britain who fondly imagined that real co-operation was possible. In late 1924 German failure to comply with the terms of Versailles relating to disarmament led to a postponement of evacuation of the northern zone of the Rhineland, but this proved merely a hiatus in the development of appeasement. Stresemann was so anxious to still Western fears that this minor crisis led to a major diplomatic initiative. On 20 January 1925 Stresemann proposed in a memorandum to D'Abernon a pact of mutual. security. The fundamentals of the proposal were simple. The existing territorial status on the Rhine was to be guaranteed and arbitration treaties were to link all the countries concerned. The notions behind these proposals were, however, more sophisticated. The German leader saw that France wanted security and that if she felt safe would be unlikely to insist on enforcement of the full rigour of Versailles. Poincaré had previously treated such an idea with contempt, but in 1925 it seemed much more plausible. Additionally, the plan had the advantage of making an Anglo-French alliance seem unnecessary to the British.

The problem of guarantees was central to British policy-making. The major legacy of the short-lived Labour government of 1924 had been Ramsay MacDonald's Geneva Protocol, an agreement which was intended to supplement and give force to the Covenant. Baldwin's administration held no real enthusiasm for the Protocol, particularly in view of the objections of the Dominions, the United States and the Service Chiefs. Such enthusiasm as existed was further reduced by the efforts of Herriot and the pro-French party in the Foreign Office to convert the Protocol into a direct British guarantee of France. The terms envisaged would, in effect, have created an Anglo-French alliance. Austen Chamberlain supported this scheme against the furious opposition of Churchill, who, in a paper to the Cabinet, refused 'to accept as an axiom that our fate was involved in that of France'.[6] Members of the government were set on a collision course.

At a special Cabinet meeting on 2 March 1925, followed by another two days later, there was full and acrimonious discussion of the rival merits of the schemes. Chamberlain was outgunned because his strongest support lay in the Foreign Office rather than the Cabinet or parliamentary party. His main supporter was Crowe—whose death later in 1925 finally ended opposition to Stresemann's proposals—who could hardly be expected to agree with D'Abernon that the Germans 'were more reliable and more bound by written engagements than many other nations'.[7] Opinion among the politicians ran strongly in favour of the mutual security pact. Quite apart from those, like Baldwin, MacDonald and Lloyd George, whose previous policies inclined them in that direction, there were also men such as Snowden, Churchill, and Balfour who were deeply suspicious of France and hence refused to entertain Chamberlain's proposals. The weakness of their arguments was not immediately obvious in 1925 and the permanent officials were unable to make their objections tell. Vansittart, admittedly from the vantage point of some thirty years later, put his finger on the weak point of appeasement, arguing that the notion of a mutual security pact was false and 'ended in fiasco because it was based on the pretence that France and Belgium were as likely to erupt as Germany'.[8]

Herriot's government was shocked by the British decision to support Stresemann's scheme, but had no alternative to co-operation. On 1 December 1925 the group of treaties subsequently called the Locarno Pact was signed in London. The pact brought together Britain, France, Belgium, Italy and Germany to guarantee the frontiers and demilitarization of the Rhineland. Britain and Italy also promised to assist France, Belgium or Germany in the event of unprovoked aggression. A second set of treaties bound together

France, Poland and Czechoslovakia in pacts for mutual military assistance to repel threat or attack. Arbitration treaties were also concluded between all the major signatories. The pact was favourably received throughout the world. Chamberlain, with all the enthusiasm of the new convert who has just glimpsed the Promised Land, declaimed, 'I believe . . . we are safeguarding peace and that we are laying the foundations of reconciliation and friendship with the enemies of a few years ago'.[9]

Signs of true reconciliation were slow to appear. Despite Allied promises, it was September 1926 before Germany entered the League —admission had been delayed by unseemly wrangling among other powers who craved status but had not the force to sustain it. Germany gave little hint of the spirit of Locarno when, in June 1926, the Treaty of Rapallo was renewed at Berlin. By coming to an agreement with the Soviet Union Stresemann made it plain that he regarded the settlement in Eastern Europe as far from satisfactory. In his efforts to minimize nationalist opposition to Locarno the Foreign Minister had stressed that the pact 'would destroy the Anglo-French Entente and open the way for sweeping territorial revisions in the East'.[10] He was not unaware of the lack of enthusiasm in Britain for defending the Eastern settlement. Indeed, even that advocate of an alliance with France, Austen Chamberlain, had told Lord Crewe (the Ambassador to Paris) on 16 February 1925, 'no British Government ever will or ever can risk the bones of a British grenadier . . . for the Polish Corridor'.[11] It was quite safe for Germany to produce a stream of complaints concerning the oppression of ethnic Germans in Eastern and Central Europe. There was little fear of Stresemann being dubbed a revanchist when so many in Britain concurred with his opinions.

The principal aim of the British government was, however, to improve relations by negotiation in three important areas: territorial adjustment, disarmament and reparations. Revision of Germany's borders was frequently discussed but could not form the centrepiece of negotiations as control of concessions lay outside British hands. The British enthusiasm for disarmament was, however, apparently boundless, while in the case of reparations a readiness to accommodate German wishes was similarly unlimited.

In 1925 it seemed as if Allied occupation of Germany was likely to prove a major obstacle to serious talks on disarmament, and it was not until August 1929 that Stresemann was told that remaining Allied forces would leave Germany the following year. French reluctance had proved the main reason for delay and caused much resentment among British politicians who felt that France was imperilling the whole cause of mutual security. In general terms British policy throughout the decade was consistent, irrespective of the alternation of parties in government. Yet there were slight differences in emphasis between Baldwin and MacDonald. Baldwin's biographers believed 'He was not a natural disarmer: although it was hard not to listen to the glowing forecasts of Austen Chamberlain nor to resist Churchill's violent drive for defence economy, he was one of the first to warn against excessive unilateral disarmament'.[12] Certainly he did not see eye to eye with Cecil, the leading advocate of disarmament, and seems to have been relieved to receive his resignation in 1927. MacDonald's commitment to disarmament was based more perhaps on faith and less on the assumption that it would only be desirable if it led to guaranteed security. Vansittart wrote, not unkindly, that MacDonald 'nursed the illusion that mankind everywhere looked to Britain for guidance'.[13] Whatever their differences in emphasis both leaders were irritated by what they saw as French backsliding. Anglo-French discord made agreement with Germany harder to reach and incidentally promoted the influence of those, like Snowden, who were Francophobes.

Disarmament negotiations were a mixture of farce and tragedy. In July 1927 it was formally reported to the League Council by the Conference of Ambassadors that German disarmament in accordance with the Versailles treaty had been completed. This was moonshine. Not only had Germany reached agreement with the U.S.S.R. at Rapallo in 1922 and Berlin in 1926 which violated the spirit of Versailles, but the whole organization of the *Reichswehr* was designed with the intention of making formal limitations invalid. The General Staff had been explicitly prohibited but, according to Wheeler-Bennett, 'Seeckt . . . and his successors worked unceasingly to train and prepare a cadre of Staff officers who, in the fullness of time, should guide the fortunes of a greater and mighty army'.[14] The revival of German military power was not confined to technical capacity. The Army held political power too, and this was consistently exerted against those parties which sought to promote disarmament. By 1930 General Groener could proudly proclaim, 'In the political structure of Germany, no stone may be moved without the *Reichswehr* casting the decisive vote'.[15]

In fact, external political factors brought about the collapse of disarmament negotiations, thus saving Stresemann and his colleagues much difficulty. The first post-Locarno initiative for disarmament came in 1927 when President Coolidge summoned a conference of Britain, Japan and the United States to Geneva to discuss naval limitations. The conference was an unmitigated disaster. It led to a bitter quarrel between Britain and the United States while Japan looked on as *tertium gaudens*. The failure of this conference had, however, a wider importance. It showed how dangerous it had been for Britain 'to enter into a new system whose functioning would principally depend upon the incalculable shifts and whims of the American democracy'.[16] It was all very well for Cecil to regard 'our two Fleets . . . as two divisions of a single Peace Fleet'[17] but his views were not shared either by London or Washington. Furthermore, by confining discussion of these problems to just three powers much ill-will was created. Cecil, who resigned after the failure of the conference, had felt that 'a failure . . . to agree on a minor question of armaments would greatly encourage warmongers in other countries'.[18] But France and Italy boycotted the conference precisely because they claimed that all 'armaments were interdependent and that the naval aspect was part of a much larger problem'[19] about which they held strong opinions. In Germany it was felt that the conference accorded ill with the Locarno ideal of treating her as an equal.

Germany took advantage of the confusion to demand a disarmament conference within twelve months. Stresemann had no real enthusiasm for disarmament but saw how this demand could bring political advantage. If the Western Powers rejected disarmament proposals, as they did Litvinov's in late 1927, then there would exist ample justification for German parity of arms. While the preparatory commission continued with apparently interminable meetings to try to find a formula to reconcile the irreconcilable, a new initiative threw all previous preparations into disarray. During the course of Franco-American discussions on an arbitration treaty Briand had suggested to Kellogg that they sign a pact renouncing war between the two countries. Briand, of course, hoped that this might be interpreted as some form of alliance. Kellogg saw the move as a potential vote-winner for the Republican Party. He therefore elaborated the draft into a pact to outlaw war. Briand was puzzled and Chamberlain stunned. If Kellogg's notions were adopted then there would have to be major changes in the Locarno Pact and the Covenant and the whole basis of British policy might need revision.

Chamberlain was very critical of the proposals. On 13 February 1928 he wrote, 'I do not think that there is any reality behind Kellogg's move. . . . It is one more instance of the common practice of the State Department to use foreign politics as a pawn in the domestic game'.[20] In spring 1928 Kellogg produced his final version of the pact to outlaw war and invited all the major states of the world to sign. All British attempts to modify the draft failed and on 27 August Baldwin reluctantly signed the pact, though he expressed reservations which effectively amounted to a Monroe Doctrine with respect to the Middle East. However, the pact was to be honoured more in the breach than the observance. As Gilbert aptly put it, 'while signed by all nations . . . [it] . . . was believed in by none'.[21] Certainly the permanent officials regarded it 'as eyewash by those who knew their job, and created no more than a passing interest among those who don't'.[22] But the pact did lead to the disarmament conference being reconvened in 1929.

Soon after the conference met there was a change of government in Britain. MacDonald and Henderson, the new Foreign Secretary, were committed to the policy of bringing peace through disarmament. Cecil was attached to the Foreign Office in order to assist this work. MacDonald attended the League Assembly in 1929, thus showing 'a great change after the negative attitude of the previous Government'.[23] Henderson was even more ardent in his enthusiasm to secure for Germany and the U.S.S.R. normal positions in international relations. He also wanted a general treaty of disarmament though he accepted that 'human nature . . . [must become] . . . very much more perfect before you will be able to do without policing forces'.[24] It was a measure of his sincerity that in May 1931 he was elected President of the Disarmament Conference which eventually met in February 1932. The Labour Government had a large fund of goodwill for mankind in general and a particular readiness to accommodate Germany.

The British attitude met with little response in Germany. Withdrawal from the Rhineland occasioned only further demands from Curtius, who had succeeded Stresemann at the Wilhelmstrasse. It is doubtful, given political developments in Germany, whether even Stresemann could have swum for long against the nationalist tide. Paradoxically, Stresemann's achievements in the field of international relations had probably only strengthened national feeling and German determination to be at least equal with other powers. But British optimism remained undiminished. Even Rumbold, well known for his lack of enthusiasm for Germany, observed that Stresemann's death 'has had a sobering effect on many people hitherto holding wild and impracticable ideas'.[25] If effect there was it was not to be of long duration. During 1930 there were ever more strident German demands for military parity with Poland and provocative speeches about the eastern frontier. In the elections of September the N.S.D.A.P. made startling gains, becoming the second largest party. Violence and unrest became increasingly common in German life.

At this point the British policy of peace through disarmament became untenable, though some time elapsed before it was abandoned. The great weakness of the policy had always been that it required Germany and France to co-operate. Statesmen in both countries had dragged their heels and by 1931 much of the work of Briand and Stresemann had been wasted. Aggressive elements were in the ascendant again in both countries. Stresemann was dead, Briand had surrendered the premiership to Tardieu and had then lost the presidential election to Doumer. Maginot insisted on 26 February 1931 that the aggressors of 1914 must necessarily accept a more severe limitation of armaments. Hitler and Hugenberg were

demanding conscription as 'the Germans are becoming increasingly
impatient of anything which seems to have the appearance of
unequal treatment'.[26] Any hope that Britain might be able to bring
the countries together was lost when MacDonald's administration
floundered into the mire of the economic crisis of 1931. The
impending collapse of the government and fracture of the Labour
Party left little energy for the pursuit of foreign affairs.

The Disarmament Conference of February 1932 was thus fore-
doomed to failure; there was no real will to achievement in Britain,
France or Germany. The conference itself was a personal tragedy for
Henderson who, after the formation of the National Government,
had to cope with an unsympathetic British delegation. MacDonald
repeatedly interfered with his work and the lack of sincerity shown
by the German, Russian and French delegations was patent. Germany withdrew from the conference in the autumn of 1932, to be
persuaded to return by MacDonald. Extremist elements were not
to be denied after Hitler's advent to power and on 14 October 1933
the German delegation withdrew finally. Rearmament in Germany
became public instead of an open secret and the French riposted by
intensifying attempts to make their defensive system impregnable.
Despite these events Henderson argued that 'many Powers are
desirous that we should continue our work without intermission'.[27]
The work continued but became increasingly irrelevant. In May
1934, as Gathorne-Hardy pithily observed, 'a compromise was
reached which preserved the Conference in a state of suspended
animation'.[28] British hopes that disarmament negotiations would
prove an easy route towards the conciliation of Germany were
thus terminated.

British politicians had hoped that by easing the terms of reparations
they could appease Germany. The Dawes plan was the first in a
series of generous offers to Germany. After Locarno it became plain
that the plan no longer suited Germany or France. The Agent for
Reparations, Parker Gilbert, initiated revision of the plan in a
memorandum sent to Köhler, the German Minister of Finance. Public
attention was now focused on Germany's method of payment.
Schacht, President of the Reichsbank since 1923, commented: 'Gil-

bert . . . realized that Germany's payments of reparations were not genuine, that the country was paying her debts not with honest export surpluses but with borrowed money. It could only be a matter of how long it would take before Germany was no longer in a position to remit foreign currency'.[29]

In September 1928 the powers announced that a committee of experts was to be set up. A definitive solution to the problem of reparations was sought. This decision was greeted with pleasure by Stresemann, as it helped ease nationalist pressure, and with relief by Poincaré, who hoped that a final settlement might lead to the receipt of more than promises. In Britain the committee was seen as a natural development from previous policy. Snowden considered that 'The Dawes Plan was never regarded as being of more than a temporary character. It involved serious interference by the Creditor Powers with the economic and commercial affairs of Germany'.[30] Macmillan believed that the Young plan, the result of the committee's deliberations, was part of 'a story of steady progress towards peace'.[31] The underlying optimistic assumption that negotiation could cure the ills of Europe prevailed among Britons of all political persuasions.

In early 1929 the experts assembled under the chairmanship of Owen Young of the United States. The nations represented were Britain, Italy, Japan, France, Belgium, Germany and the United States. The British representatives were Sir Josiah Stamp and Sir Charles Addis.[32] The experts hoped to assess the amount of German payments and the time available for payment as well as to eliminate foreign controls. However, the committee was only empowered to offer opinions, not to bind governments to its findings. This induced a lack of realism and the total of claims put forward exceeded those agreed under the Dawes plan. In 1920, at the Spa Conference, Britain had agreed to an artificially low share of reparations in order to bring the bargaining positions of victors and vanquished closer. It was soon apparent that further British sacrifices would be needed. The major beneficiaries under the new scheme would be Italy, Belgium and France. Furthermore, it was decided that German payments be divided into two classes: those which had absolute security and those which could be postponed. It was envisaged that Britain's share should fall almost entirely in the second category, thus giving her no effective security. It became clear that if Britain wished to appease Germany it remained the conviction of her erstwhile allies that she should foot the bill. Great irritation, particularly with France, was created—to the ultimate detriment of Anglo-French relations.

The work of the committee was completed in June 1929 and then became the subject of a specially convened conference at The Hague in August. The British delegation was led by Snowden, the Chancellor of the Exchequer, who had made no secret of his objections to the Young Report. In his opening address Snowden asserted, 'The House of Commons would never agree to any further sacrifices of British interests in this matter. We are agreed—and as you all know, all parties in Great Britain are agreed—upon this'.[33] From the start the Hague Conference, like the sessions of the Young committee, thus had a distinctly political aspect. Snowden dug in his heels, refused to be shifted, and in the end carried the day. His fight was directed entirely against Britain's former allies and was enthusiastically greeted in the British press. Taylor commented that for his pains '"the iron chancellor" received the Freedom of the City of London. Within less than three years, however, the money so heroically defended proved to be fairy gold'.[34] This did scant justice to Snowden's stance. Like most politicians he believed it desirable to alleviate Germany's difficulties—and, indeed, after the Young plan was agreed Germany was restored to a position of equality in economic affairs. Snowden also realized that appeasement could not be funded merely out of British resources. Contributions were needed from other powers. The British stand in 1929 was made not to satisfy national sentiment but to emphasize the continuing responsibility of all Allied governments for the preservation of peace, security and prosperity by the restoration of Germany to her rightful position in international affairs.

A second conference was held at The Hague in January 1930 to discuss implementation of the details of the Young plan. On the issue of wilful default Germany scored a minor victory. Now that the Reparations Commission was to be abolished the responsibility for defining the nature of any default and the sanctions to be employed was thrown on the Permanent Court of International Justice. However, hanging over the whole conference was the cloud of the Wall Street collapse of autumn 1929 and the threat thus posed to world economic stability. Britain put forward proposals designed to promote international banking co-operation in order to meet this danger. Britain suggested the creation of a Bank for International Settlements which would 'contribute to the stability of international finance and the growth of world trade'.[35] Despite ill-tempered displays of narrow economic nationalism the B.I.S. was eventually established at Basle but with such a limited rôle it could not properly fulfil its originally proposed functions. Snowden's view of the conference was characteristically gloomy: 'few of us entertained the hope that the decisions at which The Hague Conference had arrived would provide a lasting settlement of this problem'.[36]

British sacrifices and suggestions proved equally vain. Throughout 1930 the slump continued and, despite Brüning's best efforts, Germany proved unable to meet her debts. This situation arose principally because of increasing unwillingness of American investors to risk their money on European loans. In a last desperate attempt to remedy the situation in March 1931 the German and Austrian Governments proposed a customs union. French reaction was strongly hostile while Britain was suspicious. Rumbold argued for opposition, on the grounds that once successful the method of the *fait accompli* would be repeated, but wished Britain to try to mediate. His anti-Brüning opinions had been tempered by the elections of 1930 in which Nazi representation had risen from 12 to 107 seats; the ambassador now considered it essential to back the Chancellor. But the Laval government in France obstructed the union until on 11 May 1931 the collapse of the Kreditanstalt (Austria's largest bank) rendered further political manoeuvres superfluous. The threat to economic stability posed by this collapse caused other countries to search for increased liquidity which only France was able to provide.

The collapse of the financial system of the western world in 1931 put an end to the question of reparations and to British attempts to woo Germany through a programme of economic concession.

The Labour Government itself fell in August 1931 and Brüning was dismissed in May 1932. The National Government was interested first in internal reconstruction while Hitler, who came to power in January 1933, had no intention of ever reviving discussion on reparations. But the events of 1931 did have a profound influence on future Anglo-German relations in the sense that they soured the Anglo-French association. The selfish attitude of France in 1931 gained her many enemies. Von Papen later argued that 'the situation was grasped in Paris . . . inadequately'[37] while Rumbold wrote of 'the lack of hope which makes the situation seem to them [the Germans] so depressing, and makes it difficult for Brüning to keep them in hand'.[38] On 20 June President Hoover, exasperated by French refusals to negotiate, announced a one-year moratorium on all inter-government debts.

Hoover's action was greeted enthusiastically everywhere save in Paris. As Lloyd George pointed out, France 'did not see why the United States, Britain, Holland and Switzerland, having already lent so much money to Germany, should not go on lending her more money with which to pay France. French unemployment was then a matter of a few almost negligible thousands. France was not in the least upset by the millions of American and British workless'.[39] Britain and Germany found themselves in the same boat. Gold was being withdrawn at a frightening rate. In September Britain, followed by most of Western Europe, abandoned the gold standard. In November Brüning announced that the future transfer of reparation annuities would ruin Germany's economy. Conferences at Basle in December 1931 and Lausanne in June 1932 confirmed what all the world knew—that reparations were dead. By the end of 1932 it was plain that war debts would also not be repaid. As Snowden declared, 'The long story of Reparations and War Debts teaches the eternal truth . . . that efforts to exact such payments can only ultimately result in failure, and so far as they are paid they inflict injury both upon those who pay and those who receive'.[40]

Inability to bring France and Germany to some understanding of the common plight of Western Europe vexed and tormented Britain's makers of policy. In 1931 the need for appeasement was clear. Reading, the new Foreign Secretary, asked two senior officials

—Sargent and Ashton-Gwatkin—to prepare a paper on changing conditions in foreign policy. Their conclusions were simple: 'World recovery (the aim of our policy) depends on European recovery; European recovery on German recovery; German recovery on France's consent; France's consent on security (for all time) against attack'.[41] Vansittart saw that the important link in the chain was French obsession with security and argued that pressure should be put on France to recognize that she was strong enough. He hoped this would diminish German resentment and in turn ease French fears. It was a policy of some merit even in 1931, though more appropriate if pursued a decade earlier. Its weakness was the supposition of French recognition of the dangers of isolation and alienation from Britain. This fear was not widely felt until, perhaps, 1938. By then it was far too late.

The doctrine of appeasement had thus reached a dead end by late 1932. Failure continued to be attributed more commonly to French obsessions than German ill will. Appeasement was not discredited; it was inevitable that after a period of introspection induced by the events of 1929–32 it be revived. It was not recognized that conditions had changed profoundly and permanently. The methods of Hitler were not those of Stresemann and no amount of wishful thinking could make them so. The events of the 1920s had, too, altered British relationships with France, Italy, Japan and the United States. The basis upon which appeasement was built had been eroded and could not be replaced.

The cooling of Anglo-French relations, of which some mention has already been made, was disastrous. The aims of the two nations were not the same but there were few attempts made to understand the view-point of the other. The future Lord Lothian perceived a fundamental cause of disagreement—'psychologically they [the French] had lost the war and Germany had won it'.[42] Those who led British governments were not well suited to restore a close working relationship. Although much of his portrait of Baldwin is overdrawn, Young's comment that 'Where France was thinking of her dead, Baldwin was thinking of our unemployed'[43] was not far from the mark. MacDonald too was more concerned with a narrow view of British problems; the broad sweep of his imagination

was reserved for the activities of the League of Nations, a more
suitable arena for his style of negotiation. French leadership, with the
exception of Herriot, was no less insensitive to British fears. Poincaré
cared little for Britain, Briand found that his golden voice fell on
deaf ears, Laval and Tardieu found inspiration in their Anglophobia
for the course they were later to follow. In 1931 at the London
Conference Laval, presented with a unique opportunity to revitalize
Anglo-French relations, made 'the speech of every French politician
at every conference since the War . . . mean and cautious'.[44] Friendship or alliance could mean nothing when there was no true and
mutual understanding of problems.

A major area of dispute between France and Britain continued to
be the Middle East. Not only were there particular causes for rancour,
relating to territorial disputes, there also existed an important
difference in imperial styles. Though the British frequently made
mistakes they did not, on the whole, underestimate the dynamism
or the potential of the Arabs. In France there was an ill-founded
belief that the Arabs could be turned into Frenchmen by rigorous
implantation of the French language, law and institutions. In view
of increasing Arab consciousness of unity the British approach had
more to commend it. Unfortunately the consistency of British
policy was marred by conflicting promises to Arab leaders and by
the mill-stone of a Jewish National Home which Balfour had
so adroitly draped around his successors' necks. The excellent case
for a Jewish homeland could not, therefore, be disentangled from
purely Arab issues.

Differences in approach were highlighted after the departure of
Weygand from Syria in November 1924. Sarrail, his successor,
contrived to alienate several interest groups and from 1925–28
Syria was in a state of insurgency. Sarrail's mismanagement had
an adverse effect upon the stability of British mandated territories,
as well as giving further encouragement to unrest in French North
Africa. Britain's wish for stability in the area depended for fulfilment
on agreed self-government by Arabs and Jews in Palestine. Unrest
in French territories added an unpleasant dimension to the problem.
Sarrail was subjected to a great deal of British criticism and responded

with a cordial dislike of his supposed allies. In 1932 Britain completely undermined the French position in Syria and the Lebanon by obtaining membership of the League of Nations for an independent Iraq. France was consequently forced to make concessions in her mandates. Feeling in Paris ran high because of the lack of consultation. There was never any attempt in London and Paris to co-ordinate policy in the Arab world—with serious effects on relations both locally and generally.

British relations with her other western ally, Italy, were scarcely more successful. The basis of British policy was to convert Italy into a reliable buttress of the Versailles settlement. Britain was prepared to make concessions outside Europe—such as the cession of Jubaland in 1923—and to tolerate Italian ambitions in the Eastern Mediterranean. At all costs she wished to avoid Franco-Italian animosity or rivalry which might imperil the task of building a peaceful Europe. These hopes were stillborn.

The advent of Mussolini to power in 1922 added a serious element of discord to relations, for the *Duce* had wild imperialist and irredentist dreams. Mussolini claimed he believed in Anglo-Italian friendship[45] but actions gave the lie to his words. In 1923 he contrived to offend simultaneously the rival schools of thought in British policy-making. The bombardment of Corfu was disliked by internationalists like Cecil as an assault on the League system. Cecil, incidentally, aptly pointed out that the affair was 'an excellent example of the evil of treating our League policy as something apart from the general foreign policy of the country'.[46] Italian action was also strongly disliked by Curzon because it created unnecessary uncertainty in the Mediterranean.

All the British Foreign Secretaries of this period realized that a co-operative Italy was necessary for the fulfilment of wider aims of reconstruction and disarmament. For a brief time, following Locarno, it seemed as if British efforts had been successful. Chamberlain paid Mussolini a visit and returned strong in faith as to the dictator's good intentions. But during the next few years Italy moved into the revisionist camp and resumed her classic policy of balancing between rival power groupings in order to extract concessions. The immediate effect of Mussolini's *volte face* was minimal, for his primary areas of concern were the Balkans and the Eastern Mediterranean, and Britain showed no strong interest in an active rôle in either. The problem was that by the close of the decade it seemed to Paris that Mussolini had deliberately forged an anti-French combination in the Balkans, thus weakening France's security system.

French fears affected Britain, especially when Frenchmen argued that, 'faced particularly with the continued arming of Italy and the absence of Russia from Geneva, a strong army for defensive purposes is still necessary'.[47] Britain wished to avoid an arms race but had no substantial concession to offer Italy. Retrospectively it seems plain that Mussolini was an opportunist rather than a convinced Francophobe. Participation in conferences was to secure money, territory or prestige rather than a necessary aid to the pursuit of responsible, coherent policies. Italy, for example, sided with France in 1929 in demanding a high level of reparations, but with Britain in advocating territorial revision. Despite this evidence of cynicism and unreliability the illusion that Italy might yet prove a force for European stability died hard; in Britain in 1932 it was still very much alive.

Central to the British strategy of reconstruction was the need to maintain good relations with the United States. During this decade the two powers shared a common tongue in their diplomatic exchanges but only rarely a common language. The events of 1918–22 had produced in the United States a revulsion from close involvement with European affairs without in any way diminishing American importance. The general effects of this narrow isolationism were succinctly put by F. R. Dulles: 'By failing to direct the tremendous material power that was theirs toward a constructive internationalism, and by limiting the conscious influence of the United States on world affairs to moral suasion, the American people ignored the inescapable effects of their technology, their money, their prosperity. Nevertheless, these phenomena continued to have direct and important consequences for the rest of the globe'.[48] Less frequently realized is that in Britain there were doubts as to the desirability of American participation in European affairs and to her reliability as an ally.

American reliability had long been questioned in Britain. Curzon believed that 'the policy of the American Government was so apt to change abruptly with the changes in the Administration'.[49] Men of his generation, accustomed to the British style of a foreign policy towering above the vagaries of electoral preference, were not well equipped to understand the intricacies of American policy-making. What is more surprising is the extent to which leading politicians doubted the desirability or utility of American co-operation. According to Vansittart 'We hardly yet realized that nothing else in the world means so much as welding the users of English. Many like Austen Chamberlain still deemed the Old World more important. It was better form to be pro-German or pro-Russian than either pro-French or pro-American; to be both of the latter was deplorable. Britons seldom condescended to transatlantic politics. Of course Anglo-American relations were "paramount" and all that, but MacDonald was exceptional in meaning it'.[50]

British fears become easier to understand when the level of American ignorance about Europe is recognized. Prejudice and bigotry had been intensified by the strains placed on the myth of American unity during the period 1916–22. What were British diplomats to make of men like 'Big Bill' Thompson, three times Mayor of Chicago, whose Anglophobia was notorious even in a state full of politicians of Irish descent? On a different plane how was it possible to think of close co-operation with Presidents like Harding and Coolidge who bowed readily to the pressure of isolationists Borah and Johnson? By the time Hoover became President in 1929 it was too late to cure the effects of a prolonged bout of isolationism.

Despite these difficulties Britain remained hopeful of American co-operation. Britain needed the help of the United States in a number of areas of policy, particularly in the tasks of economic stabilization, the establishment of League authority and securing a balance of power in the Far East. Although it had become evident at the beginning of the decade that the United States would not join the League it was still envisaged that American politicians would seek to work with it. Europeans imagined that participation in organizations such as I.L.O. and the Permanent Court would not raise too many political hackles in the United States. These assumptions were invalid. It was not until 1934 that the United States joined the I.L.O. and on every occasion that membership of the Court was proposed a flood of isolationist propaganda forced the administration to demand quite impossible safeguards to protect 'American sovereignty'. Furthermore, when the League showed close interest in Latin American affairs the United States reacted by persuading Latin American states to withdraw their membership. By the end of the 1930s Brazil, Costa Rica, Chile, Guatemala, Honduras, Nicaragua and Paraguay had succumbed to American blandishments. In December 1936, at a Pan-American Conference, it was seriously suggested that an American League of Nations be created. In these circumstances to hope for American assistance in building a new world order was to chase a will o' the wisp.

The United States was much more co-operative in the task of economic reconstruction. From the start it was realized in Britain that without massive American assistance there could be no return to pre-1914 prosperity. In the United States there was opposition to the notion of economic involvement in Europe but it was far less vehement than in the case of political commitment. Nevertheless there was a general lack of understanding in the United States as to the relationship between war debts, reparations and economic prosperity. It was, after all, Coolidge himself who pressed for the repayment of loans with the comment, 'They hired the money, didn't they?' The President seemed resolved to put into practice his view that 'The business of America is business'.[51]

Coolidge succeeded Harding as President in August 1923. Despite his conservative views on business and economics it was during his term that the greatest progress was made towards reconstruction. In 1924 General Charles G. Dawes was appointed to head the committee of experts on reparations. Its report, produced on 9 April 1924, was generally favourable to British interests. The Dawes plan envisaged German control of her own resources, a stabilized *Rentenmark*, a sliding scale of reparations, repayments in German currency and a foreign loan to expedite these reforms. The London Conference of July 1924 approved all these measures. The British reaction was favourable. Even in the heat of the election campaign of 1924 Baldwin found time to congratulate MacDonald on his handling of the conference. Certainly the plan marked a substantial advance on the World Foreign War Debt Commission which Congress had set up on 9 February 1922 with instructions to collect all debts by 1947 and at a rate of interest not less than $4\frac{1}{4}\%$. Dawes, who became Vice-President in 1925, continued to exercise a benevolent influence upon Coolidge's attitude towards reparations and war debts during the rest of his term.

The years 1924–29 did not, however, witness close economic co-operation. The boom in consumption in the United States helped create an illusion of prosperity and a belief that Americans could ignore European problems. In fact there was growing impatience at European inability to meet obligations. It was not seen that the Fordney-McCumber tariff of 1922 had imposed import levies which reduced trade and hence prevented payment of war debts and reparations. Lloyd George saw the problem clearly: 'there are at least three clear and definite reasons for the dislocation of trade and industry. These are: the mishandling and faulty distribution of the world's gold supplies; the high tariff barriers to international commerce; and the special international indebtedness which is a legacy of the World War'.[52] British suppositions that none of these problems could be solved without American aid were entirely correct.

Under pressure from his advisers Coolidge agreed in 1928 to the Young Committee. Foremost in advocacy was a Governor of the Federal Reserve Bank, Strong, who was a convinced supporter of international economic co-operation. But the stock market boom of 1928–29 diverted American capital from Europe to domestic investment and so the schemes devised by Young and refined at the Hague Conferences of 1929 and 1930 were never implemented. European trade problems were intensified in 1931 by the Hawley-Smoot tariff of 1930. Hoover, faced in 1931 with a complete economic collapse in both the United States and Europe was forced to announce a moratorium on inter-governmental indebtedness. His action was in response to tremendous agitation at home and abroad. MacDonald and Snowden, reeling under the impact of the economic blizzard, needed American help to stave off catastrophe.

Their sentiments were echoed by Brüning and the Austrian Chancellor, Ender. At home, in an open letter to the *New York Times* on 5 May 1930, more than a thousand economists had advised Hoover of the adverse consequences of increased tariffs. Although by 1931 the President himself wished to lower tariffs the matter lay in the hands of Congress which consistently refused to embrace the cause of internationalism. As a result Western Europe was left to fend for itself while the United States tried to solve economic problems in isolation. By 1932 there were 13 million unemployed and Hoover was heading for a disastrous electoral defeat. Curiously, the election of Roosevelt signalled not the belated victory of the internationalists but their defeat, for the new President was committed to a policy of putting America first. By 1933 the strategy of economic reconstruction, imperfectly comprehended and worse executed by American statesmen, lay in ruins.

To encourage good Anglo-American relations Britain countenanced unrealistic American initiatives for world peace. The failure of these moves in turn alienated American opinion. Typical of these misunderstandings was the Geneva Disarmament Conference of 1927, attended by Britain, Japan and the United States. Craig's verdict was unkindly accurate: 'It was convened without adequate diplomatic preparation; it began with a public meeting at which delegates hurled widely divergent plans at each other's heads; and it ended—after weeks of futile wrangling, and after an attempt at compromise had been indignantly repudiated by the British Cabinet under the inspiration of Mr Winston Churchill—in total failure'.[53] To cap it all Chamberlain later announced a secret agreement with France, causing great offence in the United States.

In the same vein was the move to 'outlaw war'—a project beloved of the isolationists. Eventually Kellogg, the Secretary of State, adopted the proposal as his own. His Assistant Secretary, Castle, was amazed: 'For weeks the press has chorused approval of F.B.K.'s exchange of notes with Briand on out-lawing war... actually it is futile. . . . I think it is about time for the correspondence to stop. . . . The funny thing is that Olds and the Secretary seem to take it all with profound seriousness'.[54] By the Pact of Paris of 27 August 1928 fifteen states agreed to renounce war as an instrument of national policy. In fact the pact was a danger to world peace as its existence helped convince Americans there was little need for an active policy to protect security. Britain's diplomats and politicians were reduced to despair by this lack of realism. Chamberlain complained, 'I can form some opinion as to what France or Germany or Italy may be likely to do in this or that contingency. Except in a narrow field the course which will be taken by the United States is a riddle to which no one—not even themselves—can give an answer in advance. But perhaps this is only saying that the United States has no foreign policy. The ship drifts at the mercy of every gust of public opinion'.[55] These views were not unrepresentative.

Even the onset of the depression hardly diminished American enthusiasm for international peace-keeping conferences. In late 1929 the British government, prompted by the United States, issued invitations to France, Italy and Japan to a naval conference to be held in London in January 1930. The Latin nations spent most of their energies squabbling about parity and the serious question of a naval arms race was tackled by Japan, Britain and the United States in tripartite discussions. The English-speaking powers at last reached agreement on cruisers—the issue that had made the Geneva Conference futile. The final draft treated Japan very generously, amending the ratios for both cruisers and destroyers to 10:10:7. Though Japan had not attained parity she had secured local superiority in the Far East, for her forces were not so widely dispersed as those of the other powers. The three states also agreed to attend another conference in 1935, a year before the agreement was due to lapse.

The conference was regarded as a success. Long-term consequences of the concessions to Japan were foreseen by few. Objections from the Naval League, from pacifists and from a handful of diplomats and politicians, including Vansittart and Churchill, were ignored. The public mood favoured this type of contribution to peace and MacDonald was just the man to pursue such policies zealously. As Thorne commented, 'the broad context was undoubtedly one in which civilian governments and public opinion as a whole were compelling all military staffs to give ground and justify almost their very existence'.[56] If the combination of Hoover and MacDonald did little in the long run to solve international problems it did at least lend colour to the belief, widely held at the close of 1932, that Anglo-American relations were on a better footing than for some time past.

The shadow of Japanese intransigence, which was to grow so dark in the 1930s, had been apparent long before. The failure of Britain and the United States to co-operate in the Pacific and Far East created all sorts of problems. The termination in 1921 of the Anglo-Japanese Alliance had left Britain with no method of controlling Japan. In the early 1920s this hardly proved a problem but in 1924–25 two important events signalled a change in Japanese policy. In 1924 Congress passed a new Immigration Act which discriminated against the Japanese, who had already been irritated by the economic effects of the 1922 tariff—which Tokyo had seen as discriminatory against Japanese industry. In 1925 China relapsed into almost total chaos with factions and war-lords disputing the inheritance of Sun Yat-sen, who died on 12 March. These apparently unrelated events provided Japanese expansionists with both the excuses and the opportunities they needed. In Tokyo it came to be believed that a great new empire could be created in China and South-east Asia.

Britain was almost helpless to halt growing unrest in China— directed mainly against Europeans—and the growth of Japanese influence there. From time to time Britain intervened in Chinese affairs when incidents became too flagrant to pass unchecked, but as Churchill commented after the Nanking incident of 24 March 1927, 'Punishing China is like flogging a jellyfish'.[57] It was Britain's impossible task to try to protect her economic and strategic interests in the Far East without adequate resources. Japan, on the other hand, had both the resources and the motivation, for almost 82% of Japanese foreign investment was concentrated in China. The Japanese took increasing advantage of unrest in China to advance claims to preponderance in Manchuria where there were valuable minerals which Tokyo coveted.

Anglo-Japanese relations worsened as it became clear that while Britain wanted 'a united, well-ordered, prosperous and peaceful China',[58] Japan preferred its disintegration. British concern for trading interests, centred on the Treaty Ports, was more than matched, however, by her unwillingness to clash openly with the only major power in the area. The United States was not much use in restraining Japan; Hoover saw her as a barrier to the advance of Bolshevism and Assistant Secretary Johnson felt that 'the friendliest feelings between us and the Japanese . . . should continue more or less indefinitely'.[59]

In 1929 the situation deteriorated further. The slump ruined Japanese silk exports to the United States and the Chinese government, in a riposte to Japanese political pressure, boycotted her cotton products. The Hawley-Smoot tariff was seen in Tokyo as another anti-Japanese move and led to renewed demands for the creation of an area subject to exclusive Japanese economic control. Three Japanese premiers, Hamaguchi, Inukai and Inouye, who favoured good relations between Japan and the English-speaking powers were assassinated. The limitations imposed at the Naval Conference of 1930 further wounded the feelings of the expansionists. Then, in 1931, the Chinese began to show signs of independence. Demands for the ending of extraterritoriality and for tariff autonomy alarmed Japan and the Western Powers. They thus 'inopportunely invited aggression by alienating their obtuse European friends'.[60]

With Britain unable and the United States unwilling to act it was only a matter of time before Japan showed her hand. In March 1931 Johnson had told Castle, 'if Manchuria is destined to become part of Japan I do not see why it should necessarily embroil us'.[61] In Britain many agreed; Grant Jones, a consular officer of experience, had commented in 1928 that 'for Japan the control of these resources is a matter of grim necessity, and necessity knows no law'.[62] On 18 September the Japanese seized Mukden and by early 1932 had taken control of almost all Manchuria and had installed a puppet régime. The invasion came at a time of singular awkwardness for Britain. On 21 September Britain left the gold standard and shortly after Parliament was dissolved. Foreign affairs were in the hands of Reading, whose term of office lasted only from 26 August to 9 November. Policy was thus largely determined by the permanent officials.

On 21 September China appealed to the League, citing Article

XI of the Covenant. Japan was not only in breach of the Covenant but also of the Pact of Paris and the Nine Power Treaty of 1922 (which included safeguards for Chinese territorial integrity). British attempts to persuade Japan to end hostilities soon failed. Within the Foreign Office opinion polarized into two groups—headed by Lampson, the Ambassador to Peking, who argued for stern measures against Japan, and another led by Lindley, the Ambassador to Tokyo, who insisted that coercion would both fail and promote Anglophobia in Japan. The new Foreign Secretary, Simon, and his Deputy Under-Secretary, Wellesley, felt that these approaches were wrong. 'Thus', commented Louis, 'was born a policy of neutrality out of prudence'.[63]

Public reaction to the invasion was generally hostile. Internationalists believed it to be damaging to the League's prestige. Cecil set up a small committee to investigate what action might be taken against Japan if she proved obdurate. He was strongly supported by Cadogan, the Foreign Office Adviser on League Affairs. The politicians were more cautious. Most were worried about possible damage to British commercial interests in China but still more concerned to avoid offending Japan. The result was some muted criticism and many mumbled platitudes.

The issue could scarcely be avoided at Geneva. China was pressing for support and her friends were vociferous. It was plain that nothing could be achieved without the aid of the United States and on 14 October the League Council invited an American representative to attend its deliberations. In December it was decided to send a Commission of Inquiry—presided over by Lord Lytton—and early in 1932 the commission departed for China. Simon was entirely in favour of this procedure and believed that it was the course of action most likely to promote British aims. He wished not only to appease the Japanese but to work in concert with the League and the United States in order to preserve China. It may well have been true that these objectives could not all be fulfilled, but they were hardly ignoble.

Unfortunately Simon's policy sustained a serious reverse when on 24 January 1932 Japan attacked Shanghai. Pratt, Adviser on Far Eastern Affairs to the Foreign Office since 1925, believed that 'Ultimately, we will be faced with the alternatives of going to war with Japan or retiring from the Far East'.[64] The possibility of war meant that the necessity of Anglo-American co-operation became still more urgent. On 7 January Stimson, the American Secretary of State, had promulgated his doctrine of non-recognition of agreements brought about by force. Two days later Simon expressed himself satisfied by Japanese assurances that the 'open door' would be maintained in Manchuria. At a time when Anglo-American co-operation was needed the policies of the two nations began to drift apart. In London there was deep distrust of the United States. Wellesley believed that the Americans were 'quite capable of backing out after we had agreed to give our support, leaving us to clear up the resultant mess'.[65] It was not surprising, therefore, that Britain chose to try to use the machinery of the League rather than rely on Washington, though this method itself highlighted the problem of American non-membership.

On 29 January China made a further appeal to the League, claiming that Japan was in violation of Articles X and XV of the Covenant. Two weeks later the dispute was referred to the Assembly which met in special session on 3 March. The following day a resolution calling for a cease-fire and for the opening of negotiations was adopted. The smaller states of the League were by now in open revolt against what they saw as the favouritism of Britain and France towards Japan. While this was an understandable attitude it hardly did justice to Simon's efforts. Once the issue had been raised at the League the only two possible results were either condemnation of Japan or humiliation of the League as an international peace-keeping body. Simon's manoeuvres were designed to postpone the final decision, for he believed that either outcome would be detrimental to British interests. He was quite right; nor was he the only person to believe that delay could be advantageous to the cause of peace.

The Foreign Secretary and his staff seem, on the whole, to have believed that the Manchurian problem could only be solved through the League's activities. The United States' reliability was in question; France, Germany and Italy had no real interest; Britain and the Soviet Union lacked the power to compel Japan. Vansittart had written in 1931 that 'the League would be worth nothing if it did not sometimes attempt the impossible'[66] and Simon observed that 'The League devoted itself honestly and whole-heartedly to every step short of coercion and succeeded in getting the Japanese out of Shanghai. The Labour Opposition of the day clamoured for more, but coercive action, of which the brunt would have fallen on this country alone, would only have precipitated a war'.[67] Condemnation from the Left by Strachey that Simon's use of 'his immense forensic powers, and . . . by using the whole influence of Britain, stopped the League from taking action'[68] was false and misleading. Taylor's comment that Simon 'lacked the air of puzzled rectitude which enabled a Grey or a Halifax to lapse from the highest moral standards without anyone complaining or even noticing. Simon angered idealists by keeping calm and by seeing both sides of the case . . .'[69] was more apposite.

The spring and summer of 1932 were spent by Simon in vain attempts to persuade Japan to moderate her demands and the United States to work closely with Britain. British problems were intensified by the fact that whereas there was sympathy for Japanese action in Manchuria there was none for her intervention in China. On 2 October 1932 the long-awaited Lytton Report was presented. It was generally condemnatory of Japan but did recognize her special interests in Manchuria. Most importantly, as Simon pointed out, the report 'never suggested a restoration of the *status quo ante*. This would have been futile . . .'[70] The next few months were devoted to efforts by Simon to effect conciliation on the lines suggested in the report. All his work was rendered nugatory by a further Japanese onslaught on 1 January 1933. On 24 February the League voted 42 to 1 to accept its sub-committee's version of the Lytton Report. Japan promptly gave notice of her intention to resign from the League.

British Far Eastern policy lay in ruins. Japan had been alienated yet China had not been saved. The League had been humiliated and a belated attempt by Britain to impose an arms embargo on the belligerents collapsed after two weeks. France had been openly pro-Japanese and the United States unhelpful. It was the American attitude which was the key factor, for the United States was not a member of the League and never gave confidence that League action would receive her support. British attitudes were particularly affected by this fear of unreliability and also by suspicion that Americans hoped to take advantage of an Anglo-Japanese dispute to improve their commercial position in the area. Britain had neither the confidence nor the economic and military power to compel the restoration of peace. As Butler commented, 'When reduced to essentials, the Manchurian affair had demonstrated that without the certainty of whole-hearted American co-operation the League powers, that is to say the naval powers of Britain and France, were neither strong enough nor determined enough to bar the Japanese militarists in their attack on China'.[71]

The general pattern of awkward relationships with old allies was maintained in the case of Russia. There were special circumstances which made a close understanding unlikely. Britain had not treated Russia well in the years 1917–21 and intervention in the civil war had created a legacy of distrust which was hard to overcome. The attitude of the British Government towards Russia's representative in London (Litvinov) had been foolish and discourteous; in 1918 he was even arrested. Three years later Krassin, the Soviet expert on trade who had signed an agreement with Britain on 21 March 1921, was deemed not to be entitled to diplomatic immunity as Russia's government had been recognized only *de facto*. These incidents were not at all helpful. On the other side the Bolsheviks only intermittently showed awareness of how damaging to their cause was the flood of revolutionary propaganda emanating from Comintern and the Russian press.

Other matters increased mutual suspicion. The Rapallo agreement of April 1922, linking the two outcasts of Europe, convinced the British that Russia was not to be trusted. In Moscow there was little disposition to put faith in the Conservative and Conservative-dominated administrations of the 1920s. In fact the basis for co-operation was probably non-existent. After 1924 Russia's leaders were preoccupied with the power struggle which ended with Stalin's victory in 1929. Adoption of the Five Year Plan and the policy of 'Socialism in one country' diverted attention away from foreign affairs towards the task of industrialization and reconstruction. In these circumstances Russia did not wish to assume either that full membership of the European community so earnestly desired by the Labour Party or the burden of an alliance which so many Frenchmen sought.

By 1922 it was evident that the Bolsheviks were in full control and that they would neither repay Tsarist debts nor compensate British citizens for loss of property. Once these aspirations had been abandoned the Foreign Office was free to concentrate on Anglo-Russian relations in the Middle East, the Far East, Europe and the wider issue of Russia's rôle as a revolutionary power. Apprehension regarding future Russian conduct was well founded. Quite apart from a theoretical commitment to revolution there were economic, historic and geographical reasons for supposing that any Russian government, of whatever political complexion, would hardly be content with the great reduction in territory and influence which had followed defeat in 1917. It was assumed almost from the start that Russia must be reckoned a revisionist power.

The first step in creating a working relationship was *de jure* recognition of the Russian Government. On MacDonald's advent to power in 1924 this recognition was granted, though not without opposition from both Crowe in the Foreign Office and a number of diehard Tories in Parliament. In April a conference to discuss Anglo-Russian differences and to restore Russian credit was held in London. This conference met with little success as the Russians were fully aware that the Labour Government had no majority in the House of Commons and that the Liberal and Conservative majority was by no means enthusiastic for a settlement. Indeed it was in 1924 that the *Morning Post* criticized recognition in uncompromising terms—'a cardinal error . . . to accord it at a time when the Bolshevist dominion may be tottering shows singular lack of judgement on the part of men who are responsible for the government of a great Empire'.[72] The period of Labour rule was not happy in the annals of Anglo-Russian relations—principally because Comintern, under the energetic leadership of Zinoviev, persisted in its propaganda assaults. In August a Communist, J. R. Campbell, was charged under the Mutiny Act of 1797 for his propaganda appeals to the armed forces. Lloyd George, ever the opportunist, seized the chance to make trouble and in September MacDonald was defeated in a vote of censure on the handling of the case. During the following election campaign a letter, supposedly from Zinoviev, was published urging all manner of seditious activities on the British Communist Party. The general apprehension as to the purpose of Labour overtures to Russia was heightened by this letter. The election resulted in an overwhelming victory for the Conservatives, though the principal victims were Liberals rather than Labour. Whether Zinoviev's letter was genuine or not was probably of little import, for Comintern had certainly issued similar instructions to other European affiliates. Nor was its effect as profound as the more general impression of muddle and incapacity given by the handling of the Campbell case. If Labour was thought to be 'soft on Communism' it is remarkable that it was not slaughtered at the polls. In reality the main impact was prolongation of the Conservatives' impression that Russia still hoped to make a revolution in Britain.

Shortly after the election Neville Chamberlain emphasized the part that apprehension of revolutionary activity played in Conservative attitudes. He hoped, though clearly without much confidence, that 'the Soviets would renounce for ever the thought of corrupting the armed forces of this country and of bringing about over here a revolution'.[73] Russian persistence in Britain, the Far East (where attempts were made to penetrate Sun Yat-sen's movement) and in Europe alarmed and infuriated British policy-makers. In 1926 Russia was foolish enough to offer financial aid for the support of the General Strike, though this was refused by the T.U.C. In the subsequent furore Churchill urged a break in relations. This was rejected by the Cabinet, though in February 1927 a stiff note was sent to Russia urging a cessation of provocations in Britain and her Empire. In May there was a police raid on the Soviet Trade Delegation's premises, jointly occupied by Arcos—its commercial organization—which discovered some compromising material on anti-British activities. The 1921 trade agreement was abrogated and the Soviet missions were requested to leave the country. Diplomatic relations were not resumed until late in 1929, after the return of another Labour Government. By this time the fall of Zinoviev, engineered by Stalin, had seriously curtailed the activities of Comintern and fears of underground revolutionary activity were no longer so widely or strongly held even within the Conservative Party.

These vicissitudes in relations seriously hampered any attempt to bring Russia back into the mainstream of European international relations. Among all parties there were those who believed that normality could not be attained until Russia was accepted on equal terms. The British attitude was important in keeping Russia out of the League until September 1934, though a stream of Russian denunciations of the League as an organ of aggressive capitalism hardly suggested a positive enthusiasm for membership. But, as Lloyd George had commented in 1926, 'You get no peace in the world until a Government representing these valiant millions is found inside the fraternity of nations'.[74] In the end common sense prevailed but only after a decade of disastrous misunderstandings.

Britain's immediate concern was the conservation of peace in Eastern Europe. The Western Powers had been frightened by Russo-Polish conflict in the early 1920s and feared lest Russia seek to overthrow the territorial settlement of Versailles, St Germain and Trianon. Attempts by Russia in 1920 to dissipate these fears by a series of treaties with her neighbours had not been wholly successful. The gradual decline of revolutionary movements in the countries of Eastern and Central Europe made this matter seem less urgent as the years slipped by, though fears of revisionism were revived by the Treaty of Berlin of 1926. The advent of Pilsudski to power in Poland that year caused a deterioration in Russo-Polish relations and a revival of French fears as to the reliability of her alliance system. The accession of Russia to the Pact of Paris opened the way, however, to an improvement of relations between Russia and her neighbours which was welcomed in London and Paris. Litvinov, owing to Chicherin's illness the effective head of the Foreign Affairs Commissariat, promoted a Protocol of Non-Aggression in February 1929. By the summer of 1929 Danzig, Poland, Latvia, Lithuania, Estonia, Turkey, Persia and Roumania had accepted the protocol. This success lent force to MacDonald's wish to resume diplomatic relations as well as making resumption more acceptable to the non-Labour majority.

The drive for security represented by the Litvinov Protocol

seemed to harmonize with Britain's wish for Eastern European stability. There was, however, no question of any increase in British commitments to advance the cause of co-operation, though in April 1930 Henderson did sign a trade agreement. Relations in the period 1929–32 remained distant for there was no true agreement on aims. Russia was looking for security, Britain for collective security. At points there was some overlap of interest, for both governments tried to promote disarmament through international negotiation, but a strong impression remained in Britain that this was only a tactical move by Russia. Litvinov never showed any enthusiasm for schemes such as Briand's for the economic federalization of Europe. Nor did Russia scale down her savage attacks on the political and financial system of the West. It was easy for men like Lothian to believe that Litvinov's aim was 'to maintain discord in Europe'.[75] The formation of the National Government in 1931 restored to power many of those who had traditionally shown suspicion of Russia. As Winkler commented, 'Whatever its purpose, the Russian rapprochement was a disappointment. . . . The best that Henderson's colleague, Hugh Dalton, was later able to say for the policy was that it had succeeded in making Anglo-Russian relations less unsatisfactory than they would otherwise have been'.[76]

It proved equally impossible for Britain and Russia to reach agreement on traditional areas of conflict stretching from Turkey to India. It was a source of concern in Britain that the head of Narkomindel for most of the decade—Chicherin—had been a prominent member of the anti-British Asiatic Department of the Imperial Foreign Office. In Beloff's opinion, 'On the Middle East, on the frontiers of India, and, above all in China, the revolutionary propaganda of the Communist International was always a possible factor of disturbance'.[77] In Turkey the matter of potential Russian influence was satisfactorily solved by the emergence of Kemal Ataturk who plainly was no Bolshevik puppet. The conclusion of the Russo-Turkish treaty of 17 December 1925 promised to leave Turkey in peace and was welcomed in Britain. Persia was a different proposition. In 1920 the Bolsheviks had supported a revolution which had forced British troops out of the country. In 1921 Reza Khan seized power and promptly proceeded to liberate his country almost entirely from foreign influence. In 1925 he became Shah and in October 1927 concluded a neutrality pact with Russia. These developments caused considerable perturbation in London.

British goals in the Middle East were the maintenance of peace, the prevention of the spread of Russian influence and the promotion of economic contacts. In early 1921 treaties had linked together Russia, Turkey, Persia and Afghanistan. These arrangements— which ultimately turned out to be harmless—were at first seen as a step in the subversion of British power in India. In fact what was happening was the partial modernization and westernization of these countries, though this was accompanied by a rejection of the formal methods of Western control. Britain was compelled, for example, to renounce its control of Afghan foreign policy shortly after the end of the war. The notion that these strongly Islamic countries would easily adopt the revolutionary and anti-religious tenets of Bolshevism was nonsensical, though widely prevalent. Nationalists in the area were not above using Anglo-Russian rivalry, however, to promote their own aspirations and to reduce European political influence. In normal circumstances this opportunism would probably have been recognized for what it was, but the apparent success of revolutionary propaganda in Europe and the Far East rendered British politicians almost paranoic about the danger to India. As late as 1927 Joynson-Hicks, the Home Secretary, believed that 'The whole world knows that in every part where the British Empire impinges on another country there you will find Muscovite emissaries trying to stir up mischief'.[78] Arguments on these lines were lent force by increasing discontent in India after the Amritsar massacre of 1919. Thus British hostility towards Russian ambitions in these areas remained strong, though based upon historical antagonisms and fears rather than upon positive evidence of Russian activity in this period. In reality, British control everywhere was extended through increased economic contacts which supplanted and surpassed the older forms of political control and military intervention. By 1932 Russia's influence in the area was substantially reduced from the high point of 1921.

The last area of concern to both Britain and Russia was the Far East. The outbreak of civil war in China in 1922 had given

Sun Yat-sen the chance of a political comeback and in 1923–25 he, together with his Russian adviser Michael Borodin, succeeded in reviving the Kuomintang and identifying it very closely with Moscow. The British Government was particularly alarmed at some Russian successes. In 1924 the Russian-dominated Whampoa Academy had been founded and the same year Peking recognized Russia's title to the Chinese Eastern Railway. The anti-foreign bias of the Chinese, natural enough in the circumstances of a century of humiliation at European hands, was widely supposed to be financed by Comintern. In 1927 Wood, Parliamentary Secretary to Neville Chamberlain, warned that 'The Communist intrigue abroad un-doubtedly culminated in the extensive anti-British movement in China and the danger to thousands of British lives in Shanghai'.[79] It is hardly surprising that the Foreign Office should have lamented the loss of the Japanese alliance, for Japan alone seemed strong enough to resist Russian encroachment in Manchuria and political penetra-tion in China. However, events in China in 1927 brought some easing of pressure on Britain. After a series of political upheavals Chiang Kai-shek emerged victorious and in July the Chinese Communists were arrested and Borodin and his entourage expelled. By the close of 1928 Russian influence had been almost eliminated and the Chinese Government began to challenge the Russian position in Manchuria.

The Japanese invasion of Manchuria in 1931 revived again the prospect of Russian involvement. Russo-Japanese relations had not been close since 1925 and some officials hoped that a triplice of Britain, Russia and the United States might form a bar to Japan. These hopes ignored both Russian weakness and the lack of diplo-matic contact between Russia and the United States. The real British fear was a revival of Russian power. According to Louis, 'Throughout the entire Manchurian crisis loomed the spectre of Russia—a chilling vision to the Foreign Office because a wrong move might incite the Chinese to turn again to the Bolsheviks'.[80] Russia had, however, no intention of intervening in Manchuria unless forced so to do and even opened negotiations with the Japanese in order to secure a non-aggression pact—though these overtures were ultimately rejected.

Russian lack of success in dealing with the Chinese in 1929, Stalin's preoccupation with domestic affairs, poor relations with Britain and the United States and a contempt for the League all conspired to persuade Moscow to hold aloof. Stalin certainly did not wish to intervene and then be left to bear all the responsibility; this fear at least he shared with the British, who were suspicious of possible American duplicity. The Lytton Commission was given no help at all, not even when Japan tried to justify intervention by referring to subversive Russian activities. Instead of working with Britain and the United States Russia tried to drive a wedge between them by stressing the pro-Japanese elements in British policy. Britain was fully aware of these manoeuvres and soon realized that 'Japan did indeed have little to fear immediately from that quarter'.[81] The hope that Far Eastern peace could be preserved with Russian aid was unreal. Vansittart knew that the game was played out before it could even be started. Russia, the great bogey in China since the 1890s, by 1931 was anxious only to keep out of conflict; Britain was thus obliged to try to operate a strategy of balance of power without any counterbalancing forces. Resentment caused by assumption of this burden and by Russian failure to share its load created yet another unhappy memory in Anglo-Russian relations.

British foreign policy in this decade was distinguished therefore more by aspiration than by achievement. Many of the purposes were noble—restoration of economic stability, achievement of political democracy for new nations, reconciliation of enemies, development of the League of Nations and, above all, maintenance of peace. Necessarily fulfilment was limited. In part failures may be attributed to lack of perception, vision and even understanding of the other major powers. In part they must be attributed to Britain's own similar defects. Some forces were too strong perhaps even for a combination of well-intentioned powers to overcome. Narrow economic nationalism, ethnic hatreds, ideological differences and geographical remoteness were all factors which contributed to the disastrous state of the world in 1932. None of the factors for instability was easily open to correction in the 1920s. British policy in Europe was once rather unfairly characterized as one 'to amuse cynics and infuriate rivals'.[82] This was not intentional. The men of the decade—MacDonald, Henderson, Chamberlain, Simon and Reading—wanted peace and wanted a major British contribution to its permanent achievement. It is easy to analyse their mistakes and to point out their confusions, misapprehensions and, sometimes, their insensitivity. It is quite wrong to mock their efforts, for they were sincerely meant. Nor were they entirely unsuccessful, for the decade was not barren of achievement. It is perhaps just the sad truth that judgment tends to be harsh when opportunities for peace which existed in 1918 are seen to have been transmuted into opportunities for friction by 1932. But, as Petrie observed, in the end the verdict must be that if Europe missed the chance to set its house in order peacefully 'the fault does not rest with Great Britain'.[83] British policy-makers, after all, did understand the simple truth that they could not compel peace and that even if they had possessed such power such a peace could not last.

REFERENCES

1 *Life of Lord Curzon* by Earl of Ronaldshay. Vol. III. p. 345.
2 *An Ambassador of Peace* by Lord D'Abernon. Vol. II. p. 159.
3 *The Roots of Appeasement* by M. Gilbert. p. 102.
4 Ronaldshay, op. cit., Vol. III. p. 347.
5 *An Autobiography* by P. Snowden. Vol. II. p. 679.
6 *Baldwin* by K. Middlemas and J. Barnes. p. 349.
7 D'Abernon, op. cit., Vol. III. p. 139.
8 *The Mist Procession* by Lord Vansittart. p. 342.
9 *Life and Letters of Austen Chamberlain* by Sir C. Petrie. Vol. II. pp. 292-3.
10 *Stresemann and the Politics of the Weimar Republic* by H. A. Turner. p. 210.
11 Petrie, op. cit., Vol. II. p. 259.
12 Middlemas and Barnes, op. cit., p. 360.
13 Vansittart, op. cit., p. 385.
14 *The Nemesis of Power* by J. W. Wheeler-Bennett. p. 97.
15 *The German Army* by H. Rosinski. p. 174.
16 *Imperial Sunset* by M. Beloff. p. 343.
17 *All the Way* by Viscount Cecil. p. 191.
18 ibid., p. 191.
19 *Our Own Times* by S. King-Hall. p. 281.
20 Petrie, op. cit., Vol. II. p. 322.

21 Gilbert, op. cit., p. 119.
22 Vansittart, op. cit., p. 362.
23 Cecil, op. cit., p. 194.
24 *The Diplomats* ed. G. A. Craig and F. Gilbert. pp. 330–1.
25 *Sir Horace Rumbold* by M. Gilbert. p. 326.
26 ibid., p. 344.
27 *A Mirror to Geneva* by G. Slocombe. p. 248.
28 *A Short History of International Affairs* by G. M. Gathorne-Hardy. p. 356.
29 *My first Seventy-six years* by H. Schacht. p. 235.
30 Snowden, op. cit., Vol. II. p. 779.
31 *Winds of Change, 1914–39* by H. Macmillan. p. 379.
32 There is some disagreement between Schacht and Snowden as to the exact composition of the committee.
33 Snowden, op. cit., Vol. II. p. 791.
34 *English History, 1914–45* by A. J. P. Taylor. p. 272.
35 *Young Report.* p. 11.
36 Snowden, op. cit., Vol. II. pp. 837–8.
37 *Memoirs* by F. von Papen. p. 137.
38 *Sir Horace Rumbold* by M. Gilbert. p. 344.
39 *The truth about Reparations and War Debts* by D. Lloyd George. pp. 88–9.
40 Snowden, op. cit., Vol. II. p. 838.
41 *The Roots of Appeasement* by M. Gilbert. p. 131.
42 *Lord Lothian* by J. R. M. Butler. p. 118.
43 *Stanley Baldwin* by G. M. Young. p. 62.
44 *The Tragedy of Ramsay MacDonald* by L. M. Weir. pp. 341–2.
45 *Britain and the Dictators* by R. W. Seton-Watson. p. 169.
46 *A Great Experiment* by Lord Robert Cecil. p. 151.
47 *The Decline of French Patriotism, 1870–1940* by H. Tint. p. 183.
48 *America's Rise to World Power, 1898–1954* by F. R. Dulles. p. 143.
49 *British Strategy in the Far East, 1919–39* by W. R. Louis. p. 48.
50 Vansittart, op. cit., pp. 317–18.
51 From two speeches in 1925. *Oxford Dictionary of Quotations.* p. 156.
52 Lloyd George, op. cit., p. 4.
53 Craig and Gilbert, op. cit., p. 44.
54 Dulles, op. cit., p. 159.
55 Petrie, op. cit., Vol. II. p. 324.
56 *The Limits of Foreign Policy* by C. Thorne. p. 66.
57 Louis, op. cit., p. 133. Memorandum of 25 April 1927.
58 Thorne, op. cit., p. 48.
59 *After Imperialism: the search for a new order in the Far East, 1921–31* by A. Iriye. pp. 221–2.
60 Vansittart, op. cit., pp. 434–5.
61 Thorne, op. cit., p. 53.
62 Louis, op. cit., p. 175. Grant Jones to Lampson, 7 October 1928.
63 ibid., p. 179.
64 ibid., p. 188. Memorandum of 1 February 1932.
65 ibid., p. 190. Memorandum of 1 February 1932.
66 Thorne, op. cit., p. 109.

67 *Retrospect* by Viscount Simon. p. 191.
68 *Democracy and Foreign Policy: A Case History, the Sino-Japanese Dispute, 1931–33* by R. Bassett. p. 625.
69 Taylor, op. cit., p. 372.
70 Simon, op. cit., p. 189.
71 *The Lost Peace* by H. Butler. p. 43.
72 *Maisky* by G. Bilainkin. p. 38.
73 ibid., p. 38.
74 *Manchester Guardian*, 16 June 1926.
75 Craig and Gilbert, op. cit., p. 344.
76 ibid., p. 327.
77 *The Foreign Policy of Soviet Russia* by M. Beloff. Vol. I. p. 7.
78 Bilainkin, op. cit., p. 61. Speech of 4 February 1927.
79 ibid., p. 64. Speech of 25 February 1927.
80 Louis, op. cit., p. 174.
81 Thorne, op. cit., pp. 276–7.
82 *Ambassadors at Large: Britain* by E. H. Carr. p. 125.
83 *The Chamberlain Tradition* by Sir C. Petrie. p. 195.

7 Past Redress, 1933-39

> I have watched this famous island descending incontinently, fecklessly, the stairway which leads to a dark gulf. It is a fine broad stairway at the beginning, but after a bit the carpet ends. A little farther on there are only flagstones, and a little farther still these break beneath your feet.
>
> Winston Churchill, *While England Slept*

On 30 January 1933 Hitler was sworn in as Chancellor of Germany. Though he did not at once embark upon an activist foreign policy there was almost at once a change in the atmosphere of international relations. Two days later Lady Rumbold recorded, 'One can only hope that Hitler and his crowd won't force the pace. They are sure to start in before long on the Revision of the Versailles Treaty, but no one breathes it yet'.[1] The reality was plain, but there was a multitude of reasons why the makers of British foreign policy should reject the obvious.

Firstly it was generally recognized in Britain that economic conditions favoured pacific policies. There was no enthusiasm for increased spending on armaments. The Labour Party was led by a pacifist and the average Conservative would have accepted Neville Chamberlain's view that 'either we must play our part in pacification, or we must resign ourselves to the staggering prospect of spending £85 million on rearmament'.[2] Strongly associated with this viewpoint was the belief, probably correct, that Britain could only prosper in times of peace. There was thus a disposition to believe that the League of Nations, whose inadequacies had been but dimly perceived by the general public, could execute the task of pacification without undue consumption of resources. Curiously, those who were involved in the League's activities and were most

References are printed on p. 318.

committed to the principle of reasoned negotiation were often those who first recognized the League's deficiencies. Butler realized that 'The choice before Europe was not between arms *or* the Covenant, but between arms *and* the Covenant or chaos. And in the end it was chaos'.[3] In the wake of the 1931 crisis these arguments were discarded.

Another reason for the pursuit of appeasement was still more significant. It was widely believed in Britain that there was good cause for German resentment at Versailles. Europe could only be safe if Germany were appeased and fully integrated into the international security system. This had been the reasoning behind Locarno and the various schemes for the lightening of reparations payments. It made little sense when dealing with Hitler—whose potentialities in office were accurately expressed in a speech on 11 March 1933: 'I am for force, because in force I see strength, and in strength the eternal mother of rights, and in rights the root of life itself'.[4] But it continued to be believed that Hitler could be appeased and that he would be amenable to the process of reason. There were few anti-appeasers in 1933, though a number of anti-Nazis and anti-Germans. As late as November 1932 Churchill was arguing that 'The removal of the just grievances of the vanquished ought to precede the disarmament of the victors'.[5] Even Vansittart, who was in many respects the leading opponent of Germany within the Foreign Office, continued to favour some treaty revision, particularly with regard to the colonies Germany had lost in 1919.[6]

There was, too, an almost infinite capacity for self-deception in Britain concerning the nature of the Nazi régime and the personality of its leader. It was quite unnecessary, for evidence was swift to accumulate in the first weeks of the Nazi advent to power. Henderson's assessment was not untypical of one school: 'I hoped against hope that the Nazi revolution, having run its course, would revert to a normal and civilised conduct of internal and international life, that there was a limit to Hitler's ambitions and a word of truth in some at least of his assurances and statements. Many may regard my persistence as convicting me of the lack of any intellectual understanding of Nazi, or even German, mentality'.[7] It was a failure of understanding not to realize that a Nazi Germany had objectives in foreign policy which were bound to conflict with the central British objective: the preservation of peace. It was a further failing not to comprehend that the 'other Germany' had no influence at all upon the determination of policy. Cultured Germans did not, for the most part, subscribe to the Nazi outlook on life but they had participated in the surrender of fundamental political liberties in 1932–33 and, like the rest of Western Europe, paid heavily for this mistake. Their lack of power after 1933 makes all the subsequent argument and debate concerning good and bad Germans an irrelevance. It may have been true that 'eight Germans out of ten have always thought it not only legitimate but laudable to take every advantage however unfair in every walk of life'[8] or that the West Germans 'resent as an outrage to their personal dignity the suppression of all human rights—of freedom of conscience and liberty of opinion'.[9] Whether Vansittart or Thyssen was correct made no difference; Hitler was in control of Germany and could mould it as he willed. The notion that it was possible to negotiate with Hitler continued long after it deserved decent interment. As late as 1939, after the outbreak of war, Lloyd George could still urge the government to 'take into consideration any proposals for peace . . . which review all the subjects that have been the cause of all the troubles of the last few years'.[10] The 'regiment of Caligula cavalry'[11] had many eager recruits even outside the administration; the passage of time did not give them wisdom.

A powerful buttress to those sympathetic to Germany was a fear of Communism, coupled with the entirely understandable viewpoint that both Hitler and Stalin were undesirable associates—who should be induced to come to blows while the civilized world looked on as *tertius gaudens*. Gilbert aptly commented that 'Hitler claimed that the danger (the spread of Communism) was still a serious one. Many Englishmen believed him; and in answer to those who asked how we could possibly side with one tyranny against another, they answered that the evils of communism were eternal, but that the evils of Nazism could be killed by kindness'.[12] The views of Grigg typified Tory attitudes: 'In this Country Conservatives prefer the German system to the Russian because it is nationalistic in spirit and does not seek to undermine the unity of other nations by dividing them on class lines'.[13] There were some, too, on the Labour side who saw concession to Germany as the lesser of two evils. Lord Allen of Hurtwood wished to 'let Hitler have whatever he wants in Eastern Europe'.[14] There was a much larger group within the Labour Party which, while not wishing to appease Hitler, was not unaware of the dangers of consorting with Russia and took the easy line of supporting the notion of collective security. In practice, though not in theory, this meant toleration of government policy.

As if all these reasons for appeasement were not sufficient there were other factors which assisted the appeasers. Most members of the political and diplomatic establishment favoured appeasement because they believed, at least until 1938, that this was the way to promote peace. From 1938 until September 1939, and even perhaps until May 1940, appeasement was supported as it was felt to be the best way to avoid war. A positive enthusiasm was slowly transmuted into a defensive passivity. The influence of men such as Geoffrey Dawson, editor of *The Times*, and Sir Horace Wilson, Chamberlain's personal adviser, was very strong. Their opponents had fewer outlets in the press, in official circles or in Parliament. Furthermore the most prominent anti-appeaser of the decade, Churchill, had by his previous forays into political life contrived to hang a unique collection of political albatrosses around his neck—troops at Ton-y-pandy, the Dardanelles, return to the gold standard in 1925, the India Bill, and crossing the floor several times—which made him generally distrusted among men of all parties. With enemies like Churchill in the mid-1930s the National Government did not lack friends.

These are partial explanations for persistence in the policy of appeasement. The origins of the policy were simple and not ignoble. The British Government wished to promote peace and prosperity in the world so that Britain in turn could recover. In 1933 Britain was confronted with an ominously cloudy situation. Neither the United States nor the Soviet Union seemed to have much appetite for enthusiastic co-operation with Britain. The new régime in Germany was unlikely to be a force for peace. Italy and Japan had shown in Corfu and Manchuria how reliable they were as peacekeepers. The League of Nations and its attendant agencies had been a sad disappointment. France had become frightened of her own shadow and riven by real political disputes. The French Left clamoured after 1934 for alliance with Russia (a prospect terrifying to the British Right and Centre); the French Right was awaiting the moment when it could 'accept and call in the foreigner'[15] (equally terrifying to the British Left). The countries of Eastern Europe were fallen bastions of democracy. In these circumstances British policy-makers assumed that the only hope of world peace lay in British leadership and British methods of diplomacy. As it was understood that compulsion was both impossible and undesirable the process of appeasement became inevitable.

In 1933 attention was focused on Germany and Japan. The nature of the Japanese threat was quite clear after March, when withdrawal from the League was accomplished. The possibility of an alliance between Japan and either Germany or Russia now caused great alarm. In November 1933 Chamberlain feared the 'very alarming prospect . . . when Germany and Japan might come together'.[16] Strategic plans evolved to meet the contingency of a hostile Japan involved the construction of a great fortress at Singapore, for which plans had been drawn up as long ago as 1923; in 1933 construction was resumed. In autumn 1934, depressed by the failure to reach any understanding with the Americans—'the U.S.A. will give us no undertaking to resist by force any action by Japan, short of an attack on Hawaii or Honolulu'[17]—Chamberlain advocated a pact with Japan, with assurances on Chinese integrity and naval building. The problem then, and for the next few years, was that Britain had nothing to offer Japan. Britain tolerated Japanese provocation of and attacks on China in the hope that war could be avoided. The anti-Comintern pact signed by Germany and Japan on 25 November 1936 alarmed British officials but by that time policy had been reduced to the hope that Japan would bite off more than she could chew. In July 1937 Sino-Japanese hostilities finally escalated into full war and the following month, on 21 August, China and Russia signed a non-aggression pact. These events at least made it unnecessary for Britain to try to buy off the Japanese with almost non-existent assets, because it was assumed that the Chinese would fully occupy their attention and leave Japan no opportunity of attacking European possessions.

If British impotence in the Far East sprang in the first instance from her own local naval and military weakness and, secondarily, from the refusal of either the United States or Russia to help, there was in the background the threat of Germany. In autumn 1934 Chamberlain linked the Far Eastern crisis firmly to the German problem: 'if we had to contemplate the division of our forces so as to protect our Far Eastern interests, while prosecuting a war in Europe, then it must be evident that not only India, Hong Kong and Australasia would be in dire peril, but that we ourselves would stand in far greater danger of destruction by a fully armed and organised Germany. . . . The *fons et origo* of all our European troubles and anxieties is Germany'.[18] The logic was clear—in order to have any flexibility in the Far East it was essential to solve European problems. The Far East was, for the moment, to be regarded as a theatre of secondary importance. This suited Japan well enough.

The rise of Hitler led almost at once to fresh uncertainties in Europe. The first manoeuvre was a declaration by the *Führer* on 17 May 1933 that the other powers must live up to their own commitments to disarm. In October it became evident that France was not prepared to disarm further and on 14 October Hitler announced Germany's withdrawal from the Disarmament Conference and the League of Nations. His attempts to throw the blame on France met with some success as an influential group, led by Lothian, argued that 'the only thing for France to do, having missed two opportunities of settlement, was to seize what seemed a present chance of an armaments agreement for ten years'.[19] The first approaches to Germany to resume negotiations on disarmament were coldly rebuffed and an intensive rearmament programme was announced by Hitler.

In February 1934 Eden, the Lord Privy Seal, was sent to Berlin to discuss a British Memorandum of 29 January in which 'reluctant recognition to the inevitability of some German rearmament'[20] had been given. Piquancy was given to his visit by two events which undermined anti-German solidarity. News of the Stavisky affair had broken in France on 8 January, followed by unrest culminating in riots in Paris on 6 February. Meanwhile, on 26 January, Germany and Poland had concluded a non-aggression pact. This deal sapped French confidence in their security system but could hardly be cited as evidence of aggressive intentions. Although German attention was temporarily turned away, in the long run the pact was a serious threat to Poland, for she 'could only lose by any modification of the Versailles settlement which, far more than her own strength, was the main guarantee of her continued existence within the 1921 frontiers'.[21] In these circumstances Eden did well to extract some minor concessions from Berlin, but disagreements between Britain and France concerning guarantees wrecked hopes of agreement. Personal antipathy between Simon and Barthou played its part, though this must be seen in the overall context of Anglo-French distrust. Barthou's savage attacks on the bases of British policy were seen wearily by Eden as 'grand material for our isolationists at home and almost converted me into one'.[22]

Disagreements between Britain and France and the elimination of Poland as a hostile factor had set Hitler free to exercise pressure on Austria. In 1933 there had already been advance warning of German interest which Britain had sought to counter by promoting Franco-Italian friendship. The resulting Four Power Pact of March 1933, to which Britain, France, Germany and Italy subscribed, turned out to be an exercise in political jockeying rather than in active co-operation. Fears for the future of Austria were, however, growing in Rome, London and Paris. In summer 1933 Vansittart had warned that 'Austria has . . . been chosen for the first break-through of the renewed will to power'.[23] For Britain the only hope lay in Italian co-operation and as the months went by Mussolini seemed to move away from the pro-German position he had taken up earlier in the year. Simon remained unenthusiastic about an activist policy, telling Mussolini on 4 January 1934, 'We can not, of course, intervene more actively'.[24] The dictator was not put out by this clear indication that Italy was expected to shoulder the burden of resisting German penetration. He had already, following his meetings with Dollfuss in 1933, resolved so to do. The *Duce* had come to regard Dollfuss as his protégé and Austria almost as a fief.

These developments do not seem to have discouraged Hitler unduly. The suppression of Austrian parties in 1933 had provided his followers with fresh opportunities for unrest and on 30 January 1934 Hitler openly threatened the Dollfuss régime. In conditions of political turbulence the Austrian Left staged an abortive rising on 12 February. It was feared in London that this might be used as a pretext for German intervention and on 17 February in a joint declaration the governments of Britain, France and Italy agreed on 'the necessity of maintaining Austria's independence and integrity in accordance with the relevant treaties'.[25] Hitler was not to be denied and on 25 July a Nazi-inspired coup was launched and Doll-fuss killed. Western reactions were predictably strong. Mussolini promptly moved troops to the Brenner frontier in case Germany tried to take advantage of the confusion in Vienna. He told Star-hemberg, 'Perhaps the murder of Dollfuss has done some good. Perhaps the Great Powers will recognise the German danger. It may be possible to organise a great coalition against Germany'.[26] Mussolini overestimated the readiness of the Western Powers to commit themselves. There was no appetite for action in London. Simon had never wished to be involved and on this occasion, accord-ing to the British Ambassador to Vienna, Vansittart played an inglorious rôle.[27] Hitler had been stopped but not by Britain.

The strength of the French reaction was shown in the activities of Barthou in the next few months. Barthou travelled around Europe trying to construct an anti-German alliance and was enjoying some success when struck down by an assassin on 9 October. French policy for once dominated that of Britain for a brief period. The objective of Barthou and Léger (the chief official at the Quai d'Orsay) was to promote an Eastern Locarno. In 1933 the Soviet Union had offered France a bilateral agreement outside the League and this had led to further negotiation. In summer 1934 the British were told of the progress of negotiations and of Barthou's scheme for a regional agreement involving Russia, Germany, the Baltic States, Poland and Czechoslovakia which was to be supplemented by a Franco-Russian mutual assistance pact, open to German adherence. No commitment by Britain was envisaged so British consent was forthcoming. On 17 September Russia was admitted to the League of Nations and optimism was expressed in Britain concerning the revival of collective security. The French policy of balancing growing German power with the colossus of the East had a respectable ancestry but, equally, had many enemies in Britain.

Germany had no intention of accepting any agreement limiting her freedom of action in the East and received useful, if short-sighted, aid from Poland in her successful bid to elude the Barthou–Litvinov net. Hopes were high in Britain that Hitler would prove amenable, particularly as the Saar plebiscite of January 1935 (which gave a 90% + vote for reunion with Germany) was believed likely to clear up one aspect of Franco–German relations. This was a complete misjudgment. More convinced than ever of his standing in Germany, Hitler promptly revealed that Germany had an air force and on 16 March announced the restoration of conscription. In the meantime a proposed visit by Simon to discuss the Eastern Locarno proposals was postponed at Hitler's request. Phipps, the Ambassador to Berlin, had been justified in his fear that 'the result of the Saar plebiscite has been to render . . . the omens less propitious for the success of any negotiations with this country'.[28]

The tough line followed by Hitler was not unrelated to the debates over rearmament in Britain. Owing to the collapse of negotiations the British Government had decided in the summer of 1934 to rearm in modest fashion. In July the Labour and Liberal Opposition moved a vote of censure. Attlee denied that an enlarged air force would help world peace while Cripps and Samuel argued that the government had had its hand forced by Churchill and the warmongers.[29] Despite this lack of realism the government had pressed ahead with its plans and on 4 March 1935 a White Paper was published which specifically drew attention to the relationship between British rearmament and Germany's current attitude towards disarmament. Once again the Opposition vehemently attacked the proposals. Attlee argued that the White Paper was contrary to British commitments to the League and that the remedy was that 'if it is shown that someone is proposing to break the peace, let us bring the whole world opinion against her'.[30] Such naivety staggered even the innocents of the Treasury benches but it fell to Austen Chamberlain, the doyen of Tory elder statesmen, to deliver the most damning reproof: 'If war breaks out, if we become involved in a struggle . . . do you think he will hold the language he held today? If he does, he will be one of the first victims of the war, for he will be strung up by an angry, and justifiably angry, populace to the nearest lamp post'.[31] Such realism was not general, however, and Berlin knew it. Much more characteristic was Lothian's complaint that the White Paper 'touched Herr Hitler and Germany on their most sensitive complex';[32] he went on to argue that what was required was greater understanding of Germany, not greater armaments.

In these circumstances the British Government was obliged to cast about for an alternative to appeasement. Obvious possibilities were either a Franco-Italo-British bloc or an Anglo-French association buttressed by Russian support. The former was naturally more attractive to the predominantly Conservative administration and encouragement had already been given to Paris to improve relations with Rome. In January Laval, the new Foreign Minister, had concluded with Mussolini an agreement designed to defend Austria, to prevent unilateral abrogation of armaments agreements and to settle differences on colonial questions. Laval and Flandin then visited London towards the end of January and on 3 February a joint communiqué was issued offering discussions with Germany on outstanding issues. At the same time precautionary soundings by Maisky, the Russian Ambassador, had not been ill-received in London. There was thus some hope that Britain would pursue a policy of conciliation from a position of strength supported by a revitalized air force and agreements with Italy and Russia.

Towards the end of March Simon and Eden visited Berlin but made no impression on a confident Hitler. The Chancellor stressed his services as a bulwark against Communism and emphasized his wish for peace. The conference proved abortive except for the fact that Hitler learned just how disunited his opponents were. The evident displeasure in both Rome and Paris at Britain's *démarche* (which had occurred without prior consultation with her associates) did not pass unnoticed in Berlin. The process of the erosion of confidence between Hitler's opponents was thus initiated by Britain, although Simon had instructed Vansittart to consult with Maisky while the Berlin visit took place.

After Berlin Eden travelled on to Moscow where he had long discussions with Litvinov and an interview with Stalin. Litvinov tried hard to persuade him to put pressure on Poland to join an

Eastern European security pact but the lack of British interest in guarantees for these states was plain. Eden's comments revealed the limitations of British thinking: 'It would be extremely short-sighted of anyone to think it better to have a war in the east to avoid war in the west. The interest of H.M.G. in the Baltic States is not like their interest in Belgium and the Low Countries, though they are, of course, interested from the point of view of general security in Europe'.[33] Consultations with Beck in Warsaw and Beneš in Prague equally failed to produce anything more substantial than anodyne *communiqués* praising the virtues of peace and collective security.

Something of greater substance than these *papier mâché* protestations was needed to deter Germany. MacDonald and Simon were sent to negotiate with Laval and Mussolini at Stresa and produced on 11 April a strongly worded condemnation of Germany's actions and reaffirmed the three powers' commitment to Locarno and Austrian independence. Had it been the intention of any of the powers to adhere closely to the spirit of the Stresa Front it would, no doubt, have enjoyed a longer and more useful life. To reinforce this strong moral stand the British Government induced the League Council to endorse the condemnation of Germany's abrogation of arms limitation agreements. In Germany, on 21 May, Hitler promulgated the secret Reich Defence Law, so these manoeuvres hardly seem to have deterred German preparations for war.

Evidence of the disunity of the Western Powers was not long delayed. On 2 May 1935 France and Russia concluded a treaty of mutual assistance which was reinforced by a Russo-Czech agreement (contingent upon the active intervention of France) signed two weeks later. This pact lay quite outside the British conception of possible commitments and was not well received in London. Hitler promptly took advantage of British displeasure to launch a fresh initiative on 21 May. As well as offering non-aggression pacts to all Germany's neighbours except Lithuania, he suggested readiness to limit naval armaments. This immediately proved attractive to Britain and on 18 June an agreement was signed by which Germany agreed not to build beyond 35% of British naval strength. A few days before, Hoare had replaced Simon as Foreign Secretary. Truly he had inherited a poisoned chalice. French reaction to the treaty was predictably hostile. The manner of negotiations had created a dreadful impression of British bad faith and dealt a deadly blow to Anglo-French co-operation.

Various arguments were used to justify the treaty (which had been undertaken with Cabinet approval). Vansittart believed 'on the whole that the Germans should tie themselves with paper bonds, if only for a breathing-space, which I hoped to use better than proved possible'.[34] The whole-hearted appeasers, characteristically, saw the treaty as the start of a new era. Eden's critical attitude went to the heart of the matter when, in a general review of Anglo-French relations, he argued that 'the more cause they [his colleagues] gave the French to doubt British policy, the stronger the pressure on France to look elsewhere for allies, and elsewhere meant Soviet Russia'.[35] Distrust was to affect relations between the powers at a time when understanding was essential. 'In effect,' wrote Cameron, 'the search for allies had accomplished no closing of the ranks. On the contrary, it seemed only to accentuate divergences of interest and purpose'.[36]

The French and Italians were not slow to follow the path of folly and treachery. Italian relations with Abyssinia had deteriorated steadily since 1932 and on 5 December 1934 there was an incident at the Wal-wal oasis. From that moment Mussolini bent his best efforts towards a liquidation not only of the problem but also of independent Abyssinia. It seems almost certain that in their conversations of January and April 1935 Laval promised Mussolini a free hand. In March Abyssinia appealed to the League under Article XV of the Covenant, having already in January made an appeal under Article XI. After the League's failure in Manchuria the British Government believed that the dispute would be a decisive test for the principle of collective security. It was also plain that resistance to Mussolini's designs would create many problems. The Tory Right and the pacifist Left were in agreement that the use of force was undesirable, while even the stoutest defenders of Abyssinia could scarcely claim that Haile Selassie was a model ruler. Much more sinister, however, were the implications for the defence of Austria. Mussolini made it clear in May that he regarded the two questions as linked. Litvinov, Eden and Laval urged him not to involve his forces so deeply in Abyssinia as to preclude active intervention in Austria. The *Duce's* reply was, 'The independence of Austria was a European question and not one for Italy alone and he had no intention of opposing Germany in Austria unless he should receive full support from France and England'.[37] Delighted by this turn of events, Hitler immediately ordered that the German press should show sympathy for Italy in her struggles with those powers wishing to keep her in bondage. Development of this theme soon created alarm and despondency in London and Paris.

The change in Foreign Secretary also added an unwanted complication. Backbench pressure for the removal of Simon finally succeeded when Baldwin took over as premier. At first the choice of Hoare seemed sound, though he was to admit, 'From the first moment, I came under the influence of his [Vansittart's] singleness of purpose. . . . Vansittart's refrain never ceased to ring in my head. "We are terribly weak. We must gain time for becoming stronger".'[38] In effect Vansittart was the principal architect of both the Anglo-German Naval Treaty and the appeasement of Italy with Abyssinia. The former undermined French and Russian confidence while the latter convinced the Fascist Powers that Britain would prefer always to avoid confrontation. He thus damaged the very cause he wished to promote. In Eden's opinion he 'was seldom an official giving cool and disinterested advice based on study and experience . . . much more a Secretary of State in mentality than a permanent official'.[39] The combination of Hoare and Vansittart was to injure both their careers and to send British policy down a blind alley.

A further hostage to fortune was given by announcement on 27 June of the results of the Peace Ballot which showed considerable popular support for the League. Eden, who had been elevated to the newly created post of Minister for League of Nations Affairs, thus had the path of duty clearly mapped out. The prospect of Hoare and Eden, who were in effect jointly responsible for foreign policy, coming into serious conflict was much enhanced. During the summer of 1935 Britain was forced ever closer to the deadly choice between the League and Italy. Laval's government was certainly not much of a prop to the anti-appeasement faction and the Cabinet was divided.

To clarify opinion Hoare and Eden discussed the problem with Attlee, Samuel, Churchill, Lansbury, Lloyd George and Austen Chamberlain. The burden of their advice was to pursue a policy of collective security in close co-operation with France. Despite a previous readiness to consider concessions it was now decided to take a moral stand and at Geneva Hoare thundered forth his conviction that Britain stood for 'steady and collective resistance to all acts of unprovoked aggression'.[40] Ever since 25 May the dispute had been left to the participants to settle, so this reversed British policy at the League. The opinion of neutral observers, like Hymans, was that 'The British have decided to stop Mussolini'.[41]

Immediate impressions were wrong. According to Hoare and Amery the purpose of the manoeuvre was bluff and, if things went wrong, to have a clear conscience: Neville Chamberlain feared 'If things become too serious the French would run out of things first and we could show that we had done our best'.[42] Fear of French backsliding dominated British actions. Laval, like many others, was uncertain whether Britain would belatedly make concessions to Italy and hail them as a victory for peace or throw down the gauntlet to Italy. But he was certain that Mussolini was not bluffing and he also believed—and in this opinion had most of France behind him—that Germany was a greater danger than Italy and the best efforts of the Western Powers ought to be directed towards preventing 'Mussolini being driven into the German camp'.[43] The essential ingredient of active French collaboration was thus missing from the start. Laval would eagerly have embraced, and in the end did so, Vansittart's concession policy—for that suited French strategic planning. It was ironic that Vansittart's leading disciple in this matter be described as 'one of the few in whom the microscope has revealed nothing but more teeming decomposition'.[44] It suggests a certain lack of Anglo-French understanding.

Mussolini was a better judge of the inherent lack of resolution in London and Paris than the neutrals. On 3 October the invasion of Abyssinia began. The British riposte was to urge the adoption of sanctions. In debates almost the whole of the House of Commons subscribed to this policy, which had the three virtues of a high moral tone, low cost and no belligerence. It was endorsed by a plethora

of debating talent, ranging from Churchill on the Right to Greenwood on the Left. The policy, nicely tailored to the requirements of
an election campaign (which resulted in the return of the National
Government on 14 November), was soon to be abandoned when it
became clear that real sacrifices would be required. On 4 November
the League fixed 18 November for the application of sanctions.
Already there was dissension in Paris. On 12 November Laval offered
to trade the non-implementation of sanctions for the suspension of
hostilities, an offer rejected by Mussolini. On 26 November Laval
told his Cabinet that he intended to oppose oil sanctions as Italy had
indicated that these would be regarded as military in character.[45]
Allied policy was in complete disarray.

Hoare realized that the basis of collective security through
Anglo-French unity no longer existed. In early December 1935 he
and Laval, supported by a bevy of permanent officials, met in Paris.
Later attempts were made to suggest that this meeting was almost
fortuitous; in reality it was a logical continuation of Eden's talks
with Mussolini in June and of the Peterson–St Quentin discussions of
October. According to Vansittart, Hoare had been authorized by the
Cabinet 'to evolve a provisional scheme *ad referendum* both to
Cabinet and League'.[46] On 8 December Hoare and Laval reached
agreement. The proposed settlement involved three major points:
'First, an effective outlet to the sea with full sovereign rights for
Abyssinia. Secondly, in exchange for this outlet, the cession of some,
but not all, of the territory in Tigre occupied by Italy, and a frontier
rectification in the east and south-east. Thirdly, a large zone in the
south and south-west in which Italy, acting under the League,
would have the monopoly of economic development'.[47] This was
a complete breach with the policy so recently defined in the election
campaign and represented almost total victory for Laval's pressure
tactics. No wonder Laval told Hoare that 'a new chapter had opened
in Anglo-French co-operation'.[48]

News of the Hoare–Laval deal broke on 9 December. Predictably
there was a storm of moral indignation. What made matters even
worse was that there existed no reason to suppose that Mussolini
would accept the deal. The initial reaction of Baldwin and his
Cabinet was to defend Hoare from attacks in the press and the House.

On 17 December the extent of the revolt among the backbench Tories became clear and the following day the Cabinet recognized it would be suicidal to try to defend the Hoare–Laval pact. By a strange quirk of fate Mussolini decided to accept the offer on the day it was withdrawn. On 19 December Hoare offered his resignation to a sympathetic House. His listeners knew full well that he had been betrayed by his colleagues for reflecting their timidity only too accurately. Only Eden emerged with any credit from the affair, for he had denounced the proposals with vigour from the start. After several false starts in the task of finding a replacement Baldwin settled on Eden as the man who could best preserve the façade of moral commitment and on 23 December he was told, 'It looks as if it will have to be you'.[49] The myth of Eden's unflinching resolution in the face of the dictators' pressure had received its first public recognition; in retrospect Baldwin's lukewarm offer seems a more fitting estimate of the new Foreign Secretary's talents.

During the next few months nothing was done to make sanctions bite. The *Duce* regarded the efforts of the Western Powers with bitterness while Hitler looked on with amused contempt. The imposition of sanctions became a tragic and farcical irrelevance as Italian armies steadily eliminated Abyssinian resistance. On 5 May 1936 Addis Ababa fell and on 18 June Eden announced the dropping of sanctions. In the debate which followed only two Conservatives voted against the government, one of whom, Macmillan, resigned the party whip and sat henceforth as an Independent Conservative. Simon's defence of the new policy that he 'was not prepared to risk a single ship to preserve Abyssinian independence'[50] accurately reflected majority opinion. Everywhere the surrender to Italy was seen as a death-blow to the League and to collective security. Amery and the Right rejoiced, the supporters of the League were cast down and often took refuge in a vain pacifism. Small independent European powers saw the writing on the wall and in early July seven of them announced that they no longer considered themselves bound by the provisions of Article XVI of the Covenant. On 6 April 1938 the four Scandinavian states in this group declared their complete neutrality, thus completing the flight from collective security.

The achievement of British policy was thus failure on all front. The weakness and disunity of the Anglo-French association had been exposed for all to see. The government was seen as hesitant ar. l divided. The League and its sanctions had been discredited. Mussolini had been driven from the position of uncertain ally to potential enemy. The Stresa Front had been destroyed, Abyssinia had not been saved and Austria was now imperilled. Hitler had been given greatly increased room for manoeuvre of which he was quick to take advantage. As Cecil commented, 'at the best we gained an uneasy respite which lasted rather more than three years, and for that sacrificed the interests of other nations and our own reputation'.[51]

Hitler's opportunity came in March 1936. Once again he was able to take advantage of Anglo-French discord. On 27 February the long-awaited ratification of the Franco-Russian Treaty took place. A few days before this event a debate in the Commons on defence expenditure showed the Labour Party still looking to the League and collective security for defence and putting forward demands for reductions in spending on armaments. Neither of these events was conducive to mutual trust and this was clearly perceived in Berlin. On 7 March German troops re-entered the Rhineland, an action the French had feared ever since the storm over Abyssinia had arisen. Hitler's justification was that the Russian treaty was a breach of Locarno—to be answered in turn by another violation.

The Western Powers failed to rise to the occasion. In France there was indignation at German action and demands for Locarno to be honoured. Flandin, the Foreign Minister, and Sarraut, the premier, were in favour of swift action. From London, however, the news was discouraging. Corbin, the Ambassador, had a fruitless interview with Eden on 8 March. This was hardly surprising as Baldwin had already told Eden that 'there would be no support in Britain for any military action by the French'.[52] There was a consensus of opinion in the press that conflict must be avoided—and to avoid conflict it was necessary to give way to Hitler. According to Shirer, in France, 'though unable to agree on anything else the newspapers were unanimous in their insistence that nothing be done that could lead to war'.[53] *The Times* saw Hitler's move providing 'a chance to rebuild'[54] while Lothian 'would tolerate no suggestion of sanctions to turn the Germans out of "their own back garden"'.[55]

Flandin came to London to co-ordinate policy and remained to orchestrate a surrender. The possibility of Italian support was at once ruled out—quite correctly, as on 22 February Suvich had assured Hassell 'we are not going to join in any counter-action, which might be caused by the German reaction to the ratification of the Franco-Russian Pact'.[56] The military advisers of both the French and British Governments were also against any action which might lead to war. The Cabinet was in complete agreement that sanctions of any kind were out of the question. The possibility of joint staff talks was ruled out by Baldwin with the succinct phrase, 'The boys [Tory backbenchers] won't have it'.[57] It merely remained to determine the form of surrender. To preserve the proprieties it was agreed that the League Council should meet on 13 March in London. Predictably, Litvinov argued for sanctions against Germany; the source and the nature of the proposals terrified Eden and Flandin equally. In the end it was resolved that though the treaties of Versailles and Locarno had been broken Hitler should be invited to negotiate fresh security arrangements.

In the debates which followed this *débâcle* the magnitude of the reverse seems scarcely to have been comprehended. Throughout, the weakness of British forces and the justness of German claims were used to justify the heedless abandonment of specific safeguards. Believed to have been necessary in the days when warmonger Stresemann ruled in Berlin, these guarantees were clearly superfluous in the enlightened times of peace-loving Hitler. Boothby and Spears were two of the few who saw the true dimensions of defeat and how a traditional area of British concern—the Low Countries—had been imperilled. Boothby argued that if Germany were not resisted the lesser powers would hasten to make terms with her. Spears added that weakness would create increased appetite and prophesied, 'having invaded the Rhineland this year and having offered a treaty of 25 years' duration, next year they will take Austria and offer a treaty of 50 years; that after that it will be the turn of Memel and the Corridor, when they will offer a treaty of 75 years, and we can look forward to eternal peace once France and

England have disappeared'.[58] It was only the dating which was wrong with this analysis—Austria fell not in 1937 but in 1938, Memel and the Corridor not in 1938 but in 1939.

Shortly afterwards German pressure on Austria led to the Austro-German Treaty of 11 July 1936. Prior to its signature efforts had been made to resuscitate the Stresa Front, stiffened by the addition of Russia, but Suvich had rejected the offer. At the end of June Eden and Delbos, the new French Foreign Minister, tried in vain to persuade Schuschnigg to meet them at Geneva to work out a joint policy. Under pressure from Mussolini and Hitler the treaty was signed, thus removing 'the last and only mortgage on German–Italian relations'.[59] Hitler had renounced annexation and Mussolini abandoned the *Heimwehr*, for so long his instrument in Austrian affairs. But the overall result was, as Bullock commented, 'for the next eighteen months the Germans used the Agreement as a lever with which to exert increasing pressure on the Austrian Government and to extort further concessions, a process of whittling down Austrian independence'.[60]

The Austro-German Treaty and the disappearance of the Stresa Front in 'those clouds of mustard gas which hung over Addis Ababa'[61] opened the way for Italo-German co-operation in Spain, where civil war had broken out on 17 July. The outbreak of war in Spain highlighted once again the differences between Britain and France. The French were naturally concerned at the possibility of another Fascist régime on their borders and this concern was given particular sharpness by the election of a Popular Front Government, headed by Blum, on 3 May. It was hard for the victorious coalition to see not only that the Spanish Nationalists were not Fascists (though the Spanish Fascists lent them support) but also that the British Government was more alarmed by the increase in Communist strength in France. The P.C.F., in fact, had doubled its vote and increased its representation from 10 to 72 seats in the Chamber. The Spanish Civil War was deeply divisive of opinion in Britain and by an unhappy chance put the strongest critics of the government's foreign policy on opposite sides. This enabled appeasement to proceed almost unchecked while wordy, but ineffectual, battles raged around the merits of Republicans and Nationalists.

British policy was from the start one of non-intervention. In this the government was supported by France. Blum realized that open intervention might lead to a European war in which British support was doubtful, while covert intervention would only exacerbate domestic political feuds. Delbos and Eden soon agreed that peace would best be served if there were an embargo on arms to Spain. On 15 August this policy was revealed to the world. It was to have no chance of success because Mussolini intervened in strength almost from the moment the first shot was fired. After much negotiation a meeting of the Non-Intervention Committee was at last held in London on 9 September, attended by representatives of twenty-six nations. Proposals for effective supervision were made but became increasingly unrealistic as Russia and Germany joined Italy in heavy subsidies of munitions, troops and money for their preferred régime. Britain and France, however, remained undeterred and optimistic about the chances of restoring peace.

The Spanish Civil War served German interests in two particularly important ways. Firstly, it revived British suspicions of Russian revolutionary zeal and hence reduced the chances of Anglo-Franco-Russian co-operation. Secondly, the poor relationship between Italy and Britain was intensified by events in Spain and led eventually to Mussolini's accession to the anti-Comintern Pact in autumn 1937. Hitler was also aided by Russian clumsiness. The growth of Communist power in Spain, owing to the feebleness of the other parties of the Left, was not encouraged by Stalin but, equally, was not denounced. Even Maisky failed to appreciate how much the reconstruction of the Republican Government in May 1937 alarmed the British—who saw Communists but one step away from power in the heart of Western Europe.[62]

Relations between Britain and Italy sank to a new low. By autumn 1936 Eden was convinced that Italy bore the greatest responsibility for the failure of non-intervention. The Foreign Secretary also feared loss of British naval superiority in the Mediterranean if Italy were ceded the Balearic Islands. In early 1937 he extracted from Ciano, the Foreign Minister, a promise to respect the *status quo*. This was promptly violated and Eden now became 'concerned lest the insurgents should win, because the foreign powers backing them were themselves a menace to peace'.[63] Eden's policy slowly began to part company with that of the Cabinet majority, which favoured improved relations with Italy. The gap widened after Neville Chamberlain replaced Baldwin as Prime Minister in May 1937. In the same month Grandi, the Italian Ambassador, denounced the system of supervision, which had at best been inadequate and on 31 May Germany and Italy withdrew from the Non-Intervention Committee. On 12 June Britain and France managed to patch up the disagreements, by appeasing the Fascist Powers, and a week later Germany and Italy returned to the conference table. It was at this point that Stalin began to see the futility of continuing commitment in Spain and, secondly, the inherent improbability of a working alliance with Britain and France.

Eden was now compelled by Chamberlain to negotiate further with an Italian régime he had already come to distrust. The Foreign Secretary was affronted by Mussolini's demands for formal recognition of Italy's possession of Abyssinia and by his premier's apparent indifference to the issue. Attacks on British shipping by Italian submarines further raised the temperature and at a conference held at Nyon a system of patrolled zones was swiftly agreed—to which the Italians later reluctantly assented. Naval issues almost at once ceased to play an important part in Anglo-Italian relations, a success which ought to have hardened Western determination to maintain non-intervention in more robust fashion. Fear of the spread of Communism and of military weakness made this impossible. In November Britain and France agreed to approach Italy in the hope of reaching a general settlement which would eliminate all causes of friction. The stimulus was the ever growing shadow of German influence in Austria. In December Italy made it clear that *de jure* recognition of her position in Abyssinia was fundamental to successful negotiations. Eden continued to believe that conversations would in these circumstances be futile. Chamberlain disagreed.

In early 1938 differences over the emphasis of foreign policy came to a head. Chamberlain wished to open conversations at once with Italy. Eden sought some evidence of Italian good faith and changed attitudes. He cited not only past misdeeds but also the renewal of

Italian activity off Spain in January—which had been quickly ended by the revival of the Nyon patrol—as evidence in defence of his opinion. On 18 February futile discussions with Chamberlain and Grandi stiffened his resolve and at the Cabinet meeting the following day there was a complete *impasse*. On 21 February, being in a minority within the Cabinet, Eden resigned. In a statement to the House on 22 February Eden made it plain he objected both to the methods and content of Chamberlain's diplomacy. The Foreign Secretary disliked the premier's use of unofficial contacts and his personal dealings with Grandi. But, in the long term, his criticism of the content of policy was the more significant: 'Of late the conviction has steadily grown upon me that there has been too keen a desire on our part to make terms with others, rather than that others should make terms with us. . . . I do not believe that we can make progress in European appeasement . . . if we allow the impression to gain currency abroad that we yield to constant pressure'.[64]

The significance of the Spanish conflict was both particular and general in its impact on British foreign policy. It fragmented growing parliamentary opposition to the policy of appeasement into jarring sections of the Right and Left, thus giving a new lease of life to policies which had begun to seem moribund in the aftermath of the Rhineland dispute. The conflict brought to the attention of the government the weakness of the strategic position of Britain and France in the Mediterranean. The methods adopted to solve this problem gave a valuable lesson in regard to the wider problems of security, but it was ignored. The war in Spain showed all too clearly the unpleasant nature of the policies of Germany, Italy and Russia at a time when it was becoming a matter of urgency for Britain to decide which of her interests were most important and needed the greatest protection. Italian behaviour ought to have made plain the impossibility of relying on Mussolini as an ally against a revived Germany. It did not to Chamberlain and the larger part of his administration and party. The principal benefit from the war was that Britain and France had drawn closer together; the principal casualty was Anglo-French realism. In the long term the general impact of the war was that, as the alternatives of association with Russia and the Axis Powers seemed equally impossible, the Western

Powers toiled on with the limited objective of *ad hoc* measures to dispose of crises as and when they occurred. They did not plan for a future they dreaded and they feared to make a choice between two unpalatable political systems. Britain and France took refuge in the hope of Russo-German conflict rather than opting for association with one of the great Continental powers. Chamberlain's Cabinet was, perhaps, morally but not strategically perceptive and was, alas, dealing with dictators to whom moral choices seemed signs of weakness, decay and impotence. The lessons to be learned from the Spanish Civil War were clear but to implement them required a more thorough and painful re-examination of traditional foreign policy assumptions than the British cared to make.

It is far from clear that even Chamberlain's opponents properly understood the direction in which appeasement was leading Britain. It is worth noting that even in his resignation speech Eden did not utterly condemn it as a policy. His successor, Halifax, was still less critical and in his biographer's opinion 'not fitted by nature to preside over the Foreign Office at such a moment of history'.[65] Yet Churchill and other critics of the government seem, on the whole, to have approved of the appointment. Halifax had a good record in domestic and Indian politics, but he was not the man to oppose his premier with any conviction; he had too much of Baldwin's indolence to struggle against Chamberlain's misconceptions and the faulty judgment of Henderson, Ambassador to Berlin since 30 April 1937.

During 1937 the Spanish Civil War and the attendant problem of relations with Italy had been the focus of British attention. Elsewhere changes in the international scene had very much weakened the British position. In July Sino-Japanese conflict had blossomed into open war. German rearmament had proceeded apace and Hitler had ominously raised the question of the destiny of Germany's former colonies. In November Italy had signed the anti-Comintern Pact and Poland had been induced to sign a minorities treaty by which Hitler guaranteed the *status quo* in the Corridor and Danzig. The purges were in full swing in the Soviet Union and grave doubts concerning the military capacity of the Red Army had arisen following the slaughter of June 1937. On 5 October Roosevelt delivered a speech at Chicago warning of the dangers of narrow isolationism. Reaction was hostile and in the opinion of Cordell Hull, the Secretary of State, it 'had the effect of setting back for at least six months our constant educational campaign intended to create and strengthen public opinion toward international co-operation'.[66] Any hope of firm American backing against the dictators had to be abandoned in the face of the Neutrality Acts and Roosevelt's preference for moral platitudes rather than action. Vansittart's accusation that 'No country in the gathering storm so encouraged Aeolus to loose the windbags'[67] was, unhappily, only too accurate. Chamberlain agreed: 'it is always best and safest to count on nothing from the Americans but words'.[68] The United States would not join in any *démarche* against Japanese aggression when American commercial and strategic interests were plainly threatened. It was obvious nothing could be expected in the way of support in Europe. It was a year of cruel disappointment to Britain, attended by heavy expenditure on rearmament, the promotion of hostile interests and the enfeeblement of potential allies.

As Anglo-Italian relations deteriorated the question of Austrian security inevitably revived. In early 1937 there seemed no immediate threat as the Austro-German agreement was operating with moderate success. The advent of Chamberlain to power provided an important catalyst. A majority of his critics are agreed on this point; Churchill believed that his hope 'was to go down in history as a great Peacemaker'[69] while Taylor wrote that 'his motive throughout was the general pacification of Europe'.[70] The Prime Minister himself admitted: 'I believe the double policy of rearmament and better relations with Germany and Italy will carry us safely through the danger period, if only the Foreign Office will play up'.[71] In this comment there are two matters worthy of note. Firstly, better relations with Italy and Germany were bound to involve concessions to the former in Abyssinia and to the latter over the unification of the German-speaking peoples of Lithuania, Poland, Austria and Czechoslovakia with the *Reich*. In the second place the distrust of the premier for the Foreign Office led him to rely heavily on unofficial advisers and on permanent officials, like Wilson, whose expertise lay in domestic affairs. Chamberlain made no suggestion of an alliance with Russia or bolstering French links with Eastern Europe. These notions did not fall within the ambit of his consideration.

Eden's patent reluctance to pursue this policy led the premier to send Halifax, the Lord President of the Council, to meet Hitler on 19 November 1937. The talks were disappointing as the *Führer* seemed unco-operative, despite Halifax's suggestion of modifications in the European order; 'Among these questions were Danzig, Austria and Czechoslovakia. . . . But alterations should come through the course of peaceful evolution'.[72] His *démarche* was not a lone British venture. By 1937 France had abandoned her objections of 1931 to proposed Austro-German connexions. Delbos was ready to consider 'a further assimilation of Austria's domestic institutions with Germany's'[73] while Papen, the German Minister to Vienna, discovered in Paris that 'almost everyone . . . expressed the opinion that some evolutionary method must be devised for solving the problem of Austro-German relations'.[74] What the Western Powers did not know was that on 5 November at a high-level meeting Hitler had put forward proposals which involved the acquisition of both Austria and Czechoslovakia. The Halifax mission thus provided him with welcome confirmation that his goals could be attained by peaceful means.

In December 1937 Hitler put pressure on Schuschnigg for a final settlement of outstanding disputes. The Austrian was reluctant to begin negotiations as he feared German demands for the inclusion of Nazis in his Cabinet and had already resolved to take stern measures against the Austrian Nazi Party. In February 1938 Schuschnigg had a very uncomfortable meeting with Hitler at Berchtesgaden and on 9 March he announced a plebiscite to be held on 13 March to determine whether the people of Austria wished to remain independent. At once Hitler threatened invasion; on 12 March German troops moved into Austria and the *Anschluss* was accomplished. Austrian appeals for aid had been rejected everywhere. Mussolini, the protector of 1934, refused to lift a finger. The other Stresa powers offered neither diplomatic nor military support. On 11 March Halifax had told the Austrians he could not advise 'any course of action which might expose his [Schuschnigg's] country to dangers to which H.M.G. are unable to guarantee protection'.[75] France was only too pleased to fall in line and do nothing.

The annexation of Austria displeased Chamberlain because he thought this kind of 'power politics . . . made international appeasement more difficult'.[76] His assumption was that bad relations with Italy had impeded a peaceful solution and even felt that 'this might have been prevented if I had had Halifax at the F.O. instead of Anthony Eden at the time I wrote to Mussolini'.[77] He now had the man of his choice and he was also rid of Vansittart, who had been 'kicked upstairs' to the post of Chief Diplomatic Adviser and had lost his power base. There was little understanding of the long-term consequences, either strategic or political, of the disappearance of an independent Austria. The British Government addressed protests to Berlin but in the Commons there was only very muted criticism of the administration's passivity. The policy of appeasement was undented, though even Lothian feared there was now 'a momentum behind power politics which is becoming dangerous'.[78]

Success in Austria stimulated Hitler's appetite because its speed and totality were so unexpected. The strategic position of Germany had been decisively improved and that of Czechoslovakia attenuated. Hitler's greatest triumph was in the effect Austrian surrender had on the psychology of his potential opponents. On 19 March Russia suggested a four-power conference between herself, France, the United States and Britain. Chamberlain rejected this out of hand, fearing a plot by Russia to involve Britain in war with Germany. Chamberlain had support for this view from the Tory Right and most of the press. The Right's attitude towards the Austrian fiasco was exemplified by Amery who, although critical of involvement, argued it was now necessary to accept Continental entanglements. It is equally clear that Amery attributed the reverse to the foolish alienation of Italy and had in mind some revival of the Stresa Front rather than an alliance with Russia. Germany's opponents were simultaneously disunited and dissatisfied with each other.

At the time of Austria's fall it was apparent that the danger to Czechoslovakian integrity had been greatly increased. Chamberlain admitted 'You have only to look at the map to see that nothing France or we could do could possibly save Czechoslovakia from being overrun by the Germans'.[79] It was his intention, therefore, to avoid any guarantee to Czechoslovakia that carried with it the risk of a disastrous war. This reasoning was very dangerous as it led directly to the notion of abandoning France's last Central European ally and thus opening a breach with Paris. There were already signs that not only Britain was preparing to abandon the Czechs. During Papen's visit to Paris Chautemps and Bonnet informed him of no objection to 'a reorganisation into a nation of nationalities'.[80] In Canada Tweedsmuir, the Governor-General, wrote that 'The chief trouble will be if there is any real threat to Czechoslovakia; but there again . . . the frontier should be rectified'.[81] Neither from France nor the Dominions was there much support for a hardline policy. Coulondre, the French Ambassador to Moscow, did argue for the acceptance of the initiative of 19 March and stressed the urgency of 'military talks with the Soviet Union'[82] but his opinions were as unwelcome in Paris as London.

Critics of the government's policy were inhibited by lack of a sensible alternative. Churchill waffled interminably about use of the League of Nations and while Eden later observed 'the successful invasion of Austria should have pointed the danger for Czechoslovakia, even to the obtuse'[83] he did nothing immediately to support closer ties with France and Russia—the only serious alternative to appeasement. Eden's distaste for alignment with Russia was similar to that of Chamberlain, who told the Commons on 24 March, 'The inevitable consequence of any such action would be to aggravate the tendency towards the establishment of exclusive groups of nations which must . . . be inimical to the prospects of European peace'.[84] Chamberlain did not seem to be worried by groupings which excluded Russia—such as the anti-Comintern Pact or a Four Power Pact (of Germany, France, Britain and Italy) which he hoped to create as the key agreement in his appeasement policy. Once again anti-Communist feelings, revived by events in Spain, played a crucial part in destroying the chance of a Russian alliance.

Only two weeks after the *Anschluss*, on 28 March, Hitler gave Henlein, leader of the Sudeten Germans, instructions to make demands which the Czech Government could not satisfy. Within a month Henlein was busy creating unrest in Bohemia and voicing shrill complaints about the repressive nature of Beneš' government. The British reaction was feeble. On 28 April Chamberlain, Halifax, Daladier and Bonnet met in London. The result was a joint *démarche* in Prague, urging Beneš to make concessions. There was certainly no prospect of any serious Anglo-French backing for Czechoslovakia and Hitler knew it. There would be no Russian action without French determination to fight and the replacement of Paul-Boncour, who wanted a firm policy, by Bonnet made a tough line less likely still. Daladier had told Paul-Boncour 'Your policy is fine, but I don't believe France is strong enough to follow it. I'm going to pick Bonnet'.[85] The British had no regard for Russian strength; on 19 April Chilston, the British Ambassador, had reported that the Red Army was very weak and 'The Soviet Union must be counted out of European politics'.[86] Furthermore, Chamberlain believed that there were already indications of the success of his appeasement policy. On 16 April an Anglo-Italian agreement had been signed, by which Britain promised to raise the question of the *de jure* recognition of Italian possession of Abyssinia with the League; Italy and France had shortly afterwards started negotiations to improve relations. It seemed obvious that a similar policy should be pursued towards Germany.

On 21 May a crisis in Czech–German relations led to a partial mobilization of Czech forces. The crisis was overcome, but had serious repercussions. Hitler was convinced that Germany had been humiliated and became inflexible in his determination to destroy Czechoslovakia. The Western Powers failed to understand that resistance to Germany was more profitable than surrender. Indeed, British reactions to Czech firmness were dismal. On 14 May an article in the Montreal *Daily Star* argued that a smaller Czechoslovakia would be a sounder state and that the existing arrangement 'cannot survive in its present form, the British are convinced. . . . The Czechs should be practical and make the best terms with Hitler without any war at all'.[87] The author, Joseph Driscoll, was a journalist known to be in the confidence of leading members of the British Government and was a prominent advocate of appeasement. During the crisis itself Halifax and Henderson busied themselves trying to convince Prague that the story of imminent German invasion was a *canard* and that if matters got out of hand 'the only ones to profit would be the communists'.[88] Bonnet, once the crisis was over, felt able to urge, 'the Czechs must now . . . make a large and generous contribution to the cause of peace'[89] to reward Germany for her restraint!

The pattern of Anglo-French policy had been set. The two powers would not seriously consider supporting Czechoslovakia, with or without Russian aid. Chamberlain's current concern was to avoid Czech–German conflict and at different times in the summer of 1938 considered a variety of remedies. In late May his preference was for an international commission but the unwillingness of the Italians to assist (coupled with a deterioration in Anglo–Italian relations following fresh incidents in the Spanish Civil War and the break-down in Franco–Italian talks) made this impossible. This seemed but poor reward for Halifax's demand in mid-May that Abyssinia be excluded from the League. By July the premier favoured despatching a prominent politician to undertake an 'independent' enquiry into Czech affairs. This possibility, together with the notion of a plebiscite, had first been aired in May when Strang had been sent to Prague and Berlin.[90] On 26 July Chamberlain announced that Runciman was to go to Prague as an independent adviser. The Czech Government was obliged to accept the myth that they had asked for his presence, though the appointment was the brainchild of Chamberlain and Halifax. Runciman himself had grave doubts about the usefulness of his mission, not inappropriately given his lack of 'the slightest qualification for a task which would have been beyond a far abler man'.[91] In Berlin Henderson opposed the mission, believing it was 'doomed to failure before it began'.[92] The ambassador knew, of course, that Hitler had no interest in any of Runciman's likely proposals except for use as levers to prise further concessions from Prague and London.

The Runciman mission lasted from 3 August to 16 September and did nothing but convince Beneš that Britain and France intended to desert him. The assurances of Daladier on 12 July that France would honour her obligations were no longer believed. In view of Henderson's agitation for a Four Power conference (between Italy, Britain, France and Germany) at that time, Beneš was probably correct in his assumption that France would choose dishonour rather than separation from Britain. While German pressure was growing, aided by greedy governments in Budapest and Warsaw, opinion in Britain was hardening. Almost everyone feared war. Some believed that only conflict, and others merely the threat, of war, would dissuade Germany—but the majority still preferred to put their trust in appeasement. In late August Churchill advocated a joint Anglo-Franco-Russian warning to Hitler against the use of force. The veteran appeaser Lord Allen of Hurtwood began to discern a certain 'absence of confidence which will make it difficult to carry through to success those negotiations which both Germany and this country so ardently desire'.[93] The opinions of Wilson more accurately reflected official policy: 'if we two, Great Britain and Germany, can come to agreement regarding the settlement of the Czech problem, we shall simply brush aside the resistance that France or Czechoslovakia herself may offer to the decision'.[94]

On 4 September 1938 Beneš accepted Runciman's proposals for the division of Czechoslovakia into autonomous Slovak, Czech and German regions, united only for the purposes of defence, foreign relations and finance. By so doing he out-manoeuvred both Hitler and the appeasers and made it hard for them to accuse Czechoslovakia of being unwilling to compromise. It was a barren victory. Beneš' assumption that revelation of Germany's true aim—destruction of Czechoslovakia—which would then follow would in turn lead to strong Anglo-French backing was quite wrong. On 30 August at a Cabinet meeting Hore-Belisha assured colleagues that neither the general public nor the Dominions favoured the use of force. Proposals made by Litvinov on 2 September that France, Russia and Czechoslovakia begin staff talks and that together with Britain the powers warn Germany against the use of force were declined and suppressed. Subsequent attempts by Russia to persuade the Western Powers to raise the issue at the League were tersely rejected by R. A. Butler: 'Let us hope no more will come of this idea'.[95] Confronted with the alternative of betrayal or resistance it was always the intention of the Cabinet to scuttle.

By this time the most characteristic feature of British foreign policy was its managers' ability to anticipate Hitler's demands. Direction of policy in effect ceased to be the responsibility of the Cabinet as a whole and fell into the hands of a quadrumvirate of Chamberlain, Halifax, Simon and Hoare. On 7 September *The Times* suggested the possibility of the cession of the Sudetenland to Germany. Reaction to this editorial was so strong that on the following day it seemed possible British policy might yet become more resolute. Eden, Churchill, Duff Cooper, the leadership of the Labour Party, the T.U.C. (which was in conference at Blackpool) and a number of junior ministers pressed for a declaration that Britain would fight. In Paris Daladier told Phipps of his hopes of Russian help and that 'French action would follow pretty soon on any German attack upon Czechoslovakia'.[96] This resolve was soon eroded by the timidity of Chamberlain and Bonnet. On 9 September Roosevelt informed an unsurprised world that his country could not be associated with any anti-Hitler front. The anti-appeasers had lost the initiative.

At Nuremberg on 12 September Hitler was due to speak and some reference to the Sudetenland issue was expected, not least by Bonnet and Phipps who spent the day convincing each other that Anglo-French action against a German occupation would be disastrously bold.[97] The *Führer*'s diatribe incited a revolt by Henlein, which the Czechs had easily suppressed by 15 September; but by the times Beneš had shown he was in control Chamberlain had resolved to turn him out. For some time the premier had been contemplating a personal intervention in the form of a visit to Hitler. On 10 September he discussed the matter with Hoare, Halifax and Simon,[98] but he did not inform the rest of the Cabinet until 14 September, by which time he had already made his offer to Hitler.[99] French nerve had also failed. On 13 September Daladier, deserted by Bonnet and faced with a divided Cabinet, suggested a 'Three Power Conference of Germany, France and Great Britain';[100] Phipps' belief that the French had been bluffing throughout was confirmed and gave retrospective justification to Britain's unilateral action. At the Cabinet meeting on 14 September Chamberlain's action received 'unanimous and enthusiastic'[101] approval, though apprehension was expressed by Hore-Belisha and Duff Cooper. No alternative was proposed, however, and the next day Chamberlain flew to Berchtesgaden.

At the meeting Hitler made it plain that the only terms on which a peaceful solution could be agreed involved self-determination for the Sudeten Germans. Chamberlain accepted this principle and agreed to discuss it with his Cabinet. No mention was made of consultation with Prague. On 17 September the Cabinet met to hear Chamberlain's report and was in session for most of the day. Nothing was decided except to await the arrival of the French delegation the following day. But there were ominous signs of dissent. Duff Cooper argued that Hitler's assurances 'were quite unreliable' while other ministers feared the wider consequences of acceptance of the principle of self-determination.[102] When Daladier and Bonnet arrived in London it did not take long to convince them that Hitler's terms had to be accepted. The *modus operandi* involved a still larger concession, for Beneš was to be asked to cede all those areas in which Germans comprised more than half of the population. On 19 September a joint note was presented at Prague, containing this proposal together with a promise that Britain 'would be prepared . . . to join in an international guarantee of the new boundaries . . . against unprovoked aggression' and continued, 'Both . . . Governments recognise how great is the sacrifice thus required of the Czechoslovak Government in the cause of peace'.[103] As it was Chamberlain's wish to resume talks with Hitler by 21 September an early reply was also requested.

This preposterous document was discussed in Cabinet on 19 September. As it had already been despatched to Prague most of the Cabinet saw little point in trying to recall it. The quadrumvirate did not escape criticism, however. Hore-Belisha at last began to show some fighting spirit, complaining about lack of consultation of the Cabinet and observing, 'It was difficult to see how it [the rump of Czechoslovakia] could survive. . . . I was afraid that the solution proposed was no real solution. It might only be a postpone-ment of the evil day'.[104] In Paris there was not much resistance either, only Reynaud and Mandel voicing their disapproval of the base betrayal. The Czech Government refused to accept these terms and asked for arbitration under the terms of the 1925 German–Czech treaty. Beneš and his colleagues had, perhaps, been emboldened by Russian assurances that she would fulfil her obligations if called upon to do so. After all the efforts that had been made it seemed as if war could not be avoided. The British and French had one final card to play—a refusal to help Czechoslovakia. In these circumstances Bonnet and Halifax decided to inform Prague of the consequences of refusing the Anglo-French plan. At 2.00 a.m. on 21 September the British and French Ambassadors told the Czechs that unless the plan was accepted unconditionally they would be held responsible for any subsequent conflict. Britain would refuse to fight in such circumstances and France therefore announced she could not honour her treaty obligations. The Czechs, full of bitterness, were forced to surrender and the following day a new government, headed by Sirovy, came into power to facilitate the transfer of territory.

If the French showed no courage at this critical point the British had shown rank cowardice. The transactions of Halifax and Bonnet were shameful, but the craven character of British policy was best illustrated by Newton, the Ambassador to Prague, who had urged on 20 September, 'If I can deliver a kind of ultimatum to President Beneš . . . he and his Government will feel able to bow to *force majeure*'.[105] On 21 September the Cabinet met to discuss these developments and it was decided that Chamberlain should fly to Godesberg to see Hitler. At their meeting on 22 September the futility of the appeasement policy was fully exposed when Hitler announced that these concessions were insufficient; the claims of Poland and Hungary had to be met and the Sudetenland was to be occupied militarily by 1 October. The premier was staggered and affronted. Discussions the next day failed to resolve the problem and Czechoslovakia mobilized her forces. On 24 September Chamberlain returned to London.

It was at this point that the appeasement policy passed from having a moral content, however slight, and became instead one of bowing to German demands without regard to their nature. In effect Britain ceased, temporarily, to have any foreign policy save that of avoiding war. If others had to pay the price in terms of territorial concessions or shattered alliances then that was regrettable but unavoidable. Chamberlain, who had been advised by the Cabinet on 21 September to tell Hitler that military occupation of the Sudetenland in the immediate future was impossible, had not raised this point at all. At the Cabinet meeting on 24 September Chamberlain argued that Hitler's terms should be accepted, to the great astonishment of several of those who had listened to his graphic description of the impossibility of negotiating with the *Führer*. Perhaps, as Duff Cooper suggested, it was true that Hitler had 'cast a spell over Neville'.[106] Reinforcement for the appeasement lobby now came from Paris and Berlin. On 24 September Phipps reported, 'All that is best in France is against war, almost at any price'[107] and dilated on the vices of what he saw as a small, corrupt war group. Cadogan, Strang and Vansittart were among the permanent officials whom 'this telegram struck ... with a sense of outrage'.[108] The following day Henderson argued, 'Any encouragement given to the Czechs to hesitate or prevaricate will be disastrous'.[109] These were reports which the quadrumvirate were pleased to receive.

The Cabinet met three times on 25 September and in the evening there were consultations between Chamberlain and Daladier. Signs of rebellion against the appeasers multiplied. Halifax, attempting to insure his own position against all developments, pronounced himself hostile to further pressure on the Czechs. Hailsham roundly denounced Hitler's record of broken promises. Duff Cooper and Hore-Belisha argued more positively that Beneš should be supported.[110] All was in vain, the passive majority accepted the premier's proposal, already agreed with the French, that he send Wilson to talk to Hitler in a last bid for peace. Wilson's mission failed and that evening, 26 September, Hitler announced his determination to occupy the Sudetenland by 1 October. The last hope of avoiding war lay in the intervention of Mussolini, so on 27 September Perth, the Ambassador to Rome, was instructed 'to express on behalf of H.M.G. the hope that Signor Mussolini would use his influence to induce Herr Hitler to accept proposals [Chamberlain's guarantee to Hitler that Britain would ensure fulfilment of the terms agreed between Germany and Czechoslovakia]'.[111] Hitler responded swiftly to Mussolini's appeal and on 28 September agreed to postpone his intended occupation and to meet Chamberlain once more. The

Prime Minister announced this to a House which had assembled expecting war and told his relieved and overjoyed audience that the heads of government of Italy, Britain, France and Germany would consult at Munich the following day. The desire to avoid war was so strong that 'Speeches of congratulation came from every side, and . . . members of all parties crowded . . . to shake Chamberlain's hand'.[112]

The discussions at Munich were casual and unco-ordinated to a remarkable degree. In the early hours of 30 September an agreement was reached which differed little in essentials from Hitler's Godesberg Memorandum of 23 September. The Czechs had no choice but to accept or fight alone. Their fear of war was as great as that of the British and French; they chose to surrender. Before returning to London Chamberlain, true to the last to appeasement, persuaded Hitler to agree that 'the method of consultation shall be . . . adopted to deal with any other questions that may concern our two countries'.[113] It was no sacrifice for Hitler to agree to a method which had thus far brought only profit.

Chamberlain and Daladier were given enthusiastic receptions on returning to their capitals. The Prime Minister was cheered by the crowds in Downing Street while Sargent in the Foreign Office watched and commented 'you might think they were celebrating a major victory over an enemy instead of merely a betrayal of a minor ally'.[114] Daladier received similar worship but, unlike Chamberlain, seems to have had serious doubts concerning the whole affair, remarking, 'The imbeciles—if they only knew what they were acclaiming'.[115] The press was overwhelmingly adulatory in both countries. The Chamber of Deputies gave the policy a vote of confidence by 535 to 75 votes. The minority included 73 Communists. The House of Commons, in a rather longer debate, also endorsed the Munich settlement. The Labour Party voted against the policy, which was approved by 366 to 144, with 22 dissident Tories abstaining. The dissidents included many of the most able and distinguished younger men in the party, as well as a few old hands, like Sidney Herbert, Churchill and Duff Cooper. The dissidents' indictment of the government was the more effective because many of them, unlike Labour, had long argued to improved defence.

Duff Cooper, in a memorable speech, resigned from the government, saying 'The Prime Minister may be right. . . . I hope and pray he is right, but I cannot believe what he believes. . . . I have ruined, perhaps, my political career. But that is little matter; I have retained something which is to me of greater value—I can still walk about the world with my head erect'.[116] The vote was a victory for the appeasers but the debate a defeat. The policy looked as threadbare as it actually was. Mandel and Reynaud resigned, thus proving that in France too existed deep and serious doubts as to the wisdom and morality of appeasement.

Chamberlain and his supporters hardly realized the implications of their actions. They saw only that war had been avoided and not that 'for the first time in two hundred and fifty years Britain had abandoned her policy of preventing by every means in her power the dominance of Europe by a single power'.[117] The guarantees of Czechoslovakia soon vanished. On 10 October the Poles were given Teschen and on 2 November a new Czech–Hungarian frontier was agreed. These were small matters in comparison with a new British problem—that of rearmament. The quadrumvirate was not enthusiastic about full-scale rearmament because of its probable economic effects, but in the aftermath of Munich increased spending on armaments was inevitable. The administration proceeded with an uneasy combination of rearmament and continued negotiation. This policy might have made sense if, as was later claimed, the time obtained by negotiation had been used for full rearmament. It was not. Indeed it is very doubtful if the period between October 1938 and September 1939 witnessed anything more than the widening of the gap between German and Anglo-French resources. Little attempt was made to secure British capacity to take independent action— further evidence of that abdication of traditional policies condemned by Nicolson.

The effect of Munich on French morale was serious. Henceforward France became the leading advocate of appeasement, fearing abandonment by Britain if she made a stand. Anglo-German talks on economic co-operation and the former German colonies in autumn 1938 raised fears which a visit in late November by Halifax and Chamberlain was quite unable to dispel. On 6 December Ribbentrop and Bonnet signed a Declaration emphasizing the need for friendly relations. The implication of this instrument was that spheres of interest existed in Europe. In return for German abandonment of claims to Alsace, France was to take no further interest in Czechoslovakia. This was the interpretation Ribbentrop placed on the document and, in view of Bonnet's conduct in this period, there seems little reason to doubt his version. In the meantime Britain had completely surrendered to Italian demands by abandoning all pretence of concern over Spain. Despite French indignation at Italian claims against her there seemed no end to the policy of appeasement.

Although the appeasers would not admit it, the question which concerned them most was where trouble would next arise. The most obvious target was Poland, but in the autumn and winter of 1938 Hitler had in mind German–Polish co-operation against Russia. He hoped to acquire Danzig and perhaps the Corridor in return for supporting Polish claims in the Ukraine. The Poles had, however, no intention of being used by the Germans against the Russians or *vice versa*. Equally, the Russians had no intention of being left alone to face German attack. Litvinov preferred an arrangement with the Western Powers but their conduct at Munich made this seem chimerical. The shape of the Nazi–Soviet pact was already discernible; Coulondre was told, 'For us I see no other way out than a fourth partition of Poland'.[118] In October 1938 Ribbentrop had suggested to Lipski, the Polish Ambassador to Berlin, that Poland join the anti-Comintern Pact. In January 1939 Beck, the Polish Foreign Minister, visited Hitler, who offered to guarantee the Corridor in return for Danzig. None of these tempting offers was accepted. The Poles had learned from the Czechs that to embark upon territorial adjustment with Germany was a process to which there was no natural end except the destruction of independence. Poland thus refused to play the German game; Britain and France would not play Russia's. In fact Halifax became so alarmed at the prospect of German–Polish action against Russia that he feared French involvement and on 1 November urged Bonnet only to think in terms of Russian aid and not become 'entangled by Russia in war with Germany'.[119] There was thus no real basis for serious Anglo-Franco-Russian talks which might have spelt the end of appeasement.

The state of uncertainty seems to have preyed more heavily on the minds of Daladier and Chamberlain than on that of Hitler. After the settlement of immediate claims on Czechoslovakia there still remained the vexed question of a guarantee which Britain had no capability of honouring alone. France refused to join in a collective guarantee and on 8 December Halifax told the Czechs that Britain would not honour its guarantee unless effective help could be given. In view of ever-increasing German demands this was tantamount to accepting the end of an independent Czechoslovakia. Halifax and Chamberlain still hoped to avoid the destruction of the Czechs by toadying to Mussolini and in January travelled to Italy to discuss outstanding differences. They made no impression on the *Duce* or Ciano, who commented that 'the visit was a fiasco',[120] and succeeded only in offending the French who had been irritated by constant Italian demands for concessions in the Mediterranean. The quadrumvirate seemed unable even to manage the Anglo-French association properly, and their Four Power system of managing European affairs had become a corpse awaiting decent interment.

Burial took place in Czechoslovakia in March 1939. In January Hitler had openly threatened Chvalkovsky, the Czech Foreign Minister, with the total destruction of his country. Unrest in the rump state came to a head in February, following visits by Slovak leaders to Germany. The Czechs had the choice between trying to suppress the separatist movements in Slovakia and Ruthenia or accepting the disintegration of their country. On 6 March Hacha, the Czech President, dismissed the Ruthenian Government and three days later that of the Slovaks. The deposed leaders appealed to Hitler and on 14 March the Czech Government placed 'the destiny of the Czech people and country with confidence in the hands of the *Führer*'.[121] Within a few days a Protectorate had been established over Bohemia and Moravia and the state of Czechoslovakia ceased to exist.

Reactions to Hitler's latest coup were hostile. Opinion in Britain was affronted. Even Henderson recognized that 'It was the final shipwreck of my mission to Berlin'.[122] The press took a strong line against the violation of German pledges at Munich. Many M.P.s were in accord with these feelings, though all knew that nothing could now be done. Yet the initial reaction of the appeasers was mild. Chamberlain told the Commons on 15 March that as Czechoslovakia no longer existed Britain's guarantee was void. Simon gave full support and both men, while disapproving of German action and methods, made it plain they thought the work of appeasement should go on. 'The object we have in mind is of too great significance to the happiness of mankind for us lightly to give it up or set it on one side',[123] said the Prime Minister. He and the inner circle had misjudged the mood of the House. Grenfell, for the Labour Party, pointed out that there no longer existed any British foreign policy but appeasement: 'All that we witness day after day is a steady disintegration of the European system and appeasement, instead of modifying or restricting that disintegration, only gives added impetus'.[124] These views were echoed by the Tory rebels.

Chamberlain and his supporters were compelled by public opinion to shift their stance, but their faith in appeasement, though shaken, was not destroyed. On 17 March the premier told a Birmingham audience that he shared public 'indignation that . . . hopes have been so wantonly shattered'.[125] Nothing was said of new measures, such as conscription, or new men. The slight change in tone was only in response to threats of a Conservative revolt to unseat him, put Halifax in his place and make Eden Leader of the House. The possibility of a challenge to the premier continued into the summer of 1939 and led to strain between him and Halifax, who was a willing party to these intrigues.[126]

Events now conspired to push Britain into a more aggressive position. After a visit to the Foreign Office on 16 March Tilea, the Roumanian Minister, warned Halifax the next day of an imminent German threat to his country. The oil and grain of Roumania made this a matter of pressing concern. Halifax told Seeds to ask Moscow if Russia would 'if requested by Roumanian Government, actively help the latter to resist German aggression'.[127] It was further suggested by Tilea that a Polish–Roumanian treaty might help preserve peace. By 17 March the Foreign Office was deeply disturbed by Germany's actions in Czechoslovakia and her supposed threat to Roumania. Henderson was recalled as an act of protest and two days later Chamberlain drafted a declaration of collective security which on 20 March the governments of France, Poland and Russia were invited to sign.

It was at this point that the British began to encounter difficulty with both Poland and Roumania. Like most East European countries they had an abiding suspicion of any link with Russia. The Poles feared lest participation in such a pact worsen relations with Germany and Beck gave only evasive replies to Kennard, the British Ambassador. The French had also approached Beck without much success, Léger describing his policy as 'cynical and false';[128] it was now understood that only a joint approach would have any chance of weaning Poland away from her attachment to Germany. On 21 March Halifax and Bonnet met in London. Discussion revolved around the difficulty of trying to persuade Poland to commit herself to an association which included the Soviet Union. Ultimately it was agreed 'It was essential to get Poland in. Russian help would only be effective if Poland were collaborating. If Poland collaborated, Russia could give very great assistance; if not, Russia could give much less. The strongest pressure must therefore be brought to bear upon Poland'.[129] Beck, however, refused to be hurried. Poland's true apprehension was simply 'doubts about the attitude of Great Britain and France . . . and . . . of the danger of being left in isolation'.[130] Beck feared lest the Western Powers abandon Poland once she had been placed in the front line, just as Czechoslovakia had been left to her fate. The past record of the appeasers was working against their modified policy. As Vansittart put it, 'Beck mistrusted French façades, the French mistrusted his mistrust of Russia, whom they mistrusted too . . . he just meant to keep both his neighbours out of his country, and got into the black books of democracy by reluctance to commit himself for its benefit'.[131]

On 22 March Lithuania surrendered Memel and its environs to Germany. It was Hitler's easiest conquest and seems to have been regarded as inevitable by all the powers. Certainly it produced no extra sense of urgency in London, Warsaw, Paris or Bucharest. Bonnet, Halifax and Chamberlain continued talks and the French Foreign Minister reported that 'Soviet assistance would cause difficulties. The Roumanians remembered more than one Russian invasion, and some of the upper class preferred Hitler to Stalin'.[132]

Chamberlain shared Roumanian fears, confessing to 'the most profound distrust of Russia. I have no belief whatever in her ability to maintain an effective offensive, even if she wanted to. And I distrust her motives, which seem to me to have little connection with our ideas of liberty, and to be concerned only with getting every one else by the ears'.[133] The intractable diplomatic problem of 1939 can scarcely ever have been put more clearly and succinctly. Russian capacity, intention and reliability were doubted and against these fears Litvinov's statement that 'We are in agreement with the British proposal [of 20 March] and accept text of declaration. The Soviet Government will give its signatures as soon as both France and Poland have accepted the British proposal and promised their signatures'[134] availed nothing.

The debates of 16–26 March had led nowhere. Hitler, however, now came to the rescue of the Western Powers and presented them with the opportunity for a more vigorous policy. On 21 March Ribbentrop and Lipski had held talks on finding a peaceful solution to the Danzig problem. Five days later the Polish Government, perhaps alarmed by the fate of Memel, took an uncompromising line. In interviews with Ribbentrop on 26 and 27 March Lipski was subjected to the same type of tactics as Schuschnigg and Chvalkovsky before him. But his master, Beck, was made of sterner stuff than Beneš and told the German Ambassador to Warsaw that any attempt to change the *status quo* in Danzig would be regarded as an act of aggression against Poland. The ambassador protested that Beck wanted to negotiate at the point of a bayonet—the Pole replied, 'That is your own method'.[135] Polish reservists were called up and the world feared another crisis. In these circumstances the offer made on 20 March to guarantee frontiers took on a new importance. Hitherto Beck had been anxious that any negotiations remain secret; now both he and Chamberlain wanted a public declaration. Beck knew that, in the long term, Poland was in danger from Germany and wanted a guarantee from which the Western Powers would be unable to escape. Chamberlain, under pressure in Parliament, wanted to show that he was doing something constructive, though he had at that time no real fear of German intentions towards Poland. The Prime Minister seems to have been particularly alarmed by a resolution tabled in the Commons on 29 March demanding a National Government, the introduction of conscription and an increase in governmental powers 'to enable this country to put forward its maximum military effort in the shortest possible time'.[136] On 31 March Chamberlain told the Commons, 'In the event of any action which clearly threatened Polish independence . . . H.M.G. would feel themselves bound at once to lend the Polish Government all support in their power'.[137] The Prime Minister also announced that he had been empowered to state that the French Government would do the same.

Beck accepted the British guarantee, which was entirely without qualification, with alacrity. He showed less enthusiasm for participation in a joint guarantee to Roumania—where Halifax believed the greater danger lay. On 4, 5 and 6 April Beck visited London where high-level talks were held. The discussions between Halifax and Beck turned into a fencing match from which the Pole emerged the clear victor. Beck promised that if Germany attacked Britain then Poland would be a faithful ally, but was much less helpful over the subject of a Russian alliance. Indeed, he went out of his way to discourage Halifax from this policy, telling him 'Poland . . . was ready to improve her relations with Soviet Russia, but not to extend them. It was important not to provoke a conflict . . .'; nor was he much more helpful over the Roumanian issue, declaring that 'the Polish Government were loath to waste what little political capital they possessed'.[138] When Chamberlain asked what would the Polish reaction be to a British attempt to improve relations with Russia Beck replied that he believed this might provoke the very conflict which all wished to avoid. The Polish Foreign Minister was far too skilful in debate for his potential British allies and had an answer for every point. On 6 April a formal bilateral treaty was signed by Beck and Halifax which marked a new departure in British policy. As Duff Cooper argued, 'we left in the hands of one of the smaller powers the decision whether or not Great Britain goes to war'.[139] It is doubtful if the appeasers really understood the magnitude of their decision.

It is equally doubtful if the Anglo-Polish Treaty contributed anything to the preservation of peace, as Chamberlain hoped. The

Polish Government saw it as a charter for intransigence; Hitler as an insult to be avenged by the extinction of Poland. On 3 April, in response to Chamberlain's declaration of 31 March, Hitler gave orders to his General Staff to prepare plans for smashing Poland by 1 September. In the next few days Beck made it clear that if Germany wished to revise the *status quo* in Danzig it was up to her to make proposals because Poland would not make the running in offering concessions. Although the British tried hard in the next few months to change the Poles' decision, on this point Beck refused to budge—he knew that Chamberlain could not threaten to tear up the treaty if he declined to negotiate. The treaty did not impress the dictators as a serious change in policy, thus making the intransigence of Beck much more dangerous. Mussolini marched into Albania on 7 April but received no more than a mild reprimand from London. Albania had, after all, been an Italian protectorate since 1926 and Ciano believed 'British protests are more for domestic consumption than anything else'.[140] Hitler noted too that Henderson was emphasizing continually that 'nobody desired more than we did an amicable arrangement between Germany and Poland in respect of Danzig and the Corridor'.[141] The threat of the Anglo-Polish Treaty thus seemed to the Axis Powers as chimerical as earlier engagements to Czechoslovakia. It was hard for Hitler to know that promises were worth more in 1939 than in 1938.

Italian action did, however, have one important repercussion. On 13 April Chamberlain told the Commons that the British guarantee had been extended to Greece and, largely because of French pressure, to Roumania. Yugoslavia, prudently, had already declined a similarly magnanimous offer. The next day, fearing the outbreak of a European war, Roosevelt addressed messages to the Axis Powers asking for assurances against aggression in regard to some thirty countries. He received his reply on 28 April when Hitler lengthily justified all his actions and denounced both the Anglo-German Naval Treaty and the Anglo-Polish Treaty on the grounds that there was evidence of renewed attempts to encircle Germany. He gave no direct answer to the President's question but concentrated upon appealing to isolationist sentiment in the United States. Roosevelt was affronted, but powerless to act in the face of the strong peace movement at home; isolationists saw his humiliation as well deserved —'He asked for it' observed Senator Nye.[142] Failure of this ill-judged intervention convinced the British Government that no help could be expected from the United States. Trust was placed ever more heavily on militarily weak states in Eastern Europe, to which Britain became more closely linked when on 23 April the Roumanian Foreign Minister, Gafencu, informed Halifax that an agreement with Poland regarding German aggression had recently been reached.

Once it became clear that there was a serious dispute between Poland and Germany the attitude of Russia took on a new importance. On 18 March Litvinov had proposed a peace front to stop Hitler but this *démarche* had been rejected by Chamberlain. The subsequent alliance with Poland made conclusion of a treaty with Russia still more difficult, though even Bonnet now advocated negotiations. In Britain it was not understood that the Western Powers needed Russia much more than Russia needed them. It was Britain and France that were committed to the defence of ramshackle régimes, not Russia. Yet there was a dawning realism in London and Paris. On 14 April Halifax asked Maisky if Russia would bring her policy into closer alignment with Britain by endorsing the declarations to Poland and Roumania. He told Seeds of his reluctance 'to abandon my efforts to secure some measure of co-operation from the Soviet Government'.[143] Thus began the process of bringing Russia into the new security system, though the British Government showed so little consistent enthusiasm for a Russian alliance that Taylor argued, 'If British diplomacy seriously aspired to alliance with Soviet Russia in 1939, then the negotiations towards this end were the most incompetent transactions since Lord North lost the American colonies'.[144]

The truth was that the policy-makers did not yet know whether Russian aid would be needed. According to the temperature of the general European situation the Foreign Office blew hot or blew cold towards Moscow. The policy of April to September 1939 was a strange mixture of boldness and timidity, of honesty and deception. The alliances with the successor states were strongly supported verbally but not with strategic plans. Ineffective pressure was put on Warsaw to negotiate with Berlin, but there the British made it plain that they believed Germany had a good case over Danzig. At home, rearmament continued but with little sense of urgency. This combination of policies suggested that the preference for appeasement had hardly expired in Britain; neither Stalin nor Hitler, therefore, was encouraged to take British proposals seriously.

On 18 April Litvinov responded to Halifax's overtures by offering a triple alliance. This initiative was welcomed by those who realized that no effective resistance to Germany could be organized without Russian aid. The promptings of Coulondre and Churchill had, however, no effect. British policy was to insist first on a unilateral Russian guarantee to Poland and Roumania and then to review the question of a full alliance. This was putting the cart before the horse, and in Paris doubts concerning the wisdom of Chamberlain's policy accumulated. On 3 May Litvinov was replaced by Molotov and a staunch believer in co-operation with the West had given way to a veteran Stalinist who had no commitment to anything except *Realpolitik*. Negotiations dawdled and it was not until 9 May that Seeds was able to talk with authority to Molotov. The nature of the exchanges ought to have made it clear to Halifax what risk Britain was running by being so dilatory and so evasive. Molotov complained about the different replies given by France and Britain to Russian proposals but stressed that the offer was still open. Ominously he added that 'Soviet policy had not changed but . . . it was liable to be altered if the other States changed theirs . . .'; Seeds also reported that 'he commented unfavourably on our delay in answering. I repeated what I had previously said as to necessity for consulting other Governments . . . he finally pointed out that Soviet Government had always replied to us within three days instead of three weeks'.[145] Halifax and the rest of the quadrumvirate preferred to go on living in cloud-cuckoo land.

During May the situation darkened. Hitler refused obstinately to negotiate with the Poles. Indeed, throughout the summer of 1939 there was no serious diplomatic contact between Warsaw and Berlin. German diplomats passed the time by trying to convince the British and French Governments that the guarantees they had given were dangerous and provocative. The obduracy of Beck in the face of a steadily rising tide of German propaganda produced

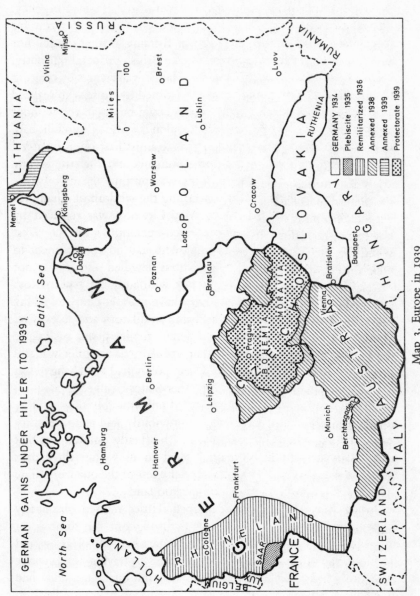

Map 3. Europe in 1939

a reversion to type among several of the appeasers. On 17 July, for example, Henderson told Halifax 'we must put Danzig back into its proper perspective. . . . It should not really be difficult to find an equitable solution . . . while permitting the re-inclusion of the city as a Free City in East Prussia'.[146] The 'peace at any price' lobby was given further encouragement by the elimination of Italy as a factor in anti-German calculations. On 22 May the Pact of Steel was signed and, in justification, Mussolini told Loraine, 'British policies were leading the whole of Europe into war. Through guarantees given to the small powers, Great Britain had brought about a very dangerous aggravation of the situation'.[147] Almost everyone in Britain now knew that nothing could be hoped for from Mussolini; strangely, the logical corollary to this deduction—that nothing could be expected from his ally—was not assumed. Even the Pact of Steel did not stimulate Halifax to negotiate more seriously with Molotov, whose country's support now offered the only possible counterweight to Axis expansion.

Relations between Britain and Poland worsened as the British persisted in their schemes for economic co-operation with Germany but refused to give Poland the loans necessary to purchase arms. Simon, as Chancellor of the Exchequer, was principally responsible for this mean and misguided policy. In the meantime the administration was coming under heavy fire in Parliament for its failure to reach agreement with Russia. The vast majority of M.P.s remained hostile to and suspicious of Russia and continued to hold these opinions at least until 1941. They, like the Cabinet, saw Russian demands as unreasonable. Henderson agreed: 'the summer months were spent in fruitless negotiation. Moscow had now become the centre of the stage, and H.M.G. and the French Government sought sincerely, but in vain, to persuade the Russian Government definitely to assume the same obligations towards Poland as we ourselves had undertaken. As soon as one alleged obstacle to Russian co-operation was overcome, Stalin produced another with unfailing regularity, and with the same persistence as we displayed in overcoming each difficulty in turn'.[148] With strong opposition to agreement with Russia in the Cabinet, Parliament and the Foreign Office it is hardly surprising that little progress was made.

In May Halifax visited Paris where Daladier told him France wanted a pact of mutual assistance with Russia. Daladier emphasized that failure to reach an agreement would be likely to stir Germany to action. The opposite point of view was the centrepiece of both Polish and British policy. Halifax was alarmed and still more so when Daladier suggested that if Germany attacked Russia without involving Poland or Roumania 'France would be involved by Franco-Soviet Pact and if this was so it would surely be impossible for us [Britain] to stand aside'.[149] Fearing a French defection the Cabinet now agreed to accept in principle the notion of a pact of mutual assistance and on 24 May Chamberlain announced this to the Commons.[150] The best way of speeding negotiations was for Halifax to visit Moscow, but he had already told Maisky that he could not entertain such a proposal.[151] Eden offered to go in his place but this idea was rejected by the quadrumvirate, as Eden must have known it would be.[152] Thus the British accepted the bases of negotiation but continued to proceed half-heartedly.

To stave off criticism of official inaction it was decided in early June to send Strang to Moscow. He arrived in Moscow on 14 June, having visited Warsaw on the way. Strang's reception in Russia was not very warm, perhaps because of his lack of status but more probably because of the inadequate nature of the proposals he had been empowered to make. Molotov told him, 'If we thought that the Soviet Government were likely to accept our proposals, we must think them nitwits and nincompoops'.[153] Negotiations made such slow progress that in *Pravda* on 29 June Zhdanov argued that the sole wish of the Western Powers was an unequal agreement in which Russia would take the greatest risks and make the largest contribution to defence. The main stumbling block was that Russia feared lest Germany be 'invited in' by the Baltic states, thus bringing her troops to the Russian frontier. This Molotov regarded as a form of indirect aggression (it had, after all, happened in Czechoslovakia in March) and wanted such a change of status to be regarded as a *casus belli*. Bonnet was willing to accept the Russian idea[154] but Halifax refused to agree to a draft that would satisfy Molotov.[155]

On 8 July a new factor emerged. Molotov demanded that signature of the treaty be delayed until a military accord had been reached.

Although Bonnet was at first irritated by this proposal he saw its logic. On 1 July he had told Ribbentrop that 'any action . . . which would tend to alter the status of Danzig . . . would activate the Franco-Polish guarantee and oblige France to render immediate aid to Poland',[156] so he was anxious to secure further support in the event of France being called upon to honour the pledge. A military accord with Russia would be excellent. Halifax would not agree to Molotov's demand and on 12 July flatly rejected it. Then, on 24 July, there was a further meeting with Molotov at which the Commissar stated that as the major political points of the mutual assistance pact had been agreed it would now be desirable to proceed with a military convention. To this the Western Powers consented three days later. Negotiations with Russia now entered their final phase.

The delegations selected by Britain and France to negotiate a military convention were hardly distinguished. Furthermore, the two missions had been given different instructions. Doumenc was told by Daladier, 'bring back an accord at any price'.[157] Drax was instructed, 'Until such time as the political agreement is concluded, the Delegation should therefore go very slowly with the conversations'.[158] In pursuance of this latter instruction the missions left Tilbury on 5 August and arrived in Leningrad on 10 August. Two days later discussions finally began. They started poorly when Admiral Drax was obliged to admit that he had no written credentials to negotiate, unlike Marshal Voroshilov and General Doumenc. Stalin's suspicion that Britain was only trying to delay progress was strongly reinforced. In the end the convention foundered on the rock of Polish intransigence. Voroshilov asked if transit facilities across Roumania and Poland were available. Drax replied that this was a matter for these states' governments. Voroshilov pointed out that it was up to Britain and France to secure permission for the passage of the Red Army. On 19 August Beck refused to accept Anglo-French advice on this point and the next morning General Stachiewicz told Kennard 'in no case could admission of Soviet troops into Poland be agreed to'.[159] Although the delegation lingered in Moscow until 25 August it could no longer serve any useful purpose. The pact of mutual assistance was dead.

While negotiations with Russia proceeded the political situation elsewhere deteriorated sharply. In July and August relations between Poland and Germany became very much worse. Britain constantly pressed the Polish Government to negotiate; Beck firmly refused. Rendered almost desperate by the apparent approach of war Chamberlain cast about for a solution. On 13 July he urged Daladier to promote a *rapprochement* with Italy, for 'Mussolini is the one man who can influence Hitler to keep the peace. . . . I don't want the crisis in Danzig to come while Mussolini feels aggrieved'.[160] The French response to this was realistic and hence discouraging. Towards the end of July ʇhe reports from Norton, British Counsellor at Warsaw, argued strongly against the policy of putting pressure on Beck to negotiate. On 26 July he argued, 'the Danzig question is only part of a very much larger problem affecting Poland and the whole of Eastern Europe, and even if Danzig were removed from the front of the stage (as it appeared to be in 1934) there is little basis for hopes that such as a "settlement" would introduce the millennium any more than did the successive "settlements" of the problems of reparations, the Rhineland, Austria, the Sudeten-Deutsch problem, Memel and, finally, Czechoslovakia'.[161] The former private secretary to Vansittart played a major part in stiffening resolve among the permanent officials at a critical time in Anglo-Polish relations and thus preventing any move towards ceding Danzig to Germany, which was the policy advocated by Henderson.

On 30 July Chamberlain was still arguing for appeasement, noting that Germany 'has a chance of getting fair and reasonable treatment from us and others, if she will give up the idea that she can force it from us'.[162] In the Commons there was some apprehension as to the likely actions of the appeasers during the recess and a motion to reassemble within three weeks was defeated by only 118 votes, less than half the Government's paper majority. Parliament rose on 4 August and almost immediately the quadrumvirate began to think of new ways to placate Hitler. Halifax, supposedly the 'iron man' of the quartet, observed on 15 August he was 'considering the suggestion that an Englishman should have a talk with Herr Hitler'.[163] Bonnet suggested that Britain threaten to renounce the guarantee unless Beck agreed to grant the Red Army right of passage.

The combination of Henderson, Halifax, Chamberlain and Bonnet—which had destroyed Czechoslovakia—now looked as if it might betray Poland.

This possibility was ended by announcement of the Molotov-Ribbentrop Pact on 23 August. Outwardly the treaty was one of non-aggression; in the secret additional protocol Germany and Russia agreed to partition Eastern Europe. The existence of this addendum was only suspected but it was clear that Russia could no longer be regarded as a potential ally for the West. The humiliation of Stalin's cynical arrangement produced very different reactions in Britain. Hoare believed that the pact showed conclusively that Chamberlain was 'proved to be right' in his contention that 'the Russians could not be trusted'.[164] Eden disagreed: 'British policy had been persistent to the point of obstinacy. The price had now to be paid'.[165] It was universally understood that the chances of avoiding war were much reduced and in sombre mood Parliament reassembled on 24 August.

The day the pact was signed the Polish Government mobilized most of its army in response to German troop movements. This action contrasted oddly with Beck's demeanour, reported by the French Ambassador as 'quite unperturbed . . . he considers that very little of importance has changed'.[166] If Beck and his colleagues had known of German attempts to seduce Britain from her guarantee there might have been a less phlegmatic reaction. Through a Swedish businessman, Dahlerus, the Germans tried to keep open unofficial channels of communication with high-ranking British politicians, businessmen and officials. The tale Dahlerus was telling was that demands for Danzig and the Corridor were Hitler's last territorial claims.

From 23 August it was realized in Britain that the Polish military position was untenable. Ciano argued that the pact made the position of Poland hopeless[167] and began fishing for a compromise which would permit co-operation on the lines of a new Four Power Pact; he made it clear that this could only be attained if Poland were abandoned and Germany reconciled. There was agreement with Ciano's opinion and some British sympathy for his suggested course of action. Pressure was put on Warsaw to negotiate with Hitler, though Kennard, the British Ambassador to Warsaw, opposed such a move; 'I am extremely doubtful whether it would really serve any useful purpose for Polish Ambassador to seek interview with Herr Hitler . . . any such approach would be sure to be construed as a sign of weakness and might even provoke the very ultimatum we wish to avoid'.[168] Despite this warning Halifax suggested to Bonnet that in the event of a German attack the Western Powers give Germany a time limit to halt hostilities and open negotiations rather than make it plain that any invasion would be followed at once by a declaration of war. The French agreed to this proposal but Polish insistence on a binding guarantee rendered the exercise nugatory. On 25 August Poland and Britain signed a Treaty of Mutual Assistance.

In certain matters the treaty was very clear. It gave clear warning that an aggressive attack on one of the signatories would be counteracted at once by the assistance of the other signatory. The treaty also covered the vexed question of indirect aggression. Unfortunately it did not make plain that Danzig would be regarded as a *casus belli*, though a pledge to defend its status was contained in a secret protocol attached to the treaty. This was madness, for it simultaneously assured Beck that there was no reason to negotiate and led Hitler to believe that the Free City was outside the scope of the alliance. It would be wrong to imagine that such an omission was accidental. Halifax was not so careless; it seems likely that he had in mind a negotiated agreement over Danzig, with Hitler making the proposals and Britain pressing them on a reluctant Poland. Without a public treaty commitment there would be little the Poles could do.

Halifax tried to keep open his unofficial lines of communication with Hitler. On 26 August he asked Mussolini to make it clear to Berlin that 'if a settlement were confined to Danzig and the Corridor, it did not seem to us that it should be impossible . . . to find a solution without war'.[169] At the same time Hitler offered his solution to the crisis. Through Henderson he suggested an agreement on colonial questions and disarmament and offered a guarantee of the British Empire. He concluded by saying that if Britain 'rejects these ideas there will be war. In no case would Great Britain emerge

stronger . . . this was his last offer'.[170] The Cabinet rejected these
proposals and Henderson was compelled to tell Hitler that anything
which threatened Polish independence could not be accepted. Yet
British actions were not as firm as their statements. France and
Britain were covertly in communication with Italy and indicated
that they feared war. News of these approaches did not take long to
reach Hitler and he remained hopeful that British refusals merely
represented a slow adjustment to the new situation, as in the period
preceding the Munich settlement.

In Britain the foes of any attempt at last minute appeasement
were gathering strength. Within the Cabinet Hore-Belisha and
Kingsley Wood insisted on a less obsequious reply to Hitler's
proposals of 25 August than Chamberlain wished to send. They
were right to fear Halifax's intentions, for on 28 August he advised
the Poles to enter 'at once into direct discussion with Germany'.[171]
Henderson met Hitler again on 29 August and was informed that a
Polish negotiator would be accepted but only within twenty-four
hours. By this time regular displays of weakness by Britain had
had an effect in Germany and on 30 August Ribbentrop read
Henderson a list of demands which included the immediate
annexation of Danzig and a plebiscite in an enlarged Corridor.
Opposition to any concessions to Germany was strong in Warsaw,
where the Polish Government was buttressed with the support of
Kennard, but in Berlin Henderson still worked frantically for peace,
trying to persuade Halifax and Chamberlain to accept the latest
German proposals. His pressure had no effect; Chamberlain had
realized that it would be 'impossible to ask Poland to give up her
rights on Danzig in advance of negotiation'.[172] A last minute
intervention by Italy to try to preserve the peace by calling a conference on 5 September was rejected by both Hitler and Chamberlain.
On 1 September Germany attacked Poland.

The British were committed to immediate support of Poland by
the treaty signed only a week earlier. There was no immediate
declaration of war on 1 September. Bonnet urged that the Italian
offer of mediation be accepted and Anglo-French entry into the war
be delayed. The British Cabinet had by this time resolved that war
was inevitable unless Germany pulled back her troops; delay was

occasioned only by a wish to synchronize the British and French declarations. In France there was still an anxiety to avoid war, so much so that on 1 September Halifax testily told Phipps, 'delays in Paris and attitude of the French Government are causing some misgivings here. We shall be grateful for anything you can do to infuse courage and determination into M. Bonnet'.[173] Yet the following day Halifax did not positively reject the idea of a conference. He was under pressure from Paris where the Cabinet wished to delay an ultimatum for forty-eight hours in the hope of reaching a settlement. At the Cabinet meeting on Sunday afternoon, 2 September, Hore-Belisha protested, 'further delay . . . might result in breaking the unity of the country. Public opinion was against yielding an inch'.[174] Finally the Cabinet decided that the British ultimatum to Germany should end at midnight that day.

In a statement made to the Commons that evening Chamberlain departed from the agreed Cabinet line (on the grounds that latest developments had made it impossible for him to consult all his colleagues) and still spoke of negotiations, placing his hope, like Bonnet, in Italian mediation. The premier gave notice of an ultimatum but placed no time limit on it. The House was both surprised and horrified. Greenwood said, 'An act of aggression took place 38 hours ago . . . I wonder how long we are prepared to vacillate at a time when Britain and all that Britain stands for, and human civilisation, are in peril'.[175] A majority of the Cabinet was enraged by the dishonesty and unconstitutionality of the latest attempt by Halifax and Chamberlain to appease Germany. A powerful group met in Simon's room and the erstwhile appeaser was deputized to tell Chamberlain that with or without French consent an ultimatum with a time limit should be sent to Germany. Desperate last-minute attempts by the Germans to prevent British entry into the war failed, though Wilson told them that if Germany withdrew 'the British Government would be prepared to let bygones be bygones'.[176] The action of the Cabinet rebels had left no time for the friends of Germany to act and at 9.00 a.m. on 3 September the British Government issued an ultimatum which expired two hours later. France declared war six hours after Britain amid Cabinet hesitancy which compared unfavourably even with the uncertainty of the

British administration. Neither country was to give any effective help to the Poles.

Announcing that Britain was at war Chamberlain, in a broadcast at 11.15 a.m., stated 'We have done all that any country could do to establish peace, but a situation in which no word given by Germany's ruler could be trusted, and no people or country could feel themselves safe, had become intolerable'.[177] Speaking to the Commons that afternoon, he mentioned 'everything that I have worked for, everything that I have hoped for, everything that I have believed in during my public life, has crashed into ruins'.[178] The personal regrets and bitterness of Chamberlain were understandable. He had mortgaged his political reputation in a lost cause. Halifax too had deep regrets, though by sleight of hand and singular good fortune he escaped much of the criticism levelled at Chamberlain. He was undeservedly fortunate, for he bore perhaps a greater share of the blame than the premier for the misguided policies pursued after Eden's resignation. But there is no justice in politics.

When Britain declared war her chosen foreign policy of the previous decades was in ruins. It had been based upon the notion of bringing Germany back into the European community of nations and reinforcing that return by a close understanding between Britain, France, Germany and Italy. Through the League it would then be possible to advance the causes of disarmament and collective security. Economic prosperity would automatically return. The goodwill of Japan and the United States was assumed; the future of relations with Russia was, for the most part, to be ignored until Moscow pursued reasonable policies. In September 1939 all these interlocking policies had collapsed. Britain was at war with Germany and in 1940 fought Italy. In 1941 Japan became an open enemy instead of the covert antagonist she had been since 1931. Russia played an important part in the diplomacy of the late 1930s but not to the advantage of the West. The United States was conspicuous by its absence from international affairs. The economic crisis had not been overcome and the League of Nations and all its works had succumbed to the pressures of political and military reality. Even the alliance with France was shaky, as events in 1940 were to demonstrate conclusively. A new world was coming into existence and new policies would be required.

The events of the next few months showed how different the world was. Long-term aims of policy, where they existed, had to be subordinated to the task of defeating Germany. In 1939 Poland was crushed and in 1940 a series of staggering blows knocked out France and a number of recent converts to the anti-German cause— Denmark, Norway, Belgium and Holland. Attempts to persuade the United States and Russia to intervene met no success until these nations were attacked—at Pearl Harbour on 6 December 1941 and in Poland on 22 June 1941. By the close of that year an essentially European war had become global and Britain's part in determining strategic plans and political actions to be taken after the end of the war secondary. After 1942 Britain was to suffer from the frustrations she had imposed on her associates in the palmy days when she decided policy. The end of the British rôle as a world power was in sight. Many observers had expected it to end in 1940 with a German invasion of Britain; few outside the English-speaking world supposed that in such circumstances Britain would fight on. Franco was an exception, telling Hitler on 23 October 1940, 'if England were conquered, the British Government and Fleet would continue the war from Canada with American support'.[179] He was almost certainly correct because the collapse of political morale which helped destroy the Third Republic was never visible in Britain.

If the appeasers had left Britain without strong allies and in a weak strategic position their policies had ensured that the nation was united. The patent failure of appeasement made it easy to transfer power in May 1940 to more aggressive leaders and to reject the German peace offers of 1939–40. In 1938 the moral case for appeasement had been destroyed; the reverses of 1940 forced those who had been distant observers or ignorant of Chamberlain's policies to recognize the terrible consequences of passivity.

A reduction in British power was inevitable in the long term. The failures of 1936–39 accelerated the decline, though another three decades were to pass before the implications of this loss of status were accepted by a majority of Britons. Unwittingly the appeasers paved the way for Britain to become a European rather than a global power. It was not without a price. Writing of the national and personal tragedies of Eastern Europe, Taylor argued 'The British people suffered comparatively little during six years of war',[180] but the traumatic experience of lost status, diminished resources and economic decline lives on in the minds of the British to this very day. Confidence in national capacity, sapped in 1914–18, was destroyed in 1939–45, though it would be unjust to blame the appeasers exclusively for these continuing conditions. The roots of British decline can be discerned far back in the nineteenth century.

The appeasers were obsessed with the past, though, strangely enough, they used very modern methods of diplomacy. These were suited neither to the times nor to the styles and abilities of their practitioners. Chamberlain relied for advice on a small group of colleagues and friends and then imposed his views on the Cabinet as a whole. In modern times this can be successful, as Nixon showed in his conduct of American foreign policy from 1969 to 1974. It was inappropriate and impossible in the 1930s when an economically weak Britain ought to have been seeking a more limited rôle in international affairs. But the policy-makers were wrestling with problems which would have been hard to solve in any age. There was little informed public discussion of their policy, not merely because the appeasers were secretive, but also because their critics were often manifestly less realistic than they were. It is easy to criticize with the benefit of hindsight. Many reservations about the wisdom of their policies were and are justified, but it would be wise to remember our own frailties of political judgment before being too harsh; after all, 'it is a complicated thing, not knowing everything'.[181]

REFERENCES

1 *Sir Horace Rumbold* by M. Gilbert. p. 367.
2 *The Life of Neville Chamberlain* by K. Feiling. p. 252. Diary for 25 March 1934.
3 *The Lost Peace* by H. Butler. p. 44.
4 Gilbert, op. cit., p. 371.
5 Quoted in Feiling, op. cit., p. 245.

6 See *The Anti-Appeasers* by N. Thompson. pp. 43–4.
7 *Failure of a Mission* by N. Henderson. p. vi.
8 *Lessons of my Life* by Lord Vansittart. p. 19.
9 *I Paid Hitler* by F. Thyssen. pp. 290–1.
10 *Old Men Forget* by Viscount Norwich (Duff Cooper). p. 267.
11 *The Origins of the Second World War* by A. J. P. Taylor. p. 153.
12 *The Roots of Appeasement* by M. Gilbert. p. 143.
13 Thompson, op. cit., p. 39. *Britain Looks at Germany* by Sir E. Grigg. p. 14.
14 *The Appeasers* by M. Gilbert and R. Gott. p. 49.
15 *Cahiers* by M. Barrès. Vol. III. p. 265.
16 *British Strategy in the Far East, 1919–39* by W. R. Louis. p. 207. Minute of 9 November 1933.
17 Feiling, op. cit., p. 253.
18 ibid., p. 254.
19 *Lord Lothian* by J. R. M. Butler. pp. 197–8. Speech of 11 November 1933.
20 *Facing the Dictators* by the Earl of Avon. p. 54.
21 *Politics in Independent Poland, 1921–39* by A. Polonsky. p. 385.
22 Eden, op. cit., p. 93.
23 *Austria, Germany and the Anschluss, 1931–38* by J. Gehl. p. 63.
24 ibid., p. 79.
25 *Documents on British Foreign Policy, 1919–39*. Second Series. Vol. VI. No. 290. Drummond to Simon, 17 February 1934. (Henceforward referred to as *D.B.F.P.*)
26 *Between Hitler and Mussolini* by Prince Starhemberg. p. 171.
27 *Diplomatic Twilight, 1930–40* by Sir Walford Selby. pp. 30–2.
28 Eden, op. cit., p. 124.
29 *Retrospect* by Viscount Simon. pp. 179–80.
30 Eden, op. cit., p. 127. Debate of 11 March 1935.
31 ibid., p. 128.
32 *The Times*, 11 March 1935.
33 Eden, op. cit., p. 149.
34 *The Mist Procession* by Lord Vansittart. p. 527.
35 Eden, op. cit., p. 99.
36 *The Diplomats* ed. by G. A. Craig and F. Gilbert. p. 387.
37 *Papers Relating to the Foreign Relations of the United States, 1931–38*. Vol. I (1935). Litvinov to Bullitt, 29 May 1935.
38 *Nine Troubled Years* by Viscount Templewood. p. 138.
39 Eden, op. cit., p. 242.
40 *The Times*, 12 September 1935.
41 Eden, op. cit., p. 262.
42 *The Unforgiving Years, 1929–40* by L. Amery. p. 174.
43 Gehl, op. cit., p. 120.
44 *Lessons of my Life* by Lord Vansittart. p. 45.
45 *Jadis* by E. Herriot. Vol. II. pp. 613–14.
46 *The Mist Procession* by Lord Vansittart. p. 538.
47 Templewood, op. cit., p. 181.
48 ibid., p. 182.
49 Eden, op. cit., p. 316.
50 *A Great Experiment* by Lord Robert Cecil. p. 278.

51 ibid., p. 279.
52 Eden, op. cit., p. 343.
53 *The Collapse of the Third Republic* by W. L. Shirer. p. 287.
54 *The Times*, 9 March 1936.
55 J. R. M. Butler, op. cit., p. 213.
56 Gehl, op. cit., p. 124.
57 Eden, op. cit., p. 362.
58 See Thompson, op. cit., pp. 112–13. Speech of 26 March 1936.
59 Gehl, op. cit., p. 133.
60 *Hitler* by A. L. C. Bullock. p. 348.
61 *Dollfuss* by G. Brook-Shepherd. p. 283.
62 *Spanish Notebooks* by I. Maisky. p. 136.
63 Eden, op. cit., p. 441.
64 ibid., p. 600.
65 *Halifax* by Lord Birkenhead. p. 607.
66 *Memoirs* by Cordell Hull. Vol. I. p. 545.
67 *The Mist Procession* by Lord Vansittart. p. 468.
68 Feiling, op. cit., p. 325.
69 *The Second World War* by W. S. Churchill. Vol. I. p. 174.
70 Taylor, op. cit., p. 174.
71 Feiling, op. cit., p. 319.
72 Gehl, op. cit., p. 163.
73 ibid., p. 165.
74 *Memoirs* by F. von Papen. p. 402.
75 D.B.F.P. Third Series. Vol. I. No. 25. Halifax to Palairet, 11 March 1938.
76 Thompson, op. cit., p. 157.
77 Feiling, op. cit., p. 342.
78 J. R. M. Butler, op. cit., p. 223.
79 Feiling, op. cit., p. 347.
80 Taylor, op. cit., p. 176.
81 *John Buchan* by J. Adam Smith. p. 443. Buchan to Anna Buchan, 14 March 1938.
82 *De Staline à Hitler: Souvenirs de deux ambassades, 1936–39* by R. Coulondre. p. 136. See also Shirer, op. cit., p. 366.
83 *The Reckoning* by the Earl of Avon. p. 8.
84 Thompson, op. cit., p. 164.
85 Shirer, op. cit., p. 376.
86 Taylor, op. cit., p. 199.
87 *Fallen Bastions* by G. E. R. Gedye. p. 401.
88 Gilbert and Gott, op. cit., p. 127.
89 D.B.F.P. Third Series. Vol. I. No. 301. Phipps to Halifax, 24 May 1938.
90 D.B.F.P. Third Series. Vol. I. Nos. 349 & 350. Strang's notes, 29 & 30 May 1938.
91 *Czechoslovakia before Munich* by J. W. Bruegel. p. 231.
92 Henderson, op. cit., p. 143.
93 *The Roots of Appeasement* by M. Gilbert. p. 172.
94 Gilbert and Gott, op. cit., p. 139.
95 D.B.F.P. Third Series. Vol. II. No. 835. Butler to Halifax, 11 September 1938.
96 D.B.F.P. Third Series. Vol. II. No. 807. Phipps to Halifax, 8 September 1938.
97 D.B.F.P. Third Series. Vol. II. No. 843. Halifax to Phipps, 12 September 1938.

98 Templewood, op. cit., p. 301.
99 *D.B.F.P.* Third Series. Vol. II. No. 862. Halifax to Henderson, 13 September 1938. See also footnotes regarding Chamberlain's plans for a personal visit.
100 *D.B.F.P.* Third Series. Vol. II. No. 858. Phipps to Halifax, 13 September 1938.
101 Norwich, op. cit., p. 228.
102 Bruegel, op. cit., p. 262.
103 *D.B.F.P.* Third Series. Vol. II. No. 937. Halifax to Newton, 19 September 1938.
104 *The Private Papers of Hore-Belisha* ed. R. J. Minney. p. 142.
105 *D.B.F.P.* Third Series. Vol. II. No. 979. Newton to Halifax, 20 September 1938.
106 Norwich, op. cit., p. 235.
107 *D.B.F.P.* Third Series. Vol. II. No. 1076. Phipps to Halifax, 24 September 1938.
108 *Home and Abroad* by Lord Strang. p. 135.
109 *D.B.F.P.* Third Series. Vol. II. No. 1082. Henderson to Halifax, 25 September 1938.
110 Bruegel, op. cit., p. 287.
111 *D.B.F.P.* Third Series. Vol. II. No. 1125. Perth to Halifax, 27 September 1938.
112 Templewood, op. cit., p. 319.
113 *D.B.F.P.* Third Series. Vol. II. No. 1228. Notes of conversation between Hitler and Chamberlain, 30 September 1938.
114 Gilbert and Gott, op. cit., p. 180.
115 *Munich, ou la drôle de paix* by H. Noguères. p. 134. See also Shirer, op. cit., p. 450.
116 Norwich, op. cit., p. 248.
117 Gilbert and Gott, op. cit., p. 180.
118 Coulondre, op. cit., p. 169. See also Taylor, op. cit., p. 244 and ff.
119 *D.B.F.P.* Third Series. Vol. III. No. 285. Halifax to Phipps, 1 November 1938.
120 *Ciano's Diary* ed. M. Muggeridge. p. 10. Entry for 12 January 1939.
121 *D.B.F.P.* Third Series. Vol. IV. No. 256. Henderson to Halifax, 15 March 1939.
122 Henderson, op. cit., p. 205.
123 *Hansard.* House of Commons. 15 March 1939.
124 Thompson, op. cit., p. 202.
125 *The Times,* 18 March 1939.
126 See Thompson, op. cit., pp. 204–6. Also *Halifax* by A. C. Johnson. pp. 511–14.
127 *D.B.F.P.* Third Series. Vol. IV. No. 389. Halifax to Seeds, 17 March 1939.
128 Craig and Gilbert, op. cit., p. 396.
129 *D.B.F.P.* Third Series. Vol. IV. No. 458. Notes on conversation between Halifax and Bonnet, 21 March 1939.
130 *D.B.F.P.* Third Series. Vol. IV. No. 471. Halifax to Kennard, 21 March 1939.
131 *The Mist Procession* by Lord Vansittart. p. 536.
132 *D.B.F.P.* Third Series. Vol. IV. No. 484. Notes on conversation between Halifax, Chamberlain and Bonnet, 22 March 1939.
133 Feiling, op. cit., p. 403. 26 March 1939.
134 *D.B.F.P.* Third Series. Vol. IV. No 490. Seeds to Halifax, 22 March 1939.
135 Bullock, op. cit., p. 498.
136 *The Reckoning* by the Earl of Avon. p. 47.
137 Feiling, op. cit., p. 403.
138 *D.B.F.P.* Third Series. Vol. V. No. 1. Notes on conversations between Halifax and Beck, 4 April 1939.

139 *The Second World War* by Viscount Norwich. p. 320.
140 Ciano, op. cit., p. 68. Entry for 10 April 1939.
141 Henderson, op. cit., p. 225.
142 *The Challenge to Isolation* by W. Langer and S. Gleason. Vol. I. p. 89.
143 *D.B.F.P.* Third Series. Vol. V. No. 170. Halifax to Seeds, 14 April 1939.
144 Taylor, op. cit., p. 280.
145 *D.B.F.P.* Third Series. Vol. V. No. 421. Seeds to Halifax, 9 May 1939.
146 *D.B.F.P.* Third Series. Vol. VI. No. 337. Henderson to Halifax, 17 July 1939.
147 Ciano, op. cit., p. 94. Entry for 27 May 1939.
148 Henderson, op. cit., p. 225.
149 *D.B.F.P.* Third Series. Vol. V. No. 576. Halifax to Cadogan, 21 May 1939.
150 *D.B.F.P.* Third Series. Vol. V. No. 609. Halifax to Seeds, 24 May 1939.
151 *Maisky* by G. Bilainkin. p. 252.
152 *The Reckoning* by the Earl of Avon. p. 55.
153 Strang, op. cit., p. 176.
154 *D.B.F.P.* Third Series. Vol. VI. No. 244. Note from Quai d'Orsay, 5 July 1939.
155 *D.B.F.P.* Third Series. Vol. VI. No. 252. Halifax to Seeds, 6 July 1939.
156 *D.B.F.P.* Third Series. Vol. VI. No. 212. Phipps to Halifax, 1 July 1939.
157 *Le Drame de 1940* by A. Beaufre. p. 124.
158 *D.B.F.P.* Third Series. Vol. VI. Appendix V. Memorandum, August 1939.
159 *D.B.F.P.* Third Series. Vol. VII. No. 87. Kennard to Halifax, 20 August 1939.
160 *D.B.F.P.* Third Series. Vol. VI. No. 317. Chamberlain to Daladier, 13 July 1939.
161 *D.B.F.P.* Third Series. Vol. VI. No. 461. Norton to Halifax, 26 July 1939.
162 Feiling, op. cit., p. 409.
163 *D.B.F.P.* Third Series. Vol. VII. No. 3. Halifax to Shepherd, 15 August 1939.
164 Templewood, op. cit., p. 370.
165 *The Reckoning* by the Earl of Avon. p. 61.
166 *Fin d'une Europe* by G. Bonnet. p. 287.
167 *D.B.F.P.* Third Series. Vol. VII. No. 214. Loraine to Halifax, 24 August 1939.
168 *D.B.F.P.* Third Series. Vol. VII. No. 270. Kennard to Halifax, 25 August 1939.
169 *D.B.F.P.* Third Series. Vol. VII. No. 327. Halifax to Loraine, 26 August 1939.
170 *D.B.F.P.* Third Series. Vol. VII. No. 283. Henderson to Halifax, 25 August 1939.
171 *D.B.F.P.* Third Series. Vol. VII. No. 411. Halifax to Kennard, 28 August 1939.
172 *D.B.F.P.* Third Series. Vol. VII. No. 627. Minute by Halifax, 31 August 1939.
173 *D.B.F.P.* Third Series. Vol. VII. No. 699. Halifax to Phipps, 1 September 1939.
174 Minney, op. cit., p. 225.
175 ibid., p. 226.
176 Gilbert and Gott, op. cit., p. 311.
177 Feiling, op. cit., p. 416.
178 ibid., p. 416.
179 Bullock, op. cit., p. 605.
180 Taylor, op. cit., p. 26.
181 In a song by Neil Diamond, 'Home is a wounded heart'.

Postscript

> The ascent of man will go on. But do not assume that it will
> go on carried by western civilization as we know it . . . We
> are waiting to be somebody's past too.
>
> Jacob Bronowski, *The Ascent of Man*

In the century which has elapsed since 1880 the face of Europe
has been completely changed. The European Powers are no longer
arbiters of the world. Indeed, it is pertinent to ask if any European
state can properly lay claim to Great Power status. Certainly the
major powers of 1880 cannot. The state of Austria-Hungary was
destroyed in the war of 1914-18, as was the Ottoman Empire.
Imperial Germany has, by a strange metamorphosis, become the
Federal Republic—a powerful economic force but limited in political
and military fields by both voluntary and compulsory restrictions.
Russia was not then and is not now a purely European power. Britain
and France, shorn of their overseas empires, have tottered uneasily
towards second-class status. Italy never was a major power, despite
the braggadocio of Mussolini. No European power has arisen to
replace the fallen great.

Professor Childe once observed that 'even in prehistoric times
barbarian societies in Europe behaved in a distinctively European
way'.[1] In fact Europe's most serious claim to influence in the post-
1941 world still lies in the cultural heritage which so strongly pene-
trates other areas of the world. But even this culture does not have
the clarity or the unity of the vanished world of yesterday. Gibbon,
writing of the ruin of Rome, was prescient when he referred to
'vicissitudes of fortune, which spares neither man nor the proudest
of his works, which buries empires and cities in a common grave'.[2]

References are printed on p. 326.

As in the case of Rome, the destruction has primarily been self-inflicted. The barbarian ideologies of Fascism and Communism were created by Europeans. The European states immolated themselves with little assistance from non-European powers. To those powers which held the greatest influence in 1914—Britain, France and Germany—must be attributed the greatest responsibility.

The three Western Powers were those best equipped to maintain the political, economic and cultural dominance of Europe. Their failure to resolve differences magnified a spark in the Balkans into a raging inferno which swept the whole of Europe. It was on the Western Front that European ascendancy bled to death. Curiously, it was representatives of non-European nations who recognized the new, changed reality most clearly. It was Trotsky who asked, 'Will Europe be able to stand all this? Will it not decay and become little better than a graveyard?'[3] From the far side of the Atlantic Scott Fitzgerald made one of his characters lament, 'All my beautiful lovely safe world blew itself up here with a great gust of high explosive love'.[4] They were, in their very different ways, outsiders who were educated in the European tradition but who saw from their vantage points the significance of the carnage in Europe.

Nor were all these possibilities entirely unforeseen in Western Europe before 1914. Statesmen knew that fearful risks were being taken but seemed to know of no other way to proceed in their tortuous diplomatic manoeuvres. But the responsibility does not rest solely on the shoulders of a small number of politicians and diplomats. It rests also on those of the peoples of Britain, France and Germany, for these nations were democracies and if ordinary people permitted themselves to be cozened and gulled by their leaders they must share the blame. The great masses of Western Europe were not helplessly illiterate, like those of Eastern Europe, but they were suffering from a much more dangerous disease: that of political illiteracy. It made some sense for Calvin Coolidge to claim in 1929 that 'the President comes more and more to stand as the champion of the rights of the whole country'.[5] It made no sense to adopt this style of policy management among the major European nations. By abdicating their infinitely precious claim to involvement in the process of decision-making the people of the three Western nations abandoned also their way of life. It was a pitiable advertisement for democracy.

Even if those who were intimately involved in the process of policy-making had all been men of goodwill and noble purpose, which they were not, this readiness to abandon responsibility would have frustrated their intentions. It was not, after all, the politicians and diplomats but the German people who gave Hitler 37·3 % of the popular vote in the elections of July 1932. It was not the politicians and diplomats who assembled clamouring for war in the Place de la Concorde in 1914. Nor did the politicians or diplomats compel the British Labour Party to adopt Lansbury's blind pacifism in the wake of the electoral disaster of 1931. Indeed, as Taylor has so pertinently observed, the justification of appeasement was precisely that 'few causes have been more popular'.[6] Politicians need to find a blend of following and leading public opinion in order to secure both immediate popularity and an escape from future strictures. But this was impossible in the period preceding both 1914 and 1939. In the decade before 1914 the public was more belligerent than British politicians. In the decade before 1939 most of the public was less warlike than its leaders. There were notable exceptions but by and large this was true. To the middle-aged, war meant a return to the appalling misery and human degradation of years of trench warfare with millions of lives squandered over a few hundred yards of territory. In the event, *blitzkrieg* methods of modern warfare were infinitely easier to bear, but the 1914–18 generation could not foresee the mobility of 1939–45 tactics. To anyone with experience of trench warfare almost *any* sacrifice was preferred to its resumption. In neither case did it make policy any easier to formulate.

In sum, therefore, a study of British foreign policy in this period suggests weakness at many levels. Frequently politicans hid from the problems which faced them. Diplomats were often guilty of misrepresentation. They knew how little the facts corresponded to the theories but, like the politicians, opted for a quiet life. Men like Vansittart were rare. The general public too must bear a fair share of the blame for foreign policy failures. In fact the weaknesses of British policy-making were derived from other flaws in the political system. In the first place policy-making in most areas of government was out of date. Britain no longer had the economic capacity to pursue 'world' policies. It was not perhaps until the 1960s that this simple fact was understood even in Whitehall. Secondly, the political system favoured those who told the public what it wished to hear rather than the truth as they saw it. Demagogy, albeit of a genteel type, was the style of the times rather than enlightened democracy. In combination these failings helped contribute to the disastrous events of these years. The wars of 1914–18 and 1939–45 were not so much a monument to human error as to the failure of a political system. As Spengler perceived, Parliamentarism was in decay and could not adapt itself to the new conditions of mass politics. It was on the basis of his experiences in the 1920s that he wrote of 'an accelerated demolition of ancient forms that leaves the path clear for Caesarism'.[7] The 1930s confirmed the validity of his dictum and the incapacity of the democracies to resist the new totalitarianism. Therein lies the tragedy of British foreign policy and, indeed, of Britain itself, for no other country was as well placed to answer the call to the defence of democracy.

REFERENCES

1 _The Prehistory of European Society_ by V. G. Childe. p. 9.
2 _The Decline and Fall of the Roman Empire_ by E. Gibbon. Vol. VI. p. 547.
3 _The Prophet Armed_ by I. Deutscher. p. 242.
4 Quoted in _The Price of Glory_ by A. Horne. p. 12.
5 Resignation Speech, 1929.
6 _The Origins of the Second World War_ by A. J. P. Taylor. p. 25.
7 _The Decline of the West_ by O. Spengler. Vol. II. p. 419.

Bibliography

The foundation of any study of British foreign policy in this period lies in the official collections of documents:

British Documents on the Origins of the War, 1898–1914 (11 vols), 1926–38.

Documents on British Foreign Policy, 1919–39 (continuing), 1946–.

German Diplomatic Documents, 1871–1914 (4 vols), 1969.

Collected Diplomatic Documents relating to the outbreak of the European War, 1915.

Documents Diplomatiques Français, 1871–1914, 1929–62.

Documents on German Foreign Policy, 1918–45, 1948–.

New Documents on the History of Munich, 1958.

Papers relating to the Foreign Relations of the United States, 1946–.

Les Evénements survenus en France de 1933 à 1945 (10 vols), 1947–54.

Hansard.

There are also other collections of original material in a number of archives of which the following are the most important:

Asquith	Bodleian Library
Balfour	British Museum
Bertie	F.O. Library
Carnock	F.O. Library
Cecil (Robert)	P.R.O.
Chamberlain (A.)	Birmingham University Library
Chamberlain (J.)	Birmingham University Library

Cromer   P.R.O.
Grey   F.O. Library
Hardinge   Cambridge University Library
Lansdowne   F.O. Library
Lascelles   F.O. Library
Lothian   Scottish R.O.
Salisbury   Christ Church Library, Oxford
Spring Rice   F.O. Library

Another source of particular importance has been the memoirs and edited papers of the leading diplomats. Among the most interesting are:

Ashton-Gwatkin, F. T. A., *The British Foreign Office*, 1949.

Beaufre, A., *Le Drame de 1940*, 1965.

Bernstorff, Count, *Erinnerungen*, 1924.

Busch, M., *Bismarck. Some secret pages of his history*, 1898.

Cambon, H., *Correspondence de Paul Cambon, 1870–1924*, 1940–6.

Coulondre, R., *De Staline à Hitler: Souvenirs de deux ambassades, 1936–39*, 1950.

D'Abernon, Lord, *An Ambassador of Peace*, 1930.

Gwynn, S., *Letters and Friendships of Sir Cecil Spring Rice*, 1929.

Hardinge, Lord, *The Old Diplomacy*, 1947.

Henderson, N., *Failure of a Mission*, 1940.

Henderson, N., *Water under the Bridges*, 1945.

Hendrick, B. J., *Life and Letters of Walter H. Page*, 1928.

Lennox, Lady, *Diary of Lord Bertie, 1914–18*, 1924.

Lockhart, R. B., *Friends, Foes and Foreigners*, 1957.

Maisky, I., *Spanish Notebooks*, 1966.

Rich, N. & Fisher, M. H., *The Holstein Papers*, 1955–63.

Selby, Sir W., *Diplomatic Twilight, 1930–40*, 1953.

Strang, Lord, *Home and Abroad*, 1956.

Vansittart, Lord, *The Mist Procession*, 1958

Vansittart, Lord, *Lessons of my Life*, 1943.

Varè, D., *Laughing Diplomat*, 1938.

The memoirs and autobiographies of other civil servants and of politicians are also essential:

Amery, L., *The Unforgiving Years, 1929–40*, 1955
Avon, Earl of, *Facing the Dictators*, 1962.
Avon, Earl of, *The Reckoning*, 1965.
Beck, J., *Dernier Rapport*, 1950.
Bethmann Hollweg, T. von, *Reflections on the World War*, 1920.
Bonnet, G., *Fin d'une Europe*, 1961.
Boothby, R., *I fight to live*, 1947.
Bülow, Prince von, *Memoirs*, 1931.
Butler, H., *The Lost Peace*, 1941.
Cecil, Lord Robert, *A Great Experiment*, 1941.
Cecil, Lord Robert, *All the way*, 1949.
Chirol, Sir V., *Fifty Years in a Changing World*, 1927.
Clemenceau, G., *Grandeurs et misères d'une victoire*, 1930.
Dalton, H., *The Fateful Years, 1931–45*, 1957.
Fitzroy, Sir A., *Memoirs*, no date.
Grey, Lord, *Twenty-five years*, 1925.
Halifax, Lord, *Fullness of days*, 1957.
Herriot, E., *Jadis*, 1952.
Hull, C., *Memoirs*, 1948.
Lloyd George, D., *War Memoirs*, 1934.
Lloyd George, D., *The truth about reparations and war debts*, 1932.
Macmillan, H., *Winds of change, 1914–39*, 1966.
Midleton, Earl of, *Records and Reactions, 1856–1939*, 1939.
Newton, Lord, *Retrospection*, 1941.
Nicolson, H., *Peacemaking, 1919*, 1964.
Norwich, Viscount, *Old Men Forget*, 1953.
Norwich, Viscount, *The Second World War*, 1939.
Oxford & Asquith, Earl of, *Memories and Reflections*, 1928.
Papen, F. von, *Memoirs*, 1952.
Paul-Boncour, J., *Entre Deux Guerres*, 1945–6.
Reith, J. C. W., *Into the wind*, 1949.
Riddell, Lord, *War Diary*, 1933.
Riddell, Lord, *Intimate Diary of the Peace Conference and after*, 1933.
Schacht, H., *My first seventy-six years*, 1955.

Shuster, M., The strangling of Persia, 1912.
Siebert, B. von, Diplomatische Aktenstücke zur Geschichte der Ententepolitik der Vorkriegsjahre, 1921.
Simon, Lord, Retrospect, 1952.
Slocombe, G., A mirror to Geneva, 1937.
Snowden, Viscount, An autobiography, 1934.
Starhemberg, Prince, Between Hitler and Mussolini, 1942.
Templewood, Viscount, Nine Troubled Years, 1954.
Thyssen, F., I Paid Hitler, 1941.
Weale, P., An indiscreet chronicle from the Pacific, 1922.
Weizsäcker, E. von, Memoirs, 1951.

There is a good deal of original material also in the following assortment of letters, papers and other writings:

Buckle, G. E., Letters of Queen Victoria (Second Series), 1928.
Buckle, G. E., Letters of Queen Victoria (Third Series), 1932.
Churchill, W. S., Great Contemporaries, 1943.
Churchill, W. S., The Second World War, 1948.
Goetz, W., Briefe Wilhelm II an den Zaren, 1894–1914, 1920.
Minney, R. J., The private papers of Hore-Belisha, 1960.
Morley, J., Memorandum on Resignation 1914, 1914.
Muggeridge, M., Ciano's Diary, 1947.
Ramm, A., Political correspondence of Mr. Gladstone and Lord Granville, 1876–86, 1961.
Ribot, A., Journal de Alexandre Ribot et correspondances inedites 1914–22, 1936.
Skazkin, S., Konets avstro-russko-germanskogo soiuza, 1879–84, 1928.
Young, O., Report, 1929.

There are a large number of useful biographies:

Andrew, C., Théophile Delcassé and the making of the Entente Cordiale, 1968.
Bilainkin, G., Maisky, 1944.
Birkenhead, Lord, Halifax, 1965.
Brook-Shepherd, G., Dollfuss, 1961.
Bullock, A. L. C., Hitler, 1964.

Butler, J. R. M., *Lord Lothian*, 1960.
Cecil, Lady Gwendolen, *Life of Robert, Marquess of Salisbury*, 1921–32.
Churchill, W. S., *Lord Randolph Churchill*, 1951.
Deutscher, I., *The Prophet Armed*, 1970.
Dugdale, B. E. C., *A. J. Balfour*, 1936.
Dugdale, E. T. S., *Maurice de Bunsen, Diplomat and Friend*, 1934.
Feiling, K., *Life of Neville Chamberlain*, 1947.
Fisher, H. A. L., *James Bryce*, 1927.
Fitzmaurice, Lord, *The Life of Lord Granville*, 1905.
Gardiner, A. G., *Life of Sir William Harcourt*, 1923.
Garvin, J. & Amery, J., *Life of Joseph Chamberlain*, 1932–69.
Gilbert, M., *Sir Horace Rumbold*, 1973.
Gilbert, M., *Servant of India*, 1966.
Gwynn, S. & Tuckwell, G., *Life of Sir Charles Dilke*, 1917.
Hammond, J. L., *C. P. Scott of the Manchester Guardian*, 1934.
James, R. R., *Rosebery*, 1963.
Johnson, A. C., *Viscount Halifax*, 1941.
Kennedy, A. L., *Salisbury, 1830–1903*, 1953.
Lee, Sir S., *King Edward VII. A biography*, 1925–7.
Mackay, R. F., *Fisher of Kilverstone*, 1973.
Maurice, Sir F., *Haldane*, 1937.
Middlemas, K. & Barnes, J., *Baldwin*, 1969.
Morley, J., *Life of Gladstone*, 1908.
Mowat, R. B., *Life of Lord Pauncefote*, 1929.
Newton, Lord, *Lord Lyons*, 1913.
Newton, Lord, *Lord Lansdowne*, 1929.
Nicolson, H., *Lord Carnock: A study in the Old Diplomacy*, 1930.
Owen, F., *Tempestuous Journey*, 1954.
Petrie, Sir C., *The Chamberlain Tradition*, 1938.
Petrie, Sir C., *Life and letters of Austen Chamberlain*, 1939.
Ponsonby, A., *Henry Ponsonby. His Life from his letters*, 1942.
Rhodes, A., *The poet as superman: D'Annunzio*, 1959.
Ronaldshay, Earl of, *Life of Lord Curzon*, 1923.
Roskill, S. W., *Hankey. Man of Secrets*, 1970.
Smith, J. A., *John Buchan*, 1965.
Smuts, J. C., *Jan Christian Smuts*, 1952.
Spender, J. & Asquith, C., *Life of Lord Oxford and Asquith*, 1932.

Trevelyan, G. M., *Grey of Fallodon*, 1937.
Weir, L. M., *The tragedy of Ramsay MacDonald*, 1938.
Wemyss, Lady, *Life and letters of Lord Wester Wemyss*, 1935.
Wilson, J., *A life of Sir Henry Campbell-Bannerman*, 1973.
Wolf, L., *Life of Lord Ripon*, 1921.
Young, G. M., *Stanley Baldwin*, 1952.
Zetland, Marquess of, *Lord Cromer*, 1932.

Original material may also be found in these publications:

The Times
The London and China Telegraph
The Nineteenth Century, 1878
The Annual Register, 1880
Colonial Zeitung
The Fortnightly Review, 1878
The Morning Post
The Daily Telegraph

The following specialist studies have been invaluable:

Anderson, M. S., *The Eastern Question, 1774–1923*, 1966.
Bourne, K., *Foreign Policy of Victorian England, 1830–1902*, 1970.
Craig, G. & Gilbert, F., *The Diplomats*, 1965.
Debicki, R., *Foreign Policy of Poland, 1919–39*, 1963.
Fischer, F., *Germany's aims in the First World War*, 1967.
Gatzke, H. W., *Germany's drive to the West*, 1966.
Gehl, J., *Austria, Germany and the Anschluss, 1931–38*, 1963.
Gilbert, M., *The roots of appeasement*, 1966.
Gilbert, M. & Gott, R., *The appeasers*, 1963.
Grenville, J. A. S., *Lord Salisbury and Foreign Policy*, 1964.
Howard, C. H. D., *Britain and the Casus Belli, 1822–1902*, 1974.
Langer, W. L., *European Alliances and Alignments*, 1964.
Langer, W. L., *The Diplomacy of Imperialism*, 1968.
Louis, W. R., *British Strategy in the Far East, 1919–39*, 1971.
Lowe, C. J., *Salisbury and the Mediterranean, 1886–96*, 1965.
Lowe, P., *Great Britain and Japan, 1911–15*, 1969.
Monger, G. W., *The end of isolation*, 1963.

Rothwell, V. H., *British War Aims and Peace Diplomacy, 1914–18,* 1971.

Shirer, W., *The collapse of the Third Republic,* 1969.

Steiner, Z. S., *The Foreign Office and Foreign Policy, 1898–1914,* 1969.

Temperley, H. & Penson, L., *The Foundations of British Foreign Policy,* 1938.

Thompson, N., *The anti-appeasers,* 1971.

Thorne, C., *The limits of Foreign Policy,* 1972.

Ward, A. & Gooch, G. P., *Cambridge History of British Foreign Policy,* 1923.

The following have been used less frequently:

Alder, G. J., *British India's Northern Frontier, 1865–95,* 1963.

Barrès, M., *Cahiers,* 1910.

Bassett, R., *Democracy and Foreign Policy: A Case History, the Sino-Japanese Dispute, 1931–33,* 1952.

Beloff, M., *Imperial Sunset,* 1969.

Beloff, M., *The Foreign Policy of Soviet Russia, 1929–41,* 1947.

Brook-Shepherd, G., *Anschluss: The Rape of Austria,* 1963.

Bruegel, J. W., *Czechoslovakia before Munich,* 1973.

Campbell, A. E., *Great Britain and the United States, 1895–1903,* 1960.

Carr, E. H., *Ambassadors at Large: Britain,* 1939.

Childe, V. G., *The prehistory of European society,* 1958.

Chung-Fu, Chang, *The Anglo-Japanese Alliance,* 1931.

Cooke, J. J., *New French Imperialism, 1880–1910,* 1973.

Crankshaw, E., *The fall of the House of Hapsburg,* 1970.

Cromer, Lord, *Modern Egypt,* 1911.

Deschanel, P., *Histoire de la politique extérieure de la France,* 1936.

Dilke, Sir C., *The present position of European politics,* 1887.

Dulles, F. R., *America's rise to world power, 1898–1954,* 1963.

Elcock, H., *Portrait of a decision,* 1972.

Eldridge, C. C., *England's Mission: The Imperial Idea in the Age of Gladstone and Disraeli, 1868–80,* 1973.

Fleming, P., *Bayonets to Lhasa,* 1961.

Fullerton, W. M., *Problems of Power,* 1920.

Gathorne-Hardy, G. M., *A short history of international affairs,* 1960.

Gedye, G. E. R., *Fallen bastions*, 1939.

Gibbon, E., *The decline and fall of the Roman Empire*, 1776.

Gopal, S., *British Policy in India, 1858–1905*, 1965.

Greaves, R. L., *Persia and the Defence of India*, 1959.

Hardie, F., *The Political Influence of the British Monarchy*, 1970.

Hardie, F., *The Abyssinian Crisis*, 1974.

Horne, A., *The Price of Glory*, 1964.

Howard, M. E., *The continental commitment*, 1974.

Iriye, A., *After Imperialism: The search for a new order in the Far East, 1921–31*, 1965.

Jäckh, E., *Die deutsch-türkische Waffenbrüderschaft*, 1915.

Keynes, J. M., *The Economic Consequences of the Peace*, 1920.

King-Hall, S., *Our own times*, 1941.

Knaplund, P., *Gladstone and Britain's Imperial Policy*, 1927.

Langer, W. & Gleason, S., *The challenge to isolation*, 1964.

Lebon, A., *La politique de la France en Afrique, 1896–98*, 1901.

Lord, W., *The Good Years*, 1960.

Marder, A. J., *British Naval Policy, 1880–1905*, 1940.

Marder, A. J., *From the Dreadnought to Scapa Flow*, 1961–70.

Marsden, A., *British Diplomacy and Tunis*, 1971.

Mayer, A. J., *Politics and Diplomacy of Peacemaking*, 1968.

Milner, Viscount, *England in Egypt*, 1920.

Moore, R. J., *Liberalism and Indian Politics, 1872–1922*, 1966.

Noguères, H., *Munich, ou la drôle de la paix*, 1963.

Pelcovits, N. A., *Old China Hands and the Foreign Office*, 1948.

Polonsky, A., *Politics in independent Poland, 1921–39*, 1972.

Robinson, R. & Gallagher, J., *Africa and the Victorians*, 1967.

Rosinski, H., *The German Army*, 1966.

Sargent, A. J., *Anglo-Chinese Commerce and Diplomacy*, 1907.

Saul, S. B., *Studies in British Overseas Trade, 1870–1914*, 1960.

Scalapino, R. A., *Democracy and the Party Movement in pre-War Japan*, 1953.

Seton-Watson, H., *Eastern Europe between the wars*, 1967.

Seton-Watson, R. W., *Britain and the dictators*, 1938.

Smith, D. M., *The Great Departure*, 1965.

Sontag, R. J., *Germany and England, background of conflict, 1848–94*, 1069.

Spender, J. A., *Fifty Years of Europe*, 1933.
Spengler, O., *The decline of the West*, 1971
Thomson, G. M., *The twelve days*, 1966.
Thornton, A. P., *The imperial idea and its enemies*, 1959.
Tint, H., *The decline of French patriotism, 1870–1940*, 1964.
Turner, H. A., *Stresemann and the politics of the Weimar Republic*, 1963.
Turner, L. C. F., *Origins of the First World War*, 1970.
Wheeler-Bennett, J. W., *The Nemesis of Power*, 1961.
Woodward, E. L., *Great Britain and the War of 1914–18*, 1967.
Young, L. K., *British Policy in China, 1895–1902*, 1970.
Zweig, S., *The World of Yesterday*, 1943.

Many articles in learned journals have also been consulted, but these are too numerous to cite in a bibliography of limited length. I would like to thank all those whose works I have consulted and drawn upon as well as those who have given facilities for the use of archive material. Without such assistance it would be almost impossible to write any historical work. Finally, I would like to draw special attention to four works, all of which I found very useful indeed. I frequently disagree with the author's interpretation of the facts but his books are important because they 'give one furiously to think'. That is essential for a historian.

Taylor, A. J. P., *The struggle for mastery in Europe*, 1957.
Taylor, A. J. P., *The Trouble Makers*, 1969.
Taylor, A. J. P., *English History, 1914–45*, 1965.
Taylor, A. J. P., *The Origins of the Second World War*, 1964.

Index